鱼米之乡

LAND OF FISH AND RICE

FUCHSIA DUNLOP

RECIPES FROM THE CULINARY HEART OF CHINA

PHOTOGRAPHY BY YUKI SUGIURA

W. W. Norton & Company

INDEPENDENT PUBLISHERS SINCE 1923

NEW YORK · LONDON

FOR DAI JIANJUN AND EVERYONE AT THE
DRAGON WELL MANOR IN HANGZHOU
AND THE AGRICULTURAL ACADEMY IN
SUICHANG, WITH LOVE AND GRATITUDE

江南好
风景旧曾谙
日出江花红胜火
春来江水绿如蓝
能不忆江南

Oh beautiful South, whose scenery I once knew so well
Those flowers lit redder than flames by the sun rising on the river
Those waters in springtime, green as the leafy indigo that lines the banks
How could I ever forget Jiangnan?

From 'Memories of Jiangnan' by Bai Juyi (772–846 AD)
白居易，忆江南词三首

THE BEAUTIFUL SOUTH

In this book, I'd like to take you on a journey to China's beautiful Lower Yangtze region, known in Chinese as Jiangnan or "south of the river." In the West, Jiangnan is known mostly for the modern metropolis of Shanghai, and yet Shanghai is just the gateway to a broader region that has been renowned in China for centuries for the beauty of its scenery, the elegance of its literary culture, the glittering wealth of its cities and the exquisite pleasures of its food. Jiangnan spans the eastern coastal provinces of Zhejiang and Jiangsu, the city of Shanghai and that part of southern Anhui province once known as Huizhou. In China, the region is known as a "land of fish and rice" (*yu mi zhi xiang*), blessed with a warm and nurturing climate, fertile land, and lakes, rivers and coastal waters that teem with fish and seafood.

My own journey there began nearly a decade ago, when I visited the old gastronomic capital of Yangzhou, and, like the Qing emperors more than two centuries before me, was captivated by its gentle way of life and glorious cuisine. Over the next few years, I made further forays into the region, visiting ancient cities including Hangzhou, Suzhou, Ningbo and Shaoxing and returning often to the modern capital, Shanghai. I wandered through old city lanes, with their street stalls and merchants' mansions, and sojourned in kitchens in all kinds of places. With local chefs and farmers, I went out fishing on lakes and foraged in the countryside for bamboo shoots and wild vegetables.

I can't remember exactly when the idea of writing a Jiangnan cookbook seeded itself in my mind, but I know that it began to grow in earnest after I walked through a moongate into the enchanted garden of the Dragon Well Manor restaurant on the outskirts of Hangzhou. There, maverick restaurateur Dai Jianjun (otherwise known as A Dai) had created a sanctuary for the kind of Chinese cooking I had often dreamed of but rarely encountered. His team of buyers were scouring the countryside for radiantly fresh produce and foodstuffs made by artisans who were preserving traditional skills. In the kitchens, his chefs were cooking in the old-fashioned way, making their own cured meats and pickles and using fine stocks instead of MSG. It seemed to me that the Dragon Well Manor was restoring to Chinese cuisine its rightful dignity, as an expression of the perfect marriage between nature and human artifice and the ideal balance between health and pleasure.

With the support and encouragement of Dai Jianjun and other leading figures in the local food scene, I fell in love with the region and its extraordinary gastronomic culture, just as I had with Sichuan a decade before. I returned often to Jiangnan over the following years, seeking out chefs, home cooks, street vendors and farmers with stories to tell and recipes to teach, and tasting some of the most wonderful food I have ever encountered. No one who has fallen in love with Jiangnan ever wants to leave. In the fourth century, the official Zhang Han is said to have abandoned his post in the north of China because of his longing for the water shield soup and sliced perch eaten in his hometown there; ever since, "thinking of perch and water shield" (*chun lu zhi si*) has been shorthand in Chinese for homesickness. While every Chinese cuisine has its charms, from the dazzling technicolor spices of the Sichuanese to the belly-warming noodle dishes of the north, I know of no other that can put one's heart so much at ease as the food of Jiangnan.

Within China, the region's food is known for its delicacy and balance. Jiangnan cooks like to emphasize the true and essential tastes (*ben wei*) of their ingredients, rather than to mask them in a riot of seasonings. Traditionally, they favor gentle tastes, which are described in Chinese by the beautiful term *qing dan*. Often translated unappealingly into English as "bland" or "insipid," it has no such pejorative meaning in Chinese: the word combines the two characters for "pure" and "light" and expresses a mildness of taste that refreshes and comforts, restoring equanimity to mind and body. This appreciation of culinary understatement is just one facet of a culture that also prizes the landscape blurred by mist, the impressionistic poem or painting, the winding path and the softness of a rainy day.

The generally even temperament of Jiangnan cooking does not imply any aversion to rich and delicious flavors. Indeed, the region is famed for its red-braised dishes, in which soy sauce, rice wine and sugar are combined to spectacular effect, for its fragrant vinegars and boozy "drunken" delicacies, and for a plethora of funky fermented foods. Overall, though, a good Jiangnan meal should leave a person feeling *shu fu*—comfortable and well. For, as any Chinese person knows, a balanced diet is the foundation of good health, and a good cook is a kind of physician (*chu dao ji yi dao*, "the way of the chef is the way of the doctor"). Heavy, meaty dishes and pungent flavors should be enjoyed in moderation and counterbalanced by lightly seasoned vegetables, cleansing broths and plain steamed rice.

Jiangnan cooking ranges from rustic food and street snacks to banquet delicacies so elaborate they are known as Kung Fu dishes (*gong fu cai*)—that is, dishes that demand the same level of technical mastery as the martial arts. It embraces myriad flavors, from the understated beauty of steamed fish and plain stir-fried greens to the outrageous pungency of stinking tofu. Even within the region there are striking differences in style, from the sweetness of Suzhou and Wuxi cooking to the fermented tastes of Shaoxing and the bright, clean seafood dishes of Ningbo. Jiangnan also has a notable tradition of Buddhist vegetarian cooking and a multitude of dainty *dim sum* snacks (or *dian xin*, as they are known in Mandarin). Famous local dishes are legion. They include beggar's chicken, the whole bird stuffed and roasted in a carapace of lotus leaves and mud; the incomparable Dongpo pork; "lion's heads," the Platonic ideal of meatballs; dainty stir-fried shrimp with Dragon Well tea leaves; and "drunken" chicken steeped in an alcoholic brine. The origins of many delicacies are bound up with historical figures or embellished by intriguing legends.

Local people believe they enjoy the finest food in the country. Whereas Cantonese food, they say, is too raw and wild, Sichuanese is too hot and northern cooking is too salty, the food of Jiangnan is both so varied that one never tires of it and so harmonious that it calms the mind as well as the palate. In the opinion of many locals, their food is perfectly balanced, particularly healthy and has universal appeal, which is why it has for so long played a leading role in Chinese state banquets and diplomacy. Jiangnan food also strikes a chord with modern Western tastes because of its clean, light flavors, the emphasis on health and seasonality, the love of fermented foods and the use of meat in moderation as part of an everyday diet rich in vegetables.

In the West, the Cantonese and Sichuanese culinary styles have become well known, while the food of Jiangnan remains neglected. This is partly, no doubt, because of the confusion of names by which the cuisines of this part of China have

Pleasure boats on the West Lake, Hangzhou, in Zhejiang province.

been known. There is Huaiyang cuisine (*huai yang cai*), which refers specifically to the style of cooking centered on old Yangzhou, often regarded as one of the "Four Great Cuisines" of China, but which is sometimes applied more generally to the food of the region. Shanghainese cuisine is another shorthand term, as is Jiangsu-Zhejiang cuisine (*su zhe cai* or *jiang zhe cai*). Moreover, in recent years, many chefs and gourmets have become champions of the local cuisines of individual provinces and cities. Amid all these rival claims, I have chosen to write of an overarching Jiangnan cuisine, embracing the cooking traditions of Zhejiang and Jiangsu provinces, southern Anhui province and Shanghai. It's a term that evokes the common geographical and culinary threads that link this diverse region and alludes to the ancient idea of Jiangnan, the beautiful south of China, as one of the heartlands of Chinese culture and gastronomy.

I hope in this book to bring you a taste of the Jiangnan region and its food. I'll invite you to sample the sleek magnificence of red-braised dishes, the mellowness of slow-cooked soups and stews, the refreshing brightness of stir-fried vegetables and the delicious ingenuity of Buddhist vegetarian cooking. I'll offer you glimpses of the iridescent beauty of the West Lake in Hangzhou, the tranquil gardens of Suzhou, the salt merchants' mansions of Yangzhou and the old canal districts of Shaoxing. I hope too to show you something of the rich landscape of the region, with its rolling hills, shady bamboo groves, ponds and streams, and the terraced paddy fields, flooded early in the season with the silvery gleam of water, and later with the quivering green of new rice shoots.

In part, this will be a journey into the Chinese past, a nostalgic glimpse of old stories and traditional dishes, but I hope it will also be in some respects a journey into China's future. The paroxysms of war and revolution, not to mention the world's fastest industrial revolution, have profoundly damaged Chinese traditional culture and the confidence of many Chinese people in their own traditions. For at least a century, many Chinese have looked towards the West for a definition of modernity and neglected the challenge of preserving and making use of their own rich heritage.

Most strangely of all, considering China's highly developed culture of nutrition and gastronomy, the Chinese have often referred to the West for "scientific" advice on how to eat, and largely failed to ask what dietary advice they might be able to offer the rest of the world. Thankfully, China's economic rise has begun to rekindle pride in the country's own heritage, particularly in the prosperous Jiangnan region. In the work of Dai Jianjun and other local gastronomic pioneers, I see what I hope will be part of a wellspring of a renewed Chinese culture that can be both modern and traditional.

It would be impossible to do justice to the cuisines of this rich and diverse region in a single book. I hope, however, that this collection of recipes and stories will at least open the door to a remarkable culinary region that is still little known in the West.

THE HISTORY OF JIANGNAN CUISINE

The great Yangtze River flows across the breadth of China, from its birthplace on the Tibetan plateau, through the central provinces to the Yangtze delta and the East China Sea. Since ancient times, the area to the south of the river's lower reaches has been called Jiangnan, or "south of the river." Long known as a land of fish and rice, it is one of the country's richest agricultural regions. Since at least the Song dynasty, some eight hundred years ago, it has also been renowned as a crucible of Chinese gastronomy. For centuries, the Chinese literati have eulogized its fine produce and exquisite cooking.

Rice has been grown in Jiangnan since Neolithic times, when the people of the Hemudu culture, near today's Ningbo, were among the earliest in the world to cultivate the grain. Just over 2,000 years ago, the Chinese historian Sima Qian wrote that famine was unknown in this region, and that local people lived mainly on rice and fish stew. Until the Middle Ages, however, the political center of China was in the north of the country, around the Yellow River basin, with its Silk Road trade links to central Asia and the West—but even in these earliest days of Chinese dynastic rule, the imperial court was hungry for the produce of the fertile south, receiving tribute shipments of fish from the barbarian tribes of the Lower Yangtze region.

From the sixth century onwards, the construction of a Grand Canal that linked Jiangnan with the northern capital gave the region a new importance as an entrepot for trade and a rich source of food and taxes. The city of Yangzhou lay at the crossroads of the new canal and the Yangtze River. It became a vital transport hub and the beating heart of the southern Chinese economy. A constant stream of taxes in the form of rice and sea salt passed through the city on their way to court, along with luxuries that included anchovies, sugared crabs and candied ginger. During the Tang dynasty (618–907 AD), Arab and other foreign merchants settled in Yangzhou, which became known as the most opulent city in China. Wang Jian, a contemporary poet, wrote of the city's thriving night markets, where crowds of people mingled under thousands of lanterns that lit up the clouds above.

In the north of China, the old dynastic heartland around the Yellow River basin was increasingly plagued by drought and raids by barbarians from the steppes. Meanwhile, the south grew in economic strength and power, buoyed up by its fertile land, gentle climate and freedom from foreign harassment. Rice played a vital role in the rising fortunes of the Jiangnan region, as new varieties made the land more productive and the population boomed. International maritime trade flourished in the coastal cities of Ningbo and Wenzhou.

It was during the Southern Song dynasty (1127–1279 AD) that Jiangnan reached a new apex of wealth and political influence. Barbarian invaders conquered the northern capital Kaifeng in 1127, and the remnants of the dynasty fled south to Hangzhou, which became not only the de facto political and cultural capital of China, but also the largest and richest city in the world. Then, as now, the city lay on the eastern side of the mesmerizing West Lake, a beautiful stillness of water ringed by green hills, its banks dotted with pavilions and towers. Within the walls of the city itself there were many-storied buildings and clean paved streets thronged with carriages, sedan chairs and mules.

There are rich descriptions of the gastronomic life of Hangzhou in the literature of the time. Specialist markets and food shops were dotted around the city; there were nearly 200 shops selling salted fish alone. From dawn until the early hours, street-sellers touted snacks to tempt the eyes and palates of passersby. In the taverns, people sipped rice wine from silver cups. Restaurants and teahouses catered to every taste and fancy, some specializing in particular regional cuisines, others serving only Buddhist vegetarian dishes or food that was chilled on ice. One contemporary source lists 234 famous local dishes, including a "hundred-flavors soup," fried crabs and hare strewn with onions. For those who preferred to dine aboard a floating pleasure boat or in a rented palace, there were catering businesses known as "tea and wine kitchens" that could lay on a feast complete with food, tableware and decorations. During this golden era, the inhabitants of Chinese cities are thought to have been the best-fed mass populations that the world had ever seen.

Eventually the Southern Song capital fell to another invasion, this time by Mongol tribes who conquered China and founded the Yuan dynasty in 1271. Within a decade the imperial capital had moved to Beijing, but Jiangnan culture continued to flourish. Not long after the fall of the Song, Marco Polo described a Hangzhou that seemed to have lost little of its luster. It was, he wrote, "without doubt the finest and most splendid city in the world," with markets selling "everything that could be desired to sustain life": wild game including stags, hares, pheasants and francolins, "as many ducks and geese as can be told," countless vegetables and fruits and improbable quantities of fish from ocean and lakes, "so vast are the numbers of those accustomed to dainty living, to the point of eating fish and meat at one meal."

The wealth and sophistication of the cities of Jiangnan, along with its plentiful produce, encouraged the development of a vibrant culture of gastronomy. The region became known across China and beyond for its scenic beauty and cultivated way of life, and people began to say that "above there is Paradise, below are Suzhou and Hangzhou." In terms of food, Song dynasty Jiangnan gave birth to what is widely recognized as the world's first true cuisine, a complex gastronomic culture in which food was not only cooked and enjoyed, but also elaborated, discussed and documented, and laid the foundations of what is now regarded as "Chinese cuisine."

With the exception of some dark periods of dynastic upheaval and civil conflict, the region prospered during the Ming (1368–1644 AD) and Qing (1644–1911 AD) dynasties. Qing dynasty Yangzhou became the national center of the lucrative salt trade, which at one time supplied an incredible quarter of China's entire tax revenue. As the salt trade boomed, the Yangzhou salt merchants grew rich. They built mansions and landscaped gardens and, like wealthy Chinese people throughout the ages, hired private chefs and entertained their friends to sumptuous dinner parties. According to local records, "scarcely a day went by without banquets and other diversions … they wallowed in luxury and pleasure."

During the final Qing dynasty, the Kangxi and Qianlong emperors were famously unable to resist the charms of the south. When, in the late eighteenth century, the Qianlong emperor visited Yangzhou, "gold was thrown around like dirt" as local dignitaries vied to impress him with lavish feasts and dazzling entertainments. A contemporary writer, Li Dou, reeled off the names of the dishes served at one notable banquet, which included bird's nest with slivered chicken, shark's fin and crabmeat soup, and bear's paw surrounded by the tongues of crucian carp. A startling number of Jiangnan dishes have origin myths connected with the Qianlong emperor's tours of the south. The emperor himself was so smitten by Jiangnan cooking that he insisted on recruiting Suzhou chefs to work in his northern court.

Yangzhou faded as an economic powerhouse with the arrival of the railways and the meteoric rise of Shanghai after the mid-nineteenth century. This new upstart gradually stole the limelight not only from Yangzhou, but also from the region's other ancient centers of culture and gastronomy. Shanghai itself became an international city and the outward-looking face of Jiangnan. Local Shanghainese cuisine absorbed flavors and cooking methods from across Jiangnan and abroad, Western-style restaurants appeared, and Chinese regional cuisines were adapted there to create hybrids such as *hai pai chuan cai* ("Shanghai-style Sichuanese cuisine").

In the early twentieth century, after the collapse of imperial rule, Jiangnan cuisine continued to represent the pinnacle of Chinese gastronomy, partly because of the dominance of leading Jiangnan figures such as Chiang Kai-shek in the new Republican

Interior of the Lu Mansion, built by salt merchant
Lu Shaoxu, in Yangzhou, Jiangsu province.

A farmer gathers the underwater fruits of Euryale ferox, source of the starchy foxnut or "Suzhou chickpea," in Jiangsu province.

government. Like most aspects of Chinese culture, however, it was affected by the vicissitudes of war and revolution. Then, in the 1990s, as China began to reform and open up, the culinary traditions of the region were eclipsed first by Cantonese cuisine, which acquired a new aura of prestige with the growing wealth of the Cantonese south, and later by the sudden craze for Sichuanese cooking around the turn of the century. But now, as the Chinese confront the negative consequences of rapid economic development, and many begin to look for a deeper connection with their traditional culture, lovers of Jiangnan food often express the hope that renewed inspiration can be found in the gentle and delightful flavors of this historic culinary region.

INGREDIENTS

The landscape of Jiangnan, with its rivers and canals, lakes and ponds, mountains and fields, mudflats and rocky coastline, yields an extraordinary bounty of produce for the kitchen. Pork is the favorite meat in this region, as in much of China, and the principal ingredient in of some of its most irresistible recipes. Fresh or salted, stewed or stir-fried, simmered into stocks or rendered into lard, the meat is an indispensable player in Jiangnan cooking, while beef and goat make occasional appearances on the dinner table. Chicken is chief among what Jiangnan people used to call "the feathered tribes" (*yu zu*), not only as an ingredient in its own right, but also as the invisible heart and soul of the stocks used to enrich all kinds of dishes (the eighteenth-century gourmet Yuan Mei wrote that the chicken was like a virtuous person who never received due credit because his good works were performed in secret). Duck is widely eaten, most famously in Nanjing. Great white geese, calm and stately, are also prized, particularly in Yangzhou, where street vendors specializing in saltwater goose ply their trade across the old city. Wild fowl such as francolins, wild ducks, pheasants and partridges are traditional delicacies, but these days rarely seen.

The people of Jiangnan, as befits the inhabitants of a land of fish and rice, eat a stunning variety of fish, seafood and crustaceans. In the markets of Ningbo, long hairtails (*dai yu*) gleam silver beside the sequinned glamour of grenadier anchovies (*dao yu*, or "knife fish"). There are slippery squid, octopuses and cuttlefish; cured cuttlefish roe is a particular delicacy. Among the numerous shellfish, the most unusual is perhaps the Ningbo mud snail (*ni luo*, or *Bullacta exarata*), which is divine when eaten raw, ice-cold and "drunken," complete with its thin, crunchy shell. Salted sea crab, chopped and served raw on the shell with a glistening crown of coral, is another Ningbo speciality with a bracing marine flavor and a slick, slimy texture. The seafood of Ningbo is so fine and fresh that it's often simply steamed or blanched in salted water. Delicious and nutritious seaweeds, including laver, kelp and string lettuce, are gathered on the seashores around Ningbo and Zhoushan.

Aside from seafood (known as "sea delicacies," *hai xian*), the Chinese have a collective term for its freshwater equivalent. "River delicacies" (*he xian*) describes the full gamut of freshwater fish, shellfish and other creatures, which are equally important in Jiangnan cookery. Paddy eels, freshwater shrimp and various kinds of crab are eaten, along with river mussels and, occasionally, crayfish. Among the many fish that swim in the region's lakes, rivers and streams, the small, silvery crucian carp are used to make gorgeous, milky-rich broths, while larger carp varieties are prized for their clean, relatively boneless flesh. One of the grandest local fish is the shimmering Reeves shad, which used to return from the ocean every spring to spawn in the Yangtze and Qiantang rivers. Another freshwater treat is the Chinese perch or Mandarin fish, a fierce-looking creature with delicate flesh that is perfect when lightly steamed.

Through the ages, the Jiangnan literati have been lavish in their praise of the region's fish and seafood; the Song dynasty poet Su Dongpo mentioned "wantonly gazing at the silvery knife fish coming out of the nets." No one, however, has written of Jiangnan water creatures with more infatuation than the seventeenth-century playwright Li Yu: "when it comes to crabs," he said, "while my heart lusts after them and my mouth enjoys their delectable taste (and in my whole life there has not been a single day when I have forgotten them), I can't even begin to describe or make clear why I love them, why I adore their sweet taste, and why I can never forget them … From the first day of the crab season until the last day they are sold, I … do not let a single evening pass without eating them … Dear crab, dear crab, you and I, are we to be lifelong companions?"

Dried and salted fish and seafood have been staples of the Jiangnan larder since the thirteenth century. Sea fish are often salt-fermented and wind-dried to make *xiang*, a pungent relish that is particularly loved in Zhejiang province. Strongly flavored, it is often used to jazz up milder ingredients such as fresh pork or vegetables. Salt-cured, wind-dried sea eel is steamed and served as an appetizer, while dried shrimp are ubiquitous in the region's cookery. For those interested in extreme cuisine, the infamous stinky mandarin fish of Tunxi near the Yellow Mountain is seriously funky, with a stinging aroma and an almost cheesy taste. It is said to have been invented accidentally by fishmongers returning to southern Anhui from the Yangtze River; after a week of being knocked about with salt in a bucket, so the story goes, the fish they brought back to their families had a strange smell and a most unusual flavor…

A seemingly limitless range of vegetables, varying by season and location, wild and cultivated, fresh and pickled, are eaten in Jiangnan. Varieties of the Brassica cabbage family are particularly important: favorites include green bok choy and Chinese cabbage, and the potherb mustard that is pickled to make "snow vegetable" (*xue cai*). Jiangnan people also have an unusual predilection for shepherd's purse (*ji cai*), a tiny-leafed wild relative of the Brassicae that is often used in soups, stir-fries and dumpling stuffings. Various types of bamboo shoot, fresh, dried or salted, are enjoyed in different seasons, as are squashes including the shiny green gourd, silk gourd and winter melon. Among the root vegetables, taro, white Asian radishes and sweet potatoes are widely consumed.

Some of the region's most wonderful and distinctive vegetables are water-born. There is wild rice stem (otherwise known as water bamboo), with its tender, bamboo-like shoots, crisp water chestnuts and the strange, horned fruits called water caltrops. Many parts of the lotus plant are used in Jiangnan cookery, including its leaves, seeds and plump underwater stems. Other local specialities include a type of water reed eaten in Nanjing (*lu hao*) and the slippery weed called water shield that haunted the homesick soul of Zhang Han all those centuries ago. Perhaps most fascinating is the euryale seed or foxnut (*qian shi*), a sticky, starchy sphere the size of a pearl that is made into tonic soups and banquet delicacies. The seed is laboriously extracted from the pomegranate-like underwater fruits of a plant with great round leaves that sit on the surface of a pond like tea trays. Each fruit has what looks like a beak, which is why the seeds are known in Suzhou as "chicken-head rice" (*ji tou mi*, sometimes translated as "Suzhou chickpeas").

Salted fish, hung up to dry in the old city of Yangzhou,
Jiangsu province.

Farmer gathering soybeans, Zhejiang province.

A love and appreciation of vegetables flows through the culture of the region. The thirteenth-century writer Lin Hong extolled the virtues of vegetable eating in his cookery book *Simple Offerings of a Mountain Dweller*. He included recipes for foraged foods and home-grown vegetables, many of them with lyrical names such as Three Crisp Ingredients of the Mountain Household—a salad of blanched bamboo shoot, mushrooms and goji berry leaves. The seventeenth-century poet and playwright Li Yu, a Jiangsu native, found beauty in the naturalness of vegetables: "When I speak of the Tao of eating and drinking, finely minced meat is not as good as meat in its natural state, and even such meat is not as good as vegetables in terms of the closeness of each to nature." In modern Jiangnan, people take particular pleasure in eating seasonal produce, and restaurant menus always vary with the cycle of the year.

Foraged vegetables have a cachet for discerning eaters: traditional favorites include Indian aster (*ma lan tou*) and spiky-leaved "sesame vegetable" (*zhi ma cai*), a wild variety of rocket. Many farmed vegetables that are not often available commercially, like pumpkin and sweet potato leaves, are served on farmhouse dinner tables. Some of the vegetables eaten in the region today have been part of local diets for millennia, including bamboo shoot, shepherd's purse and lotus root, as well as now-rarer plants such as mallow (*kui*) and betony (*huo*). Others are more recent foreign imports, like the tomato, which is used more in the polyglot cities of Shanghai and Ningbo than in other parts of the region, and is still known as a "barbarian eggplant" (*fan qie*).

FLAVORS

A deep respect for ingredients lies at the heart of Jiangnan cookery. Typically, cooks like to highlight the essential or "root" tastes (*ben wei*) of their ingredients, choosing seasonings and cooking methods that will make them shine. Seasonings are added not to dazzle the senses, but to frame the quiet beauty of the ingredients themselves. This is why Jiangnan cooks are so obsessed with sourcing the finest ingredients in their appropriate seasons, such as the first bamboo shoots of the spring, the plumpest autumn crabs or the sweetest greens gathered after a winter frost. The eighteenth-century gourmet Yuan Mei, one of the greatest exponents of the arts of Jiangnan cooking, wrote that the success of a feast was six parts down to the work of the cook, and four parts down to the efforts of the person who went to the market, a maxim that could still be applied today.

Local chefs excel at smoothing over the rough edges of their raw ingredients. They often begin by purging fish, meat and poultry of what the Chinese see as the less pleasant aspects of their natural flavors, known as "fishy tastes" (*xing wei*). This can be done by using purifying aromatics such as Shaoxing wine, ginger and spring onion in marinades and cooking, or by blanching raw meat and poultry in boiling water that is then discarded. Strongly flavored animal foods such as paddy eels may be seasoned with garlic, cilantro and spices to subdue their "fishy" flavors. These techniques may sound esoteric to anyone not immersed in Chinese food culture, but they really do refine the flavors of animal ingredients. Some vegetable ingredients are also tamed before cooking: radishes might be blanched to remove any harsh pepperiness, bamboo shoot to purge it of natural toxins.

The purpose of seasonings is not to overwhelm the innate taste of ingredients, but to enhance them with umami savoriness (*ti xian wei*), or to round out or "harmonize" the flavors of a dish (*he wei*). A fresh fish, for example, may be marinated in ginger and spring onion to refine away any coarseness of flavor, then steamed with slices of ham to amplify its umami qualities. Fresh vegetables are often stir-fried with a little lard or seasoned with stock to give them a luxurious taste and mouthfeel without obliterating their natural flavors. Tiny amounts of sugar are added to otherwise savory dishes to round out and "harmonize" a sauce. When a fine ingredient is cooked without any extraneous seasoning, such as a free-range chicken in its own broth, the resulting dish may be described as embodying the bird's "original juices and flavors" (*yuan zhi yuan wei*).

Jiangnan cooks rely mainly on a small battery of vital seasonings. Soy sauce is used for its savory taste and rich, dark color, particularly in "red-braised" dishes; it may be either a seasoning or a dip. Traditional local soy sauces are both intensely savory and very dark in color; the finest, made in Shaoxing, are known as "mother-and-son" soy sauces (*mu zi jiang you*) and have a zingy, peaty depth of flavor. Dark, thick fermented sauces made from soybeans (*dou ban jiang*) and wheat (*tian mian jiang*), which have bolder, earthier flavors than soy sauce, are also used. Soy sauce, the liquid run-off from fermented soybeans, is actually a relative upstart compared to these ancient condiments that evolved out of the fermented meat and fish pastes eaten in Confucian times; the first written mention of soy sauce (*jiang you*) occurs only in the thirteenth century, in a cookbook written by the Jiangnan author Lin Hong.

The people of Jiangnan have a particular affinity with vinegar, which has long been regarded as one of the "seven essentials" of daily life (along with firewood, rice, oil, salt, fermented sauce and tea). Rice vinegar is not only a key flavoring in sweet-and-sour dishes, but also ubiquitous as a table condiment. Local people employ it to dispel the "fishiness" of shrimp, fish and crab, which is why it is often served with them as a dip. It is also consumed to warm the stomach, awaken the appetite and cut through the oiliness of food. The old Yangtze River port of Zhenjiang (also known as Chinkiang) is home to one of China's most celebrated vinegars, a rich, dark brown brew made from glutinous rice. Red or "rosy" rice vinegar is also used widely in Zhejiang cooking. Across Jiangnan, vinegar is often the only condiment on the dinner table.

The city of Shaoxing in Zhejiang province has been a center of rice wine production for more than two millennia, and its famous "yellow wine" (*huang jiu*), named for its amber color, is an essential seasoning as well as a drink. It is the key flavoring in "drunken" dishes and is used to purge the "fishy tastes" of meat, fish and poultry. Stronger, vodka-like liquors are also occasionally used in Jiangnan cooking, for example in the classic Shanghai dish of stir-fried alfalfa sprouts. A wonderful by-product of the Shaoxing wine industry, which, sadly, is hard to find outside the region, is *jiu zao*, made from the boozy mulch left over from wine production. This brownish paste has a captivating aroma with smoky, fruity, earthy and floral notes, and various culinary uses. It is made into a pickling brine (*zao lu*) for steeping cooked ingredients such as edamame beans or shrimp, to make what are known as *zao* dishes. It can also be stirred into the mud used for sealing wine jars or clothing a "beggar's chicken," or layered with dried fish in clay jars, which gives the fish a gorgeous fragrance.

Sugar is another key seasoning, used more liberally in the famously sweet dishes of Suzhou and Wuxi than in other parts of the region. Ordinary white sugar made from cane or beet can be used in most recipes, but rock sugar lends a particularly lovely taste to fruit infusions and sweet tonic soups, while brown sugar is sometimes

Canal scene, Shaoxing, Zhejiang province.

Jinhua ham for sale in Hangzhou, Zhejiang province.

employed for its color and complex flavor. Traditionally, a liquid made from burned sugar (*tang se*, "sugar color") was used to add color and luster to stewed dishes, but this has fallen out of favor in recent years because of concerns about its possible carcinogenic properties; most chefs these days use dark soy sauce instead.

Ginger and spring onion are ubiquitous and vital, both in marinades and stocks (to dispel "fishiness"), and as the signature flavoring in some dishes, such as appetizers dressed in spring onion oil. In general, cooks in Jiangnan steer away from garlic, chilli and pepper, with a few exceptions: rural dwellers, especially in mountainous areas, sometimes pep up their cooking with chilli, while garlic and pepper are essential seasonings in some classic dishes, such as slivered eels with sizzling oil, again for their role in dispelling "fishiness." Dried spices have a role to play in many recipes, most notably star anise and cassia bark, but also others including *tsao-kuo* (Chinese cardamom, or *cao guo*), licorice root and "sand ginger" (*shan nai*). Stocks, lard and chicken oil are essential umami flavorings in the traditional Jiangnan kitchen, although these days many commercial chefs rely on MSG. In vegetarian cooking, umami flavors can be enhanced with dried mushrooms, soy sauce, sesame oil, soybean sprouts, bamboo shoot and other delicious plant foods.

Aside from these basic seasonings, salted, pickled and cured ingredients lend umami qualities to all kinds of dishes. The renowned Jinhua ham from southern Zhejiang province is often used to boost the savoriness of understated ingredients such as bamboo shoot and tofu, and to magnify the umami tastes of soups and stocks. Another notable ham is produced in Rugao, Jiangsu province. Salt pork, which is cheaper than ham, softer in texture and can more easily be made at home, is used in a similar way, along with dried shrimp and salted fish. According to legend, Jinhua ham dates back to the Song dynasty, when a great band of local men traveled to the northern capital to defend a patriotic official from slander. They salted their provisions of pork to last for the long journey, and by the time they reached their destination the meat, sun-dried and windswept, tasted extraordinary. The official, in a fit of nostalgia, christened it "hometown pork" (*jia xiang rou*), a name that is still sometimes used locally for Jinhua's salted meats. His followers, meanwhile, struck by the bright red hue of the pork hind legs, called them "fire legs" (*huo tui*)—the supposed origin of the common Chinese term for ham.

Probably no other pickled vegetable is as widely used in Jiangnan cooking as snow vegetable, made from salted potherb mustard, a variety of Brassica with jagged leaves and a strong, mustardy taste. Snow vegetable is particularly good with fish, shellfish, beans and broths, to all of which it lends a refreshing sourness. In Shaoxing, *mei gan cai*, a dark, aromatic dried vegetable made by pickling and then sun-drying mustard greens, has a central place in local hearts and myriad culinary applications. Pickles and preserves are often used as cooking ingredients; many are also served as relishes to "send the rice down" (*xia fan*).

In sweet dishes, one of the most distinctive flavors is the scented osmanthus, whose yellow blossoms are brined and then sugared for use in sweet soups, pastries, dumplings and other delicacies. On autumn evenings, the bewitching scent of these tiny blooms hangs heavy in the air of city streets and gardens across the region. Although it's not really a seasoning, red yeasted rice is another interesting local ingredient, made from rice grains covered in the mold *Monascus purpureus*, which stains them a deep purplish red. Ground up or steeped in water, the rice is used as a natural food coloring to decorate sweet pastries and dumplings, and to give a rosy hue to meat and poultry.

CULINARY THEMES

The "red-braising" (*hong shao*) cooking method, in which ingredients are stewed with soy sauce, wine and sugar, is found all over China, but the cooks of Jiangnan are its true masters, using it to coax pork belly into ecstatic tenderness, create magic out of fish tails, and make vegetables like bamboo shoot taste rich and opulent. There are countless variations on the red-braised theme, from treacly Shanghainese red-braised pork to the ambrosial Dongpo pork of Hangzhou. The name, incidentally, refers to the deep "red" color given by the soy sauce (dishes cooked without soy sauce may be referred to as "white-flavored," *bai wei*).

One of the most striking characteristics of the region's food is the practice of cooking fresh and salted ingredients together, which local chefs describe as *xian xian he yi* (a unity of fresh and salted). Traditionally, this was rooted in frugality, since small amounts of strong, salted foods could be used to heighten the flavors of cheap, plain ingredients such as tofu and vegetables to make them more palatable. It's a theme that recurs in numerous dishes, including Ningbo's famous yellow croaker soup with pickled greens, Shaoxing's steamed chicken with salted fish and Shanghai's bamboo shoot soup with fresh and salted pork.

Sweet dishes play a minor role across most of Jiangnan, but achieve a notorious prominence in the cooking of Suzhou and Wuxi, and to a lesser extent Shanghai. In Suzhou, you might come across "squirrel fish," a mandarin perch artfully cut and then bathed in a bright red sweet-sour sauce; a starter of finely chopped ham mixed with fried pine nuts and granulated sugar; or even, if you're really lucky, one of the most rare and glorious of banquet dishes, "honeyed" ham with lotus seeds. In Shanghai, you may find the sauce of your red-braised pork reduced to a thick, syrupy glaze. However, as local gourmets are always keen to point out, even in these places, the sweet tastes should be balanced on a menu with those that are "even and mild" (*ping dan*); stir-fried vegetables, perhaps, or a light, refreshing broth.

Although much of Jiangnan cooking is designed to create a gentle and seductive harmony of tastes, there is also a fascinating strain of what they call "stinky and rotten" (*chou mei*) flavors. These are the Chinese equivalents of the thrilling, funky tastes of moldy cheeses and well-hung game. Stinking tofu, with its aroma that smacks you in the face at about fifty yards, can be found all over the region, but the spiritual home of smelly foods is Shaoxing, where fermentation—of both wine and food—is a way of life. Here, locals traditionally use a brine made from rotted amaranth stalks to cure ingredients such as tofu, bamboo shoot, squash and young rape shoots, all of which acquire weird and wonderful flavors after a spell in the murky broth. These unusual foods are thought to have been born out of past periods of poverty, when local people had to use all their ingenuity to create palatable relishes when they could afford neither meat nor fish.

One intriguing strand of Hangzhou cooking is so-called "southern ingredients cooked in a northern style" (*nan liao bei peng*), thought to be a legacy of the flight south of the imperial court during the Song dynasty some 800 years ago. The wave of immigrants carried south during the flight of the Song court included officials and rich merchants, but also working people, among them chefs. Hangzhou, known then as Lin'an, became a melting pot of northern and southern culinary influences; one contemporary source lambasted the promiscuity of the fusion food of the era. In modern Hangzhou, chefs and gourmets point out certain delicacies that seem

Woksmith, Zhenjiang, Jiangsu province.

to stand apart from the dominant local style, such as West Lake vinegar fish and Mrs. Song's thick fish soup, as southern interpretations of old northern dishes.

Traces of north-south culinary influence may also be seen in Hangzhou "cat's ears," which echo a similar kind of pasta shell made in northern Xi'an, and in the sesame-studded pastries found across the region, which appear to be dainty southern versions of the "barbarian pastries" (*hu bing*) of the old Silk Road. Even the "soup dumpling" (*xiao long bao*), now famed as a Shanghainese speciality, is known in Jiangnan by the old northern word for such dumplings, *man tou*, and bears a striking resemblance to the steamed dumplings of Kaifeng, the old Northern Song capital.

Ever since the Song dynasty, the people of Jiangnan have enjoyed imitation dishes, in which food is cleverly engineered to tease and cheat the senses. In Song dynasty Hangzhou, diners-out could amuse themselves with imitation river globefish and imitation barbecued river deer. These days, any visitor to a Buddhist vegetarian restaurant will marvel at the vegetarian "roast duck" and "crabmeat" that so closely resemble their originals in appearance, taste and texture, yet are made entirely from vegetable ingredients. Aside from Buddhist cooking, Jiangnan gourmets delight in the conceit of making one ingredient appear to be something quite different, for example by laboriously boning out and stewing pig's trotters to make a lip-sticking delicacy known as "better-than-bear's-paw" (*sai xiong zhang*).

At the highest levels of Jiangnan banqueting, gourmets seek out rare and esoteric delicacies. These might be exotic ingredients such as peach tree sap, or simply a particular part of a plant or animal: fish cheeks, the tenderest tips of new bamboo shoots or the innermost hearts of green bok choy. Moralists through the ages have deplored such preferences as atrociously decadent, but in many cases there is actually little waste: the rest of the fish and bamboo shoot, and the outer vegetable leaves, will be used in other dishes. A discerning eater might also and equally take delight in eating cheap foodstuffs prepared with great skill, examples of "cooking coarse food exquisitely" (*cu cai xi zuo*).

Most relevant, perhaps, to modern concerns, is the wonderful Jiangnan practice of "vegetarian ingredients cooked meatily" (*su cai hun zuo*), in which vegetable foods are cooked with a little meat, poultry or fish to season and enrich them. In banquet cookery, stocks, lard, chicken oil or morsels of dried seafood or ham may be added to the season's vegetables, lending them a delicious flavor and luster without overwhelming their natural beauty. On an everyday level, most people in both town and country eat a wide variety of healthy vegetables, their flavors enhanced by small amounts of lard, pork or home-cured meats. This aspect of Jiangnan gastronomy can be an inspiration for anyone wishing to reduce the amount of meat they consume without any sacrifice of gastronomic pleasure.

SATISFYING THE SENSES AND THE MIND

For Jiangnan gourmets, as for those across China, a fine meal is a multi-sensory experience involving not only taste, but also "color, fragrance, flavor and form," and even the vessels and utensils used to serve a dish (*se xiang wei xing qi*). Serious Jiangnan cooks pay particular attention to the visual appeal of their food, striving, for example, to "match colors" (*pei se*). A well-planned menu will feature a pleasing variety of ingredients and cooking methods, and will also be color balanced: dark rosy

Fisherman on his houseboat, Jiangsu province.

pink ham might set off bright green peas or ivory-white taro in a single dish; in terms of the overall menu, lively greens might balance a sleek red-braised meat, while a pale soup might contrast with the treacly darkness of soy-cured duck.

Elegant cutting underpins the beauty of Jiangnan cooking, and local chefs are known for their dexterity with the cleaver. The cooks of Yangzhou are renowned for their virtuoso cutting skills, and the city for its "three knives": the cook's cleaver, the scissors and the pedicurist's knife (a foot massage is another of the city's treats). Chefs there are trained to reduce a block of silken tofu to a dreamy mass of hairlike strands, to transform the flesh of fish into "chrysanthemums" and to cut clumsy chicken gizzards into elegant frills. One Yangzhou chef told me he and his colleagues could each cut a block of tofu into 5,000 filaments. In the past, but rarely in modern times, chefs took the art of cutting to awe-inspiring extremes. Guests at a banquet might be presented with a display platter framing a collage made up of dozens of ingredients, meticulously cut and arranged in the form, perhaps, of a cockerel resplendent with multicolored feathers or a landscape of white cranes among a stand of pine trees; or a soup served in a hollowed-out watermelon carved with intricate intaglio designs.

The Chinese take a far greater pleasure in texture and mouthfeel than most other cultures. Some tactile qualities of food are particularly prized. *Cui* refers to the pleasant, snappy crispness of fresh celery or a fast-fried chicken gizzard; *nuo* to the soft, huggy stickiness of glutinous rice. *Hua nen* combines the words for slippery and tender, describing perfectly the mouthfeel of freshwater shrimp that have been poached in oil and then lightly stir-fried. While many Westerners dislike gristle and chewiness, the Chinese adore a certain tensile quality in their meat. Chicken wings and legs are savored over breast meat because they contain muscles that have moved and worked, developing characteristics of strength and stretchiness (*ren*); they are strong and chewy (*jiao jing*), the opposite of soft and cottony. Texture and mouthfeel are just as important in any Chinese discussion of food as visual beauty and flavor.

This precise appreciation of texture means that the subtle command of heat, known by chefs as *huo hou* (literally "fire and timing") has a central importance in Jiangnan cookery. An accomplished chef will develop a sixth sense for the temperature of the oil in his wok, keeping it low to preserve the cloudlike softness of egg white, driving it high for stir-frying. In Ningbo, the finest chefs are said to be so well schooled in *huo hou* that they can braise a whole eel so that its skin remains intact, despite being so tender that it will disintegrate if you play a tune nearby!

A fine Jiangnan repast will delight not only the senses, but also the mind. For beyond the pleasures of aromas, colors, tableware and multifarious sensations for the tongue and palate, there is serious fun to be had in thinking about food. Perhaps it's the knowledge that the stir-fried cabbage tips on the table were picked only this morning at the height of their perfection, or that the fish came from a celebrated lake or stream. Maybe it's the extraordinary *trompe l'oeil* of a vegetarian "Dongpo pork" conjured up from a thick slice of winter melon, or some crisp "eels" made from mushrooms. It might be the lyricism of a dish's name, its legendary origins or the way it nods to a classical Chinese novel that brings a knowing smile to the lips. In China, the enjoyment of food is not seen as a baser pleasure because of its roots in physical appetite and the need for nourishment. Gastronomy is part of culture, and good food has the power to move mind and spirit, connecting us not only with our family and friends, but also with our history and heritage, and with the rhythms and essences of the natural world.

A CULTURE OF GASTRONOMY

Through the ages, the educated people of Jiangnan, more than anywhere else in China, have not only savored their food, but have also been moved to write about it in poetry, prose and recipe books, which is why Jiangnan food is often described as the cuisine of the literati. Many of China's best-known gastronomic writers lived in or visited Jiangnan, including the Song dynasty poets Su Dongpo, who served as governor of Hangzhou, and Lu You, who spent many years in Shaoxing. Both men wrote widely and evocatively of the region's food.

Ni Zan, a leading landscape painter of the fourteenth century and a native of Wuxi, penned his own cookery book, *The Dietary System of the Cloud Forest Studio*, while the Suzhou-born official Han Yi is thought to have been the author of a collection of recipes from the Jiangnan region that was published in the early fifteenth century. One Yangzhou salt merchant, Tong Yuejian, was the probable author of a great culinary compendium of the Qing dynasty, *The Harmonious Cauldron*. Most famously, the eighteenth-century gastronome Yuan Mei named his remarkable cookery book, *Food Lists of the Garden of Contentment,* after his estate in Nanjing. For the Chinese literati, good taste in food was a mark of self-cultivation, and gastronomy a delight both sensual and intellectual.

Many notable gourmets took a stand against ostentatious and extravagant food, suggesting that real discrimination lay in a kind of gastronomic modesty. Yuan Mei was scornful of people who lusted after expensive ingredients and were unable to see that a well-cooked dish of tofu could be far superior to one made with bird's nest or "vulgar fellows" like sea cucumber. Many men of letters recoiled from gluttonous excess and yearned for the simplicity of rural life. Su Dongpo spent several happy years of exile in impoverished areas, tilling the land and cooking for his wife and concubine, while the "poor scholar" Shen Fu, author of *Six Records of a Floating Life* (1809), extolled the virtues of frugal eating and described the pleasures of simple suppers shared with his beloved wife.

There's an old tale by the poet Tao Yuanming (also known as Tao Qian), "The Peach Blossom Spring," which has embedded itself in the Chinese imagination. Written more than 1,500 years ago, it tells of a fisherman who stumbles upon a forgotten, old-fashioned world where people live in bucolic harmony, far from the corrupting influence of society. This utopian story has inspired people of many generations, from the scholar-officials who retired to the countryside to forage and cook to the organic farmers and gastronomic traditionalists of today. For Chinese idealists, simple, balanced, seasonal eating is not just a matter of diet, but an expression of the rejection of materialist aspirations and a yearning for a more harmonious relationship with the natural world.

Some of the values of the Chinese literati seem strikingly attuned to those of the modern locavore and environmental movements. There's the obsession with seasonal produce, grown and gathered according to the fortnightly solar terms of the old agricultural calendar, and the idea that human beings should live in harmony with the natural world (*tian ren he yi*). Like their modern equivalents, the gourmets of Song dynasty Hangzhou were concerned with provenance and appreciated foraged foods. Many of the recipes in Lin Hong's thirteenth-century cookbook, *Pure Offerings of a Mountain Hermit*, feature wild game and foraged plants, and have lyrical and exotic names that would not sound out of place on

Dai Jianjun's organic farm, Suichang, Zhejiang province.

the menu of a modern Nordic restaurant, such as honey cakes with pine pollen, "snow and sunset soup," "pocket of mountain and sea" and "treasures in an icy pot."

Many traditional Jiangnan dishes still have witty or poetic names. A dish in which two contrasting ingredients are cooked together, such as a stir-fry of wild rice stem and celtuce or a steamed duo of fresh and salted fish, may be described as "civil-and-military" (*wen wu*), a reference to the complementary opposites of traditional Chinese administration. Delicate, custardy egg white concoctions are named after the snowy cotton rose hibiscus flower (*fu rong*). More elaborately, one of the old-fashioned gems of Ningbo cooking is slow-cooked turtle with rock sugar, which since 1852 has been called Grasping the Turtle's Head (*du zhan ao tou*) in honor of a brilliant young scholar who ate it on his way to take the civil service examinations in Beijing. The name is a reference to the way the top scholar of every year group would receive his honors while standing beside a marble sculpture of a turtle on the steps of the imperial palace.

The names and legends of Jiangnan dishes reveal much about the more general culture of the region: not only the traditional esteem for scholarly achievement, but also a fascination with the Qianlong emperor's southern tours, the wit and lyricism |of the Chinese language, a love of nature, the sense of helplessness felt by ordinary people in the face of corruption, popular affection for upright officials committed to the common good and, above all, the pleasure and delight that Chinese people everywhere take in food.

Although the annals of Jiangnan gastronomy are dominated by men, the region also has its gastronomic heroines. Song dynasty Hangzhou had a minor but notable tradition of women cooks. One famous dish, Mrs. Song's thick fish soup, is named after a female professional chef of the time, while *Madame Wu's Recipe Book*, written by a woman in the same era, is the earliest extant Chinese cookbook in which precise measurements are given. There is also the tale of Dong Xiaowan, the lovely concubine of a gifted scholar of the late Ming dynasty, whose delicacy of character was reflected in her exquisite cooking. Other spirited women feature in the folklore around specific dishes, such as Peihong, the inventor of a favorite Shaoxing pickle, and the nameless woman who made the first Hangzhou West Lake fish in vinegar sauce.

Some of the most celebrated Jiangnan dishes are fantastically complicated and demand exotic ingredients, days of labor and intricate, dainty knifework. But while the exceptional wealth of the region and the sophistication of its urban elite may have fostered the development of a complex haute cuisine, the local traditions of frugal folk cooking are equally fascinating. In Shaoxing, the origin myths of many dishes involve downtrodden servants trying to outwit their miserly masters, or poor scholars and vagrants who make culinary discoveries out of hunger and desperation. The street snacks and homemade pickles of the region are just as enticing as its banquet delicacies. All over Jiangnan, delicious food, rich in lore and legend, is made by farmers, snack sellers and ordinary domestic cooks. In China, the love of good food is not just the preserve of the rich, but permeates the whole of society, from the palace and the mansion down to the farmhouse and the city street.

APPETIZERS

In Jiangnan, formal meals always begin with a selection of appetizers to set the mood and whet the appetite. There might be salads and pickles, cured and "drunken" meats or crisp-fried little fish in syrup: a mixture of salty, sour, sweet and umami flavors. When it comes to entertaining at home, cold dishes are particularly convenient for the cook, since they can be prepared in advance, leaving time to tend to the stove after guests have arrived. And for less formal occasions, "little dishes" (*xiao cai*) of salty cured meats, fried peanuts and the like are the traditional accompaniments to a leisurely evening of wine or beer and conversation, and were once served at taverns across the region. Many people in Jiangnan buy some of their snacks and appetizers from delicatessens or specialist street vendors, particularly when it comes to cold cuts such as saltwater duck or goose, and time-consuming delicacies like stuffed lotus root and spiced wheat gluten.

Once, when I visited Suzhou, I was invited into a kitchen at the back of the local culinary association offices where two master chefs were preparing dinner for a group of local dignitaries. A grand old soup was simmering away on a backburner, breathing out exquisite aromas; the huge clay pot contained a whole hen, a duck and a pigeon, along with a pork hock and a chunk of cured ham. An array of cold dishes were already laid out on plates, ready to be served, with a centerpiece of "oil-exploded" shrimp steeped in syrup and wine surrounded by eight further little dishes. There was cured duck in a rosy pink sauce, salted chicken, barbecued beef and wine-fragrant strips of pig's stomach. And to "match the meaty dishes with vegetables" (*hun su da pei*), there was sweet lotus root stuffed with glutinous rice, a cucumber salad, cabbage infused with a rumor of chilli, and slivered jellyfish. It was just a taste of the delicate diversity of Jiangnan appetizers.

"Drunken" dishes, made by steeping raw or cooked ingredients—often poultry and seafood—

in Shaoxing rice wine, are typical of the region and a particular speciality of Shaoxing. Less well known outside Jiangnan are what are known as *zao* dishes, which are flavored with *jiu zao,* the boozy mulch of grains left over after making Shaoxing wine. Dried out, it looks like compost, but has a captivating smell. In Shaoxing, people pack dried fish or cooked chicken into jars with layers of dried *jiu zao* mixed with strong rice liquor, and store them until the fish or chicken is boozily aromatic. The *jiu zao* can also be simmered with water, salt, wine and spices, then strained to produce a gorgeously fragrant liquid called *zao lu.* This potion can be used for steeping edamame beans in their pods, cooked chicken, cooked shrimp and cooked pig's stomach, to all of which it imparts its distinctive and alluring flavor. *Jiu zao* can also be used to make delicate and delectable sauces for hot fish and seafood dishes. I've never seen this unusual ingredient for sale outside the region, and the only place I've found *zao lu* is in New York's Chinatown, where it was sold as

"superior pickle sauce." Drunken dishes can more easily be made outside the region, though; see the recipe for drunken chicken on page 71.

Some appetizers need to be made or finished shortly before cooking, while others, such as Hangzhou vegetarian roast goose or Spiced wheat gluten with four delights, can be made a day or two in advance and kept in the fridge. When planning a selection of appetizers for a Chinese meal, try to include contrasting ingredients, colors, tastes and textures and, if your guests eat meat, a balance of meaty and vegetarian dishes. And do, of course, feel free to include Jiangnan appetizers in a non-Chinese meal. Chinese sweet-sour pickles go magnificently with European cold cuts of meat and poultry, and leftover saltwater duck or Zhenjiang terrine, for example, are fabulous in sandwiches. The Shanghai pickled radish in the Basic Recipes chapter (see page 328) may also be served as an appetizer.

Crisp seaweed with peanuts

tai cai hua sheng mi 苔菜花生米

This delectable appetizer, a speciality of the coastal city of Ningbo, combines the crisp dark frizz of deep-fried seaweed with fragrant red peanuts. A sprinkling of sugar sets off the salty, umami taste of the vegetable. It's traditionally made with a kind of branched string lettuce or gutweed that grows like a carpet of strandy green hair along the shoreline near Ningbo, and has a mesmerizing fragrance and flavor. It's known as *tai cai* or *tai tiao* in Chinese, and is used in both sweet pastries and savory dishes. I've never found branched string lettuce for sale outside China, but once when I was walking along a beach in southern England I caught its unmistakable scent on the wind. I returned to London with bagfuls of seaweed, which I dried out and used in a few Ningbo dishes.

If you can find clean, wild branched string lettuce, which you will recognize from its resemblance to skeins of green hair, do dry it and use it in the following recipe. Otherwise, I offer you a favorite cheat of Chinese restaurants in the UK, which often serve "crispy seaweed" made from deep-fried cabbage leaves: delicious, and strikingly similar in effect to the original dish.

Crisp seaweed with peanuts, made with branched string lettuce, above, and with spring cabbage, below

¾ oz (25g) dried branched string lettuce, or 5 dark green outer leaves of spring cabbage, or 4 oz (100g) green or purple curly kale	5 oz (150g) red-skinned peanuts 1⅓ cups (300ml) cooking oil 3 tsp granulated sugar Salt

If using spring cabbage, cut out and discard the thick stem from the center of each leaf. Lay the leaves on top of each other, roll them up and slice as thinly as possible. You should end up with 1–2mm strips of cabbage. If using kale, strip the curly leaves from the stems and break them into small pieces. If using dried seaweed, separate it into strands following the line of the "hair" and then cut it into ⅛ in (5mm) pieces.

Put the peanuts in a seasoned wok with the cooking oil and heat gently to 260–275°F (130–140°C) until there is a gentle fizzing around the nuts—it's easiest to use a thermometer for this. Deep-fry at this temperature for 15–20 minutes, until the nuts are glossy, crisp and fragrant (if you taste one, carefully, you will be able to tell when it has lost its raw crunch). Remove with a slotted spoon and drain on paper towels.

Reheat the oil to 350°F (180°C). Add the cabbage or kale in two or three batches and deep-fry for a couple of minutes, or until crisp. Remove with a slotted spoon and drain on paper towels. If using seaweed, heat the oil to 300–320°F (150–160°C) and deep-fry very briefly until crisp. Remove with a slotted spoon and drain on paper towels.

Mix the peanuts and cabbage "seaweed" together, season with salt, then add the sugar and serve. If you are using real branched string lettuce, you won't need any salt.

Quick cucumber salad

liang ban huang gua 凉拌黄瓜

At dinnertime, people loiter on the pavement outside a tiny, ordinary-looking townhouse in a tree-lined lane of Shanghai's former French Concession, waiting for a table at one of the city's most adored local restaurants. For more than 20 years, the chefs at Old Jesse have been turning out mouthwatering renditions of Shanghainese cuisine, from stir-fried green soybeans with pickled greens to boned pig's trotters with "eight-treasure" stuffing. This recipe is based on one of their simplest appetizers, a sweet-sour, garlicky salad that's quick to make and a refreshing contrast to richer dishes. If you don't have the mellow brown rice vinegar they use at the restaurant, balsamic vinegar would make a good substitute.

The common Chinese name for cucumber is "yellow squash" (*huang gua*), which is why you will often find it served in Zhejiang province as one of the traditional "five yellows" at the Dragon Boat Festival of the fifth lunar month (the other "yellow" foods might include yellow croaker, "yellow" paddy eels, salted duck-egg yolks and Shaoxing "yellow wine").

Quick cucumber salad; Sweet-and-sour radishes (page 40)

1 cucumber (about 12 oz/375g)
½ tsp salt
1½ tbsp superfine sugar
2 tbsp finely chopped garlic
1 tbsp Chinkiang vinegar
1 tsp light soy sauce

Trim both ends off the cucumber and lay it across your chopping board. Use the flat side of a Chinese cleaver or a rolling pin to smack it gently several times, turning it each time, to break it open and loosen the flesh without smashing it to smithereens.

Cut the cucumber in half lengthways, then into two or three long strips. Lay the strips parallel and cut them into bite-sized pieces. Add the salt, mix well and leave in a colander for at least 10 minutes to drain.

Drain off as much of the liquid that has emerged from the cucumber as possible. Add the sugar and set it aside for a minute or two until it dissolves, then add the rest of the ingredients, stir well and serve.

Slippery cucumber salad

This is a dish taught to me by chef Sun Fugen in Suzhou. Cut the cucumber into thin slices and leave in the salt for several hours, then squeeze out as much water as possible. Add superfine sugar to taste, some finely chopped garlic and a little sliced pickled chilli. The longer salting gives the cucumber an intriguing texture: floppy yet crisp.

Cucumber with sweet fermented sauce dip

Cut the cucumber into batons and serve with sweet fermented sauce dip (see page 333). At the Dragon Well Manor restaurant in Hangzhou, this is the way they serve their whole baby cucumbers: crisp, delicate and picked earlier the same day.

Sweet-and-sour radishes

tang cu xiao luo bo 糖醋小萝卜

The Chinese tend to favor the large white radish commonly known in English by its Japanese name, daikon (or its south Asian one, mooli), but small pink radishes like these are occasionally eaten. I enjoyed them in this dish as part of a radiantly beautiful autumn lunch at my friend He Yuxiu's flat in Shanghai, where they were served alongside a pile of steamed hairy crabs as red as fire engines, a lazy tangle of paddy eels and wild rice stem, and a dish of juicy alfalfa sprouts.

See photograph on page 39

2 bunches small red radishes, (about 14 oz/400g after topping and tailing)
2 tsp salt

3 tbsp superfine sugar
1½ tbsp Chinkiang vinegar
¾ tsp sesame oil

Top and tail the radishes. Fold them up in a clean tea towel and pat them into a single layer underneath the cloth. Smack them with the flat side of a Chinese cleaver or a rolling pin to crack them all open, without smashing them to smithereens. Put the radishes in a bowl, add the salt and mix well. Set aside for at least a couple of hours.

Rinse the radishes, then squeeze out as much water as possible, either by pressing them in a colander or wrapping them in a clean tea towel and squeezing it out. Put the radishes in a bowl, add the sugar and mix well. Set aside for a few minutes to allow the sugar to dissolve, then stir in the vinegar. Just before serving, stir in the sesame oil.

Slivered white Asian radish and jellyfish salad

cong you hai zhe pi 葱油海蜇皮

The people of Jiangnan have a particular liking for jellyfish, which is often served as an appetizer. Their smooth umbrellas are known as "jellyfish skin," while the frilly, crinkled arms with which the jellyfish stuffs food into its mouth are known as "jellyfish head." Both are flavorless and enjoyed for the pleasure of their textures. The "skin" is a delightful mixture of slipperiness and crispness, while the amber-colored "head" has a bright, electrifying crunch.

In Shanghai, the "head" may be dressed in spring onion oil or in a dark, mature rice vinegar; in Hangzhou it's often served with a dip of soy sauce, vinegar and chopped garlic. The "skin," which is regarded as the more desirable part, is typically served like this, its transparent ribbons mingling with the supple crispness of the radish.

Three different species of jellyfish are eaten in China. The creature is known, appropriately, as "ocean sting." The idea of eating it might seem strange to foreigners, but in my experience few people find it weird in practice. It's one of the best foods with which to begin to appreciate the Chinese love of texture. These days, you can buy ready-to-eat jellyfish in many Chinese groceries—just the thing for those jellyfish emergencies!

14 oz (400g) white Asian radish
¾ tsp salt
1 pack ready-to-eat jellyfish (about 6 oz/170g)
3 spring onions
2 tbsp cooking oil
¾ tsp superfine sugar

Peel and trim the radish. Cut it into thin slices, then into slivers. Put them in a bowl, add the salt and scrunch it in with your fingers. Set aside for half an hour or so in a colander to draw out the liquid.

Squeeze the radish slivers to remove as much liquid as possible. If the jellyfish comes in large pieces, cut it into ⅕ in (5mm) ribbons. Separate the white and green parts of the spring onion. Smack the whites briskly with the flat side of a Chinese cleaver or a rolling pin to loosen their fibers. Thinly slice the greens and put them in a small heatproof bowl.

Heat the oil in a seasoned wok over a medium flame. Add the spring onion whites and stir-fry until they are a rich brown color and wonderfully fragrant. Remove them, leaving behind as much oil as possible. Pour the hot oil over the spring onion greens: it should sizzle fiercely. Add the spring onions with their oil and the sugar to the radish slivers. Mix everything together well with chopsticks, then allow to cool. Finally, stir in the jellyfish. Pile the mixture up on a dish to serve.

Ningbo soy sauce greens
ning bo kao cai 宁波燩菜

At first glance, these sleek, darkened vegetables might not compete for your attention with more glamorous Zhejiang specialities, but they are absolutely scrumptious and juicily aromatic. Fresh greens are blanched, briefly stir-fried and then simmered gently in soy sauce, wine and sugar until the liquid has reduced to a dark, roasty glaze. They're normally served at room temperature and have a lazy, bittersweet flavor reminiscent of roasted chicory and Italian slow-grilled vegetables.

The dish is a speciality of Ningbo, where it's made with a local variety of mustard green known as *tian cai xin*, but I've followed the practice in nearby Shanghai and used green bok choy. Smaller heads with a greater proportion of dark leaf to fleshy stem are best, if you can find them. I've also used the same method with curly kale, which tastes delicious but looks less pretty. Some people add a little blanched, sliced bamboo shoot to the greens. I learned how to make this dish in the kitchens of the Zhuangyuan Lou restaurant in Ningbo, thanks to chef Chen Xiaoliang.

1 dried shiitake mushroom	3 tbsp cooking oil
4 spring onions, white parts only	2 tbsp Shaoxing wine
8 medium-sized heads green bok choy, preferably 6 in (15cm) long (about 2 lbs/1kg in total)	2 tbsp light soy sauce
	1 tbsp dark soy sauce
	2 tsp superfine sugar
	1 tsp sesame oil

Soak the shiitake mushroom for at least half an hour in boiling water. When it has softened, slice off and discard the stem. Smack the spring onions lightly with the flat side of a Chinese cleaver or a rolling pin to loosen their fibers. Wash and trim the bok choy, discarding any yellow leaves.

Bring a large pan of water to the boil. If the heads of bok choy are larger than 6 in, cut them in half or quarters lengthways, otherwise, leave them whole. Blanch briefly in the boiling water to wilt the leaves. Drain and shake dry.

Heat the oil in a seasoned wok over a high flame. Add the spring onions and stir-fry until they smell wonderful. Add the bok choy pieces and stir-fry for a minute or two to clothe them in the oil, then add the whole shiitake mushroom, wine, both soy sauces and sugar and mix well. Bring to the boil, cover and reduce the heat to medium. Simmer gently for 20–30 minutes, stirring occasionally. You will find that a lot of water initially emerges from the bok choy; when this happens, remove the lid and allow it to evaporate. Keep an eye on the wok to make sure the vegetables don't boil dry.

When the vegetables are sleek, dark and much reduced in volume, and only a little syrupy sauce is left, turn off the heat and stir in the sesame oil. Use chopsticks to pile the bok choy neatly in a serving dish and top with the shiitake mushroom. Allow to cool before serving at room temperature.

Chrysanthemum leaves with pine nuts

song ren hao cai 松仁蒿菜

The green leaves of the garland chrysanthemum, or crown daisy, have a meadowy, herby taste that is most refreshing. They can be found in good Chinese supermarkets, where they are sold as *tong hao* or *hao cai* (there are two common varieties with differently shaped leaves but similar flavors). The leaves may be blanched and then stir-fried with lard, garlic and salt, but they are more usually made into salads, often with added pine nuts or finely chopped tofu; my friend Rose calls these dishes "Chinese tabbouleh."

This recipe comes from the Dragon Well Manor restaurant in Hangzhou. Don't try to use any other type of chrysanthemum leaf that you might find in your garden, as most are inedible. The same method can be used to serve curly green kale, to delicious effect. A similar salad is made in the region with the tender spring leaves of *ma lan tou* or Indian aster (*Kalimeris indica*), a herbaceous plant with daisy-like flowers with yellow hearts and purple petals.

A small handful of pine nuts	2 oz (50g) firm tofu
1 lb (500g) garland chrysanthemum (crown daisy) leaves	2 tsp sesame oil
	Salt

Preheat the oven to 250°F (120°C). Roast the pine nuts on a lipped baking tray for 5–10 minutes, until golden. Keep an eye on them, as they burn easily. Tip them out quickly onto a plate to cool.

Wash the chrysanthemum leaves and discard any thick stalks. Bring a pan of water to the boil, add the leaves and blanch for 10–20 seconds, until wilted. Turn them out into a colander and rinse them immediately under the cold tap to cool completely. Squeeze as much water as possible out of the leaves, then chop them finely. Finely chop the firm tofu.

Mix the leaves and tofu in a bowl, add the sesame oil and season with salt. Stir well. Pile the leaves on a serving dish, or press them into a cup and invert it to make a tidy mound. Garnish with the pine nuts.

"Thousand sheet" chrysanthemum rolls

Blanch approximately 200g tofu sheet in boiling water, then refresh under the cold tap, shake well and spread out to dry. Blanch, chop and season the chrysanthemum leaves as in the main recipe. Place the tofu on your work surface and arrange a ½ in (1.5cm) deep row of chopped greens along one end; roll up until the tofu is two or three layers thick. Trim off any excess tofu. Cut the roll into 2½ in (6cm) sections. Repeat with the rest of the tofu, then pile the rolls up on a serving plate.

Spicy Chinese cabbage

la bai cai 辣白菜

This is a gorgeous little Shanghainese starter that can be made well in advance of your meal. After a long salting and draining, the cabbage is soft but retains a little bite, and is thrillingly infused with scorched chilli. The salting greatly reduces the volume, so you'll end up with a fairly small portion, but it's easy to double the recipe if you are cooking for a crowd.

The chilli plays a marginal role in Jiangnan cooking, and it's tempting to see dishes like this one as the product of Sichuanese influences in Shanghai, which has long been a melting pot of cultural and culinary influences from across China and the world. The city even has its own, somewhat toned-down version of Sichuanese flavors in *hai pai chuan cai*, the so-called "Shanghai-style" Sichuan cuisine.

1 Chinese cabbage (about 1⅓ lbs/600g)	¾ tsp whole Sichuan peppercorns
2½ tsp salt	3 dried chillies
	2 tbsp cooking oil

Rinse the Chinese cabbage whole, then put it on a chopping board and slice across the grain into ⅕ in (5mm) strips. Put them in a bowl. Add the salt and Sichuan peppercorns and use your hand to scrunch them into the cabbage strips, which will become slightly floppy. Cover the cabbage with an inverted small plate that sits directly on it and put a heavy weight on top (I use old-fashioned weights in a plastic freezer bag, but a heavy stone will do). Leave it in the fridge or a cool place for several hours or overnight.

Remove the weight and plate. Drain the cabbage, squeezing to extract as much liquid as you can. Pick out and discard as many of the Sichuan peppercorns as possible. Snip the chillies into 1 in (2cm) sections and discard the seeds.

Heat the oil in a seasoned wok until smoking. Turn off the heat, immediately add the chillies and stir them for a few seconds until fragrant and darkening, but not burned. Swiftly add the drained cabbage and stir to clothe it in the fragrant oil. Serve at room temperature.

Sour-and-hot Chinese cabbage

Add 1½ tsp Chinkiang vinegar and ¾ tsp sesame oil to the main recipe.

Celtuce salad with spring onion oil

cong you wo sun 葱油莴笋

Celtuce, also known as stem or asparagus lettuce, can be hard to find outside China, but it's an extraordinarily delicious and versatile vegetable and I wanted to include a couple of recipes for it here. If you do find it in a Chinese supermarket or farmers' market, snap it up immediately! The leafy tips are fabulous stir-fried with nothing more than oil and salt, but they must be used very fresh because they wilt quickly.

The stems, however, are the real treasures. Shorn of their fibrous outer layer, they are delicate, translucent and the prettiest pale green (see photograph on page 191), with a subtle, nutty flavor that one of my friends has described as being like buttery popcorn. They are often eaten uncooked, as in this recipe, but can also be stir-fried or added to slow-simmered stews. Their jade-like color, light flavor and crispness offer a particularly pleasing contrast to meaty ingredients.

This easy salad makes a fine accompaniment to noodles or dumplings for lunch, and can also be served as an appetizer with other dishes.

2 celtuce stems (about 1½ lbs/700g)	2 tbsp cooking oil
4 tbsp thinly sliced spring onions, green parts only	1 tsp superfine sugar Salt

Use a potato peeler to remove the fibrous outer layer of the celtuce stems. Slice the stems thinly, then cut the slices into slivers. Put the slivers in a bowl, add 1 teaspoon salt and mix thoroughly. Set them aside in a colander for half an hour or so.

Drain off any water that has emerged from the celtuce and squeeze the strips tightly to get rid of as much liquid as possible. Put the spring onions in a small heatproof bowl.

Heat the oil in a seasoned wok until the edges of the wok are beginning to smoke. Pour the hot oil over the spring onions: it should sizzle fiercely. Pour the spring onions and oil onto the celtuce, add the sugar and extra salt to taste and mix well. Pile up on a dish to serve.

White Asian radish with spring onion oil

Exactly the same method can be used to prepare slivers of peeled white Asian radish.

Nanjing New Year's salad

jin ling su shen jin 金陵素什锦

In Nanjing, the capital of Jiangsu province, a colorful cooked salad like this is an essential part of the New Year's Eve feast, and makes a pleasing contrast to the lavish "big fish, big meat" (*da yu da rou*) character of the other celebratory dishes. It is traditionally made in large quantities so that it can be eaten gradually over the lazy first few days of the year. The salad should include at least ten different vegetables; some restaurants make it with eighteen, which is why another name for the dish is Eighteen Fresh Ingredients (*shi ba xian*).

Some of the vegetables typically included have an auspicious symbolism, like "golden" lily flowers, "silver" bamboo shoot and soybean sprouts, which resemble the archaic *ruyi* scepter, an ornamental backscratcher made from precious materials. In Shanghai restaurants, red and green bell peppers and cucumber are often added. Celtuce, lotus root, arrowhead, winter bamboo shoot, tofu skin, snow peas and fresh mushrooms all make fine additions.

I've tasted many different versions of this dish in Nanjing and Shanghai; the following recipe is my own amalgam. Feel free to tweak it as you see fit, and compose your own salad like a symphony of color. What you want is a pretty mix of hues, made harmonious by the strandy cut of all the ingredients; a hint of sweetness shot through with pickle pungency; and a gentle toastiness from the sesame oil. Double the quantities if you want a salad to tide you through the New Year holiday.

A few dried wood-ear mushrooms
3 dried shiitake mushrooms
A handful of dried lily flowers (about ¾ oz/25g; optional)
2 celery sticks (about 5 oz/150g)
4 oz (100g) carrots
A bunch of spinach (about 4 oz/100g)
¼ red bell pepper
1½ oz (40g) fresh ginger
4 oz (100g) soybean or mungbean beansprouts
4 oz (100g) chopped snow vegetable or Chinese black pickled cucumber
1 tbsp superfine sugar
½ tbsp sesame oil
Cooking oil, as needed
Salt

Put the wood-ear and shiitake mushrooms and lily flowers, if using, in a bowl and soak in plenty of boiling water for at least half an hour.

Meanwhile, trim and de-string the celery and cut it into 2¾ in (7cm) sections, then into strips ⅛ in (3–4mm) wide. Peel and trim the carrots and cut them into thin slices, then into similar strips. Do the same with the red bell pepper. Trim the spinach and cut it into 2¾ in (7cm) strips. Peel the ginger and cut it into fine slivers.

When the wood-ear and shiitake mushrooms are fully reconstituted, discard any stalks and knotty bits, then cut them into thin slices. Drain the lily flowers, if using.

Heat a seasoned wok over a high flame. Add ½ tablespoon cooking oil, tip in the ginger and stir-fry until it smells wonderful. Add the mushrooms and lily flowers and stir-fry until hot and fragrant, seasoning with salt. Remove from the wok and set aside.

Return the wok to a high flame, add another ½ tablespoon cooking oil, tip in the celery strips and stir-fry until hot—just to "break their rawness." Season with salt, then remove and set aside. Repeat for all the other vegetable ingredients individually, adding a little more oil each time and seasoning lightly to taste with salt. When the vegetables have cooled, mix them together in a big salad bowl. Add the sugar and sesame oil, stir thoroughly and serve.

Lily bulb and celery salad

bai he ban xi qin 百合拌西芹

The Sunday market on the outskirts of Shanghai was like a rugby scrum. We pushed our way through the crowds and decibels. To one side, live crabs, gunmetal green, sidled around in their leggy way; to the other, shiny, dark eels seethed snakily in tubs of water. There were vegetable stalls piled with the season's produce: tiny, clover-shaped leaves of alfalfa; the ivory ziggurats of peeled wild rice stem; slender, waif-like chives; dirty lily bulbs that would be washed and peeled apart into crystalline petals.

Mrs. He charged ahead, greeting her neighbors in Shanghainese as she went. She had her eels weighed and gutted and picked out her lily bulbs and pickles, a winter bamboo shoot and a clutch of small yellow croakers. Back at her flat, one of the dishes she made was this salad of bright green celery and pearly wisps of lily bulb, with their starchy crispness and subtle hint of sweetness. It was an exquisite example of culinary minimalism, seasoned with nothing but a whisper of sesame oil and a hint of salt.

Juicy shiitake mushrooms (page 52); Lily bulb and celery salad

4 celery sticks (about 7 oz/200g)
1 large day lily bulb (about 4 oz/100g)
½ tbsp cooking oil
1 tsp sesame oil
Salt

Trim and de-string the celery sticks and cut them diagonally into bite-sized pieces. Pull the lily bulb into individual petal-like lobes. Use a small knife to trim off the base and any broken or discolored sections, so that you end up with pure whiteness.

Bring a small pan of water to the boil and add the cooking oil. Tip in the celery and blanch for 30–60 seconds. Add the lily bulb and blanch for another 30 seconds or so: you just want to "break the rawness" of the vegetables, which should retain their crispness. Tip the vegetables into a colander and cool immediately under the cold tap. Shake them dry. Put them in a bowl, add the sesame oil and mix well. Season with salt, and serve.

Juicy shiitake mushrooms

lu wei xiao xiang gu 卤味小香菇

Versions of this delectable appetizer can be found all over the Jiangnan region. The juicy mushrooms look perfectly normal but are replete with secret invisible flavors that magnify their deliciousness. It's one of the simpler examples of Kung Fu cooking, in which the effort, or *gong fu*, is hidden in the final dish, and you are just invited to enjoy the effect. In the main recipe the mushrooms are simmered in stock, then dressed in sesame oil, so they just taste like magically enhanced versions of themselves. I've included a little spice in the vegetarian variation, so that the mushrooms are more juicily aromatic. In some kitchens dried shrimp eggs are added to the seasoning broth; in others the mushrooms are garnished with a few bright gingko or pine nuts. Any leftovers can be sliced up and added to congee, soupy rice, fried rice or noodles.

If you can, choose small, dainty dried mushrooms to make this dish. It keeps well in the fridge for a couple of days.

See photograph on page 50

1½ oz (40g) dried shiitake mushrooms (7 oz/200g after soaking)
1 spring onion, white part only
1 tbsp cooking oil
⅓ oz (10g) fresh ginger, peeled and sliced

2 cups (500ml) good chicken stock
1 tbsp Shaoxing wine
½ tsp salt
2 tsp superfine sugar
1 tsp sesame oil
A few toasted pine nuts (optional)

Put the shiitake mushrooms in a bowl and soak in plenty of boiling water for at least half an hour, until softened. When they are fully reconstituted, slice off and discard their stalks and squeeze them dry.

Smack the spring onion lightly with the flat side of a Chinese cleaver or a rolling pin to loosen its fibers. Heat the cooking oil in a seasoned wok over a high flame. Add the ginger and spring onion and stir-fry briefly until they smell wonderful. Add the drained mushrooms and continue to stir-fry for a minute or so until fragrant.

Add the stock, Shaoxing wine, salt and sugar. Bring to the boil, then turn down the heat and simmer gently for at least 40 minutes.

Increase the heat to high to reduce the broth. When it has reduced to little more than a glaze, turn off the heat and stir in the sesame oil. Leave to cool, garnish with toasted pine nuts if desired, and serve.

Vegetarian version

Follow the recipe above, but reserve and strain the mushroom-soaking water and use 2 cups (500ml) of it instead of the stock. Add an extra 1 tsp superfine sugar, 1 tbsp light soy sauce, ¼ tsp dark soy sauce, half a star anise and a small piece of cassia bark or cinnamon stick to the broth. This is also delicious.

Hand-torn mushrooms

shou si jun gu 手撕菌菇

This is my attempt to re-create a delicious and unusual starter served at the Fu 1088 restaurant in Shanghai: a golden tumble of deep-fried mushrooms dressed in fragrant spring onion oil, with a hint of sweetness. At the restaurant, according to one of the waiters, they make it with a more exotic selection of mushrooms including "monkeyhead" mushrooms, "tea tree" mushrooms and "pig's stomach" mushrooms. At home, I've used the more easily available oyster and king oyster mushrooms. You may feel you're starting off with an excessive amount of mushrooms, but they will shrink considerably in the deep-frying oil.

9 oz (250g) king oyster mushrooms
9 oz (250g) oyster mushrooms
6 tbsp thinly sliced spring onions, green parts only

4 tbsp cooking oil, plus extra for deep-frying
½ tsp salt
½ tsp superfine sugar

Tear the mushrooms lengthways into strips about 5mm wide. Heat the deep-frying oil to 375°F (190°C). Deep-fry the mushrooms in batches until they have reduced in volume by about half and are tinged with gold. Remove with a slotted spoon and drain on paper towels.

Reheat the deep-frying oil to 375°F (190°C) and fry the mushrooms in batches again, until they turn a rich brown. Remove and drain on paper towels.

Put the spring onions in a heatproof bowl. Heat 4 tablespoons fresh cooking oil in a wok over a high flame until a little smoke is coming off the sides of the wok. Pour the oil over the spring onions—in order to extract their fragrance, the oil must be hot enough to produce a violent sizzle, so it's best to test the temperature by dripping a small amount over the onions first. If there's a vigorous sizzle, pour over the rest of the oil. Add the salt and sugar and mix well. Toss in the fried mushrooms, adding a little more salt to taste if you wish, then serve.

Lotus root stuffed with glutinous rice

gui hua tang ou 桂花糖藕

In one of the old canal lanes of Shaoxing I came across a man selling stuffed lotus root from a cart on the back of his bicycle. He had a great cooking pot filled with them and a metal basin displaying a few, glossy with syrup. This sticky, fragrant delicacy is served as an appetizer or snack all over Zhejiang and in Shanghai, usually alongside savory dishes. The best is said to be made with plump lotus roots from Huzhou in northern Zhejiang, which have about nine round holes running through them. In the past, the roots were cooked with lye water made from the ash left after burning rice husks, which helped to tenderize them and lent them a distinctive alkaline flavor.

Some cooks simply serve slices of this stuffed lotus root with a sprinkling of white sugar, but I like the luxurious gloss of a syrup. If you can lay your hands on a jar of osmanthus blossom jam, add some for a wonderful fragrance, and use short-grain glutinous rice if you can find it (Japanese shops sell this as "sweet rice").

Lotus root stuffed with glutinous rice; Spiced wheat gluten with four delights (page 56)

¼ cup (50g) short-grain glutinous rice, preferably Japanese sweet rice
2 sections lotus root (about 15 oz/425g)
4 oz (100g) rock sugar or superfine sugar
1 tbsp osmanthus blossom jam (optional)

Rinse the rice well, then soak it in cold water for at least 2 hours or overnight. Drain well.

Trim the lotus roots so that they have a bit of the mid-section join left at both ends. Peel them and slice off the top ½ in (1cm) of each section to make a lid. Poke a chopstick into the holes that run through the roots to clear any obstructions. Stuff the drained rice into the holes, using a chopstick to poke it in, until all the holes are filled (a slightly fiddly job). Replace the "lids" and secure each one with three or four bamboo skewers. Rinse any bits of rice off the outside of the roots.

Put the roots in a saucepan and cover generously with water. Bring to the boil over a high flame, then half-cover and simmer for 2 hours, topping up with hot water as necessary. (Alternatively, cover with water and pressure-cook at high pressure for 30 minutes, then allow to reduce pressure naturally.) As it cooks, the lotus and the water it cooks in will blush a deep, rosy pink. When they are tender, remove the roots from the liquid and allow to cool.

When the roots are cool, remove and discard the lids and skewers. Cut the roots into ½ in (1cm) slices. Put ½ cup (100ml) of the pink cooking liquid in a small pan with the sugar and heat gently, stirring, to dissolve it. Increase the heat and boil for 1 minute, or until syrupy. Add the osmanthus blossom jam, if using, stir well, and pour over the sliced lotus roots. Serve at room temperature.

Spiced wheat gluten with four delights

si xi kao fu 四喜烤麸

This dark golden tumble, aromatic with spices, looks almost like cubes of brown bread threaded with strands of lily flower and pieces of mushroom. Juicily delicious and a little sweet, it is one of Shanghai's most distinctive appetizers. It is almost unknown in the West, but every friend to whom I've served it at home has loved it immediately. The dish is made with *kao fu*: wheat gluten that has been leavened with yeast and then steamed to make a kind of loaf with a springy, spongey consistency. In Shanghai markets you can buy it fresh; elsewhere, you will find it in packets, cubed and dried. This dish is thought to have evolved from a simpler version that was once served at the vast Tiantong Buddhist temple near Ningbo, one of the centers of Zen Buddhism in China. Chefs in the vegetarian restaurants of Shanghai refined the recipe using techniques borrowed from Suzhou and Yangzhou cooking, adding dried mushrooms and lily flowers and giving it a delicate sweetness.

The recipe has several stages, which makes it something of a hassle to make, but in my experience it's worth it. The finished dish keeps well in the fridge, and seems to taste most delicious after it's been kept for two days. The degree of sweetness is a matter of taste: do add extra sugar if you wish.

See photograph on page 55

4½ oz (125g) dried or 10 oz (275g) fresh kao fu
A small handful of dried lily flowers
A few dried wood-ear mushrooms
3 dried shiitake mushrooms
1½ oz (40g) raw peanuts, in their skins
1¾ cups (400ml) cooking oil, plus extra for frying
⅓ oz (10g) fresh ginger, lightly crushed
2½ tbsp light soy sauce
½ tbsp dark soy sauce
1½ tbsp Shaoxing wine
2½ tbsp superfine sugar
1 star anise
1 tsp sesame oil

If using dried kao fu, cover it with cold water and leave to soak for 3 hours or overnight. If using fresh, blanch it in boiling water, then drain and cut it into 1½ in (3cm) cubes. In separate bowls, soak the lily flowers, wood-ear and shiitake mushrooms and peanuts in boiling water for at least half an hour. While the peanuts are still warm, massage them with your fingertips to remove the skins. Rinse them with cold water; the skins will float so you can easily discard them. Drain the dried kao fu and squeeze it gently to remove excess water. Bring a pan of water to the boil, add the kao fu and blanch it for 1–2 minutes. Rinse in cold water, then gently squeeze it out as much as possible.

Heat the oil in a seasoned wok to 350–400°F (180–200°C); it should produce a vigorous sizzle. Fry the kao fu in batches until golden and crisp, then remove and drain on paper towels. Drain the shiitake mushrooms and strain and reserve the soaking liquid. Remove the stalks and cut the caps into two or three pieces. Drain and gently squeeze the lily flowers and wood-ears. Remove any knotty bits, then tear them into bite-sized pieces. Boil the kettle.

Brush out the wok and reheat it with 1 tablespoon oil. Add the ginger and shiitake and stir-fry briefly until fragrant. Add the mushroom-soaking liquid topped up with hot water to make 3 cups (750ml). Add the kao fu and peanuts, along with the soy sauces, wine, sugar and star anise. Bring to the boil, then cover and simmer gently for 20 minutes, stirring occasionally.

Add the wood-ears and lily flowers, then increase the heat to high. Cook, stirring, to reduce the sauce to a shallow, flavorful pool of liquid. Allow to cool. Before serving, sprinkle over the sesame oil and stir it gently in.

Hangzhou Buddhist "roast goose"

su shao'e 素烧鹅

In the southern Yangtze region, more than in any other part of China, the Buddhist tradition of making vegetarian dishes that cunningly mimic the appearance, texture and taste of meat has escaped from the monasteries into mainstream food culture. Vegetarian "ham," vegetarian "crabmeat" and vegetarian "roast fowl" have become beloved and characteristic dishes on many local menus. This practice of ingenious fakery dates back many centuries: in thirteenth-century Hangzhou, one Buddhist vegetarian restaurant was entertaining its customers with such delights as fried "eel" with noodles, "skewered fowl" and "donkey offal." These days, the people of the city like to eat "roast goose" made of layers of tofu skin seasoned with soy sauce, ginger, wine and sugar. In Shanghai, "roast duck" stuffed with mushrooms and bamboo shoot or carrot is more popular (see the variation on page 59). The glossy roasted "skin" of both is so realistic I hope it will make you smile.

You'll need a steamer at least 10 in (25cm) in diameter. If you don't have a steamer, put a metal trivet (or a small washed-out tuna tin with both ends removed) in your wok, stand a plate on top and cover it with a lid to use the wok for steaming. You'll also need a few bamboo skewers to secure the rolls.

See page 58 for a photograph that includes "roast goose" at the bottom of the page; Shanghainese Buddhist "roast duck" is pictured at the top

6 sheets dried tofu skin, 24 in (60cm) in diameter
Cooking oil, for deep-frying
1–2 tsp sesame oil

For the flavoring broth:
2 oz (50g) rock sugar (or ordinary superfine sugar)
½ oz (15g) fresh ginger, peeled and sliced
3 tbsp Shaoxing wine
2 tbsp light soy sauce
½ tsp salt
1¾ cups (400ml) unsalted vegetable stock or water

If using rock sugar, crush it into small pieces with a pestle and mortar. Put all the ingredients for the flavoring broth in a pan with the stock or water. Bring slowly to the boil, stirring to dissolve the sugar completely. Set aside.

With a pair of scissors, trim off but retain the hard edges of the sheets of tofu. Cut the sheets into semicircular halves. On a clean work surface, lay out one unbroken semicircle with the straight edge closest to you. Use a pastry brush to brush the sheet generously with the flavored broth—you will find that the wrinkled surface of the tofu retains a surprising amount of liquid.

Lay another unbroken sheet on top of the first one, this time with the curved edge towards you. Brush generously with liquid. Repeat with the remaining sheets, laying each one in the opposite direction to the one before it (don't worry about little tears or holes in the upper layers). Dunk the retained trimmings into the flavored broth, then spread them out along the edge of the layered skins closest to you. Turn the edge nearest to you over the hard bits and tuck it in. Fold in the left- and right-hand edges of the layered sheets to make a rectangle.

Take the rolled edge closest to you and fold the nearest third of the rectangle over the second third (as if you were folding puff pastry). Now turn your attention to the far edge. Turn the rough edges in, then fold the far third in to make a long rectangular packet. Fold the packet in half, right to left, to make your "goose" parcel. Use three bamboo skewers to secure the three open sides of the parcel. Put the parcel, seam down, in the steamer and steam over a high flame for 7 minutes—no longer, or you will lose the layering effect that is important for this dish. Leave to cool completely. ▶

When the "goose" has cooled, heat the oil for deep-frying to 350°F (180°C)—about 400ml will do if you are using a wok. Taking care to keep the wok stable, gently slide the "goose" into the hot oil. Fry, turning once, until golden and puckered. Be aware that it will color quickly. Carefully remove the "goose" from the oil and place it in a deep dish. Strain the remains of the flavoring broth over it and leave to cool before serving.

Remove the "goose" from the broth to serve, and pick out and discard the skewers. Brush with the sesame oil, then cut widthways into 1 in (2cm) slices. Pile up neatly on a dish to serve. This dish keeps for several days in the fridge, but try to let it return to room temperature before serving.

Shanghainese Buddhist "roast duck"

Follow the recipe above, except that you will need only 5 sheets of tofu, and the following stuffing: soak 4 dried shiitake mushrooms in boiling water for at least half an hour, and then cut the caps into thin slices. Retain the soaking water. Cut 3 oz (75g) carrot into thin slices. Heat 1 tbsp cooking oil over a high flame. Add 1 tsp finely chopped ginger and sizzle briefly until it smells wonderful, then add the mushrooms and carrot and stir-fry until the carrot is supple. Stir in 1 tbsp Shaoxing wine. Add 1 tsp light soy sauce and 1 tsp sugar, remove from the wok and allow to cool.

Prepare the tofu sheets with the flavoring broth as in the main recipe. Lay the stuffing along one of the shorter ends of the rectangle, with the trimmings. Roll it up from the shorter end, tucking in the sides as you go, to enclose the stuffing. Secure with skewers, steam, deep-fry and steep as in the main recipe. Brush with sesame oil before cutting and serving.

Cool steamed eggplant with a garlicky dressing

liang ban qie zi 凉拌茄子

This Shanghainese appetizer is absurdly easy to make and wondrously satisfying. Steaming brings out a gentle, unfamilar side to a vegetable that is more commonly fried, baked or grilled, and, simple as they are, the seasonings taste sublime. Use Mediterranean eggplant or, if you can find them, the slender purple Chinese variety. I was introduced to this recipe by my Shanghainese friend Jason Li.

Mashed fava beans with snow vegetable (page 62); Cool steamed eggplant with a garlicky dressing

1 lb (500g) eggplant
2 tbsp light soy sauce
1 tsp Chinkiang vinegar
¼ tsp sugar
1 tbsp finely chopped garlic
1 tbsp finely chopped fresh ginger
1½ tbsp thinly sliced spring onions, green parts only
2 tbsp cooking oil

Cut the eggplant lengthways into ½ in (1cm) slices, then cut these into ½ in (1cm) strips. Cut the strips into bite-sized lengths and pile them into a bowl that will fit inside your steamer basket. Place the bowl in the steamer basket and steam over a high flame for 20 minutes, until tender. Combine the soy sauce, vinegar and sugar in a small bowl.

Shortly before you wish to serve them, pile the eggplant in a serving dish and top them with the garlic, ginger and spring onion. Heat the oil in a seasoned wok or saucepan over a high flame until it is very hot. Carefully ladle the hot oil over the garlic, ginger and spring onions—it should produce a dramatic sizzle. Pour the soy sauce mixture over the eggplant. Gently stir in the seasonings and serve.

Mashed fava beans with snow vegetable

dou ban su 豆瓣酥

My first Jiangnan meal was at the Ningbo Residents' Association restaurant in Hong Kong, a hidden enclave of traditional Ningbo food in the heart of the island's entertainment district. With my friend Rose, a fluent speaker of Ningbo dialect, as my guide, I tasted my first raw mud snails pickled in Shaoxing wine, steamed clams in a delicate custard, smoked duck eggs and this delectable appetizer of mashed fava beans with pickled greens. Since then I've eaten many versions of the dish, which is a favorite in both Ningbo and Shanghai.

I've suggested making it with fresh fava beans, but you can also make it with the dried beans which can be bought ready-skinned in Middle Eastern shops (soak them overnight, boil until tender, then add to the stir-fried snow vegetable as in the recipe). You can also use the fresh skinned beans whole rather than mashed: just boil them, then stir-fry with the snow vegetable and allow to cool to room temperature before serving. Some Chinese supermarkets sell frozen shelled and skinned fava beans, which save a lot of time.

See photograph on page 60

10 oz (300g) shelled fava beans (around 3 lbs/1kg in the pod)	3 tbsp chopped snow vegetable
3 tbsp cooking oil	Salt

Bring a pan of lightly salted water to the boil. Add the beans and boil them until completely tender. Plunge into cold water or rinse under the cold tap to cool them quickly, then pop the beans out of their skins (if they are very small and tender, you can leave the skins on if you don't mind a chunkier mash). Mash the beans coarsely, using a potato masher in a pan or a Chinese cleaver on a chopping board. Boil the kettle.

Heat a seasoned wok over a medium flame. Add the oil, then the snow vegetable and stir-fry briefly until fragrant. Add the mashed beans and continue to stir-fry until piping hot, adding a little hot water if necessary to keep the mash loose, and seasoning with salt. Leave the mash to cool, then press it into a lightly oiled rice bowl. Turn it out onto a dish to serve.

Shanghai "smoked" fish

lao shang hai xun yu 老上海熏鱼

Strangely, "smoked" fish, a popular Shanghainese appetizer, isn't smoked at all: it seems to derive its name from the resemblance to smoked fish with its caramel-dark color and smoky intensity of flavor. It is made by marinating boneless slices of fish, then deep-frying them and steeping them in a flavoring broth that is dark with soy sauce and aromatic with spices, with a hint of sweetness. This recipe is a particular speciality of Shanghai, but versions of it are served across the region. In Shaoxing, where cooks like to reduce the flavoring broth to a treacly glaze, it used to be regarded as a special treat, eaten only at the New Year and other festivals.

The dish is normally made with the middle section of a grass carp, which yields good, boneless slices. As an alternative, gray mullet works well: a whole gray mullet weighing 3 lbs (1.5kg) will give you a fillet of about 1¾ lbs (750g). You can also use sea bass, chopped through the backbone into thick diagonal slices.

1¾ lbs (750g) filleted grass carp, black carp or gray mullet
1¾ cups (400ml) cooking oil
Sesame oil, to serve

For the marinade:
¾ oz (20g) fresh ginger, skin on
2 spring onions, white parts only
1½ tbsp Shaoxing wine
2 tsp light soy sauce
2 tsp dark soy sauce

For the flavoring broth:
¾ oz (20g) fresh ginger, skin on
2 spring onions, white parts only
1 star anise
A piece of cassia bark or a cinnamon stick
¼ tsp five-spice powder, plus extra to serve (optional)
Ground white pepper
1½ tbsp dark soy sauce
4 tbsp light soy sauce
9 tbsp superfine sugar
1 tbsp Shaoxing wine

Remove any bones from the fish. Scrape away any black membrane on each fillet, rinse well and pat dry with paper towels. Lay each fillet on a chopping board and slice off the thinner section. Holding the knife at an angle to your board, cut the thicker part into ½ in (1cm) slices, starting at the tail end. Then, with your knife perpendicular to the board, cut the thinner part into pieces around the same size. Smack the ginger and spring onions with the flat side of a Chinese cleaver or a rolling pin to loosen their fibers and add to the fish along with the other marinade ingredients. Mix well and set aside in the fridge for about 1 hour.

Make the flavoring broth. Smack the ginger and spring onion lightly as before. Put them in a saucepan with 2 cups (500ml) water and the other flavoring broth ingredients. Bring to the boil slowly, stirring to dissolve the sugar. Simmer for 5 minutes, then set aside until the fish is ready.

Remove the ginger and spring onions from the marinade. Place the fish slices on paper towels to drain. Bring the broth to the boil, then set aside.

Heat the cooking oil in a wok to 350°F (180°C). Fry the fish slices in batches until crisp and golden. Remove them with chopsticks and drop into the hot flavoring broth to steep for 2–3 minutes. Fish them out and set them aside to cool. Repeat with the rest of the fish, then pile the pieces up neatly on a serving dish. Sprinkle with 2 teaspoons sesame oil and a little five-spice powder, if desired. Serve at room temperature.

Smoked duck eggs

yan xun tang xin dan 烟熏溏心蛋

With their shiny, molten yolks and delicate smoky aroma, these eggs make an irresistible appetizer. I first tasted them at the Ningbo Residents' Association in Hong Kong, and have been enjoying them practically ever since at one of my favorite Shanghai restaurants, Fu 1088. At Fu 1088, they top each egg with a tiny leaf of cilantro and about half a teaspoon of black caviar, which looks pretty and tastes delicious. The eggs are also delectable when dipped into Sichuan pepper salt or, less authentically, celery salt.

6 duck eggs
Iced water
3 tbsp dark soy sauce
1 tbsp light soy sauce
4 tbsp black tea leaves
5 tbsp superfine sugar

A bunch of spring onions
A few sprigs of cilantro,
   to garnish (optional)
Salt or Sichuan pepper salt
   (see page 333), to serve

Put the duck eggs in a saucepan and cover generously with cold water. Bring them to the boil, stirring gently with a long-handled spoon (the stirring helps to center the yolks). Simmer for 1 minute, then turn off the heat, cover and leave to steep undisturbed in the hot water for 3 minutes. Remove, immerse in iced water and crackle the shells all over by knocking them against the base of the container or other hard surface. Once the eggs have cooled, shell them carefully.

Put the soy sauces in a bowl with 3 tablespoons cold water. Working in batches, roll the eggs in the dark liquid for about a minute, turning them occasionally for even coloring, then drain on paper towels.

Wash and trim the spring onions and smack them gently with the flat side of a Chinese cleaver or rolling pin to loosen their fibers. Put them in a steamer basket and arrange the eggs on top.

Put the tea leaves in a bowl and add just enough hot water to cover them. Soak for a minute, then drain and, when cool enough to handle, squeeze them dry. Line the base of a seasoned wok with two layers of aluminum foil. Scatter the sugar, then the damp tea leaves, over the foil. Heat the wok over a high flame until plenty of smoke is rising from the tea leaves. Put the steamer basket with the eggs into the wok, cover with a lid, then turn off the heat and let them sit in the smoke for 3 minutes.

To serve, cut the eggs in half and arrange on a serving dish. Garnish each egg with a tiny piece of cilantro, if you wish. Serve with salt or Sichuan pepper salt.

Nanjing saltwater duck

yan shui ya 盐水鸭

Some 800 years ago, during the Southern Song dynasty, the plump, succulent ducks of Nanjing were already renowned as the finest under heaven. By the end of the Ming dynasty, two duck dishes had risen to fame: the roast fowl said to be the ancestor of Peking duck, and this one. In a beauty contest, Nanjing saltwater duck would never triumph over its sleek, coppery rival, but don't let the dove-gray modesty of its appearance deceive you, because it's unexpectedly fabulous: tender, savory and elegantly spiced.

In China, saltwater duck is such a celebrated local product that loudspeakers enunciate its virtues on trains stopping at Nanjing station—you might even be able to buy some on board. Enjoy the duck as an appetizer or a snack with wine; it's just the kind of delicacy characters in the racy Ming dynasty novel *The Plum in the Golden Vase* send their servants out to fetch between bouts of illicit lovemaking, as an accompaniment to a flask of wine.

Saltwater duck is made all year round, but the finest is said to be the "osmanthus duck" made in the autumn, when the osmanthus flowers bloom and the wind brings relief from the sultry summer heat.

Don't think of Nanjing saltwater duck only in a Chinese context; it makes a wonderful addition to sandwiches and salads, and a fine accompaniment to other cold cuts. The master stock, enriched by the flavors of the duck, can be strained, frozen and used another time. Do keep the leg bones: they make a good stock to use for soup or congee.

See photograph on page 68

2 duck breasts (about ¾ lb/350g)
2 duck legs (about 1 lb/500g)

For the salt rub:
2½ tbsp salt
1 tbsp whole Sichuan peppercorns

For the master broth:
2 star anise
2 bay leaves
A piece of cassia bark or cinnamon stick (about 2½ x 1 in/6 x 2cm)
1 tsao-kuo (black cardamom) pod, smacked
2 cloves, their powdery heads pinched off and discarded
3 spring onions, white parts only
¾ oz (20g) fresh ginger, skin on
2 tbsp salt

To make the salt rub, stir the salt in a dry wok over a medium flame. When it is hot, add the Sichuan pepper and continue to stir until the pepper smells wonderful and the salt has yellowed slightly. Remove and leave to cool. When it has cooled enough to handle, rub it all over the pieces of duck. Cover and leave them in the fridge for 4–5 hours.

While the duck is being salted, prepare the master broth. Put all the spices, tied into a small muslin bundle if you wish, in a large pan with 2 quarts (2 liters) water. Gently smack the spring onion and ginger with the flat side of a Chinese cleaver or a rolling pin to loosen their fibers. Add them to the pan with the 2 tablespoons salt, bring to the boil and simmer gently for 20 minutes. Set the broth aside.

When the duck has finished salting, rinse it well and pat dry on paper towels. Bring the broth to the boil again. Add the pieces of duck and cover them with a plate so they are kept fully immersed in the liquid. Bring to the boil, cover and turn off the heat. Leave to steep for 20 minutes. Bring the broth to the boil a second time, then cover, turn off the heat and leave to steep for another 15 minutes.

Remove the duck pieces from the broth and allow to cool completely, retaining the broth. Cut the meat into slices before serving. Chinese cooks usually chop through the bone, but you may wish to remove the meat from the leg bones before cutting it. Serve the sliced duck with a spoonful or two of the cooking broth, to make it juicy.

Hangzhou spiced soy-sauce duck

hang zhou lu ya 杭州卤鸭

For centuries, the Chinese have had a flourishing trade in takeaway food. In Song dynasty Hangzhou, the streets were dotted with cookshops offering hot steamed buns and dumplings, roasted geese, cooked pork and sweetmeats. And all over today's Jiangnan you find cooked food stalls and shops selling meat, fish, poultry and salads that can be taken home and eaten alongside other, home-cooked dishes. In Suzhou, people queue up for cold pork in a sweet sauce given a bright pink luster by red yeasted rice, while the Shanghainese jostle for position at counters selling sweet-and-sour ribs, deep-fried fish and glossy pork hocks.

This Hangzhou appetizer is addictive: cool slices of duck bathed in a luxurious dark sauce, with an edge of spice and an undercurrent of sweetness. Traditionally, it is eaten during the Great Summer solar term of the lunar calendar.

You will end up some leftover sauce, which has its own culinary uses. Diluted with a little stock or water, it can be used to red-braise deep-fried tofu or wheat gluten, plain white tofu, or vegetables such as winter melon, taro or radishes. If you just reheat it, it is simply delicious drizzled over a bowlful of plain rice or congee. The duck itself keeps well for a few days in the fridge. The same method can be used to cook squab pigeons.

See photograph on page 69

1 spring onion, white part only
½ oz (15g) fresh ginger, skin on
2 duck breasts and 2 duck legs (about 2 lbs/850g)
1 cup (100ml) light soy sauce
2½ tbsp dark soy sauce
3 oz (75g) superfine sugar
½ star anise
A piece of cassia bark or a cinnamon stick

Smack the spring onion and ginger lightly with the flat side of a Chinese cleaver or a rolling pin to loosen their fibers. Put them in a pan large enough to hold the pieces of duck fairly snugly. Add the soy sauces, sugar, spring onion, ginger, star anise and cassia, top up with 3 cups (700ml) water and bring to the boil.

Add the duck pieces, arranging them so that they are immersed in the liquid. Bring to the boil over a medium flame, skim, then turn down the heat and simmer for 20 minutes; the liquid should bubble gently.

The next step is to reduce the liquid: I find it easiest to do this by transferring everything into a wok, where the larger surface area makes reducing much faster. Turn the heat up high and reduce the liquid by about two thirds, ladling it constantly over the duck. Skim off the surface layer of oil as far as possible, along with any impurities. Pick out and discard the spices, ginger and spring onion as you go along. You will end up with a dark, shiny, treacly sauce.

Remove the duck from the sauce and leave to cool completely, reserving the sauce. To serve, cut the duck into bite-sized pieces and arrange them on a serving dish. Reheat some of the cooking juices and pour them over the duck.

Black "char siu" pork

In Shanghai, the Jardin du Jade restaurant serves a gorgeous black char siu pork which is made by a similar method: strips of skinless pork belly, with a little fat but not too much, are parboiled and then simmered in a sweet, soy-sauce broth like the one in this recipe. Afterwards, the cooled pork is sliced and served with a libation of the dark cooking juices. I adore this dish.

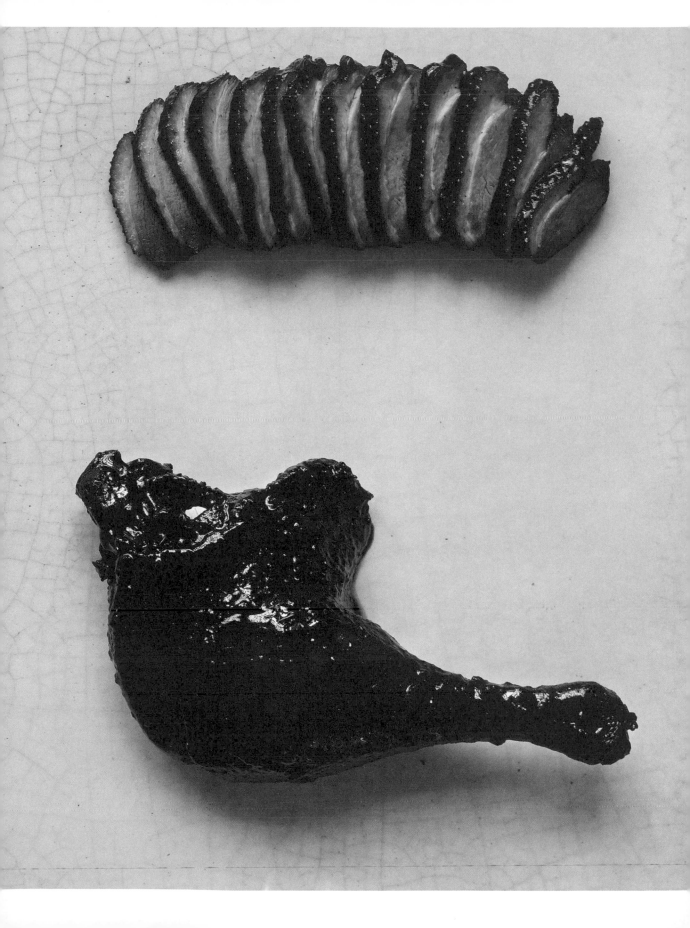

White chopped chicken with soy sauce

bai zhan ji 白斩鸡

White chopped chicken is served as an appetizer across the Jiangnan region, as it is in the Cantonese south. The simplest of Chinese chicken dishes, it relies not only on careful control of cooking temperature, but also on the quality of the bird. In Shanghai, where it's a particular favorite, they like to use the local "triple yellow" chickens, so named because of their yellow skin, beaks and feet. Do make sure you use a fine free-range chicken, preferably one with golden skin. The bird is steeped in very hot water, then chilled quickly in iced water, so the flesh has a magnificent succulence with just a hint of tautness. Even the breast, so often cottony in texture when cooked by other methods, should be sleek, juicy and delicious.

In China, they serve the meat chopped, on the bone, into bite-sized strips, but you can remove it from the bone if you wish. For maximum simplicity, eat it with just a dip of a really good, rich soy sauce. At home I often use an organic Japanese-style tamari that has both the dark treacly color and the saltiness of old-fashioned Chinese soy sauces. Otherwise, you might like to dip it in a zesty relish made from spring onion and ginger (see variation).

This cooking method can leave the chicken a little pink at the bones; if this bothers you, return it to the boil for a third time and steep for a further 5 minutes. To make sure the chicken is cooked to internationally approved standards, use a meat thermometer to check that the innermost parts are heated to 165°F (74°C).

1 free-range chicken (about 4 lbs/1.8kg)	Sesame oil, to taste
Iced water, for steeping	A rich, flavorful soy sauce, to dip

Bring 5 quarts (4.5 liters) water to the boil in a large stockpot. Carefully put the chicken in the boiling water, breast-side down, then lift it out again, letting the water drain out of its cavity. Put it back in the water (this helps even out the temperature of the water inside and outside the bird—some recipes recommend doing it several times). Bring the water back to the boil, immediately turn the heat down low and simmer extremely gently for 8 minutes. After this, remove from the heat, cover with a close-fitting lid and leave undisturbed for 20 minutes.

Heat again over a high flame until the liquid is just beginning to boil. Remove from the heat, cover again and leave to steep for another 15 minutes. Fill another large pan with iced water.

When the chicken is ready, carefully remove it from the cooking liquid and let the hot water drain out of its cavity. Place it in the iced water and leave for 15 minutes.

Remove it from the iced water, then drain and pat it dry with paper towels. Rub the skin with a little sesame oil to give it a fragrant gloss. Leave to cool completely.

Before serving, cut the chicken, on or off the bone as you please, into bite-sized pieces. Use the cooking liquid as stock, perhaps to make a chicken congee (see page 239). Serve with soy sauce to dip.

Ginger and spring onion dip

This relish is unbelievably delicious and can be served alongside the soy sauce dip. Put 2 tbsp very finely chopped fresh ginger and 1 tbsp very finely chopped spring onion white in a dish. Heat 1½ tbsp cooking oil until very hot, then pour it over them, producing a vigorous sizzle. Stir in 1 tbsp very finely chopped spring onion greens, 1 tsp salt and ½ tsp sugar.

Drunken chicken

zui ji 醉鸡

Drunken dishes form a whole genre of delicacies in the ancient wine-producing city of Shaoxing. In some of them the ingredients are more literally drunken than you might want to imagine: live crabs and shrimp are immersed in a boozy liquor until they expire. Served cold, these sozzled sea creatures have a cool, slimy texture and an ambrosial taste, especially the female freshwater crabs adorned with shining red coral. The first time I tried one, in Shanghai, I was almost speechless with pleasure and amazement.

Happily, drunken chicken—a Shaoxing speciality—does not demand the sousing of live creatures in alcohol. The chicken is simply poached and then steeped in a seasoned wine liquor. Traditionally, it is served very cold in a Shaoxing clay wine jar; the texture of the meat should be a little firm and brisk. In the days before refrigeration, drunken dishes were only eaten in cold weather—in Yangzhou people say you should stop eating drunken crab after the Lantern Festival that concludes the Lunar New Year holiday.

For dishes like this, in which wine is the dominant flavor, do buy one intended for drinking, rather than a cooking wine.

To make sure the chicken is cooked to internationally approved standards, use a meat thermometer to check that the innermost parts are heated to 165°F (74°C).

¾ oz (20g) fresh ginger, skin on
2 spring onions, white parts only
2 chicken breasts (about 10 oz/300g)
2 chicken legs (thighs and drumsticks separated, about 1–1½ lbs/500–600g)
Iced water, for steeping
1 tbsp salt
1¼ cups (225ml) good Shaoxing Huadiao wine
½ tbsp strong Chinese liquor (optional)

Smack the ginger and spring onion lightly with the flat side of a Chinese cleaver or a rolling pin to loosen their fibers. Bring 1½ quarts (1.5 liters) water to the boil in a large saucepan. Add the chicken pieces, ginger and spring onion and bring to the boil. Turn down the heat and simmer very gently for 3 minutes, then turn the heat off, cover the pan and leave to steep undisturbed for 25 minutes.

Fill a large saucepan with iced water. When the chicken pieces have been steeped, remove them from the pan and put them in the iced water for 10 minutes. Remove and drain them and leave to cool completely.

Strain 1¼ cups (275ml) of the chicken cooking liquid into a jug. Add the salt and stir to dissolve, then add the Shaoxing wine and strong liquor, if using. Set aside to cool completely.

Remove the bones from the chicken thighs and drumsticks. Cut the meat widthways into ½–1 in (1–2cm) strips through the skin. Put the cooled chicken pieces in a pot just large enough to hold them and pour over the cooled stock mixture. Cover and leave in the fridge for at least 24 hours (it keeps well in the fridge for a few days). Serve cold.

Cold chicken with spring onion oil

cong you ji 葱油鸡

This understated, refreshing dish is popular in Shanghai, where it is made with the small, yellow-skinned local chicken, which is poached whole, chopped on the bone and then dressed in an aromatic oil speckled with the greens of spring onion. I'm suggesting boned chicken legs, but if you prefer to use breasts, or indeed a whole chicken, please go ahead. As with any dish of this simplicity, success depends on the quality of your ingredients, so make sure you choose good free-range chicken and a rich stock.

Chinese cooks like to poach their chicken until only just cooked and still a little pink at the bones. To make sure the chicken is cooked to internationally approved standards, use a meat thermometer to check that the innermost parts are heated to 165°F (74°C).

¾ oz (20g) fresh ginger in one piece, plus 2 tsp finely chopped
2 spring onions, white parts only
2 star anise
A small piece of cassia bark or cinnamon stick
1 tbsp Shaoxing wine

2 boned chicken legs (about 1½ lbs/675g on the bone or 1 lb/500g boned)
4 spring onions, green parts only, sliced (about 6 tbsp)
½ tsp sesame oil
3 tbsp cooking oil
½ cup (100ml) good chicken stock
Salt and ground white pepper

Bring 1½ quarts (1.5 liters) water to the boil in a large pan. Smack the whole piece of ginger and spring onion whites lightly with the flat side of a Chinese cleaver or a rolling pin to loosen their fibers. Add the chicken pieces to the pan, return to the boil and skim. Add the ginger and spring onion whites along with the star anise, cassia and Shaoxing wine. Turn down the heat and simmer very gently for 3 minutes, then turn the heat off, cover the pan and leave to steep undisturbed for 25 minutes.

Fill a large saucepan with iced water. When the chicken pieces have been steeped, remove them from their pan and place in the iced water for 10 minutes, then drain well. Pat the skin dry with paper towels, then brush with the sesame oil. Leave to cool completely.

Cut the chicken into bite-sized strips and pile up tidily in a serving dish. Shortly before serving, heat the oil over a high flame until the surface is beginning to shimmer. Turn off the heat, add the spring onion greens and chopped ginger and stir rapidly until fragrant (the spring onions should remain green). Add the stock, bring to the boil and season with salt and pepper: the sauce needs to be quite salty to season the chicken. Pour over the chicken and serve.

Zhenjiang crystal pork terrine

zhen jiang shui jing xiao rou 镇江水晶肴肉

In China, the old Yangtze river town of Zhenjiang is famed not only for its vinegar, but also for this delectable terrine, a speciality of the Yanchun restaurant. Made with pork hock, which is traditionally cured with saltpeter, boiled and then pressed, it has a pretty pink-and-white color, with a halo of "crystal" clear aspic. The terrine is usually eaten as an appetizer with a dip of vinegar spiked with ginger. In 1949, it received the accolade of being included on the menu of a banquet held in Beijing to mark the founding of the People's Republic of China. According to legend, one of the Taoist Immortals, Zhang Guolao, was once flying over Zhenjiang on his white mule when he sniffed the glorious perfume of crystal pork terrine on the wind. He was on his way to a party in honor of the Queen Mother of the West, but its scent so beguiled him that he forgot all about the feast, and instead whooshed himself down into the mortal world to taste it.

This recipe is based on one in a textbook by Chen Zhongming of the culinary department of the Yangzhou Business School. You need to start curing the meat 4–5 days before you wish to eat it. You'll need a pair of rectangular containers about 2 in (5cm) deep; one to hold the meat and one to place on top so you can weigh it down to press it. You will also need curing salts: I use "continental curing salts," which are 99.6 percent salt and 0.4 percent sodium nitrite. The powdered alum, which helps clarify the aspic, can be found in Indian groceries or online. Ask your butcher to bone the pork hocks for you so that they can be laid out flat.

2 pork front hocks, boned (3 lbs/1.7kg after boning)
2 oz (50g) continental curing salt
2 spring onions
1½ oz (40g) fresh ginger, skin on
1 tsp Sichuan peppercorns
½ star anise
3 oz (80g) salt
1 tbsp Shaoxing wine
¼ tsp alum powder
3 tablespoons Chinkiang vinegar, to serve
¾ oz (20g) fresh ginger, cut into slivers, to serve

Place one boned hock on your chopping board, skin-side down. Use a skewer to prick the meat all over. Place it, skin-side down, in a nonreactive container. Sprinkle half the curing salt over it and use both hands to rub it in thoroughly. Repeat with the other hock. Cover and leave in the fridge for 3–4 days, turning the hocks every day. After curing, remove the hocks and rinse them well. Soak them for about 2 hours in cold water, changing the water a couple of times.

Smack the spring onions with the flat side of a Chinese cleaver or a rolling pin to loosen their fibers. Slice the ginger. Place the spring onions, ginger, Sichuan peppercorns and star anise on a piece of muslin and tie them up to make a bundle.

Remove the hocks from the soaking water and scrape the skin clean. Pluck out any bristles with tweezers. Rinse the hocks in warm water, then drain. Place them, skin-side up, in a pan and cover with about 1 quart (1.2 liters) water. Bring to the boil, skim, then add the spice bundle, the salt and Shaoxing wine. Return to the boil, then simmer gently for about 3 hours, until tender, topping up with hot water if necessary.

Once cooked, discard the spice bundle. Gently place the hocks next to each other, skin-side down, in a 2 in (5cm) deep rectangular container. Put another container the same size on top, add some heavy weights and press the meat for 20 minutes. Carefully strain the cooking liquor back into the pan and return it to the boil. Add the alum, then strain 2 cups (500ml) of the liquid over the pork, prodding it with a chopstick to make sure any air pockets are filled. Cool, then chill overnight, until set.

Turn the terrine out of the container, cut it into ½ in (1cm) slices and pile them neatly on a plate. Pour the vinegar into dipping dishes, add the slivered ginger and serve alongside the pork for dipping.

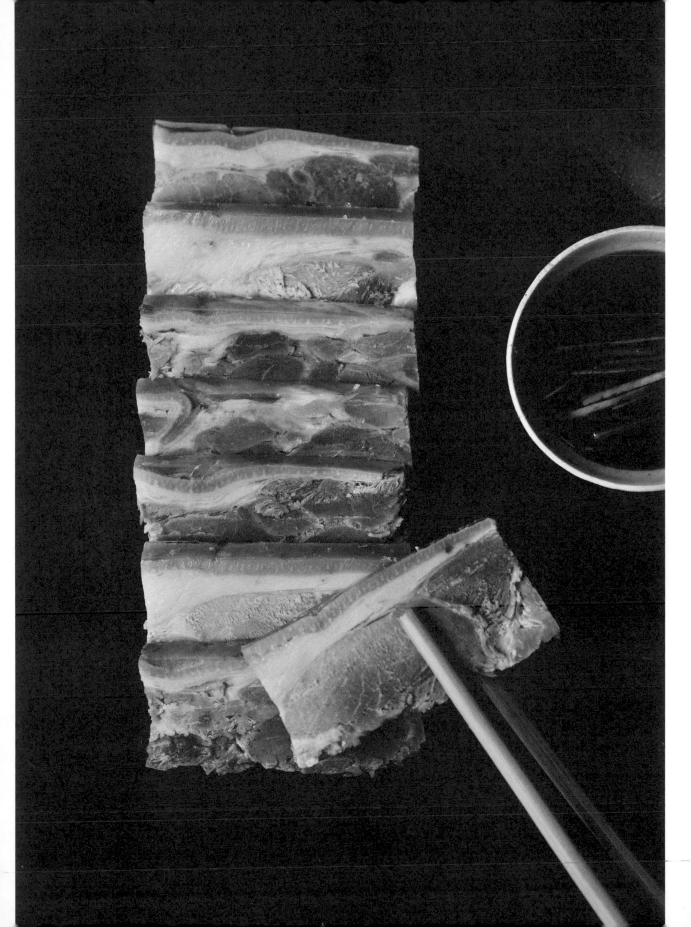

Eight-treasure spicy relish

ba bao la jiang 八宝辣酱

This hearty relish, with its earthy fermented flavor and hint of chilli, is typical of Shanghai and Suzhou cooking. There are no hard-and-fast rules about what goes into it, except that it's normally a mixture of meaty and vegetarian ingredients with a pleasing variety of textures. As a Shanghai market vendor once told me, it's a "great hotchpotch" made from whatever bits and pieces you have to hand; the local equivalent, perhaps, of Cantonese chop suey. Some cooks add gingko nuts, chestnuts or sesame seeds; others cooked ham or tofu skin; crunchy chicken gizzard is another favorite. In Shanghai restaurants they usually finish the dish with a pretty garnish of pale, slippery river shrimp and bright green peas.

The relish can be served straight as an appetizer, added to a wokful of stir-fried rice cake or eaten with rice or noodles. It's known as an "on-the-road dish" because it keeps well and can easily be packed up and taken on a trip. The relish became well known in restaurants in the early twentieth century, but many people trace its ancestry back to the famous eggplant confection described in the eighteenth-century novel *Dream of Red Mansions*: a delectable medley of small cubes of fried eggplant, chicken breast, mushrooms, bamboo shoot, spiced tofu and dried fruit and nuts.

Some recipes use a mixture of fermented wheat sauce and the darker, earthier Shanghainese soybean sauce, but I've simplified things by using the former alone. Purists would insist that each cubed ingredient is fried separately before they are mixed.

6 dried shiitake mushrooms
¾ oz (25g) dried shrimp
About 3 tbsp Shaoxing wine
4 oz (100g) raw peanuts
4 oz (100g) chicken breast or boneless thigh
2 tsp potato starch
4 oz (100g) pork tenderloin
4½ oz (125g) bamboo shoot
4 oz (100g) firm tofu
4 oz (100g) shelled green soybeans
3 oz (75g) sweet fermented sauce (see page 337)
1½ tbsp chilli and garlic sauce
½ cup (100ml) stock
1 tbsp superfine sugar
½ tbsp dark soy sauce
About 4 tbsp cooking oil
Salt

Cover the shiitake mushrooms with boiling water and set aside for half an hour to soften. Put the dried shrimp in a bowl with 1 tablespoon Shaoxing wine and cover with hot water.

Bring a pan of salted water to the boil, add the peanuts and simmer for 20 minutes. (If you wish, you can then flush them with cold water and massage off their skins.) Drain well.

Cut the chicken into ½ in (1cm) cubes. Add ⅛ teaspoon salt, ½ teaspoon potato starch and 1 tsp Shaoxing wine and mix well. Do the same with the pork. Cut the bamboo shoot and firm tofu into ½ in (1cm) cubes. Drain the soaked shiitake, remove their stalks and cut the caps into ½ in (1cm) cubes. Drain the shrimp. Bring a pan of water to the boil. Blanch the tofu, green soybeans and bamboo shoot for about 1 minute, then drain well.

Heat 1 tablespoon oil in a seasoned wok. Add the pork and chicken and stir-fry until cooked through; remove and set aside. Heat a little more oil, add the shiitake and shrimp and stir-fry until fragrant, then add the bamboo shoot, soybeans and tofu and stir-fry until piping hot. Remove and set aside.

Heat another 2 tablespoons oil in the wok over a medium flame. Add the sweet fermented sauce and garlic and chilli sauce and stir-fry until wonderfully fragrant. Add the remaining Shaoxing wine, then all the pre-fried ingredients. Add the stock, sugar and dark soy sauce and turn up the heat to high. Stir until everything is piping hot and the liquid has reduced by about half. If you want to thicken the sauce, mix 1 teaspoon potato starch with 2 teaspoons water and add just enough of the mixture, in a couple of stages, to thicken the sauce to a lustrous gravy that clings to the ingredients. Serve hot or cool, as you please.

MEAT

The chunk of pork sits on a golden plinth, so tender that the meat seems to droop under its mantle of succulent, honey-colored skin; you can imagine the aroma of the rice wine, the melting opulence of the fat, the enticing hint of sweetness … actually, however, the pork is a hard piece of agate that has been meticulously carved and colored by master craftsmen. The famous "meat-shaped stone" is one of the treasures of the Forbidden City, spirited out of mainland China by the nationalists at the end of the civil war and now on display in the National Palace Museum in Taipei. For me, it's always been an emblem of the Chinese love affair with pork, for in no other culture can I imagine so much devotion applied to evoking the sensory pleasures of the meat in such a permanent form.

Pork is beloved across much of China, but no one understands the gastronomic mysteries of the meat better than the people of the Jiangnan region, with their ham, their salt pork and, above all, their masterful use of rice wine, soy sauce and sugar to transform this most common of meats into something sublime. For that is the contradictory nature of pork: it is both mundane and heavenly. Ordinary pork, cut into small pieces and often stir-fried with vegetables, is the stuff of everyday eating; grander cuts and lavish quantities are the traditional centerpieces of rural feasts and celebrations. Although Chinese food snobs may may look down on pork because it lacks the glamour of expensive delicacies like bird's nest and turtle, it's usually more delicious, as any true gourmet knows. The eleventh-century poet Su Dongpo, also known as Su Shi, expressed this perfectly in his poem "Eating Pork":

That good pork of Huangzhou
It's cheap as dirt,
The rich disdain it,
The poor have no idea how to cook it.
But with a slow fire and just a little water,
When it's cooked just right, it's certainly delicious.
Have a bowlful every morning
And you'll be so richly satisfied that you won't have
*   a care in the world.*

The most adored cut of pork is the belly, which the Chinese call "five-flowered meat" (*wu hua rou*) for its layering of fat and lean meat, and which is the star of many of the region's most notable dishes. Aside from the belly, Jiangnan cooks have ingenious ways of using every inch of the pig: stir-frying the lean flesh, mincing the streaky meat for stuffed buns and dumplings, rendering the fat into lard and simmering the skin to make jellied stock (the liquid elixir in steamed "soup dumplings" or *xiao long bao*), or slowly deep-frying it into puffy golden pieces. A Chinese granny may advise you to eat trotters and hocks, both rich in collagen, to beautify your complexion; bones are used in stocks and soups. As for offal, a sliced boiled pig's heart is delicious with a soy sauce dip, while ears can be made into a layered terrine. Liver might be stir-fried with Chinese chives; strips of stomach and tongue are magnificent steeped in an aromatic brine. In Yangzhou, where the salt merchants wined and dined the Qianlong emperor, a slow-cooked pig's head, served with fluffy white buns and pickled garlic, is one of the centerpieces of the gastronomic extravaganza known as the Three-Head Feast, at which it is served alongside the head of a giant carp and "lion's head" meatballs.

Salted and cured pork is particularly important in Jiangnan cooking. Many people still cure their own pork, and in winter the courtyards of old Yangzhou are hung with great sides of salted meat studded with Sichuan peppercorns. The cured pork is sometimes just sliced, steamed and served as a dish in its own right, perhaps with lotus leaf buns. More often, it is used in small quantities to lend umami deliciousness to vegetarian ingredients.

The famous cured ham of Jinhua in southern Zhejiang province is dense, dark pink and as intensely flavored as its equivalents in Spain and Italy, although, unlike them, it is not eaten raw. Jinhua ham appears both as savory flavoring and garnish; larger pieces of ham may be used to ratchet up the umami factor in stocks and soups. In Shanghai and Hangzhou, specialist ham shops can advise on which cut, and what vintage, to use for every classic dish (according to the eighteenth-century gourmet Yuan Mei, "the difference between good ham and bad ham is like the difference between high heaven and the deepest ocean"). A prime chunk of ham is the main ingredient in the delectable Suzhou banquet dish honeyed ham with lotus seeds (*mi zhi huo fang*).

Aside from pork, beef and goat meat play more minor roles in Jiangnan cooking, and tend only to take center stage in Muslim restaurants.

Shanghai red-braised pork with eggs

shang hai hong shao rou 上海红烧肉

Red-braised pork, in which chunks of pork belly are simmered with soy sauce, rice wine and sugar, is beloved across China, and there are many regional variations. In Jiangnan, and especially Shanghai, they like theirs dark, sleek and seductively sweet. The pork is only cooked for about an hour in total, so the meat and fat retain a little spring in their step. A secondary ingredient is often added, such as bamboo shoot, deep-fried tofu, cuttlefish, salted fish or, as in this recipe, hard-boiled eggs. The dish is a perfect accompaniment to plain white rice; I do recommend that you serve it also with something light and refreshing, such as stir-fried greens.

At the Dragon Well Manor restaurant in Hangzhou, they call this dish Motherly Love Pork because of an old local story. Once upon a time, they say, there was a woman whose son had traveled to Beijing to sit the imperial civil service examinations. Eagerly awaiting his return, she cooked up his favorite dish, a slow-simmered stew of pork and eggs. But the road was long and the traveling uncertain, so her son didn't arrive when expected, and she took the pot off the stove and went to bed. The next day, she warmed up the stew and waited again for him, but he didn't arrive. By the time her son actually reached home on the third day, the stew had been heated up three times, and the meat was inconceivably tender and unctuous, the sauce dark and profound.

6 eggs, small if possible
¾ oz (20g) fresh ginger, skin on
1 spring onion, white part only
1¾ lb (750g) pork belly, skin on
1 tbsp cooking oil
1 star anise
A small piece of cassia bark or cinnamon stick
3 tbsp Shaoxing wine
3 cups (700ml) stock or hot water
2 tbsp light soy sauce
1½ tbsp plus 1 tsp dark soy sauce
3 tbsp superfine sugar or 1½ oz (40g) rock sugar

Hard-boil the eggs in a pan of boiling water, then cool and shell them. In each egg, make 6–8 shallow slashes lengthways to allow the flavors of the stew to enter. Smack the ginger and spring onion gently with the flat side of a Chinese cleaver or a rolling pin to loosen their fibers.

Put the pork in a pan, cover with cold water, bring to the boil over a high flame and boil for 5 minutes. Drain and rinse it under the cold tap. When cool enough to handle, cut the meat through the skin into 1–1½ in (2–3cm) cubes (if your piece of belly is thick, you may want to cut each piece in half so they end up more cube-like).

Heat the oil in a seasoned wok over a high flame. Add the ginger, spring onion, star anise and cassia and stir-fry briefly until they smell wonderful. Add the pork and fry for another 1–2 minutes until the meat is faintly golden and some of the oil is running out of the fat. Splash the Shaoxing wine around the edges of the pan. Add the hard-boiled eggs and stock or hot water, along with the light soy sauce, 2 tablespoons dark soy sauce and the sugar. Bring to the boil, then cover and simmer for 45 minutes, stirring occasionally.

Pour into a pot or a bowl, allow to cool, then chill overnight. In the morning, remove the layer of pale fat that has settled on the surface. Tip the meat and jellied liquid back into a wok, reheat gently, then boil over a high flame to reduce the sauce, stirring constantly. Remove and discard the ginger, spring ▸

onion and whole spices. After 10–15 minutes, when the liquid has reduced by about half, stir in the remaining dark soy sauce.

Shortly before you wish to serve, bring to the boil over a high flame and reduce the sauce to about an inch of dark, sleek gravy. Turn out into a serving dish. Then go and welcome your son back from his imperial civil service examinations!

If you have any leftovers—unlikely, in my experience—you can reheat them with a little water and some dried bamboo shoot, winter melon, tofu knots, deep-fried tofu puffs or radishes. In fact, you might wish, like some of my Chinese friends, to red-braise odd scraps of fatty pork just to cook vegetables, because it makes them so delicious.

Shanghai red-braised pork

Omit the eggs and increase the amount of pork to 1kg. Use only 1½ tbsp light soy sauce, 1½ tbsp plus 1 tsp dark soy sauce, 2½ tbsp sugar and 2 cups (500ml) hot water.

Red-braised pork with chestnuts

Add a quantity of peeled, cooked chestnuts roughly equal in volume to the pork when you reheat and reduce the stew. This is a scrumptious variation made by Zhejiang chef Zhu Yinfeng.

Ningbo red-braised pork with salted fish

Omit the eggs, and use only 1 tbsp light soy sauce, 1 tbsp sugar and 2 cups (500ml) stock or water. Soak some dried yellow croaker in cold water to soften, then cut it into bite-sized pieces. Add the fish to the pork when you reheat and reduce the stew. Garnish with a few lengths of spring onion greens.

Ningbo pork with fermented tofu juices

tai cai xiao fang kao 苔菜小方燎

Ningbo chefs are best known for their delicate ways with fish and seafood, but the city also prides itself on some rich stewed dishes, such as turtle, slow-cooked with rock sugar into an ecstasy of sticky voluptuousness. Fresh turtles are even harder to come by in the West than they are in China, but I hope you'll be satisfied by this fragrant slow-cooked pork, another classic Ningbo stew. The pork is traditionally served with a garnish of deep-fried branched string lettuce seaweed from the Ningbo coast, but it's also delicious on its own. If you wish to achieve a similar flavor and mouthfeel to the seaweed, I suggest deep-fried cabbage leaves, which sound unlikely but are remarkably good (see page 36). If you can find the seaweed, whole or flaked and ready-to-use, it will add a sparkle of magic to the recipe. This dish is just one of the many versions of pork slow-cooked with the pink juices of red fermented tofu or, in Suzhou and Wuxi, with red yeasted rice, wine and sugar.

2 lbs (900g) boned pork belly in one piece, skin on
2 spring onions, white parts only
2 tbsp cooking oil
½–¾ oz (15–20g) fresh ginger, crushed slightly
3 tbsp Shaoxing wine
3½ tbsp liquid from a jar of red fermented tofu
4 tsp superfine sugar
1 tbsp light soy sauce

1 tsp dark soy sauce
About 2 cups (500ml) stock or water
A good handful of deep-fried cabbage leaves or seaweed, or 1 tbsp aonori-ko seaweed flakes (optional; see page 36)
A few pinches of granulated sugar to garnish the seaweed, if using

If you want to cook the dish in the oven, preheat it to 250°F (120°C). I usually put my small clay cooking pot in the oven at this stage to warm it up.

Bring a pan of water to the boil, add the pork and cook for 15 minutes, until part-cooked. Drain and rinse the meat, then cut it through the skin into 1 in (2cm) cubes. Trim the spring onions and smack them with the flat side of a Chinese cleaver or a rolling pin to loosen their fibers.

Heat the oil in a seasoned wok over a high flame. Add the spring onions and ginger and stir-fry until they smell wonderful, then add the pork, wine, fermented tofu liquid, sugar, light soy sauce and ½ teaspoon of the dark soy sauce, with enough stock or water to just cover the meat. Bring to the boil, then cover and simmer over a low flame or in the oven for 1 hour, until tender. Spoon the liquid over the pork occasionally.

When the pork has cooked, transfer the pan to a high flame, remove the lid and boil rapidly, spooning the liquid over the pork, until it has reduced to a thick, syrupy consistency. Add the remaining dark soy sauce as the liquid reduces. If you are using the deep-fried cabbage or seaweed, first arrange the pork chunks on a serving dish and pour a little sauce over them, then pile up the cabbage or seaweed on the other end of the dish and sprinkle lightly with granulated sugar. If using aonori-ko seaweed flakes, simply sprinkle them over the finished dish. Serve.

Wuxi meaty pork ribs

wu xi rou gu tou 无锡肉骨头

A speciality of the old canal town of Wuxi, these chunky pork ribs are clothed in a gorgeous, aromatic gravy with a bit of the sweetness for which the local cooking is renowned. According to local lore, the recipe originated in the Nanchan Buddhist Temple. The gist of the story is that during the Southern Song dynasty, a visiting monk called Jigong gave the owner of a local cooked-meat shop some invaluable tips on the art of stewing meat (somewhat curiously, since Chinese Buddhist monks are normally vegetarians). Jigong cooked his meat slowly, overnight, in one of the temple's incense burners, making all the young monks "drool with greed," and the shop owner adopted his method.

This is one of several Jiangnan legends about meat-eating Buddhist monks; I'm not sure if this means that a little meat-eating was tolerated in monastic communities, that laypeople just enjoy telling tales about the hypocrisy of clerics, or if it's simply an illustration of the Chinese infatuation with pork, a meat so delicious that even committed vegetarians are not immune to its delights.

You'll need a big, meaty tranche of spare ribs. I've given instructions for cutting them in the traditional Wuxi way, but you can, of course, use other cuts of rib. The red yeasted rice gives a gorgeous pink tint to the sauce but is unnecessary in terms of flavor. Note that the ribs must be salted overnight before cooking.

2 lbs (850g) meaty pork ribs, in one piece
1 tbsp salt
2 tbsp red yeasted rice (optional)
¾ oz (20g) fresh ginger, skin on
2 spring onions, white parts only
2 tbsp Shaoxing wine
1 star anise
A small piece of cassia bark or cinnamon stick
2 tbsp light soy sauce
½ tsp dark soy sauce
3 tbsp superfine sugar
2½ cups (600ml) stock or water
1 tsp potato starch mixed with 2 tsp cold water

Ask your butcher to saw the whole tranche of ribs crossways into two or three pieces, cutting through the rib bones at 2–2½ in (5–6cm) intervals. When you get home, make a cut through the meat between every other rib, so you end up with fat squares of meat, each with two embedded lengths of bone. Put the rib pieces in a container, add the salt, mix well and chill overnight.

If you are using the red yeasted rice, put it in a bowl or mortar and just cover it with hot water. Leave to steep for at least half an hour, then mash with a pestle. Put the salted ribs in a pan, cover with cold water and bring to the boil. Boil for 1–2 minutes, skim, then drain in a colander. Rinse well. Smack the ginger and spring onions lightly with the flat side of a Chinese cleaver or a rolling pin to loosen their fibers.

Put the ribs in the cleaned pan or a clay pot. Add the ginger and spring onions, Shaoxing wine, spices, soy sauces, sugar and stock or water. If you are using the red yeasted rice, strain the mashed rice liquid through a tea strainer into the pot. For best results, rinse the residue a few times with the liquid in the pot to extract as much color as possible, then discard the residue. Bring everything to the boil, then cover and simmer over a medium flame for 1 hour.

Remove the lid, discard the ginger, spring onion and spices, then turn up the heat to reduce the sauce to about 1 in (2cm) deep, stirring frequently and spooning the liquid over the meat. Give the potato starch mixture a stir and add just enough to thicken it to a luxurious gravy, then serve.

Dongpo pork

dong po rou 东坡肉

This sumptuous dish, named after the Song dynasty poet Su Dongpo, is a Hangzhou speciality. Large square chunks of pork belly are slow-cooked with soy sauce, sugar and Shaoxing wine until they are so exquisitely tender that they melt away at a chopstick's touch. While serving as governor of Hangzhou in the late eleventh century, Su Dongpo organized the dredging of the city's beautiful West Lake, which had become clogged. According to local lore, the grateful townspeople sent him gifts of his favorite meat for Chinese New Year; touched by their kindness, the poet-governor instructed a servant to red-braise the pork and return it with a gift of wine. The servant mistakenly thought he'd been told to cook the pork with the wine, and the resulting dish was so magnificent it has never been forgotten.

The supposed rule with Dongpo pork is to let wine take the place of water in the stew, but in practice most chefs add a little water. Although it's traditionally cooked on the stovetop, a low oven works very well too. The final dish is so rich and intense that one square of pork, served with plain rice, is usually enough for each person. Make it a day in advance and chill it if you want to remove the layer of solid fat that will collect on the surface. Do not make this dish with everyday Shaoxing cooking wine; invest in a bottle of five- or ten-year aged drinking wine, which can be found in good Chinese supermarkets. Happily, although this is one of the finest dishes in the whole pantheon of Chinese cooking, it's very easy to make.

1 x 5 in (1 x 12cm) wide strip of unscored, skin-on, boneless pork belly (about 2 lbs/1kg, or 3 lbs/1.3kg bone-in)
2 spring onions
1 oz (30g) fresh ginger, skin on
4 tbsp superfine sugar
5½ tbsp light soy sauce
½ tbsp dark soy sauce
1½ cups (250ml) good Shaoxing wine
Plain white rice or steamed lotus leaf buns (see page 289), to serve

If using an oven, preheat it to 250°F (110°C). Bring a large pan of water to the boil, add the pork and cook for about 5 minutes. Drain it well and rinse under the cold tap. Place the pork, skin-side up, on a chopping board and cut it as accurately as possible into 2 in (5cm) squares. Keep any trimmings.

If you have one, lay a bamboo mat in the bottom of a heavy-bottomed pan to prevent sticking. Crush the spring onions and ginger slightly with the flat side of a Chinese cleaver or a rolling pin and put them in the pan. Add the pork trimmings and arrange the pork chunks, skin-side down, on top. Add the sugar, soy sauces and Shaoxing wine. If you are using a traditional Chinese clay pot, warm it gently over a low flame to prevent cracking, then bring it to the boil over a high flame; if you are using a more robust pan, bring it to the boil directly. Boil rapidly for 1–2 minutes to give the skin a rich, soy-dark color. Cover and cook gently for 2½ hours over a very low flame or in the oven. Keep an eye on it to make sure it doesn't boil dry; add a little hot water if necessary.

Remove and discard the ginger and spring onions. For best results, leave the pork to cool in the pan and chill overnight. Scrape off and remove the layer of white fat on the surface (this can be used for other purposes, such as frying potatoes or stir-frying mushrooms).

Reheat the pork in the pan, turning the pieces skin-side up as soon as the juices have loosened. You want to end up with a dark, slightly syrupy sauce: if there is too much liquid, strain it off, fast-boil to reduce it, then return it to the pan. Serve the meat and its juices with plain white rice or steamed lotus leaf buns.

Clear-simmered lion's head meatballs

qing dun shi zi tou 清炖狮子头

Lion's head meatballs are one of the crowning glories of Jiangnan cooking—almost cloud-like spheres of pork so tender they can be eaten with a spoon. One of the centerpieces of the famous Three-Head Feast of Yangzhou, they epitomise the phrase "richly fat without being greasy" (*fei er bu ni*). Legend says that the dish, originally called Sunflower Chopped Pork, was invented during the Sui dynasty by a Yangzhou chef who wanted to please the emperor by composing dishes in honor of local scenic spots—in this case, Sunflower Hill.

Later, during the Tang dynasty, a local nobleman's chef re-created the dish to the delight of his guests, who thought the meatballs so resembled lion's heads with their flowing manes of leafy vegetables that they renamed them on the spot. Personally, I've never been struck by the resemblance, but I adore the dish. Even the cooking juices are exquisite drizzled over a bowl of plain white rice.

The essential trick for this recipe is to cut the pork by hand; if you cheat by using machine-minced pork, the meatballs will have a mealy rather than voluptuous texture (true lion's heads, made with hand-chopped meat, always look slightly coarse and chunky). I advise you to chill the meat in the freezer for an hour or so beforehand, otherwise the cutting is extremely hard work. Don't even think of using lean pork. As Zhang Hao, the Yangzhou chef who tutored me in this recipe, explained: "The lion's heads must melt in your mouth; they should be as tender as tofu. Lean meat will make them leathery, like a steak" (this comment gives you some clue as to ▶

8 Chinese cabbage leaves
⅓ oz (10g) fresh ginger, skin on
1 spring onion, white part only
2 cups (500ml) chicken or chicken and pork stock
1 tbsp Shaoxing wine
½ tsp salt
3 tbsp potato starch mixed with 3 tbsp cold water

For the meatballs:
1 lb (500g) skinless, boneless pork belly
2 tsp finely chopped fresh ginger
2 tsp finely chopped spring onion, white part only
1½ tbsp Shaoxing wine
1½ tsp salt
⅓ cup (75ml) cold stock or water
1 egg white
1½ tbsp potato starch mixed with 1 tbsp cold water

Put the pork belly in the freezer until slightly hardened but not frozen; 1–2 hours should do the trick. Bring a pan of water to the boil and blanch the Chinese cabbage leaves until floppy. Refresh in cold water, then drain and set aside.

Remove the pork from the freezer and use a sharp knife to cut it into ⅙ in (4–5mm) slices. Lay these slices on your board and cut them into ⅙ in (4–5mm) strips, then into tiny cubes the size of pomegranate seeds. (Traditionally, the leaner meat is cut into slightly smaller ⅛ in/3–4mm pieces).

To make the meatballs, put the meat in a big mixing bowl. Add the chopped ginger and spring onion, Shaoxing wine and salt and mix vigorously, stirring in one direction—it's easiest to do this with your hand. (Chinese chefs always stir in one direction so that all the fibers of the meat line up, making it very smooth.) Keep slapping handfuls of the mixture hard against the bowl for a few minutes, until the meat becomes springy and sticky in consistency. Still stirring by hand in one direction, add the water gradually. Finally, add the egg white and the potato starch mixture, and continue to stir in one direction until incorporated.

Warm a Chinese clay pot or a casserole dish by filling it with hot water, then pouring the water out. Smack the piece of ginger and spring onion white gently with the flat side of a Chinese cleaver or a rolling pin to loosen their fibers. Cover the base of the pot with half the cabbage leaves in a single layer. ▶

what many Chinese people think about "Western" food!).

In Yangzhou restaurants the meatballs are normally removed from their cooking liquid and served individually in a clear broth, with another ingredient that varies with the season: blanched bok choy or Chinese cabbage in winter, bamboo shoot in spring, freshwater mussels in the summer. In the autumn, the pork is often enriched with hairy crab meat, and a morsel of crab coral is pressed into the top of each meatball like the jewel in a crown. Lion's head meatballs may also be deep-fried and then red-braised. Some people like to stir some coarsely chopped water chestnut into the meat, for a bit of crunch amid the tenderness.

Add the stock and 1 cup (250ml) water and bring to the boil over a medium flame. Add the Shaoxing wine and salt, and the smacked ginger and spring onion. Turn the heat down to a simmer.

Have the potato starch and water mixture to hand. Divide the pork mixture into four, then use both hands to shape each quarter into a large globe. Give the starch mixture a stir and use your hand to smear a thin layer around each meatball—this will give them a nice gloss. Gently drop the meatballs into your simmering broth. When all the meatballs are in the pot, cover them with a single layer of the remaining cabbage leaves. If necessary, top up the liquid with a little hot stock or water—it should just about cover the meatballs. Turn the heat up until the water is bubbling around the edges of the pot. Cover with the lid, turn down the heat and simmer very gently for 2 hours. Remove the top layer of cabbage leaves to serve.

Lion's head meatballs with hairy crab meat

Mix 4 oz (100g) crabmeat into the pork mixture with a little ground pepper, then make an indentation in the top of each meatball and press in some crab coral. I have made this recipe with saltwater crabmeat; it was pretty delicious, but not quite the same thing.

Red-braised lion's head meatballs

This variation is particularly popular in Shanghai. Make meatballs the size of small tangerines, deep-fry them until golden, then red-braise in the manner of red-braised pork (see page 80). Reduce the sauce until syrupy. Serve the meatballs on a bed of blanched green bok choy, with the reduced sauce poured over them.

Hangzhou sweet-and-sour pork

tang cu li ji 糖醋里脊

This is a delicious variation on the sweet-and-sour pork theme, and less gaudy than the Cantonese restaurant version. It's the kind of dish that you might find at dinner in a Hangzhou home, and was taught to me by master chef Hu Zhongying of the Hangzhou Restaurant.

10 oz (275g) pork tenderloin
¾ tsp salt
2 tsp Shaoxing wine
2 tbsp potato starch
4 tbsp all-purpose flour
1 tsp sesame oil (optional)
A small handful of spring onions, green parts only, cut into 2 in (5cm) lengths
Cooking oil, for deep-frying

For the sauce:
3 tbsp superfine sugar
2 tbsp Chinkiang vinegar
1 tbsp Shaoxing wine
2 tsp light soy sauce
1 tsp potato starch mixed with 2 tsp cold water

Cut the pork into bite-sized slices, about ½ in (1cm) thick. Add the salt and Shaoxing wine and mix well. Mix the potato starch and flour with about 5 tablespoons water to make a thick batter. Add it to the pork and stir well to coat all the pieces. Combine all the sauce ingredients in a bowl.

In a seasoned wok, heat the oil for deep-frying to 350°F (150°C). Use a pair of chopsticks to drop pieces of pork into the oil in batches. Fry for about 3 minutes, until crisp and just cooked through, then remove and set aside. Reheat the oil to 375–400°F (190–200°C). Fry the pork again until golden and crisp; set aside. Pour off the oil into a heatproof container.

Return the pork pieces to a dry wok over a high flame. Give the sauce a quick stir and immediately pour it into the base of the wok. When the sauce boils and starts to thicken, stir vigorously to coat the pieces in the sauce, which will quickly reduce to a treacly glaze. Add the spring onion greens and turn a couple of times to give them a lick of heat. Remove from the heat, stir in the sesame oil, if using, and serve.

Shaoxing slow-cooked pork with dried fermented greens

gan cai men rou 干菜焖肉

Many old canal towns in the Jiangnan region have been spoiled by reckless development, but pockets of Shaoxing still retain their historic charm. In the alleys around Cangqiao street, residents play cards and drink tea on canalside terraces. Little silvery fish lie drying on bamboo mats in the sun. Doorways offer glimpses of local life: a family sitting around a square table with bowls of food, chopsticks in hand; old men chatting in a teahouse near an ancient stone bridge clothed in creepers.

On warm days, everywhere in the city's old streets hangs the scent of *mei gan cai* (dried fermented greens), the city's most famous preserve, made by pickling and sun-drying mustard greens. *Mei gan cai* was originally a poor man's food, used to bring a savory deliciousness to cheap vegetable ingredients, but these days it is most famously used in a pork belly stew. According to legend, this dish was first cooked in the Ming dynasty by Xu Wei, a poor Shaoxing artist who was given some pork but had no money to spend on seasonings. All he had at home was a clay jar of *mei gan cai*, so he cooked the pork with some of it, and the result was so bewitchingly fragrant that all his neighbors asked him what he was eating.

In Shaoxing restaurants, the cooked meat and fermented greens are normally packed into a bowl and steamed before being turned out, dome-like, onto a serving dish, but you can simply stew them together if you prefer.

3 good handfuls of Shaoxing dried fermented greens (about 3 oz/75g)
1¼ lbs (550g) pork belly, skin on
1 spring onion, white part only
1 tbsp cooking oil
A few slices of peeled fresh ginger
2½ cups (600ml) stock or water
½ tbsp light soy sauce
½ tbsp dark soy sauce
2 tsp superfine sugar
3 tbsp Shaoxing wine
½ star anise
A small piece of cassia bark or cinnamon stick
Salt
Lotus leaf buns, to serve (optional; see page 289)

Put the dried fermented greens in a bowl and cover with cold water. Squeeze them with your hands to rinse off any excess salt. Put them in a colander and rinse again under the cold tap, then squeeze dry.

Bring a pan of water to the boil, add the pork and cook for 5 minutes. Drain and rinse under the cold tap, then cut it into 1–1½ in (2–3cm) cubes through the skin. Smack the spring onion with the flat side of a Chinese cleaver or a rolling pin to loosen its fibers.

Heat the oil in a seasoned wok over a high flame. Add the ginger and spring onion and stir-fry briefly until fragrant. Add the meat and stir-fry for a few minutes until fragrant and slightly tinged with gold. Add the stock or water, along with the fermented greens, soy sauces, sugar, wine and spices. Bring to the boil over a high flame, then cover and cook very gently for 2 hours. Before serving, turn the heat up high to reduce the sauce, seasoning with salt to taste if you need it (you probably won't). Remove the ginger and spring onion before serving.

An optional final step is to use chopsticks to pluck the pieces of pork out of the stew and place them, skin-side down, in the base of a bowl that will fit into your steamer. Fill the sides and top of the bowl with the fermented greens. Steam over a high flame for about 20 minutes to heat through, then turn out onto a dish to serve.

Steamed chopped pork with salted fish

xiang zheng rou bing 鲞蒸肉饼

Like all dishes made with *xiang*, the salted sea fish beloved in Zhejiang province and the Cantonese south, this one has a wild, funky aroma that may, to the uninitiated, seem disconcerting at first. In some ways, however, it's not so different from the more familiar Mediterranean leg of lamb spiked with anchovies and chunks of garlic that melt into the flesh as it cooks, perfuming it with a bold pungency that is sweetened by heat.

In Zhejiang, this dish tends to be popular with the older generation, who remember the bitter old days when a tiny slice of the pungent fish might be all someone had to "send down" a whole bowlful of rice. It is sometimes known as a "lazy cake" (*lan duo bing*), apparently because the meat is slapped down on the plate rather than carefully shaped into spheres, like meatballs. Serve it with plain white rice and a simple stir-fried green vegetable for an easy and satisfying supper—and be sure to spoon the glorious juices over the rice. Hand-chopping the meat really does give a more delectable texture, so I strongly advise it.

10 oz (300g) skinless, boneless pork belly (or coarsely ground fatty minced pork)	1 tbsp Shaoxing wine
	2 tsp finely chopped fresh ginger
1½ oz (45g) Vietnamese salted mackerel or 2 oz (60g) Chinese dried yellow croaker	1½ tsp light soy sauce
	1 tbsp potato starch
	3 tbsp stock
2 dried shiitake mushrooms	1 tbsp thinly sliced spring onions, green parts only

If possible, put the meat in the freezer for an hour or two before you begin, which will make the cutting much easier. If you are using dried croaker, soak it in cold water for at least 1 hour, then cut it open, winkle out the bones and finely chop it. If you are using the moister salted mackerel, just cut it into small pieces, discarding the bones. Cover the shiitake mushrooms with boiling water and leave to soak for at least half an hour, then remove the stalks and finely chop the caps.

Cut the pork into 2 in (5mm) slices. Cut the slices into strips and then into small dice. The idea is to end up with a coarse, chunky mince. Put it in a mixing bowl and add everything else except the salted fish and spring onions, and mix well. Stir in the croaker, if using (salted mackerel should be added later). Stir vigorously with your hand until the pork has a sticky texture. Spread it out into a circle in a shallow dish that will fit in your steamer: the meat should be 1–1½ in (2–3cm) deep.

Cut the salted mackerel, if using, into slices and place these on top of the pork. Cover the dish with a plate or aluminum foil. Place it in a steamer and steam over high heat for about 25 minutes, until cooked through. Serve scattered with the spring onion greens.

Steamed pork with salted duck eggs

For a delicious variation, use 2 salted duck eggs instead of the salted fish. Break the eggs and separate the waxy yolks from the liquid whites. Stir the whites into the pork mixture, omitting the soy sauce because the eggs themselves are very salty. Slice the yolks and arrange them on top of the pork patty before steaming it.

Steamed pork in lotus leaves

he ye fen zheng rou 荷叶粉蒸肉

In the summer, lotus leaves sprawl languidly over glittering ponds and lakes all over the Jiangnan region. Here, they are used to wrap marinated pork clothed in a spiced rice meal that becomes soft, sticky and soothing after steaming, rather like a savory version of an English steamed treacle pudding. The pork, as you might imagine, is hauntingly soft and aromatic. If you are using a traditional steamer for this recipe, make sure the water doesn't boil dry during the long cooking. Alternatively, use a pressure cooker and steam for half an hour; in my experience, this gives an even more fabulous result.

Chinese supermarkets sometimes sell ready-made spiced rice meal for making dishes like this, which is usually labeled "steam powder" (*zheng rou fen*). Otherwise, you can make your own: put 7 oz (200g) Thai fragrant rice, one star anise and a couple of pieces of cassia bark or cinnamon stick in a dry wok and stir over a medium flame for 10–15 minutes, until the rice is brittle, yellowed and aromatic. Allow to cool, then pick out and discard the spices. Grind in a food processor until the rice has a consistency like fine couscous. If by any chance you can use fresh lotus leaves, blanch them in boiling water before using.

1⅓ lbs (600g) boneless pork belly, skin on
1 dried lotus leaf
4 oz (100g) spiced rice meal (see headnote)
2 tsp sesame oil

For the marinade:
3 tbsp sweet fermented sauce (see page 337)

3 tbsp light soy sauce
1 tsp dark soy sauce
2½ tbsp Shaoxing wine
2 tbsp superfine sugar
2 tbsp finely chopped fresh ginger
2 tbsp finely chopped spring onion

Cut the pork, through the skin, into ½ in (1cm) slices. Cut each piece into two: you want to end up with bite-sized pieces that are 2½–3 in (6–8cm) long, ½ in (1cm) wide and as deep as the piece of belly. Put them in a bowl, add the marinade ingredients and mix well. Cover and set aside in the fridge or a cool place for at least 1 hour to marinate.

Soak the lotus leaf for a few minutes in boiling water to make it supple. You may have to turn it as you dunk it in the hot water until it softens enough to fit into your bowl.

When you are ready to start cooking, add the rice meal to the pork and mix well so that every slice of meat is coated. Lay the lotus leaf, shiny side up, in a shallow heatproof bowl large enough to take the pork, but that will fit into your steamer (you will need to tuck the center of the leaf under so that it will lie flat). The leaf will flop over the edges of the bowl. Place the slices of pork, skin-side up, in neat rows to fill the bowl. Fold the leaf over to cover the pork snugly, then trim off the excess with a pair of scissors. Put it in a steamer and steam over a high flame for 2 hours. If you have a pressure cooker, steam at high pressure for 30 minutes, then allow the pressure to release naturally. Lift the top part of the leaf and sprinkle with sesame oil before serving.

Slow-cooked pork hock with rock sugar

bing tang yuan ti 冰糖元蹄

A slow-cooked pork hock makes a magnificent centerpiece for a family meal, and this particular recipe is glorious, with its glossy rock-sugar sauce. The skin and fat become soft and voluptuous, and the meat so tender it slips easily from the bone. You can make the dish in advance and simply reheat and reduce the liquid before you wish to serve it. As you can imagine, it's wildly rich, and best served with plain white rice or lotus leaf buns (see page 289).

The recipe is based on instructions given to me by two village ladies at the Pig's Inn in southern Anhui Province, a guest house in a rambling mansion that once belonged to a Huizhou merchant. Like the other grand old houses of the region, it has tall, whitewashed walls with ornately carved lintels fashioned from pale gray stone. Inside there are courtyards, gardens and wood-paneled rooms. When I visited in November, bright red persimmons hung on the bare, dark branches of a tree in the front courtyard like Chinese lanterns.

1 pork hock (about 2 lbs/950g)
1 oz (30g) fresh ginger, skin on
1 spring onion, white part only
½ cup (100ml) good Shaoxing wine
3 tbsp Chinese red rice vinegar
½ tbsp dark soy sauce
3½ tbsp light soy sauce
1 star anise
A piece of cassia bark or a cinnamon stick
4 oz (100g) rock sugar
8 small heads green bok choy, to garnish (optional)

Place the hock on a chopping board with the straighter side uppermost and make a deep incision into the thickest part, cutting along the line of the bone and right down to it. Open the hock out slightly around the cut, then make two parallel cuts into the thick flesh on either side of the bone. This will enable you to open out the thicker end a bit so you can stand the hock upright. Use kitchen scissors or a knife to trim the skin around the edge into a neatish circle.

Smack the ginger and spring onion lightly with the flat side of a Chinese cleaver or a rolling pin to loosen their fibers. Bring a pan of water to the boil, add the hock, return to the boil and blanch for 2 minutes. Remove it and rinse under the cold tap. When cool enough to handle, use tweezers to remove any stray bristles. Place the hock in a pan or clay pot with all the other ingredients except the bok choy, if using, and enough water to cover—about 1½ quarts (1.5 liters). Bring to the boil, then cover and simmer for about 3 hours, until utterly tender—you want the hock to keep its shape, but the meat to be almost falling off the bone. Turn it occasionally to make sure it's not sticking.

If you plan to garnish it, blanch the bok choy in boiling water with a little salt and a dash of cooking oil, then refresh in cold water. Drain well just before using.

Strain the cooking liquid into a wok, turn the heat up high and stir as the liquid reduces. When it is starting to become syrupy, add the hock (discard the ginger, spring onion and spices) and spoon the sauce over it. When you have a dark, glossy pool of sauce that makes the hock look gorgeous and shining, transfer it to a serving dish and spoon over the remains of the sauce. Surround it with a halo of blanched green bok choy, if you wish.

Shaoxing "small stir-fry"

shao xing xiao chao 绍兴小炒

On one of my longer visits to Shaoxing, I dined with chef Mao Tianyao at the famous Xianheng Tavern many times; we would share a few dishes with a cup or two of Shaoxing wine and he would dazzle me with his passion and erudition on the subject of Shaoxing food. After a couple of meals I realized that we had abandoned the restaurant menu, and that he was asking the kitchen to rustle up the kinds of simple, healthy and delectable dishes local people ate at home. Many, in classic Shaoxing style, were vegetables cooked with pickles and preserves to give them funky or deeply savory flavors. One of the most amazing was a stir-fry of fresh amaranth greens with young rape shoots that had been cured in a stinky tofu brine.

When I asked him to tell me about his own favorite dish, Mao didn't hesitate: it was a Shaoxing *xiao chao*, or "small stir-fry," made with pork, preserved mustard tuber, bamboo shoot and yellow chives, perhaps with some firm tofu or mushrooms added. This everyday dish, he said, was the archetypal dish for a household supper, the equivalent, perhaps, of twice-cooked pork for the Sichuanese. *Xiao chao* is the term used across Jiangnan to describe a simple stir-fried medley of whatever odds and ends you have in your kitchen, typically including a variety of vegetable ingredients and a little meat. The following recipe is based on the Shaoxing *xiao chao* we shared that evening.

4 oz (100g) lean pork	2 tbsp cooking oil
½ tsp Shaoxing wine	3 tbsp stock
½ tsp light soy sauce	¾ tsp rice vinegar (red
½ tsp soy sauce	or Chinkiang)
4½ oz (125g) Chinese yellow chives	A few lengths of spring onion, green parts only
5 oz (150g) bamboo shoot	Salt
3 oz (75g) preserved mustard tuber	

Cut the pork into thin slices, and then into slivers. Put them in a bowl, add the wine and soy sauces and mix well. Cut the chives into 2½ in (6cm) lengths. Cut the bamboo shoot into slivers and blanch in boiling water; drain well. Rinse the preserved mustard tuber and cut it into slivers.

Heat the oil in a seasoned wok over a high flame. Add the pork and stir-fry. As soon as the pieces have separated, add the preserved mustard tuber and bamboo shoot and continue to stir-fry until the pork is just cooked and everything is piping hot. Add the stock and stir until it has mostly evaporated. Add the chives and continue to stir until hot and fragrant, then season with salt. Stir in the vinegar, then remove from the wok and serve with a scattering of spring onion greens.

Slivered pork with flowering chives

jiu cai hua chao rou si 韭菜花炒肉丝

If you have supper in a Chinese home, you will very likely taste at least one dish like this: slivers of pork stir-fried with some kind of vegetable. Cooked in this manner, a little meat goes a long way, so it's not only healthy and delicious, but also economical. Think of this as a master recipe for any stir-fry that follows the basic formula of slivered meat plus slivered vegetable. Instead of pork, you can use beef, lamb, chicken, pigeon breast, turkey … and instead of the flowering chives, you can use another vegetable of your choice, or a mixture of vegetables, or firm tofu, spiced or plain. Chunkier or more watery vegetables, such as celery, lotus root, snow peas or carrot, will benefit from blanching before you stir-fry them, to "break their rawness" (*duan sheng*) and speed up the cooking time. The pre-frying of the meat keeps it beautifully tender. Flowering chives are simply the flowering stems of Chinese garlic chives.

4 oz (100g) pork tenderloin
6 oz (175g) flowering chives
3 tbsp cooking oil
A few thin slivers of peeled
    fresh ginger
A few thin slivers of red bell
    pepper (optional)
1 tsp sesame oil
Salt

For the marinade:
½ tsp Shaoxing wine
½ tsp light soy sauce
2 tsp potato starch
1 tbsp cold water or
    beaten egg

Cut the pork into thin slices and then into thin slivers. Add the marinade ingredients and mix well. Remove the flower buds from the end of each chive, and cut the chives into 2–2½ in (5–6cm) lengths. (The buds can be used in other dishes, including omelets.)

Heat 2 tablespoons oil in a seasoned wok over a high flame. Add the pork and stir-fry until just cooked; remove from the wok and set aside. Return the wok to a high heat, with the remaining cooking oil if you need it. Add the ginger and stir-fry for a moment until fragrant; then add the chives and red bell pepper, if using, and stir-fry until piping hot and fragrant. Return the pork to the wok and season with salt. Remove from the heat, stir in the sesame oil and serve.

Goat and radish stew

bai tang yang rou 白汤羊肉

We sat in a drawing room stacked with old paintings and calligraphies. Large picture windows opened onto an orchard and a meadow of grass and wildflowers, red, pink and white. Inside, there was a tea table, a great slab of wood scattered with teapots and bowls—the paraphernalia of the tea-drinking scholar. As we chatted, we sipped delicate, almost transparent tea made from the white tea leaves of Anyi in Zhejiang province.

My friend Sansan and I were visiting another friend in Gaochun, a well-preserved old town in southern Jiangsu. After tea, we wandered through the streets at dusk, among the terracotta-painted wooden shop fronts and whitewashed brick walls. This is one of the dishes we had for supper that day: a refreshing soup of goat meat and radish. As you will have gathered from the predominance of pork dishes in this chapter, pork is the principal meat of the Jiangnan region, but goat and beef make occasional appearances.

In the last couple of years, goat meat has become more widely available at farmers' markets, specialist shops and halal butchers, and it has a wonderful, edgy flavor that is perfectly complemented by the pure white radish. I first made this dish at home to mark the new Year of the Goat. Mutton or lamb shanks would work equally well.

1¾ lb (775g) goat leg in one piece, on the bone
¾ oz (20g) fresh ginger, skin on
2 spring onions, white parts only
A small piece of cassia bark or cinnamon stick
½ star anise
3 tbsp Shaoxing wine
1 lb (500g) white Asian radish
A few lengths of spring onion, green parts only
Chilli sauce of your choice, for dipping
Salt

Bring a large pan of water to the boil. Blanch the goat for 5 minutes, then drain and rinse well. Cover it with fresh water and bring to the boil. Skim.

Crush the ginger and spring onions slightly with the flat side of a Chinese cleaver or a rolling pin to loosen their fibers, and add them to the pan along with the spices and Shaoxing wine. Bring it back to the boil, then half-cover the pan and leave to boil over a medium flame for 1¼ hours, topping up with hot water as necessary. Turn off the heat and carefully remove the goat from the pan. Once cool enough to handle, remove the meat from the bone, cut it into bite-sized chunks and return it to the pan, along with the bone.

Peel and trim the radish and roll-cut it (see page 350) into bite-sized pieces. Bring a pan of water to the boil, add the radish and cook for 3 minutes to dispel any pepperiness. Drain. Add the radish to the pan, bring it to the boil and simmer until the radish is tender—about 20 minutes.

Before serving, discard the bone, season with salt, then garnish with the spring onion. Serve with a dip of chilli sauce for the meat.

POULTRY AND EGGS

The Lower Yangtze region is not just a land of fish and rice, but also of poultry. In the countryside, chickens peck around while ducks waddle and swim across a watery landscape of ponds and paddy fields. In most households, chickens are traditionally eaten for special occasions rather than everyday meals; until recently birds were always sold live rather than in packaged pieces. Every Chinese person knows that the finest chickens are free-range farmhouse birds (or as one Chinese friend rather sweetly explained to me in English, "freelance chickens"!).

If you can lay your hands on a good free-range bird, you may find clumps of golden fat inside its body cavity; heat these in a pan over a high flame until the oil runs out, then strain, cool and chill it, discarding the solids. This pure, delicious "chicken oil" can be added to soups, stir-fries and steamed fish just before serving, to heighten umami flavors. Rich chicken stocks, with or without added pork or ham, are the hidden backbone of many classic Jiangnan dishes.

Ducks are eaten all over the region but are particularly associated with Nanjing, where saltwater duck is a speciality. In general, Chinese people tend to eat duck in restaurants or buy it cooked from specialist vendors. Some Jiangnan duck dishes are fantastically complicated and demand advanced kitchen skills, like the "eight-treasure duck" of Shanghai, a steamed, boned bird stuffed with seasoned glutinous rice or, even more challenging, the "eight-treasure calabash duck" of Yangzhou, in which the fowl is boned, stuffed, sewn up, deep-fried and then steamed or stewed (see page 116).

Aside from fresh poultry, Jiangnan people have a marked predilection for cured, brined and dry-salted birds, which can be steamed and served straight up as an appetizer or cut into tiny pieces and added to other dishes.

As you might guess, Jiangnan cooks make imaginative use of almost every part of the bird. Local people reckon the choicest cuts are the so-called "squawk, jump and fly": the neck, feet and wings. Before the advent of factory farming and freezing, chicken's feet and duck webs were an extraordinary luxury—just think of how many ducks and how much labor it takes to create a single dish of piled-up, boned-out webs.

One interesting speciality of Gaochun, south of Nanjing, is "treasure in the palm of the hand," a curious snack made from two cured duck hearts clasped in a duck's foot, then bound tightly in a length of duck's intestine. Lacquered by their curing, these tidbits hang in bunches outside the shops of the old town; after a quick steaming, they are fragrant, chewy and delicious.

There are many gorgeous Jiangnan recipes for the eggs of different birds. Hen's eggs may be stir-fried, steamed or made into omelets; they are also delectable when hard boiled and stewed with stock, spices and tea leaves, or tucked into a potful of red-braised pork. Traditionally, people in Hangzhou offer poached eggs in hot water sweetened with sugar to honored guests such as a daughter's husband-to-be. Local people also prize a "head egg," the first egg laid by a hen, which is thought to be especially nutritious.

Duck eggs are often salt-cured, hard-boiled and eaten as a relish with congee. Quail and pigeon eggs are seen more in banquet cookery than on the everyday supper table; pigeon eggs, which retain their wobbly translucency after cooking, make a beautiful addition to a clear banquet soup.

Fertilized eggs (known as "live eggs") are among the more unusual poultry delicacies of Jiangnan. In Nanjing, the ladies especially like to eat "living pearls": live hen's eggs, hard-boiled and served with a salt-and-Sichuan pepper dip, which are thought to be a fortifying food. My local friend Lingling says women there often eat four or five at a go, not only for their taste, but also because they nourish the complexion. In Shaoxing, they prefer hard-boiled fertilized goose eggs dipped in soy sauce.

One of the wealthy salt merchants of Yangzhou, Huang Zhiyuan, is said to have taken the gastronomy of eggs to ludicrous lengths. Huang was the owner of the Ge Yuan, an elegant mansion and classical garden that still stands in the old city. According to one published tale, he liked to eat bird's nest, ginseng and hen's eggs for breakfast. However, when he found out that the eggs were costing him a tael of silver apiece, even he felt this was exorbitant, so he summoned his personal chef and accused him of cheating. The chef, affronted, handed in his resignation, insisting that the eggs he served were exceptional. Mr. Huang hired another chef, and then another, but each chef presented him with eggs that were markedly inferior. So he re-employed his original chef and discovered that the expensive eggs were laid by chickens that had been fed on ground-up medicinal ingredients such as ginseng and jujubes. Finally he understood why they were so exquisite, so he accepted the cost and resumed his old breakfasting habit.

Chicken with young ginger

nen jiang chao zi ji 嫩姜炒仔鸡

Mencius, the Chinese sage of ancient times, famously said that "the gentleman keeps his distance from the kitchen"— a line that is often used to explain the disdain that scholarly gourmets have traditionally expressed for actual cooking. Even Yuan Mei, author of the classic eighteenth-century cookbook *Food Lists of the Garden of Contentment*, is not thought to have personally tried his hand at the wok or chopping board, although he treated his favored chef with great respect.

I'm often reminded of Yuan Mei and his chef when I spend time with Hangzhou restaurateur Dai Jianjun and his personal chef Zhu Yinfeng at his retreat in rural Zhejiang. Every day, after presenting his dishes, chef Zhu joins Dai at the table and receives a meticulous commentary on his cooking.

This is one of Zhu Yinfeng's dishes, a succulent stir-fry of chicken with crisp young ginger. I originally learned to make it with ginger that Zhu and I had plucked out of the earth that morning, in the shade of a stand of peach trees. Ginger is a gorgeous, prehistoric-looking plant, with dramatic sprays of spear-like leaves that recall the colors and shapes of a Rousseau painting. Dig down beneath the leaves and you will find clusters of yellow rhizomes with pink tips singing out their fresh, zippy fragrance.

For this dish, use plump, tender ginger that is not too fibrous—a small piece should break off cleanly, with no fibers poking out of the cut.

3 oz (75g) plump fresh ginger
1 spring onion, white part only
¾ lb (350g) boned chicken thighs
2 tbsp cooking oil or lard
1 tbsp Shaoxing wine
¼ tsp potato starch mixed with ½ tsp cold water
A few 2 in (5cm) lengths of spring onion, green parts only
1 tsp sesame oil
Ground white pepper

For the marinade:
½ tsp salt
½ tbsp Shaoxing wine
2 tsp potato starch
2 tsp cold water

For the sauce:
1 tsp light soy sauce
½ tsp dark soy sauce
½ tsp superfine sugar
2 tbsp stock or water

Peel the ginger and cut it into 2mm slices. Smack the spring onion white gently with the flat side of a Chinese cleaver or a rolling pin to loosen its fibers. Cut the chicken into 1 in (2cm) cubes, put it in a bowl with the marinade ingredients and stir well.

Combine the sauce ingredients in a small bowl. Heat the oil in a seasoned wok over a high flame. Add the ginger and spring onion white and stir-fry until they smell wonderfully fragrant. Add the chicken and continue to stir-fry over a high heat, separating the pieces as you go.

When the chicken is cooked through and beginning to color, splash in the Shaoxing wine, then give the sauce a stir and add to the wok. Bring it to a fast boil and season with a pinch or two of pepper to taste. Give the starch mixture a stir and add it to the wok, stirring as the liquid thickens to a glossy sauce. Add the spring onion greens and give them a brief lick of heat. Finally, off the heat, stir in the sesame oil, then serve.

Beggar's chicken

jiao hua tong ji 叫化童鸡

Beggar's chicken is a dramatic centerpiece of a dish: a whole chicken wrapped in leaves and encased in baked mud that must be smashed apart with a mallet. The method used to make it is a relic of ancient times. Legend tells that a local beggar once stole a chicken for his supper. Lacking a pot, he simply wrapped the bird in mud and baked it in the embers of his fire. When it was done, he cracked open the clay sarcophagus, stripped off the skin and feathers, and the bird inside was so wondrously fragrant that people nearby came rushing to see what he'd done. Later, chefs refined the original recipe, which became a famous speciality of Hangzhou and of Changshu, both of which cities lay claim to it.

In Hangzhou, the bird is wrapped in clay mixed with the aromatic mulch left over from making Shaoxing wine. At home, I use a salted pastry crust, which works just as well as a means of encasing the bird, and can be smashed apart at the table like clay. Both methods keep the chicken wondrously juicy, infused with the haunting fragrance of lotus leaves. Don't throw away the leftover lotus leaves: add them to a pot of rice or congee the next day, with any leftover scraps of chicken and juices salvaged from the pan, and they will transform it into something ambrosial.

A kind of dried ginger known as *shan nai* or *sha jiang* ("sand ginger") is used in seasoning the chicken. This can be found in good Chinese supermarkets, but the recipe will work without it.

See photographs on pages 110–11

1 chicken (3–3½ lbs/1.5–1.7kg)
Sichuan pepper salt, to serve (see page 333)

For the marinade:
A small piece of sand ginger
¾ oz (20g) fresh ginger, skin on
2 spring onions, white parts only
2½ tbsp light soy sauce
½ tsp dark soy sauce
3 tbsp Shaoxing wine
1 tsp superfine sugar
½ tsp salt

For the stuffing:
10 spring onions or 5 oz (150g) baby leeks, white parts only
4 oz (100g) skinless pork belly
2 tbsp lard
1½ tbsp Shaoxing wine
1 tbsp light soy sauce
¼ tsp salt

For the salt-crust pastry:
4 cups (500g) all-purpose flour
1¾ cups (500g) fine salt

For the wrapping:
2 whole dried lotus leaves
3 oz (75g) lard

Preheat the oven to 425°F (220°C). Pound the sand ginger to a coarse powder with a pestle and mortar.

First, prepare the chicken. Slice through the skin between the legs and the body, but don't sever the legs—just pull them away from the body. Break the hip and knee joints of each leg so they hang loose. If the feet are still attached, chop them off just below the drumstick joint and discard. Make an incision along the length of each drumstick, all the way to the bone, and wiggle out the bones. Use a Chinese cleaver or heavy knife to chop off the bones as close as possible to the foot joints. Cut, wiggle and chop off the thigh bones in the same way. Cut gently into each wing close to the joints, without severing them, then wiggle out the main bones (this can be a little fiddly). Turn your cleaver upside down and use the spine to make about five hard chops down each wing tip: this will make them floppy without severing them. If your chicken still has its head, do the same to the neck, to make it floppy without severing it. Finally, use the flat of the blade to smack the breast bone hard several times, so the body of the chicken collapses slightly. Put it in a large bowl, ready for the marinade.

Smack the fresh ginger and spring onion whites gently with the flat side of the Chinese cleaver or a rolling pin to loosen their fibers, then put them in the cavity of the chicken. Mix all the other marinade ingredients in a small bowl and pour them over and into the chicken, using your hands to spread the marinade over it. Set aside for at least half an hour, turning occasionally.

Make the stuffing. Cut the spring onion whites or leeks and the pork into slivers. Heat the lard in a seasoned wok over a high flame. Add the spring onion and stir-fry for a few seconds until fragrant. Add the pork and continue to stir-fry until it has changed color. Add the other stuffing ingredients, mix well, then remove them from the wok and set aside.

Mix the flour and salt in a big bowl and add enough water to make a dough that can be rolled. Cover with a damp cloth and set aside. Put the lotus leaves in a wide pan or deep baking tray. Cover with a kettleful of boiling water and leave to soak for 1–2 minutes until supple (lotus leaves are huge, so you may have to move them around to make sure they are completely soaked). Put one drained lotus leaf, shiny side down, on the work surface, folding down the slightly conical center so it lies flat. Cover with two overlapping 24 in (60cm) lengths of aluminum foil. Put the other leaf, shiny side down, on top of the first one.

Remove the chicken from the marinade and put it breast-side up in the center of the leaves. Discard the ginger and spring onion. Put the stuffing and its juices in the cavity of the bird. Fold the flap of skin at the base of the bird over the body. If the head remains, fold it into the body too. Pull the legs and fold them tightly across the body, then pull in the wings and fold them tightly across, on the diagonal. Press the lard into the body at the base of the bird. Wrap the bird tightly in the first leaf, then in the foil, and finally in the outer leaf. Use kitchen twine to tie it tightly like a parcel, then tie it across both diagonals so you have a British flag pattern of twine.

Roll the dough into a large rectangle, ⅙ in (4–5mm) thick and wide enough to enclose the bird. Put the chicken upside down on the pastry and wrap it tightly, sealing the overlapping edges with a little water. Turn the bird over and put it on a rectangle of parchment paper in a baking tray. Roast for 40 minutes, then reduce the temperature to 300–325°F (150–160°C) and cook for another 2 hours. The crust will be hard and dark brown. Allow to rest for 20 minutes before serving, then put the parcel on a wooden board and take it to the table with a wooden mallet to smash open the shell (do not serve it on a ceramic plate, which will very likely end up in pieces!). Be prepared for small pieces of pastry to fly about as you crack open the crust. Remove the crust, use scissors to snip the twine, and unwrap your gorgeous, juicy, steaming bird, curled lazily in an aromatic cradle of leaf.

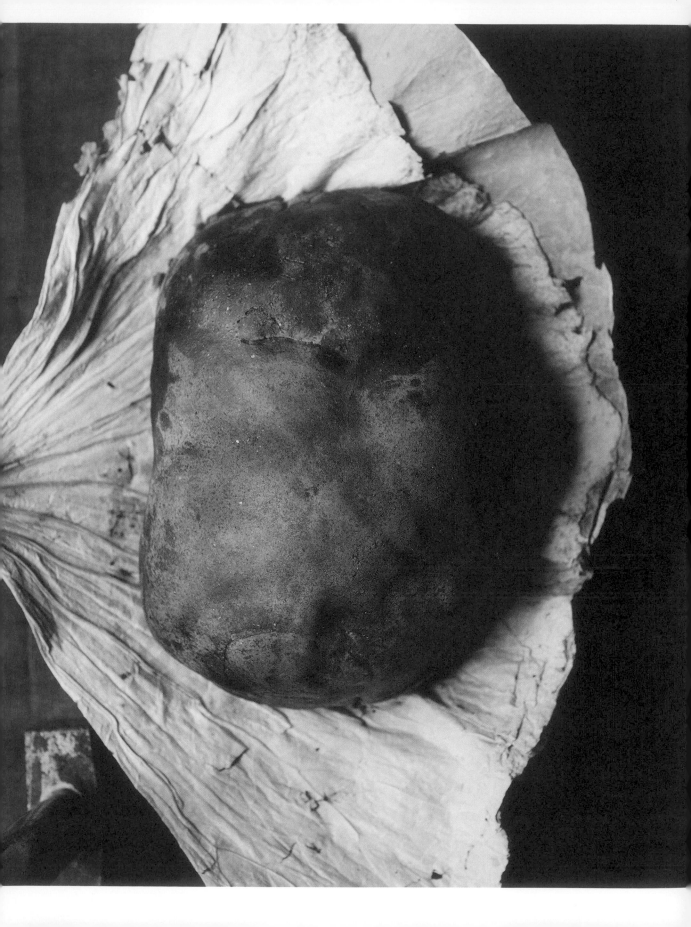

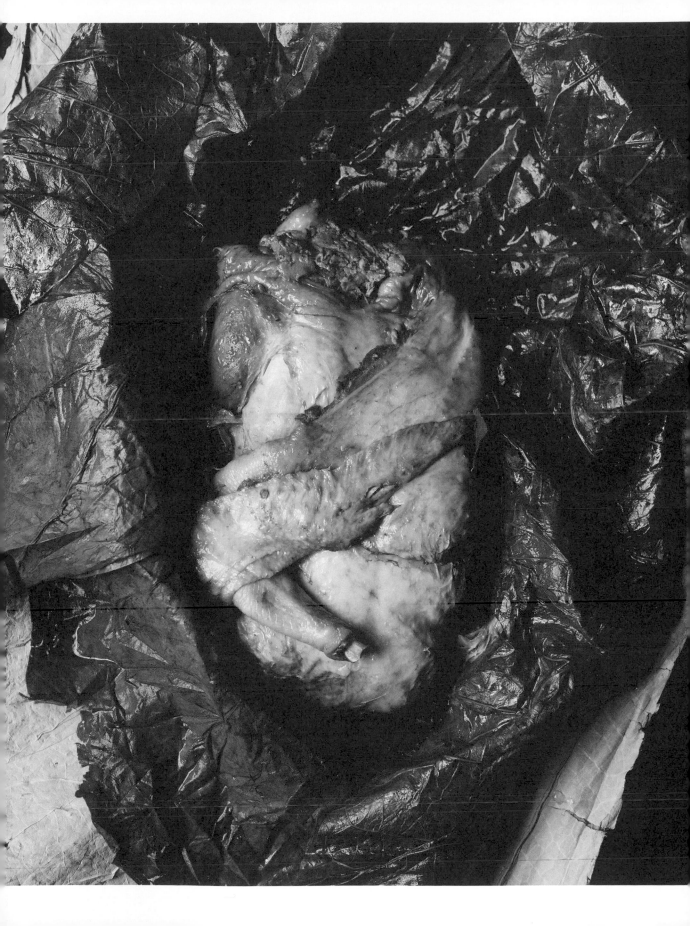

Stewed chicken with chestnuts

ban li shao ji 板栗烧鸡

The Jiangnan chestnut season begins in September, when the tender young nuts, pale and crisp, can be harvested. Later in the season and during the winter, after they have swelled, they may be used in sweetmeats, soups or stews like this one. There are many versions of the dish; this one, from Suzhou, includes the textural contrasts of crunchy bamboo shoot and succulent mushrooms. In China, it would normally be made with chopped chicken on the bone, but the recipe works well with boned leg meat. If you wish, you can turn up the heat at the end to reduce the broth to a thicker sauce, or thicken the liquid with a mixture of potato starch and cold water. The recipe is strikingly similar to one in Yuan Mei's eighteenth-century cookbook.

This dish is one of a family of what are known as "yellow-smothered" or "yellow-stewed" (*huang men*) dishes, in which the main ingredient is simmered in a covered pot, usually with some soy sauce for color, but not enough to give the dark treacliness characteristic of red-braised dishes. I normally use tinned or vacuum-packed chestnuts, but if you wish to cook and peel your own, slice off the bases of the raw chestnuts and boil them for a couple of minutes, then drain. When cool enough to handle, remove their shells and inner skins as far as possible.

6 dried shiitake mushrooms
14 oz (400g) boned chicken legs or thighs
3 oz (75g) winter bamboo shoot (optional)
2 spring onions, white parts only
¾ oz (20g) fresh ginger, skin on
2 tbsp lard or cooking oil
9 oz (250g) cooked peeled chestnuts

2 tbsp Shaoxing wine
2 cups (500ml) chicken stock
2 tbsp light soy sauce
2 tsp dark soy sauce
1 tbsp superfine sugar
½ tsp salt
A few 2 in (5cm) lengths of spring onion, green parts only
1 tsp sesame oil

Cover the dried mushrooms with boiling water and leave to soak for at least half an hour. Cut the chicken evenly into bite-sized chunks. Remove the shiitake stalks and quarter the caps. Cut the bamboo shoot, if using, into 2 in (5mm) thick bite-sized slices and blanch these in boiling water; drain. Smack the spring onion whites lightly with the flat side of a Chinese cleaver or a rolling pin to loosen their fibers. Slice the ginger.

Heat the oil in a seasoned wok over a high flame. Add the ginger and spring onion whites and stir-fry until they smell wonderful. Push them to the side of the wok, add the chicken and spread it out into a single layer. Fry until it colors lightly without moving it around too much, except to turn it. Add all the other ingredients except the spring onion greens and sesame oil. Bring to the boil, then cover and simmer for 15–20 minutes (I usually transfer the mixture from the wok to a saucepan or clay pot for the simmering, and to serve).

Before serving, increase the heat to reduce the sauce if you wish, and season with a little extra salt if desired. Add the spring onion greens and cover for a few seconds to give them a lick of heat. Off the heat, stir in the sesame oil, then serve.

Bowl-steamed chicken with salted fish

xiang kou ji 鲞扣鸡

Steaming is one of the most ancient and characteristic of Chinese cooking methods, although it has been eclipsed by stir-frying in most people's perceptions of Chinese cuisine. Pottery steamers have been found among the relics of Chinese Neolithic sites, including the Hemudu site in Zhejiang. Steaming is still one of the finest ways of preserving the innate or "root" flavor (*ben wei*) of ingredients, without the transformations of searing, browning or tossing at high temperatures in a wok. In the past, it was also used because it was an economical means of cooking a few separate dishes in the steam of the rice pot, thus saving fuel.

The following dish is a favorite in Shaoxing and Hangzhou. It is a *kou* dish, which is to say one in which ingredients are fitted neatly into a bowl, steamed, then turned out onto a serving dish in the form of a dome. In this case, strips of partially cooked chicken are interleaved with slices of pungent salted fish. The salted fish is a treasured ingredient in Zhejiang, but it's an acquired taste for those who did not grow up with it. It has a funky, complex flavor reminiscent of ripe washed-rind cheeses, which perks up the gentle chicken flesh in a darkly magnificent way. Chinese people don't expect Westerners to like their salted fish. The first time I served this dish to non-Chinese guests, I warned them that they might dislike it—but they adored it, and one of my friends described the dish as "a revelation."

2 oz (50g) Chinese salted mackerel or 2½ oz (65g) dried yellow croaker	1 spring onion
	3 slices fresh ginger, skin on
2 boned chicken legs or thighs only (about 1 lb/550g)	1 tbsp Shaoxing wine
	3 tbsp chicken stock or water
	1 tbsp thinly sliced spring onions, green parts only

If you are using dried yellow croaker, soak it in cold water for at least 1 hour. Bring a pan of water to the boil, add the chicken and poach it for about 5 minutes, until semi-cooked. Drain and rinse it in cold water to cool. Pick out the spine of your salted fish, along with as many bones as possible, then cut the fish into slices.

Cut each boned chicken leg into two, separating thigh and drumstick. Lay each piece skin-side up on a chopping board and cut it evenly into 1 in (2cm) strips, keeping the slices together in their original positions as far as possible. Scoop each set of slices up with a large knife or Chinese cleaver and place them in a 2 cups (500ml) heatproof bowl so that the slices are lined up with the skin against the inside of the bowl. Tuck slices of salted fish at regular intervals in between the chicken slices. When the inside of the bowl is covered, fill the bowl with any remaining pieces of chicken and morsels of salted fish.

Smack the spring onion with the flat side of a Chinese cleaver or a rolling pin to loosen its fibers and cut it in half. Put the spring onion and ginger on the chicken and add the Shaoxing wine and chicken stock or water. Cover the bowl with a heatproof plate or aluminum foil, place it in a steamer basket and steam over a high flame for 30 minutes.

To serve, remove the plate or foil, cover the bowl with a serving dish and swiftly invert it, so the chicken falls out in a dome surrounded by its cooking juices. Garnish with the spring onion greens. Don't forget to spoon the wild, heady juices over your rice.

Stir-fried chicken hotchpotch

chao shi jian 炒时件

This recipe is based on one I enjoyed at the Dragon Well Manor restaurant in Hangzhou. There, they made it with the assorted offal of four chickens: livers, hearts, intestines and gizzards. The contrasting textures of the crisp intestines and gizzards and the tender livers and hearts is delectable, but the same method can also be used to make a marvelous quick stir-fry of chicken livers alone, mixed with hearts if you have them. It doesn't look particularly elegant but it tastes wonderful. With plain rice and a simple green vegetable, this makes a satisfying supper for a couple of people.

6 oz (175g) chicken livers (or livers and hearts)	1 tsp light soy sauce
	¼ tsp dark soy sauce
3 garlic cloves and an equivalent amount of fresh ginger	A pinch of superfine sugar
	½ tsp sesame oil
2 spring onions, green parts only	
	For the marinade:
3 tbsp cooking oil or lard	¼ tsp salt
2 tsp Shaoxing wine	1 tsp Shaoxing wine
	2 tsp potato starch

Cut the chicken livers into 2 in (5mm) slices and put them in a bowl. Add the marinade ingredients and mix well. Peel and slice the garlic and ginger and cut the spring onion greens into 2½ in (6cm) lengths.

Heat 2 tablespoons of the cooking oil or lard in a seasoned wok over a high flame. Add the chicken livers and stir-fry rapidly to separate the slices. When they are half cooked, remove them from the wok and set aside. Return the wok to the heat with the remaining lard or oil and the ginger and garlic and stir-fry briefly until the latter are wonderfully fragrant. Return the livers to the wok and stir them into the fragrant oil. Splash the Shaoxing wine around the edges of the pan and season with the soy sauces and a pinch of sugar. Stir in the spring onion greens to give them a brief lick of heat. Finally, remove from the heat, stir in the sesame oil and serve. The livers should be barely cooked and still juicy.

Chicken livers with Chinese chives

Slice, marinate and pre-fry the chicken livers as in the main recipe. Instead of ginger and garlic, fry 4 oz (100g) Chinese chives cut into 2½ oz (6cm) sections until hot and fragrant, with some ground chilli if you wish. Return the livers to the wok, season to taste with light soy sauce and serve.

Eight-treasure stuffed calabash duck

ba bao hu lu ya 八宝葫芦鸭

At the highest echelons of banquet cookery, Jiangnan chefs are known for their Kung Fu dishes: elaborate concoctions that demand time, expense, virtuoso cooking skills, and often a bit of madness. In the past, the salt merchants of Yangzhou and the rich citizens of Suzhou feted visiting emperors with multiple Kung Fu delicacies; one historical account of a banquet describes a host of complex dishes including steamed camel's hump and mock leopard's fetus! These days, few restaurants are equipped to serve the more elaborate traditional dishes, but one exception is the Lu Mansion in Yangzhou, which is encouraged by the local government to fly the flag of classic Yangzhou cooking. I was lucky enough to spend a few days in the kitchen there, learning the ropes of the Three-Head Feast, including legendary dishes such as slow-cooked pig's head and this extraordinary eight-treasure duck. The boned duck is stuffed with glutinous rice, sewn up, tied around the waist to resemble a lucky calabash gourd, deep-fried, stewed, and finally served with a sauce reduction.

This, then, is a just a taste of crazy, complicated, wonderful Kung Fu cooking, and it's probably the most challenging recipe in the book, but a fantastic dish for a special occasion. To make it, you will need a pair of good kitchen scissors; a heavy chopping cleaver; a needle and strong cotton thread; a thin ribbon or some string made of uncolored, natural fiber; and a certain amount of patience. While the recipe may take time, I hope you'll agree that the end result is spectacular.

1 oven-ready duck (about 4 lb/2kg)
5 tsp dark soy sauce
1 oz (30g) fresh ginger, skin on
2 spring onions
1 star anise
4 tbsp Shaoxing wine
2 tbsp light soy sauce
2 tsp superfine sugar
1 tbsp potato starch mixed with 2 tbsp cold water
Cooking oil, for deep-frying
Salt
Several small heads of green bok choy and strips of red bell pepper, to garnish (optional)

For the stuffing:
½ cup (100g) glutinous rice
2 dried shiitake mushrooms
2 oz (50g) bamboo shoot
2 oz (50g) raw chicken breast
1½ oz (40g) Spanish or Chinese cured ham, steamed briefly
2 oz (50g) ready-to-use lotus seeds
2 oz (50g) green soybeans
1½ tbsp cooking oil
2 tsp finely chopped fresh ginger
2 tsp finely chopped spring onions, white part only
4 tsp light soy sauce
½ tsp dark soy sauce
¼ tsp salt

First, make the stuffing. Cover the glutinous rice with cold water and leave to soak overnight, or for at least 4 hours. Cover the shiitake mushrooms in boiling water and leave to soak for at least half an hour.

Remove and discard the mushroom stalks and cut the caps into ½ in (1cm) dice. Cut the bamboo shoot into 1cm dice and do the same with the chicken breast. Cut the ham into slightly smaller dice. Bring a pan or wok of water to the boil. Add the lotus seeds, green soybeans and bamboo shoot dice and blanch for 30 seconds, then remove and drain. Drain the soaked rice.

Heat the cooking oil in a seasoned wok over a high flame. Add the ginger and spring onion and stir-fry briefly until fragrant; add the shiitake and ham and stir-fry until they are also fragrant. Add the chicken and stir-fry until just cooked through, then add the bamboo shoot, lotus seeds and soybeans. When everything is piping hot, stir in the rice, the light and dark soy sauces and salt. Set aside to cool.

Next, bone the duck: break the joints that connect the legs and wings to the body and break the internal joints in legs and wings, taking care not to damage the skin of the bird. Lay the bird ▶

breast-side down on a chopping board and use kitchen scissors to snip down the center of the skin along the neckbone to the top of the torso—this will create an opening large enough to remove the carcass of the bird. Now carefully peel the skin and flesh away from the carcass, snipping close to the ribcage to detach the flesh from the bones as you go, and taking great care not to damage the skin. Don't try to rush this—it requires patience and care. Cut through the broken shoulder joints when you reach them, and keep snipping. At some point you may find it easier to start snipping from the bottom end of the bird. Keep snipping until you can remove the entire rib cage from the bird. Keep this for another use (it will make a wonderful stock).

Now, working from the inside of the bird, snip along the leg bones, cutting away the flesh from the bone. When you reach the first joint, you should be able to winkle out and discard the bone (which you can also add to the stockpot). Keep snipping until you reach the end of the drumstick—at this point, use a heavy cleaver to chop through the bone, leaving the nub at the end of the drumstick attached to the flesh and skin. (You don't want to cut out this nub, or you will end up with a hole at the end of each leg.) Repeat for the other leg, then for the upper bone of the wings. Chop off the ends of the wings, just below the joints. Now snip into the parson's nose at the base of the bird, and remove and discard the small, gray-yellow, kidney-shaped glands on either side.

Bring a large pan of water to the boil. Turn the duck inside out and blanch it briefly in the hot water, then rinse it well under the cold tap and turn it right-side in again. Use a needle and strong cotton thread to sew up any holes in the skin, and to sew up the hole in the base of the bird.

Push the cooled stuffing through the neck and into the bird, poking it into the furthest reaches. The bird should only be loosely filled, otherwise it may burst during cooking. Sew up the hole in the neck. Use some natural ribbon or string to tie it tightly around the middle to make a "waist," like a calabash gourd. Wipe any stray rice grains off the skin of the boned bird, then smear it all over with 2 teaspoons of the dark soy sauce. Slice the skin-on ginger and cut the spring onions into 2 in (5cm) lengths. Boil the kettle.

In a stable, seasoned wok, heat the oil for deep-frying to 320°F (160°C). Very carefully, lower the bird into the oil and deep-fry until golden brown, turning it once for even coloring. Carefully remove it from the oil and set aside.

In a saucepan large enough to take your duck lying down, heat 2 tablespoons of the deep-frying oil over a high flame. Add the sliced ginger, spring onions and star anise and stir-fry until

wonderfully fragrant. Add some hot water from the kettle, add the duck, then top with enough hot water to cover. Add the Shaoxing wine, light soy sauce, 2 teaspoons of the dark soy sauce and the sugar. Bring to the boil and season with salt. Cover the pan, turn down the heat and simmer for 1½ hours.

If using, trim the bok choy, discarding any tired leaves. Cut a small cross in the base of each head and insert a small strip of red bell pepper into each cross. Bring a pan of water to the boil. Blanch the bok choy until just wilted, then refresh it under the cold tap. Drain well and set aside.

To finish the duck, remove it from the pan and put it on a serving dish. Strain 1⅓ cups (300ml) of the cooking liquid into a wok, bring it to the boil and season with salt. Add the remaining 1 teaspoon dark soy sauce. Give the potato starch mixture a stir and gradually add enough to thicken the juices to a lazy gravy-like consistency, so they will cling to the bird. Pour this gravy over the duck. Garnish, if you wish, with a circle of the blanched bok choy. Serve the duck whole and carve it at the table, taking care to remove any pieces of sewing thread before eating!

Golden scrambled eggs with shrimp

xia ren chao dan 虾仁炒蛋

One warm day in May, with the breeze whispering in the bamboo and the lotus leaves lying lazily on the surface of the pond, I spent the morning sitting in the garden of the Dragon Well Manor restaurant in Hangzhou. At lunchtime, I sat among friends at a table spread with the most exquisite repast: crisp river shrimp cradled in golden eggs, darkly glistening red-braised pork with tofu puffs, a lively stir-fry of fresh green soybeans, fluffy white rice and a dreamy broth in which floated the tenderest, most ethereal little cabbage leaves.

It was, like all meals at the Manor, full of quiet, understated joy and the perfection of the season. In this recipe, I've suggested you use saltwater shrimp rather than freshwater shrimp, but have otherwise followed the instructions of the Manor's head chef, Chen Xiaoming.

4 oz (100g) uncooked
  saltwater shrimp
3 large eggs
1½ tsp potato starch
3 tbsp thinly sliced spring
  onions, green parts only

½ tbsp Shaoxing wine
3 tbsp cooking oil
Salt and ground white
  pepper

Rinse and devein the shrimp, then shake them dry and put them in a bowl. Separate one of the eggs. Add 1 teaspoon egg white and ¼ teaspoon salt to the shrimp and chill them in the fridge for 1 hour before cooking.

Remove the shrimp from the fridge and stir in the potato starch. Beat the remaining white and yolk of the separated egg with the two other eggs and season with salt and white pepper. Stir in the spring onions and Shaoxing wine.

Heat the oil in a seasoned wok over a high flame. When hot, turn down the heat, add the shrimp and stir-fry until nearly—but not completely—cooked. Remove them with a slotted spoon and drop them into the egg mixture. Return the wok to a high flame. When the oil is hot again, add the egg mixture and stir-fry until nearly cooked. Stop stirring and allow the egg to become golden, flipping it over once to color the other side. Break up the eggs and pile them onto a serving dish.

Ningbo omelet with dried shrimp and Chinese chives

jiu cai xia pi ta dan 韭菜虾皮煸蛋

Eggs and Chinese chives always make a fine marriage, and they are especially good when enhanced by the umami taste of the dried shrimp in the following recipe. The cooking method is known as *ta*, and refers to frying ingredients against the flat surface of a wok or frying pan without moving them around. Chinese cooks usually do this in a wok, but if you have a flat frying pan to hand, it's actually more convenient. It is very important to season the surface of the pan, or use a non-stick pan, so the egg doesn't stick. Sliced spring onion greens or yellow hothouse chives can be used instead of the green Chinese chives, if you prefer.

3 oz (75g) Chinese or garlic chives
3 tbsp cooking oil
¾ oz (25g) papery dried shrimp
4 large eggs
½ tbsp Shaoxing wine
Salt and ground white pepper

Trim off and discard the white ends off the chives, and cut the green leaves into 2 in (5mm) sections. Heat 1 tablespoon cooking oil in your wok or pan, then stir-fry the shrimp until they smell delicious and are faintly golden. Remove and set aside.

Beat the eggs, add the Shaoxing wine, shrimp and chives, and season with salt and pepper. Pour the remaining cooking oil into a hot, seasoned wok or frying pan. When it is hot, pour in the egg mixture. Use a wok scoop to push in from the sides of the omelet several times, allowing the runny egg mixture to fill the space you have created. When there is no longer enough runny egg to do this, leave the omelet to fry over a medium flame until the base is golden and the eggs are nearly set.

Cover the omelet with a plate and carefully invert the pan so the omelet turns out onto the plate, then slide it back into the pan and cook the other side until golden. Slide the omelet onto a chopping board. Cut it into 1½ in (4cm) strips, then cut the strips diagonally into chopstickable slices. Pile up on a serving dish.

Galloping eggs with slivered pork

rou si pao dan 肉丝跑蛋

This fluffy omelet laced with slivered pork and spring onion, a speciality of Hangzhou, is one of those Chinese supper dishes that is so much more delicious than the sum of its parts. It makes a fine supper with a green vegetable and rice. Omelets like these are sometimes described in cookery books as "roasted eggs" (*pao dan*), which sounds the same in Chinese as "galloping eggs" (*pao dan*), but the latter name, which is the one I was given by chef Zhu Yinfeng when he taught me the recipe, conjures up such a wonderfully appropriate image of rapid, bubbling movement that I had to use it.

The same method can be used to make omelets with fresh shrimp, soaked and shredded dried scallop or slivered ham. And if you don't fancy ladling around boiling hot oil, the omelet is fairly puffy and extremely delicious if simply cooked in very hot oil in a frying pan.

4 oz (100g) lean pork
½ cup (100ml) cooking oil
3 large eggs
4 tbsp thinly sliced spring onions, green parts only
Salt and ground white pepper

For the marinade:
¼ tsp salt
1 tsp Shaoxing wine
½ tsp potato starch mixed with ½ tsp cold water

Cut the pork into very thin slivers, add the marinade ingredients and mix well. Stir in ½ tablespoon cooking oil. Beat the eggs, seasoning them with salt and white pepper. Add 3 tablespoons of the spring onions and stir them in.

Make sure your wok is stable before you start to cook. Heat 1 tablespoon cooking oil in a seasoned wok over a medium flame. Add the pork and stir swiftly to separate the slivers. When they are just cooked, remove them from the pan and tip them into the egg mixture, stirring them in.

Heat the remaining cooking oil in the wok over a high flame until the surface begins to shimmer. Take the bowl containing the egg mixture in your weaker hand. Scoop up a ladleful of hot oil from the wok with the other hand, pour the egg mixture into the wok and immediately pour the ladleful of hot oil into the center of the egg mixture, taking great care as you do this. The egg will bubble up dramatically.

When the omelet is golden underneath, drain off the excess oil and turn it over to cook the other side. When the other side is golden, sprinkle over the remaining spring onions, flip it over briefly to give them a lick of heat, then slide the omelet onto a serving dish. Cut it up into slices like a pizza to serve.

Dai Jianjun's vegetarian "crabmeat"

a dai su xie fen 啊戴素蟹粉

Dai Jianjun, the owner of the Dragon Well Manor restaurant in Hangzhou, normally takes the role of gentleman instructor to his personal chef, but on one occasion he gave me a dish he said he had cooked himself. We were visiting a chicken farm in the hills outside Hangzhou and he disappeared into the kitchen, reappearing a few minutes later with a fragrant dish of "vegetarian crabmeat": scrambled eggs laced with the traditional crabmeat seasonings of ginger and vinegar. Dai is a bit of a tease, and I'll never know if he really cooked the dish himself, but it was delicious, and strikingly reminiscent of stir-fried hairy crab, so I thought it should bear his name in this book.

The dish is a soft tangle of yellow yolk and egg white, with just a hint of sweetness amid the scintillating fragrance of ginger and rice vinegar. The cooked eggs have the same rich curdiness as stir-fried crabmeat, and will make anyone who has tasted the latter smile in surprise and recognition. The key to this recipe is to add the eggs unbeaten to the wok, so they are not evenly blended in the final dish, creating the illusion of the white and brown meat of the crab. The dish will look most convincing if you use eggs with deeply colored yolks.

4 medium eggs
1½ tbsp finely chopped fresh ginger
¼ tsp salt
¾ tsp superfine sugar
A good pinch of ground white pepper
2 tbsp cooking oil
1 tbsp Chinkiang vinegar

Break the eggs into a bowl. Add 1 tablespoon of the chopped ginger, along with the salt, sugar and pepper. Do not mix.

Heat the cooking oil in a seasoned wok over a high flame. Add the remaining ginger and stir-fry very briefly until you can smell its fragrance, then add the egg mixture and stir-fry gently to scramble. When the eggs are just about cooked, stir in the vinegar. Remove from the wok and serve immediately.

Hibiscus-blossom egg white with fresh fava beans

fu rong can dou 芙蓉蚕豆

This simple but dreamily delicious dish is made of pillowy, cloud-like egg white and fresh fava beans, finished with a sprinkling of dark pink ham. The egg white, scrambled gently to preserve its tenderness, resembles the loose, unbuttoned white flowers of the cotton or Confederate rose, *Hibiscus mutabilis*, hence its name. I first tasted this dish in a small restaurant in Yangzhou run by chef Yang Bin. It's typical of Yangzhou cooking in its delicacy, its seasonality, and the elegant way in which the rosy ham is used to complement the white egg and bright green beans. The crux of this dish is *huo hou*, the control of heat and timing. The egg white must be scrambled at a modest temperature; if you overheat it, it will lose its soft, custardy texture.

2¼ tsp potato starch
4 large egg whites
2 cups (500ml) chicken stock
5 oz (150g) shelled, skinned
    fava beans (about 1¼
    lbs/550g in their pods)

1 cup (200ml) cooking oil
2 tsp finely chopped Spanish
    or Chinese cured ham,
    steamed briefly
Salt

Mix 2 teaspoons of the potato starch with 2 teaspoons water. Gently stir it into the egg whites and season with salt (you don't want to make them frothy).

Bring the stock to the boil and season with salt. Add the fava beans, return to the boil and simmer for a few minutes until tender—they will also have absorbed the savory flavor of the stock. Remove the beans from the stock and set aside.

Heat the oil in a seasoned wok to 250°F (120°C). Pour in the egg white mixture and stir gently over a medium flame as it sets into lazy billows, taking great care not to let the oil get too hot or the egg white will toughen. Remove it with a slotted spoon and set aside.

Mix the remaining potato starch with 1 teaspoon water. Brush and wipe out the wok to remove most of the oil, then add ½ cup (100ml) of the seasoned stock and bring to the boil over a high flame. Add the beans and quickly reheat them. Add the egg white and stir swiftly but gently to incorporate. Give the potato starch mixture a stir and pour it into the wok, stirring gently as the stock thickens. Turn it out onto a serving dish, scatter over the chopped ham and serve immediately.

Shanghai golden egg dumplings with Chinese cabbage

shang hai dan jiao 上海蛋饺

Golden egg dumplings are traditionally a New Year's treat in Shanghai and the wider Jiangnan region. They are made by folding tiny omelets over little mounds of stuffing: somewhat fiddly, but fun. The dumplings may simply be steamed before eating, but more typically are added to a potful of ingredients to make a soupy stew crowned by their golden halo. On special occasions, such dishes can be complex compositions of different ingredients laid out in concentric circles in a great big pot, including perhaps meatballs, chunks of pork belly, hard-boiled quail eggs and stuffed wheat gluten or tofu. The following dish is a much simpler version than these festive extravaganzas, and is based on one I enjoyed at the Shunfeng Harbor restaurant in Shanghai. Do try to use a wonderfully rich and flavorful stock, since it needs to flavor the pale-tasting cabbage and sweet potato noodles.

Traditionally, the dumplings are made using an oiled ladle held over a gas flame, and the cook tilts the ladle to spread the egg mixture easily. However, they can also be made in a flat pan, and if you want the skins to be as round as possible, you can use a 3 in (9cm) round metal biscuit cutter to keep them under control—ideally, use a biscuit cutter with a heatproof handle; otherwise, you will need a potholder. Many people add some chopped water chestnut to the pork mixture, for a little crunch.

4 oz (100g) dried sweet potato noodles
14 oz (400g) Chinese cabbage
5 oz (150g) minced pork
2 tsp Shaoxing wine
1 tsp finely chopped fresh ginger
1 tsp finely chopped spring onion
4 large eggs
1 quart (1 liter) stock
1 tbsp lard
¾ tsp dark soy sauce
2½ tsp light soy sauce
1 tbsp thinly sliced spring onions, green parts only
Cooking oil
Salt and ground white pepper

Put the sweet potato noodles in a bowl, cover with cold water and leave to soak for at least 2 hours. (You can soak them for half an hour in hot water, but they will be more likely to disintegrate during cooking.) Cut the Chinese cabbage into 1–1½ in (2–3cm) ribbons, discarding any hard stalky bits. Put the pork in a bowl and add ¼ teaspoon salt, 1 teaspoon of the Shaoxing wine and the chopped ginger and spring onion. Mix well. Beat the eggs with the remaining Shaoxing wine, ¼ teaspoon salt and 1 teaspoon cooking oil.

Pour 1 tablespoon cooking oil into a frying pan and heat over a high flame until faint smoke starts coming off the sides of the pan. Pour any excess oil into a heatproof container, then add a little fresh, cool oil and swirl it around the cooking surface. Over a gentle flame, put a 3 in (9cm) metal biscuit cutter in the pan and pour about 1½ tablespoons beaten egg into the ring. When the egg is half set but still runny on top, put about 1 teaspoon of the pork mixture onto it, off center. Remove the ring with a potholder or chopsticks. Use a spatula to flip half the egg skin over the pork and press the edges down, to make a dumpling. (Some beaten egg may run out of the circle; if you are very fastidious you may trim this off!) Remove the dumpling, which should be golden on both sides, and set aside; the pork does not need to be cooked through at this stage. Repeat with the rest of the egg and pork mixtures. You should end up with about 10 dumplings. (If you are not going to use them immediately, steam them over a high flame for 5 minutes to cook the pork through, then allow to cool and chill in the fridge.)

Drain the sweet potato noodles well, then put them in a heavy-bottomed pan with a lid that you can also use as a serving vessel. Put the sliced cabbage on top and add the stock, lard and soy sauces. Put the dumplings on the surface of the pot in an overlapping circle. Bring to the boil and season with salt and pepper. Cover and simmer over a medium flame for about 10 minutes, until the cabbage is silkily tender. Serve with a sprinkling of spring onion greens.

Salt pork, cabbage and egg dumpling soup

At the Old Jesse restaurant in Shanghai they serve this delicious soup: place a few slices of blanched Chinese ham or salt pork (unsmoked bacon, gammon or pancetta work well) in a clay pot with plenty of sliced Chinese cabbage. Cover with stock, then crown with the egg dumplings. Bring to the boil, season with salt to taste and simmer for 8–10 minutes, until the cabbage is tender.

FISH AND SEAFOOD

My friend Rose's cousin Lin Wei had brought me to one of his favorite restaurants, a small place near the old docks in Dinghai. As usual with restaurants in Ningbo and Zhoushan, there was no printed menu, but instead a ravishing display of ingredients by the entrance, many of them still alive. Small, intelligent-looking octopuses hovered in one tank of water, alongside another filled with "jumping fish"—reptilian, prehistoric-looking mudskippers with wing-like fins. There were sand eels, razor clams, cockles and mussels, tiny "pumpkin seed" clams, strutting crabs and lurking mantis shrimp. On a bed of ice lay sea fish shining in shades of pewter, gold and rosy pink. And who knew that the Chinese also eat that Galician speciality, goose-necked barnacles, known here as "Buddha's hands" and gathered on the Dongji islands of Zhoushan?

Land of Fish and Rice is no idle name for the Jiangnan region, for the range of water creatures eaten here is extraordinary. The Zhoushan archipelago, east of Ningbo, is one of China's most important fisheries, supplying some 500 varieties of fish and shellfish that also include the yellow croaker, eel, mackerel, pomfret, tonguefish, Chinese herring and Bombay duck, which is known as "tofu fish" because of its soft, custardy flesh. Freshwater creatures, including fish, eels and crustaceans, are equally important. The large grass carp, black carp and bighead carp have fairly boneless flesh that can be cut into slices or slivers or pulverised into a sticky paste that an accomplished chef can fashion into cloud-like fish balls.

The head and tail of the bighead carp, cooked in various ways, are legendary specialities of the Jiangnan region. Fish tails are prized as hardworking muscles with a pleasing quality of tautness; they are what the Chinese call "live meat" (*huo rou*), in contrast to the soft "dead meat" (*si rou*) of, say, a factory-farmed chicken breast. The splendid, old-fashioned dish Red-Braised Paddle (*hong shao hua shui*) is made with one huge black carp tail, and named for the way the fish swishes its tail through the water. An elderly calligrapher once showed me how to pick apart the sides of the tail with my fingers and suck out the ravishing nectar between them—we left almost nothing besides thin spears of cartilage on our plates. Slippery catfish are occasionally eaten; one of the most incredible Chinese delicacies I've ever tasted was Catfish Basking in Honors (*tu bu lou lian*), an old Hangzhou dish made with the cheeks of 200 little catfish—400 cheeks in all, in a single bowl! Richard Nixon was offered the same dish when he visited Hangzhou in 1972.

Shelling tiny freshwater shrimp is fiddly and tedious, but they are utterly delightful when poached gently in hot oil before a swift turn in the wok. Slippery-crisp in texture, they appear in many classic Suzhou dishes. Unshelled freshwater shrimp can be deep-fried in very hot oil so their shells puff up crisply, then bathed in a sweet-sour sauce. More exotic are ghostly white shrimp, considered to be one of the "three treasures" of the Tai Lake, along with the grenadier anchovy and the silver fish, a salangid white fish. The latter—tiny, scaleless, jade-white creatures—are said to have come into existence when the beautiful concubines of King Fucha of Wu cast thousands of jade hair pins into the lake, where they were magically transformed into fish. (The scraps from the concubines' dinner tables metamorphosed into the shrimp and anchovies.)

No other water creature inspires such passion, and even hysteria, as the mitten or hairy crab, a modest-looking creature with mossy claws and legs adorned with spiky yellow hairs. Every autumn the crabs swell with roe and semen, and the people of Suzhou and Shanghai embark on a frenzy of crab-eating. The crabs are most commonly steamed and served whole with a dip of ginger-infused vinegar and plenty of Shaoxing wine; eating them is a riot of mess and pleasure. In the crab season, many restaurants offer entire menus of hairy crab dishes, including steamed dumplings with crabmeat stuffing, crabmeat with silken tofu and the devastatingly delicious crabmeat with sheets of mung bean noodle (*xie fen fen pi*).

An entire book could be written on the pleasures of Jiangnan water foods and the cornucopia of local recipes. Many of the ingredients described here, however, are difficult or impossible to obtain outside the region. I hope that the modest selection of recipes in this chapter will give you a taste of Jiangnan fish cookery, and will encourage you to visit the region to taste some of the other specialities for yourself.

Some tips on cooking fish

Freshness is paramount. Look out for fish with bright, gleaming eyes, blood-red gills, shiny skin and flesh that bounces back when prodded.

To refine the flavor of a fish, rub it inside and out with salt and Shaoxing wine, put a piece of crushed ginger and spring onion in its belly and set it aside for 10–15 minutes. Discard any juices that emerge and pat it dry before cooking.

When frying fish, make sure that the surface of your wok is seasoned well and rub the skin with a little salt to prevent sticking. Frying a fish in lard, or cooking oil mixed with a little lard, makes it particularly delicious.

When steaming a fish, place it on top of a couple of spring onions to allow steam to circulate beneath it. If you cannot fit a whole fish in your wok or steamer, cut it in half widthways at a steep angle, then reassemble it on a serving dish after cooking. A bit of sauce or a garnish of cilantro or spring onion will hide the join!

Try not to overcook fish. As the Qing dynasty gourmet Yuan Mei advised: "When it is time to eat your fish, if its flesh holds together and is as white as jade, this is what we call "live meat"; if it is powder-white and does not cohere, this is what we call "dead meat". Obviously, to take a fresh fish and make it seem unfresh is pitiful."

Treat your fish gently and with respect, because cooking fish is an important and delicate matter, as the ancient sage Laozi acknowledged when he said: "governing a great country is like cooking small fish."

Clear-steamed sea bass

qing zheng xian yu 清蒸鮮魚

This recipe uses the techniques and seasonings traditionally applied to one of the most celebrated Jiangnan fish, the Reeves shad, to cook the more easily available sea bass. (If by any chance you can lay your hands on a true Reeves shad or its close relative the hilsa, please refer to the variation overleaf.) It's a beautiful dish, in which chicken stock and other umami ingredients enhance the flavor of the fish.

The Reeves shad itself is a glittering queen of a fish that was served to the Qianlong emperor when he visited Yangzhou in the eighteenth century. Traditionally, it was eaten during a short season from the fourth to the sixth lunar months and, steamed, was often the principal dish at Jiangnan banquets. Unusually, the fish is steamed in its oily scales, which partially melt in the heat of cooking, infusing the flesh with their luxurious fragrance. Chefs enhance its flavor with pickled cucumbers or a triumvirate of sliced ham, bamboo shoot and shiitake mushrooms, clothe it in luxurious caul fat and anoint it with Shaoxing wine and sweet, boozy glutinous rice. Inevitably, Chinese men of letters through the ages have been moved to poetry by the taste of this fish, including the Song dynasty poet Su Dongpo, who wrote:

Young ginger shoots, purple vinegar,
the silvery shad
Raise the snowy bowl more than two
feet high!
The springtime breath of the peach blossom
lingers
Oh the taste of this surpasses even that of those
ancient delicacies, perch and water shield. ▶

1 dried shiitake mushroom
A few rectangular slices of bamboo shoot
1 oz (30g) fresh ginger, skin on
3 spring onions, white parts only
1 sea bass (about 1½ lbs/650g), scaled and gutted
A few rectangular slices of Spanish or Chinese cured ham, steamed briefly
4 tbsp Shaoxing wine
½ cup (100ml) clear chicken stock
3 tbsp light soy sauce
½ tsp superfine sugar
3 tbsp fermented glutinous rice
1 tbsp chicken oil or lard
Salt and ground white pepper

For the dipping sauce:
1 tbsp finely chopped fresh ginger
2 tbsp Chinkiang vinegar

Cover the shiitake mushroom in boiling water and leave to soak for at least half an hour. Bring a pan of water to the boil and blanch the bamboo shoot slices, then drain them. Smack the ginger and spring onion whites with the flat side of a Chinese cleaver or a rolling pin to loosen their fibers.

Put the fish on a chopping board. Holding your knife at an angle to the board, make a few parallel diagonal slashes into the thickest part of the flesh. Repeat on the other side. Rub the fish inside and out with a little salt and 1 tablespoon of the Shaoxing wine. Put half the ginger and one of the spring onion whites in its belly and set aside for 10–15 minutes.

When the mushroom has softened, remove the stalk and cut the cap in half. If you wish to be a bit fancy, make lots of tiny parallel cuts perpendicular to the cut edge, so you can fan out the mushroom on the fish. Mix the chopped ginger and vinegar for the dip in a dipping dish.

Put the remaining spring onion whites in the base of a serving bowl deep enough to hold the fish and some liquid, but which will also fit into your steamer. (If a whole fish doesn't fit in your steamer, hold your knife at a steep angle to the board and cut the fish in half. Place the two pieces parallel to each other in the dish.) Lay the fish across the spring onions. Arrange the bamboo shoot and ham slices along the center of the fish, with a shiitake half at either end. ▶

Much later, in the Qing dynasty, another writer, Xie Tang, compared the fish to Xi Shi, the legendary beauty of ancient times.

Sadly, pollution and the construction of hydroelectric dams mean that it's no longer possible to taste the fish fresh out of the Yangtze river at Zhenjiang and Yangzhou. The Reeves shad served in Jiangnan restaurants these days are mostly imported, frozen, from India. One can only dream of the taste of the native fish, freshly netted and steamed, but even the frozen one, cooked in the traditional manner, is exquisitely delicious. The fish has rich, oily flesh, rather like the Japanese amberjack or hamachi. At home in London I have made the classic recipe with frozen hilsa (or ilish), a similar variety of shad that I've found in the Bangladeshi quarter of Brick Lane, but I more commonly steam sea bass in the same manner, but without its scales. The juices of either are fabulous spooned over rice.

Mix together the remaining Shaoxing wine, stock, soy sauce and sugar and pour it around the fish. Spoon the fermented glutinous rice down the center of the fish. Place the ginger beside the fish and the chicken oil or lard on top of it. Steam over a medium flame for about 10 minutes, until you can push a blunt chopstick easily into the thickest part of the fish.

Remove and discard the ginger. Strain the cooking juices into a bowl and season them with a little ground white pepper. Tidy up the sliced ham arrangement on the fish, then pour over the cooking juices. Serve with the vinegar-and-ginger dip.

Classic clear-steamed Reeves shad

Instead of a sea bass, use a whole Reeves shad or hilsa fish (2 lbs/850g before gutting). You will also need 2 shiitake mushrooms and double the amount of ham and bamboo shoot. Defrost the fish before you begin. Assuming you are dealing with a whole fish, do not remove its scales. Make a slit along its belly and pull out its guts. Lift up the gill flaps and pull out the gills, then insert a heavy chopping knife into the head and cut it in half lengthways, chopping through the top of the head. Starting at the head end, slice the whole fish in half, cutting close to the backbone, so you remove the top half of the fish, attached to half the head, and ending at the tail. You should now have two half fish, each with half a head, and one half with a tail. If you wish, you can also remove the backbone.

Rinse well and scrape away any black membrane inside the belly cavity. Blanch the fish in boiling water to clean it, then rinse in cold water. Place the two halves, head ends together, alongside each other on a dish and proceed according to the main recipe, except that you should steam the fish for 20 minutes over a low flame.

Traditionally, the entire fish is covered in a sheet of caul fat before steaming, instead of the lard or chicken oil.

Steamed sea bass with snow vegetable

xue cai zheng lu yu 雪菜蒸鲈鱼

In the past, when the cities of Jiangnan were threaded by canals, and the rivers, lakes and streams all teemed with fish and other creatures, water was the focus of local life. Traders and fisherfolk lived and worked on their boats, farmers gathered underwater crops from their liquid fields, and the rich hired pleasure craft for floating excursions. These days, most of the city canals have been filled and the water-dwellers have moved onto dry land, but in a few places the old way of life lingers. Once, in rural Jiangsu, I met an old fisherman who had spent his whole life on a wooden sampan like his father and grandfather before him. He sat on his boat patiently hooking worms onto his long fishing line.

This is a simply gorgeous way to cook a good, fresh fish. The gently sour flavor of the snow vegetable, enriched by a hint of lard or oil, perfectly complements the delicacy of its flesh, and the juices of fish and pickle mingle in the most delicious manner at the bottom of the dish. Like many recipes in this book, this one comes from chef Zhu Yinfeng, who demonstrated it with a Chinese mandarin fish plucked from a nearby lake barely an hour before, and his home-pickled snow vegetable.

If you can't fit a whole fish in your steamer, you can either hold your knife at an angle, cut the fish in half widthways and steam the halves together or, as I've done here, curve it into a bowl. If you have a large steamer and would like to try a more professional approach, please see the method on the opposite page. The same seasonings can be used to steam fillets of fish.

1 sea bass (about 1 lb/500g), scaled and gutted	1½ tbsp Shaoxing wine
1 oz (30g) fresh ginger, skin on	3 tbsp lard or cooking oil
2 spring onions, white parts only	4 oz (100g) snow vegetable
	2 tbsp sliced spring onions, green parts only
	Salt

Put the fish on your chopping board and, holding your knife at an angle to the board, make a few parallel diagonal slashes into the thickest part of the fish. Repeat on the other side. Cut the piece of ginger in half. Use the flat side of a Chinese cleaver or a rolling pin to smack the ginger and spring onion whites to loosen their fibers. Put the fish on a plate and rub it inside and out with 1 tablespoon of the Shaoxing wine and ½ teaspoon salt. Put one piece each of ginger and spring onion into the cavity of the fish. Leave to marinate for about 15 minutes.

Remove the ginger and spring onion from the marinade and pat the fish dry on paper towels. Place the fish in a bowl that will fit into your steamer, curling it around the inside of the bowl.

Heat the oil or lard in a seasoned wok over a high flame. Add the snow vegetable and stir-fry until it smells delicious. Stir in the remaining Shaoxing wine and 1 tablespoon water. Ladle the mixture over the fish. Put the remaining piece of ginger and spring onion on the fish, cover and steam over a medium flame for 8–9 minutes, until you can push a blunt chopstick easily into the thickest part of the flesh.

Remove the dish from the steamer and carefully pour the cooking juices into a small bowl. Remove and discard the ginger and spring onion. Scatter the spring onion greens over the fish, and then pour over the cooking juices, which will moisten the top of the fish and make it look most appetizing. Serve.

An alternative way of steaming a whole fish

This method is used mainly in restaurants. Put the fish on your chopping board. Holding your cleaver or knife parallel to the board, cut the flesh away from the top side of the tail, then extend the belly opening so you have one long cut running from head to tail. Open out the fish by pulling apart both sides of the belly and using a heavy knife or cleaver to cut through the little bones along one side of the backbone, without cutting through the flesh: this will enable you to open the fish and lay it flat. Use the same heavy knife or cleaver to make a chop down the center of the underside of the head, so you can open it out too. The two fish halves, attached along one side and placed on your board with the skin facing up, will look like a pair of fish. Proceed as in the main recipe, but reduce the cooking time to 6–8 minutes, until you can push a blunt chopstick easily into the thickest part of the flesh.

West Lake fish in vinegar sauce

xi hu cu yu 西湖醋鱼

This is one of Hangzhou's most celebrated dishes, and a speciality of the Louwailou restaurant at the edge of the West Lake. Traditionally, it is made with a grass carp that has been fasted for two days to purge it of any muddiness of flavor. The fish, briefly boiled, is bathed in a sauce fragrant with vinegar and ginger, with a chorus of sweetness and a base note of salt; its flesh is tender with an edge of tautness. At its best, the dish is said to recall, in its harmony of flavors, the taste of freshwater crab.

Like many Hangzhou dishes, this one comes with a tale of its origin. Two brothers named Song, they say, plied their trade as fishermen on the West Lake. One day, a brutal local official took a fancy to the elder brother's wife, and killed him with the aim of forcing her to become his concubine. The younger brother and the widow rushed to the local government to report this crime, but they were rudely evicted and the brother beaten. Fearing for his life, the younger brother prepared to flee the city. The night before his departure, his sister-in-law cooked him a fish with sugar and vinegar. It was, she said, meant to remind him that in future, sweeter times, he should never forget the bitter suffering of the past, and that he should come back one day and avenge his brother's death.

Years passed, and the younger brother became an official himself and returned to Hangzhou, but he was unable to find his sister-in-law. However, one day, dining in a local household, he tasted a fish dish that reminded him of the flavors of that parting meal. It turned out that the ▶

1 sea bass or West Lake grass carp (about 2 lbs/850g), scaled and gutted	4 tbsp superfine sugar
2½ tbsp light soy sauce	5½ tbsp Chinese red or rose vinegar
2 tbsp finely chopped fresh ginger	3 tbsp potato starch mixed with 3 tbsp cold water

First, prepare your fish. Lay the fish across the chopping board with the tail facing to the right if you are right-handed, or to the left if left-handed. Then, holding your knife parallel to the board, cut away the top half of the fish, starting at the base of the tail and cutting just above the backbone. When you reach the head, turn the fish so you can cut the head in half—you should end up with two pieces of fish, each with half the head. The thicker piece with the backbone is called the "male" (*xiong*), and the other piece the "female" (*ci*).

Lay the male piece, skin-side up, on the board and, holding your knife at an angle, make five deep, slanting parallel cuts into the thickest part of the flesh towards the head, taking care not to cut all the way through. With the third cut, do cut all the way through the backbone, cutting the piece of fish into two. Rinse the three pieces of fish under the cold tap.

Bring 1½ quarts (1.5 liters) water to the boil in a wok over a high flame. Skin-side up, add the male head piece, the tail piece and finally the female piece of fish. Shake the wok very gently to prevent sticking. Cover and bring it back to the boil. Skim the liquid, then cover and boil for 2–3 minutes, until just cooked. It is ready when you can poke a blunt chopstick into the thickest part of the flesh.

Remove the wok from the heat and drain off all but 1¼ cups (250ml) of the water. Return the wok to the heat and scatter the soy sauce and 1½ tbsp of the ginger into the pooled liquid around the fish. Gently swirl the liquid around the fish so it absorbs some of the flavors, then carefully slide the fish out onto a serving plate, leaving the liquid behind. Reassemble the two halves, the heads both at one end of the plate. Handle the fish carefully after boiling, but don't worry if it looks a little messy when you arrange it on the plate: the thick glossy sauce will smooth over a multitude of sins. ▶

household's cook was indeed his long-long sister-in-law, and the two were joyfully reunited. The fish evoked in him such nostalgia that he resigned his official commission and returned to his former life as a fisherman.

For best results, use Zhejiang "rose" rice vinegar or Chinese red vinegar. This recipe follows exactly the method shown to me by chef Dong Jinmu, veteran of the Louwailou restaurant in Hangzhou. The fish is boiled rather than poached to keep the flesh a little taut.

Return the liquid to a medium flame, add the sugar and stir to dissolve. Add the vinegar, return to a vigorous boil and immediately turn down the heat. Don't overheat the sauce once you've added the vinegar, or you'll lose much of its fragrance. Give the potato starch mixture a stir and add it in stages, mixing well between each addition, until the sauce has thickened to a lazy gravy that will cling to the fish.

Pour the sauce evenly over the fish. Sprinkle over the remaining ginger as a garnish and serve.

Red-braised fish

hong shao xian yu 红烧鲜鱼

Red-braised fish is a favorite dish on domestic supper tables across the Lower Yangtze region. A whole fish is fried until its skin is slightly caramelized, then cooked with Shaoxing wine, dark soy sauce and sugar until tender and bathed in a sleek, luxurious sauce (skin-on fillets may also be used). The sauce itself is magnificent soaked into plain white rice; any leftovers can be reheated with vegetables or tofu. One common variation on this recipe is the "spring onion-braised" crucian carp, in which the fish is red-braised with a whole bunch of slender spring onions; tender and silky after cooking, they are laid neatly over the fish before serving.

This method works equally well with freshwater fish and sea fish such as bream and bass. Chinese cooks often fry their fish in lard, or a mixture of lard and vegetable oil, to enhance its flavor. I was lucky enough to be given lessons in the art of red-braising by chefs Dong Jinmu of the Dragon Well Manor restaurant and Zhu Yinfeng of the Agricultural Academy, and this recipe is based on their teaching. Any leftover sauce will set to a jelly: in the old days, a friend in Nanjing told me, people would cut up the jellied stock with its fragments of fish and eat it as an appetizer.

A similar method is used to to red-braise the heads and tails of bighead carp.

1 sea bream or sea bass (about 1¾ lbs/800g), scaled and gutted
¾ oz (20g) fresh ginger, skin on
1 spring onion
2 tbsp lard or cooking oil
3 tbsp Shaoxing wine
1½ tbsp dark soy sauce
2 tsp superfine sugar
2 tbsp thinly sliced spring onions, green parts only
Salt

For the marinade:
1 tbsp Shaoxing wine
¼ tsp salt
2 tsp dark soy sauce

Make 3 or 4 parallel diagonal slashes through the thickest part of the fish, then a couple in the opposite direction, to make a broad crisscross pattern. Rub the fish inside and out with the marinade wine and salt and leave for a few minutes. Smack the ginger and spring onion with the flat side of a Chinese cleaver or a rolling pin to loosen their fibers. Tie the spring onion into a knot, if it's long and slender enough to make this possible.

When you are ready to cook, boil the kettle. Pat the fish dry with paper towels, then rub both sides with the 2 teaspoons dark soy sauce. Heat the lard or cooking oil in a seasoned wok over a high flame. Add the fish, turn the heat down to medium and fry until browned. Turn the fish, add the ginger and spring onion and fry until the other side is colored and the ginger and onion are fragrant. (Try not to move the fish around too much to avoid breaking the skin; just tilt the wok gently to make sure it is evenly colored.) Add the Shaoxing wine, 1½ tablespoons dark soy sauce, the sugar and 1 cup (200ml) hot water from the kettle. Bring to the boil over a high flame. Cover with a lid and cook over a medium flame for about 4 minutes. Carefully turn the fish, cover and cook for about another 4 minutes, until the thickest part of the fish is cooked through.

Transfer the fish to a serving plate, discarding the ginger and spring onions. Turn up the heat to reduce the sauce to a dark, glossy gravy. Pour the sauce over the fish, scatter with spring onion greens and serve.

"Squirrel fish" in sweet-and-sour sauce

song shu yu 松鼠鱼

The old city of Suzhou was a center of Jiangnan literati culture. Within the whitewashed walls of landscaped gardens commissioned by the wealthy, people could rest in a pavilion and gaze at carefully composed views of lakes, rockeries, miniature hills and stands of quivering bamboo, the wildness of nature framed for their delectation. Sweet-and-sour "squirrel fish" is a Suzhou classic and the signature dish of the old Pine and Crane restaurant, where the Qianlong emperor is said to have tasted and praised it during one of his incognito forays into the city. It's a dazzling performance of knifework: a mandarin fish is boned and then scored into frills that separate in the deep-frying oil into a delight of golden crispness. The fish, reunited with its head on the serving dish, bathed in a gorgeous red sauce and garnished with tiny river shrimp and peas, is thought to resemble a squirrel, hence the name. In its sweetness and dainty appearance, the dish is typical of Suzhou cooking. The modern dish is thought to have evolved from an older recipe of the same name that appears in the Qing dynasty cookbook The Harmonious Cauldron (tiao ding ji).

The classic dish is extremely complicated to make, but fantastically delicious and with almost universal appeal. In the following recipe, I have slightly simplified the cutting by using two fish fillets instead of a boned, split fish, but the preparation still demands care and concentration. If you'd like to make it easier still, use the variation, made with a straightforward pan-fried fish, and inspired by a version made by my friends Jason Li and He Yuxiu.

1 fresh sea bass (about 1 lb/500g), filleted on the skin
1½ tbsp tomato paste
1 tbsp potato starch mixed with 2 tbsp cold water
At least 2 cups (500ml) cooking oil, for deep-frying

For the marinade:
⅓ oz (10g) fresh ginger, skin on
1 spring onion
¼ tsp salt
½ tbsp Shaoxing wine

For the starch coating:
2 tbsp potato starch mixed with 2 tbsp cold water
4 oz (100g) dry potato starch

For the sauce:
1½ tbsp Chinese red vinegar
2 tbsp superfine sugar
½ tsp salt
½ cup (100ml) stock or water

For the garnish:
1 tbsp pine nuts
1 tbsp frozen peas

Put one of the fillets skin-side down on the chopping board. Holding your knife perpendicular to the board, make parallel cuts along the length of the fish at ½ in (1cm) intervals; the cuts should go deep into the fish but not through the skin. Then, holding your knife at a 30-degree angle to the board and cutting towards the head end, make deep cuts at right angles to your original ones, again at ½ in (1cm) intervals, and again taking care not to cut through the skin. Repeat with the other fillet and put them both in a bowl. Smack the ginger and spring onion for the marinade lightly with the flat side of a Chinese cleaver or a rolling pin to loosen their fibers and add them to the fish with the other marinade ingredients. Mix well and set aside.

Combine the sauce ingredients in a bowl and mix well. Put the pine nuts in a wok with enough oil to cover and heat gently to about 200–250°F (100–120°C), stirring, until the oil fizzes gently around the nuts. Fry until lightly golden and fragrant, taking care not to let them darken. Remove with a slotted spoon and set aside on paper towels. Blanch the peas in boiling water, then set them aside.

Shortly before you wish to serve the fish, remove the ginger and spring onion from the marinade and pat the fillets dry. Drip the potato starch and water mixture for the starch coating all over the fish, making sure it goes deep into the cut frills. Handle the fish gently so you don't lose any of the frills. ▶

Heat the oil for deep-frying to 350°F (180°C). Hold each fish fillet up by the tail and dredge it in the dry potato starch, again making sure they are completely coated, deep into the cut frills—this ensures that the frills don't stick together during cooking.

Hold a fillet upside down, with one hand at each end, so the frills fall open, and lower it carefully into the hot oil. Repeat for the other fillet. Deep-fry the fillets for 3–4 minutes, ladling over the hot oil, until cooked through and gorgeously crisp and golden (keep the oil hot enough to sizzle fairly energetically around the fish). Transfer the fillets to a serving dish, then carefully pour the oil into a heatproof container and rinse out the wok if necessary.

Return the wok to a medium flame with 1 tablespoon oil. Add the tomato paste and stir-fry for a moment until it smells delicious. Give the sauce ingredients a stir and pour them into the wok. Turn the heat up high to boil the liquid, stirring to dissolve the sugar. Give the 1 tablespoon potato starch mixture a stir and add it, in stages, to the wok, stirring as the liquid thickens. Add just enough to thicken the sauce so that it will cling to the fish fillets. Stir in 2 tablespoons of the hot deep-frying oil. Pour the sauce over the fish fillets, scatter with the pine nuts and peas and serve immediately.

Simple pan-fried "squirrel fish"

This is an easier version of the dish. Instead of sea bass fillets, use a whole sea bream (about 1¼ lbs/550g), scaled and gutted. Slice off the head (discard or use this, as you wish). Put the fish on a chopping board and make deep parallel diagonal cuts into the flesh at 1 in (2cm) intervals. Make similar cuts at right angles to these, so you end up with a crisscross pattern. Marinate as in the main recipe.

Instead of deep-frying, heat 5 tbsp oil over a high flame in a seasoned wok. Sprinkle a little salt on the base of the wok to prevent sticking. Pat dry the fish and its head (if using), and slide into the oil. Cover the wok and fry the fish for about 3 minutes, then turn and do the same on the other side. Do not move the fish around until each side is golden and crisp—this will encourage the skin to remain intact. Make sure the fish is cooked through by poking a chopstick into the thickest part of the flesh. Remove the fish from the wok and place it on a serving dish, along with its head if you wish. Make the sauce and pour it over as in the main recipe, and scatter with peas and pine nuts to serve.

Stir-fried fish morsels with pine nuts

song ren yu mi 松仁鱼米

This delicate stir-fry was an early-twentieth-century speciality of the Yangzhou Hotel in Shanghai, where they made it with the silky flesh of either the mandarin fish or the black carp. At home, I've made it with both sea bass and flounder, which have slightly different flavors but are suitably delicate in mouthfeel. The tender morsels of the fish, cut into tiny cubes or "rice grains," contrasts beautifully with the fragrant crispness of the pine nuts.

Perhaps for reasons of economy, many restaurants use a mixture of fish morsels and sweet corn instead of fish alone; this variation has a certain poetry to it, because the word for corn kernels (*yu mi*, "jade rice") sounds the same as that for fish morsels (*yu mi*). If you wish to try this, add precooked sweet corn to the wok with the peppers and make sure it is piping hot before you add the velvety fish and crisp nuts. When cutting the fish, try to slice off and discard as much dark skin and brown flesh as you can, because the beauty of the dish lies not only in the delicacy of its cutting, but also the jade-like purity of the flesh.

10 oz (300g) skinless flounder or sea bass fillet
1 oz (30g) pine nuts
1 spring onion, white part only
A 1 in (2cm) strip of green bell pepper
A 1 in (2cm) strip of red bell pepper
2 tbsp chicken stock
½ tsp potato starch mixed with 2 tsp cold water
1 tsp sesame oil
1¾ cups (400ml) cooking oil
Salt

For the marinade:
¾ tsp salt
1 tbsp Shaoxing wine
1½ tbsp egg white
1½ tbsp potato starch
Ground white pepper

Trim off and discard any dark parts of the fish fillets and pick out any remaining bones. Cut it into 2½ in (6mm) strips, then into 2½ in (6mm) cubes. Add the marinade ingredients, mix well and then cover and chill for at least half an hour.

Put the pine nuts in a wok with enough of the oil to cover them and heat slowly to about 250°F (120°C), stirring often. Fry the nuts until golden, then remove and set aside on paper towels. Smack the spring onion white gently with the flat side of a Chinese cleaver or a rolling pin to loosen its fibers. Cut the green and red bell pepper into tiny cubes.

Add 2 teaspoons cooking oil to the fish and mix well—this will help to prevent the pieces from sticking together. Pour the rest of the oil into the wok and heat to about 260°F (130°C). Add the fish and stir gently to separate the pieces. Fry for 1 minute or so, taking care not to let the oil get hotter than about 275°F (140°C). The oil should hiss very gently around the fish, which should remain uncolored and exquisitely tender. Remove from the oil with a slotted spoon and set aside.

Drain off all but 2 tablespoons of the oil. Add the spring onion and stir-fry over a high flame until you can smell its fragrance. Add the green and red bell pepper and turn briefly in the oil. Add the stock with a small pinch of salt, bring to the boil, then tip in the fish and pine nuts. Stir rapidly to mix. Give the starch mixture a quick stir and pour it into the wok. Stir swiftly as the juices thicken, then, off the heat, mix in the sesame oil. Serve.

Fish fillets in seaweed batter

tai tiao yu liu 苔条鱼柳

If you like English fish and chips, you will enjoy this dainty Ningbo version. Thin strips of tender fish are clothed in a thick batter speckled with delicious seaweed, deep fried and then eaten with a refreshing vinegar dip. In Ningbo they make it with yellow croaker, but grouper, or slippery flat fish such as flounder and sole, also work very well. The seaweed is *tai tiao*, a kind of sun-dried string lettuce or gutweed. At home I've made it with dried, ground *aonori-ko* seaweed flakes from a Japanese supermarket, which includes gutweed and has a very similar flavor.

9 oz (250g) skinless flounder, sole or grouper fillet
Around 2 cups (500ml) cooking oil, for deep-frying
Chinkiang or Chinese red vinegar, to serve

For the marinade:
⅓ oz (10g) fresh ginger, skin on
1 spring onion, white part only
½ tsp salt
½ tbsp Shaoxing wine

For the batter:
½ cup (60g) all-purpose flour
2 tbsp potato flour
½ tsp baking powder
¼ tsp salt
2 tbsp seaweed flakes

Cut the fish evenly into small strips, 2–2½ in (5–6cm) long and ½–1 in (1–2cm) wide, and put them in a bowl. Smack the ginger and spring onion white lightly with the flat side of a Chinese cleaver or a rolling pin to loosen their fibers and add them to the fish with the other marinade ingredients. Mix well.

Mix together the flours, baking powder and salt for the batter in a bowl. Gradually stir in ½ cup (100ml) cold water to make a thick, smooth batter. Finally, stir in the seaweed flakes.

Heat the oil in a wok to 300°F (150°C). Trail the pieces of fish through the batter, ensuring they are evenly coated, and drop them into the hot oil, using chopsticks to separate them. The oil should fizz around the pieces. Fry for 1–2 minutes at this temperature, turning the strips from time to time, until the outside of the batter is firm. Remove the fish from the wok and set aside.

Reheat the oil to 350°F (180°C). Add all the fish strips and fry again until golden, turning for even coloring. Serve immediately with a dip of vinegar.

Zhoushan fish chowder

jin tang fan qie tu duo shao yu 金汤番茄土豆烧鱼

At night, the strip of shoreline on the edge of Dinghai, the main town of the Zhoushan archipelago, is taken over by an orgy of seafood eating. Dozens of stalls line the strand, each one displaying its wares on crushed ice or in tubs of water. There are swimming crabs and silvery, kite-shaped pomfret, yellow croakers and shining ribbonfish, razor clams and shrimp, squid and cuttlefish … Behind this bounty of the seas, the chefs toss their woks over furious flames, cooking up dish after dish for a raucous, riotous crowd of customers. Singers and fortune-tellers drift in and out. My friend Rose's cousin Lin Wei and I sat with his friends amid the cacophony, eating crabs with our fingers, guzzling the savory white meat from a shatter of shell and entrails, slurping up razor clams seasoned with garlic and chilli, scoffing steamed fish and shrimp, and leaving on the table a devastation of whisker, carapace and bone. Lin Wei plied me with red bayberry wine from the nearby Buddhist island of Putuoshan "to drive out the coldness of the crabs."

One of the dishes I particularly enjoyed that night was a kind of chowder made with a "tiger-head" fish, potatoes and tomatoes. As satisfying as bouillabaisse, the dish seemed more Mediterranean than Chinese, except for the tell-tale hint of ginger and spring onion (the people of Shanghai and Ningbo sometimes use tomato and potato in what seems like a European way, perhaps a legacy of their semi-colonial histories). The rich broth is tinted golden by the tomatoes and made silky by the addition of mashed potato.

9 oz (250g) cooked potatoes, peeled
2 ripe tomatoes (about 7 oz/200g)
1 red snapper or grouper (about 1½–1¾ lbs/700–800g), fillets and backbone separated
3 tbsp Shaoxing wine
2 spring onions, white parts only
2 tbsp cooking oil
¾ oz (20g) fresh ginger, peeled and sliced
1 tbsp thinly sliced spring onions, green parts only (optional)
Salt and ground white pepper

Mash 4 oz (100g) of the potatoes and cut the rest of them into thick slices. Cut the tomatoes into sixths or eighths. Cut the fish fillets into bite-sized chunks and put them in a bowl with ⅛ teaspoon salt and 1 tablespoon of the Shaoxing wine. Put it in the fridge while you prepare the soup.

Cut the fish backbone into about 3 pieces. Smack the spring onion whites lightly with the flat side of a Chinese cleaver or a rolling pin to loosen their fibers. Boil the kettle.

Heat the oil in a seasoned wok over a high flame. Add the fish backbone and fry until golden; do not stir, just tilt the wok to cook it evenly. Turn the pieces over, add the ginger and spring onion whites and fry until the backbone is golden on the other side. Add the remaining Shaoxing wine and let it sizzle for a moment, then pour in about 1 quart (1 liter) hot water from the kettle. Bring to the boil, skim, then cover and boil for about 10 minutes until you have a rich fish stock. Remove and discard the backbone.

Add the tomatoes and both mashed and sliced potatoes to the broth. Bring to the boil and simmer until the tomatoes are tender and the broth is a light orange color. Season with salt. Add the fish chunks, with a little more boiling water to cover if necessary, then return to the boil and simmer for 2 minutes, until the fish is just cooked. Season with pepper, pour into a serving tureen and garnish with the spring onion greens, if using.

You can make this recipe with a whole fish, or ask your fishmonger to cut the fillets from the bones—just make sure you keep the backbone, to make the base of the soup. If you like, add some roll-cut chunks of peeled silk gourd to the broth with the chunks of fish flesh.

The original method, with a whole fish

Do not fillet the fish; instead, make a few diagonal slashes into the thickest part of the flesh on both sides. Heat the oil in a seasoned wok and fry the fish until golden on both sides. Add the ginger and spring onions towards the end of cooking, allowing them to sizzle out their fragrances. Cover generously with boiling water, boil and skim. Add the tomatoes and mashed and sliced potatoes, return to the boil, season with salt and simmer for 10 minutes. Finally, add pepper to taste, and serve with a scattering of spring onions, if you like.

Ningbo crab chowder

Instead of a fish, use a couple of live swimming crabs (around 6 oz/175g each), cleaned and chopped into sections. Crack the front claws with the blunt spine of a heavy cleaver or a nutcracker so they will be easier to eat. Proceed as for a whole fish, frying the crab before you add the other ingredients. Be prepared for some messy eating. This is a scrumptious variation.

Soupy fish with snow vegetable

xue cai da tang xian yu 雪菜大汤鲜鱼

In its original version, made with a large yellow croaker, this is one of the most famous Ningbo dishes. The tender, silky fish lazes in a rich broth made with snow vegetable and bamboo shoot. It's a lovely marriage of flavors, and perfectly expresses both the lightness of Ningbo cooking and the local predilection for combining fresh and salted ingredients.

The snow vegetable is widely eaten in Jiangnan, but is particularly adored by Ningbo people, who call it by a dialect word, "salty choppings" (*xian ji*), and have a little ditty: "If three days go by without a taste of pickled vegetable soup, your feet will be so sore they bring tears to your eyes." Rather charmingly, there is also a local saying that yellow croaker and pickle soup is so delicious that "it makes your eyebrows fall off"! In the past, the dish was made with a large wild yellow croaker, but these are so rare now that they sell for prices equivalent to hundreds of dollars. At home I've used the same method to cook sea bass, which is also delicious.

1 yellow croaker or sea bass (about 1 lb/500g), scaled and gutted
1½ tbsp Shaoxing wine
2 spring onions
2 oz (50g) sliced bamboo shoot

2 tbsp lard or cooking oil
3 oz (75g) snow vegetable, chopped coarsely
⅓ oz (10g) fresh ginger, peeled and sliced
Salt and ground white pepper

Trim off and discard the fins of the fish and make 4 or 5 parallel diagonal cuts into each side. Rub ¼ teaspoon salt and ½ tablespoon Shaoxing wine into the fish, inside and out, and set aside. Boil the kettle.

Trim the spring onions and separate the white and green parts. Smack the whites gently with the flat side of a Chinese cleaver or a rolling pin to loosen their fibers. If you wish to garnish the dish, cut the greens into 1½ in (4cm) sections. Blanch the bamboo shoot for 1–2 minutes in boiling water, then drain well.

Rinse the fish and pat it dry with paper towels. Heat the lard or oil in a seasoned wok until smoking. Add the ginger and spring onion whites and stir-fry briefly until you can smell their fragrance. Remove with a slotted spoon and set aside. Carefully slide the fish into the wok and fry over a high flame until tinged with gold on each side. Try not to move the fish around too much to help keep it intact; instead, tilt the wok for even frying.

Add the remaining Shaoxing wine and let it burn off. Just cover the fish with hot water (about 2½ cups/600ml) and bring to the boil. Return the ginger and spring onion whites to the wok. Cover and simmer over a medium flame for 7–8 minutes, then add the bamboo shoot and snow vegetable. Cover the pan again and boil vigorously for another 2–3 minutes, until the soup is milky white. Season with salt and a little white pepper. Gently transfer the fish to a deep serving dish and pour over the soup and vegetables. Use chopsticks to fish out the bamboo slices and lay them prettily over the fish. Garnish with the spring onion greens, if using, and serve.

Pan-fried ribbonfish

gan jian dai yu 干煎带鱼

The ribbonfish or hairtail looks like a shiny silver girdle, which is why its Chinese name is "beltfish." Laid out in rows in the markets of Shanghai and Ningbo, where they are a particular favorite, these long, flat creatures, with their bright metallic sheen, are astonishingly beautiful. If you can't find them fresh, you will probably be able to find them frozen in good Chinese supermarkets. Often, they are simply pan-fried, as in the following recipe, but they can also be steamed. To eat the fish, pull out the pin-like bones from the side of each piece with your teeth or fingers; you will then find the flesh comes away easily from the backbone. Any leftover fried fish can be simmered in a little stock with dark soy sauce, Shaoxing wine and sugar, to make red-braised ribbonfish for another meal.

1 lb (450g) ribbonfish, fresh or frozen and defrosted
½ oz (15g) fresh ginger, skin on
1 spring onion, white part only
½ tbsp Shaoxing wine
½ tsp salt
Around 1 cup (200ml) cooking oil

Make diagonal cuts into the thickest part of the fish at 1 in (2cm) intervals, then cut it into 2–2½ in (5–6cm) sections. Put them in a bowl. Smack the ginger and spring onion with the flat side of a Chinese cleaver or a rolling pin to loosen their fibers, then add them to the fish, along with the Shaoxing wine and salt. Mix well and set aside in the fridge for 2–3 hours.

Pat the fish pieces dry with paper towels. Pour ⅛ in (3–4mm) cooking oil into a flat frying pan with a seasoned or non-stick surface and heat over a high flame. When the oil is hot, turn the heat down to medium and add the fish pieces in a single layer. Fry for 5–10 minutes, until crisp and golden, then turn over and repeat on the other side. It is very important not to move the fish around until it has developed a crisp, golden layer, to avoid breaking the skin. Serve with rice and other dishes.

Fresh clam custard

ge li dun dan 蛤蜊炖蛋

In this Ningbo dish, clams, mouths wide open, peep out of a pale lake of silken custard. Usually, when I've eaten this, the custard has been a pale egg yellow in color, but in one marvelous Ningbo restaurant they add a little dark soy sauce, which gives it the color of café au lait; I've added this as an optional ingredient. Do steam the eggs gently—if the heat is too fierce, they will froth up and become coarse in texture. When I've had this dish in Ningbo it has been served plain, so you can really appreciate the tastes of the eggs and clams; in the Cantonese south they often finish the cooked custard with a little light soy sauce and sesame oil, which is also delicious.

10 oz (300g) live littleneck clams or similar
½ oz (15g) fresh ginger, skin on
1 spring onion, white part only
2 large or 3 medium eggs
1 tbsp Shaoxing wine
¼ tsp dark soy sauce (optional)
1 tbsp thinly sliced spring onions, green parts only
Salt

If you suspect the clams are sandy, soak them for half an hour or so in cold water from the tap to purge them before you begin. Wash them throughly in cold water. Discard any that have broken shells, or that remain open when tapped.

Smack the ginger and spring onion with the flat side of a Chinese cleaver or a rolling pin to loosen their fibers and put them in a saucepan or wok with 1 cup (200ml) water. Bring to the boil over a high flame, add the clams, cover and cook for 2–3 minutes, until the shells have opened. Quickly remove the clams with a slotted spoon and set aside. Leave a good handful of clams in their shells; remove the meat from the others with chopsticks and discard the shells.

Boil the kettle. Beat the eggs with ¼ teaspoon salt until well blended. Pour ¾ cup (150ml) of the clam cooking liquid slowly into the egg mixture, leaving any sandy residue in the pan. Add the Shaoxing wine and dark soy sauce, if using, and mix well. Skim off and discard any froth on the surface. Stir in the shelled clams.

Bring water to the boil under your steamer. Warm a shallow bowl large enough to hold the clams and the egg mixture by filling it with hot water from the kettle, then pour off the water. Scatter the unshelled clams, smiley side up, across the base of the bowl. Pour over the egg and shelled clam mixture. Put the dish of eggs and clams in your steamer basket and steam over a medium flame for about 12 minutes, until the eggs have set into a very delicate custard. Scatter with the spring onion greens, cover and steam for a few seconds more, then serve.

Clams with spring onion oil

cong you ge li 葱油蛤蜊

This recipe is my re-creation of a dish I enjoyed with my friend Rose in the Ningbo restaurant Good Harvest Day in Shanghai: a glorious pile of shellfish singing with the fragrances of garlic and spring onion, with a satisfying harmony of good soy sauce. There, they made it with the tiny, fingernail-sized clams beloved by the people of Ningbo, who call them "melon seeds from the ocean," a reference, perhaps, not only to their diminutive size, but also to the way you have to rummage through piles of shells to winkle out those tiny kernels of pleasure. At home I've made it with littleneck clams, which are almost dangerously delicious. Roll up your sleeves and dive in with fingers and chopsticks. Pour any remaining juices over your rice, or mop them up with a piece of bread.

By the way, you don't have to discard the leftover cooking liquor: stir it into some beaten eggs and steam gently for a simple variation of the clam custard recipe on page 153. As with any dish where soy sauce is a principal seasoning, please do make sure that you use a really excellent brand.

1¾ lbs (800g) live littleneck clams
2 spring onions, white parts only
⅓ oz (10g) fresh ginger, peeled and sliced
2 tbsp Shaoxing wine

To finish:
2 tbsp light soy sauce
5 tbsp cooking oil
2 tbsp finely chopped garlic
7 tbsp thinly sliced spring onions, green parts only

Wash the clams very thoroughly in cold water and discard any with cracked shells, or that do not close when you tap them briskly. Measure out the soy sauce into a small bowl. Smack the spring onion whites lightly with the flat side of a Chinese cleaver or a rolling pin to loosen their fibers.

Fill a lidded saucepan large enough to hold the clams with ½ in (1cm) water. Add the ginger, spring onion whites and Shaoxing wine and bring to the boil. Add the clams, cover the pan and cook over a high flame for about 3 minutes, until they have all opened and are just cooked through. Remove with a slotted spoon and pile up on a serving dish. Add 2 tablespoons of the cooking liquor to the soy sauce (discard the rest, or use in a steamed egg custard as described in the headnote).

Heat the oil in a wok over a high flame. Add the garlic and stir-fry very briefly until it smells wonderful. Switch off the heat, tip in the green spring onion and stir into the sizzling oil. Pour the oil, with the spring onions and garlic, all over the clams, then pour over the soy sauce mixture and serve.

Steamed clams with snow vegetable

This is another Ningbo speciality. As in the main recipe, heat the clams in a covered pan with Shaoxing wine, ginger and spring onion until they open. Place them in a serving dish that will fit into your steamer (for maximum elegance, remove the top of each clamshell). Scatter over 2 tbsp Shaoxing wine and 3 oz (80g) chopped snow vegetable. Put the dish in a steamer and steam over a high flame for 1–2 minutes to heat through. While the clams are steaming, heat 5 tbsp cooking oil over a high flame. Pile 5 tbsp thinly sliced spring onion greens onto the clams, then pour over the oil – it should be hot enough to produce a vigorous sizzle.

Stir-fried cockles with Chinese chives

jiu cai chao wu ge 韭菜炒乌蛤

This incredibly quick and extremely delicious stir-fry is based on a similar dish made with small freshwater snails from the Dragon Well Manor restaurant in Hangzhou. I've made it with shelled cockles, but you could equally use clams or other shellfish. If you buy live cockles or clams, put them in a saucepan with water to a depth of ½ in (1cm); heat over a high flame for a couple of minutes, until the shells have all opened, then pick out the meat; strain the cooking liquor and use it in place of the stock in the recipe.

5 oz (150g) Chinese chives
2 tbsp cooking oil
3½ oz (90g) shelled, cooked
  cockle meat

2 tbsp stock
Salt

Trim the chives and cut them into 1 in (2cm) sections. Heat a seasoned wok over a high flame. Add the oil, heat until very hot, then add the chives. Stir-fry briefly until you can smell their wonderful fragrance, then add the cockles. Continue to stir-fry just until everything is piping hot. Add the stock, bring to the boil, stir and season with salt. Serve.

Stir-fried fava beans with Chinese chives

This is a lovely vegetarian dish I ate in Ningbo. Instead of cockles, use shelled, peeled fava beans which you have pre-cooked in boiling water.

Oil-exploded shrimp

you bao xia 油爆虾

One spring afternoon we set off by boat to explore the lake near restaurateur Dai Jianjun's farm in southern Zhejiang. A fisherman rowed up and offered us some live shrimp he had caught a few moments before. Back at the farm that evening, Dai's chef, Zhu Yinfeng, cooked them up in typical Zhejiang style, deep-frying and then stir-frying them over a high flame with a sweet, rich sauce laced with rice wine and vinegar. The deep-frying in very hot oil is known as "oil-exploding" (*you bao*), and it shocks the papery shrimp shells away from the flesh, making them delectably crisp and crunchy. The fragrant sauce clings to the shrimp like lacquer, so they look as beautiful as they taste.

Small freshwater shrimp are particularly dainty in this recipe, but you can also achieve a marvelous effect using saltwater shrimp, which is what I do at home. In Zhejiang, they cook the shrimp with their heads; you may include or omit these as you please, but the shells and tails are essential to the character of the dish.

Be warned that this dish has what my father calls a "high grapple factor" and be prepared for some messy eating! Use your teeth and tongue to extract the flesh of the shrimp and leave the bits of hard shell on the plate.

¾ lb (350g) uncooked unpeeled shrimp (a little more if you want to cook them without heads)
1 spring onion, white part only
A few slices of peeled fresh ginger

2½ tsp Chinkiang or red rice vinegar
2 cups (500ml) cooking oil

For the sauce:
2 tsp Shaoxing wine
3 tsp light soy sauce
5 tsp superfine sugar

Use a sharp knife to trim the spikes from the head of the shrimp (or their entire heads if you are discarding these), and their legs. Use a darning needle to remove, as far as possible, the black veins that run along their backs, just under the shell. Rinse them thoroughly and shake dry. Smack the spring onion white lightly with the flat side of a Chinese cleaver or a rolling pin to loosen its fibers. Combine the sauce ingredients in a small bowl, and have the vinegar measured out and ready in another small bowl.

Heat the oil in a seasoned wok over a high flame to 400°F (200°C). Have another pan or a heatproof container to hand. Carefully tip the shrimp into the hot oil and deep-fry for 10–20 seconds (depending on size), stirring constantly, until they have curled up and changed color. Remove with a slotted spoon and set aside.

Let the oil return to its original temperature. Add the shrimp and fry for another 20 seconds or so, until the shells are crisp and tinged golden. Remove with a slotted spoon and set aside. Pour all but about 1 tablespoon of the oil into your heatproof container, then return the wok to a high flame with the spring onion white and ginger. Stir-fry until they smell wonderful. Add the shrimp, stir once, then give the sauce a stir and pour it in. Stir rapidly as the sauce boils and becomes syrupy. Splash the vinegar around the edges of the shrimp and stir over a high flame for another 5 seconds or so to fuse the flavors. Serve.

Stir-fried shrimp with Dragon Well tea

long jing xia ren 龙井虾仁

Just beyond the willow-lined shores of the West Lake in Hangzhou rise the Dragon Well hills, where tea-pickers in straw hats pluck the tenderest new leaves from rows of tea bushes. True Dragon Well tea, which is grown only in this small area on the western outskirts of the city, has a delicate, nutty flavor and is one of the most prized green teas in China. The tea leaves are graded by size and season: the finest are picked early in the year, before Qingming, the Festival of Pure Brightness.

This dish, a seasonal delicacy, is very similar to "clear-fried shrimp" (*qing chao xia ren*), but has a delightful hint of the fragrance of Dragon Well tea. Once, a local chef made it for me with tea leaves he had picked himself only an hour or two before in the Dragon Well tea fields. It is traditionally made with tiny freshwater shrimp, which are laboriously peeled by hand and have an impeccably tender, silky and springy texture. At home I make it with saltwater shrimp. Dragon Well tea is sold by specialist tea vendors in the West; if you can't find it, use another green tea in its place.

The pre-frying in hot but not sizzling oil is a technique used across Jiangnan for keeping delicate seafood such as shrimp and sliced fish tender and slippery. The oil temperature is critical: as veteran Suzhou chef Sun Fugen told me, if the oil is too hot, the shrimp acquire a yellow tinge; if it's too cold, "their clothes fall off"—which is to say that they lose their slippery starch coating.

1 lb (450g) raw peeled shrimp (about 1¾ lbs/750g unpeeled)
¾ tsp salt
2 tbsp egg white
3 tbsp potato starch
1 tbsp Dragon Well tea leaves or other green tea
1¾ cups (400ml) cooking oil
1 tbsp Shaoxing wine
½ tsp potato starch mixed with 1 tbsp cold water
Chinkiang or red rice vinegar, to serve

Use a sharp knife to make a slit along the back and front of each shrimp, and remove and discard the dark veins with a darning needle. Rinse the shrimp in a colander under the cold tap. Drain and pat dry with paper towels. Put them in a bowl with the salt and egg white and stir vigorously with your hand, in one direction, until they have a slightly springy texture. Add the starch and mix well, until they are evenly clothed in starch and egg white. Cover and chill for at least 2 hours.

Boil the kettle. Put the tea leaves in a bowl with 4 tablespoons hot water (Dragon Well tea is best infused with water just below boiling point, at 185–195°F/85–90°C). Leave to infuse for 1 minute, then strain out the tea leaves, retaining both them and the infused liquid.

Stir 2 teaspoons oil into the shrimp to separate them as they cook. Heat the remaining oil in a seasoned wok over a high flame to 250–260°F (120–130°C). Add the shrimp and separate them with chopsticks. Stir them gently until they have curled up, become opaque and are very nearly cooked through; remove them with a slotted spoon. Take great care not to let the oil overheat. The idea is to keep the shrimp very tender and succulent, not to sizzle them; if the oil reaches 275°F (140°C) you will begin to lose some of their succulence.

Drain all but 1 tablespoon oil from the wok. Return it to a high flame and add the shrimp, Shaoxing wine, tea leaves and 2 tablespoons of the tea infusion, and stir rapidly to incorporate. Stir the starch mixture and pour it into the wok, stirring. As soon as the juices have thickened, remove the shrimp from the wok and serve with a dish of vinegar for dipping.

TOFU

Tofu is a genius food, a technological marvel. Soybeans are the richest source of plant protein, containing an array of vital amino acids in the proportions best suited for human absorption. Unless eaten young and green, however, they are unpalatable and indigestible. The Chinese discovered early on that the beans could be made edible by lengthy boiling or sprouting, and they harnessed the power of fermentation to make soybean relishes that were both nutritious and delicious. Tofu, which according to legend was invented by King Liu An in the second century BC, represented another great leap in understanding how to unlock the dazzling dietary benefits of the bean. Although its historical origins are disputed, by the time of the Song dynasty, tofu was widely eaten and enjoyed in the Jiangnan region, and it has been a pillar of the Chinese diet ever since.

In a traditional tofu workshop in Zhejiang province, yellow soybeans lie soaking in great basins on the floor. Nearby, a pair of heavy millstones rest on their wooden frame above an enormous wok set into a wood-burning range. Beginning his morning's work, the tofu-maker drains his beans, now soaked and swollen, and feeds them gradually into the small opening in the upper stone, along with a trickle of water. He turns the wooden handle and the soymilk begins to ooze dreamily from between the stones.

This is the old-fashioned way of making tofu. The stone-ground milk will later be strained, boiled and simmered, then curdled with gypsum or mineral salts. The fresh curds, the "flower of the bean" (*dou hua*), can be eaten just as they are, soft and comforting as custard. Otherwise, they may be poured into a muslin-lined mold and pressed to make tofu.

In the West, tofu is often viewed disparagingly as a substitute food, useful only for vegetarians trying to plug the hole left when meat is removed from a "normal" diet. But in China, tofu is eaten not only by Buddhist vegetarians, but by practically everyone else too, alongside meat. Tofu in China is a shape-shifting food with myriad forms. It may be pressed to varying degrees of firmness, simmered in spices, wood-smoked, deep-fried into golden puffs, made into sheets as thick as leather or as thin as cellophane, or fermented into relishes that are addictively delicious. Outside Buddhist monasteries, tofu is often cooked with meat, fish, lard or stock, to enrich it with umami flavors.

The people of Jiangnan make particularly inventive use of pressed tofu sheets and tofu skins. The former, made by pressing the warm curds between layers of muslin, are often sliced into ribbons and used in stir-fries, salads and soups. Sometimes, small strips are tied into knots that make a toothsome addition to soups and stews, including red-braised pork. Otherwise, they may be used as wrappers for rolls of blanched chrysantheum leaves, or parcels of minced pork to be simmered in broth. Specialist workshops flavor and color sheet tofu with soy sauce, sugar and spices, then press it into ham-shaped molds to make a vegetarian simulacrum of ham, complete with flesh-like fibers. The thinner "tofu skins," whipped off the top of a potful of simmering soymilk and hung up until dry, are golden, transparent and thin as a cicada's wing. They can be used as wrappers for deep-fried snacks, or flavored and layered loosely to make vegetarian "duck" or "goose." Tiny scraps of leftover tofu skin are often added to stir-fried greens for an injection of protein and a pleasant contrast of color and texture.

There are numerous local tofu specialities, especially when it comes to the "dry-and-fragrant tofus" (*xiang gan*), made by infusing firm tofu with the flavors of spice or smoke, and fermented tofus. Stinking tofu, that infamous snack, is the best known. It is made by steeping thick squares of tofu in a pickling brine made from rotted vegetables. Uncooked—stone-white and speckled with mold— it looks remarkably unappetizing, but after deep-frying and slathered in chilli sauce, it tastes delicious. In Ningbo, the local stinking tofu may be served steamed as part of a "Stinking Trio" (*san chou*) with fermented amaranth stalks and winter melon.

In Shaoxing, tofu sheets are rolled up and then left in a pot for a few days to partially decompose; these "fermented thousand layers" (*mei qian zhang*) have a fierce, stinging smell and a wild, heady flavor reminiscent of ripe Camembert. But perhaps the most marvelous of all these fermented tofus is the "hairy tofu" of old Huizhou in southern Anhui province (*mao dou fu*). In the markets, slabs of hairy tofu lurk on wooden pallets under a thick white fur coat of mold—the product, locals assure me, of a particular local microclimate and humidity. Hairy tofu is most commonly pan-fried until golden all over, then eaten with a pickled chilli dip. It has a faintly cheesy texture, and a delicate, earthy flavor with a hint of sourness that recalls the taste of Welsh rarebit.

While some of these more exotic tofu concoctions are rarely found outside the region, the range of tofu products available in the West is increasing all the time. I hope that the following recipes will show a few of the ways in which tofu can be a delightful part of a varied and balanced diet, whether vegetarian or otherwise.

Scalded tofu slivers

tang gan si 烫干丝

Scalded tofu slivers is one of the essential dishes of the Yangzhou tea breakfast, a leisurely ritual that is little known outside the city. The tofu slivers, typically served alongside steamed buns and dumplings, are cool and smooth in their delicate sauce, with its murmur of ginger and hint of sweetness, speckled with the umami deliciousness of shrimp and pickle. This is a sister dish to the grander boiled tofu slivers on page 166, but quicker and easier to make. With a stir-fried green vegetable and rice, it also makes a simple, healthy lunch or supper.

The tofu made in Yangzhou is famously smooth and firm. A skilled local chef can lay a block of it on a wooden board and shave it into exactly uniform slices, which he then cuts into perfectly even slivers as thin as matchsticks. I won't pretend that at home, with a looser pressed tofu and my own inferior cutting skills, I've achieved the same aesthetic precision, but the dish remains delightful. Vegetarians may simply omit the dried shrimp and use plain water in the sauce.

8 oz (225g) plain firm tofu
Salt
½ tbsp small dried shrimp
⅓ oz (10g) fresh ginger, peeled
1½ tbsp finely chopped
    Sichuan preserved
    vegetable
2 tsp sesame oil

Salt
A sprig of cilantro,
    to garnish

For the sauce:
2 tbsp light soy sauce
½ tsp dark soy sauce
1 tsp superfine sugar

Cut the tofu into very thin slices and then into thin slivers. Place them in a bowl with a good pinch of salt and cover generously with boiling water. Leave to cool.

Put the dried shrimp in a small bowl and cover with boiling water. Leave for at least half an hour to soften. Cut the ginger into very thin slices and then into tiny slivers. Put in a bowl, cover with cold water and set aside. Drain the tofu in a colander. Return it to the bowl with another pinch of salt and cover with fresh boiling water. Leave for at least 2 minutes.

Put the shrimp with 6 tablespoons of their soaking water in a pan and bring to the boil (if there isn't enough, make up the quantity with plain water). Boil for 30 seconds or so, then add the sauce ingredients with 5 tablespoons water and return to the boil, stirring to dissolve the sugar. Set aside.

When you are ready to serve, drain the tofu slivers and pile them up in a serving dish. Drain the ginger and place it on the tofu with the preserved vegetable. Pour over the sauce and shrimp. Sprinkle over the sesame oil and garnish with the cilantro. Give the dish a good stir before eating.

Boiled firm tofu slivers in chicken stock

ji huo zhu gan si 鸡火煮干丝

In the past, Yangzhou was regarded as one of China's most elegant destinations for pleasure and relaxation, and the historic quarter of the city, with its lanes and canals, salt merchants' mansions and Slender West Lake Park, still has an old-fashioned charm. For centuries it was also one of the centers of Chinese gastronomy, and the city lays claim to many famous dishes, including this one. Several sources trace its origins back to a more elaborate "nine-sliver soup" (*jiu si tang*) that was served as a banquet dish for the Qianlong emperor, and which included slivered sea cucumber, dried razor clams and bird's nest among its ingredients.

These days, many ostentatious restaurant versions involve freshwater shrimp, chicken slivers, chicken gizzard and liver, dried shrimp eggs and sliced bamboo shoot, while more elegant, pared-down renditions employ only pea shoots and slivers of ham. This recipe is somewhere between the two, and I hope you'll find it delicious.

The tofu slivers are twice soaked in boiling water to dispel what the Chinese refer to as their "beany fishy taste" (*dou xing wei*)—that is, the less appealing aspect of the flavor of soybeans. Typically of Yangzhou cooking, this dish involves careful attention to color, with green leaves and needles of dark pink ham used as a counterpoint to the pallor of the tofu.

8 oz (225g) plain firm tofu
4 oz (100g) cooked chicken breast
½ oz (15g) lean Spanish or Chinese cured ham, sliced 1mm thick
A handful of pea shoots or baby spinach leaves
2¾ cups (650ml) chicken stock
1 oz (25g) lard or chicken oil
Salt

Cut the tofu into very thin slices and then into thin slivers. Put them in a bowl with a good pinch of salt and cover generously with boiling water. Leave to cool.

Cut or tear the chicken into thin slivers. Boil or steam the ham and, when cool, cut into thin shreds. Bring a pan of water to the boil and blanch the pea shoots or spinach leaves very briefly to wilt them; refresh immediately in cold water, then shake dry.

Drain the tofu in a colander, then return it to the bowl with another pinch of salt, cover with fresh boiling water and leave for at least 2 minutes.

Bring the stock to the boil in a wok. Add the tofu and shake gently to immerse. Tuck the chicken into the stock at one side of the wok. Add the lard and boil fast for about 10 minutes, until the stock has emulsified and become milky, stirring occasionally with chopsticks so the tofu strands don't stick together. Season with salt, cover and simmer gently for another 2 minutes.

Pile the tofu up in a deep serving dish with the chicken slivers on top. Pour over the rest of the stock. Arrange the green leaves prettily around the tofu, garnish with the slivered ham and serve.

(If you wish to make the full, classic version of this dish, you will also need small amounts of cooked chicken gizzard and liver, cut into slivers, sliced bamboo shoot, blanched pea shoots, dried shrimp eggs and a few uncooked shrimp, which should be lightly coated in starch paste and briefly stir-fried in lard. Add the chicken offal, shrimp eggs and bamboo shoot to the wok along with the chicken slivers. Garnish with the cooked shrimp, pea shoots and ham.)

Zhoushan pan-fried tofu

xiang jian dou fu 香煎豆腐

We drove over the endless bridge across the bay from Ningbo, low over the water, with no land visible on either side. Eventually we reached the mud flats and ponds of Zhoushan, and then drove into the gentle hills, covered in small trees and feathery bamboo.

Later, my friend Lin Wei and his companions took me to one of their favorite Dinghai restaurants, where we chose our dishes from a display of ingredients on the ground floor. We ended up eating raw salt-cured crab, spiced cuttlefish, red-braised pomfrets, steamed tonguefish, enormous king shrimp and clams with celery, as well as an array of vegetable dishes that included this one. The tofu had been pre-steeped in brine, which gave it a surprisingly delicious flavor, especially when scattered with morsels of ham and spring onion.

1 tbsp salt
1½ lbs (600g) plain white tofu
2 tbsp cooking oil
2 tbsp very finely chopped
   Spanish or Chinese cured
   ham, steamed briefly
2 tbsp thinly sliced spring
   onions, green parts only

Pour 2½ cups (600ml) cold water into a pan, add the salt and stir to dissolve. Slice off the firm outer skin of the tofu block (you can keep this and use it in a stir-fry or a salad). Cut the rest of the tofu into bite-sized slices about ½ in (1cm) thick. Put the tofu slices in the salted water, leave to soak for 45 minutes, then drain.

Heat the cooking oil in a seasoned frying pan. Add the tofu slices in a single layer and fry over a medium flame until beautifully golden on both sides. You may need to cook them in a couple of batches.

When the tofu is nearly ready, sprinkle it with the ham and spring onions, cover the pan for a few seconds to give them a brief burst of heat, then transfer to a serving dish. Serve hot or cool.

Tofu ribbons with salt pork and green bok choy

xian rou bai ye tang cai 咸肉百叶棠菜

This is a particularly harmonious combination of pale, ribbony tofu, savory salt pork and fresh, juicy greens. The recipe is based on some advice from a salt pork vendor in a Shanghai market. It's typical of Jiangnan cooking in the use of a little meat and stock to make vegetarian ingredients taste sumptuous. With rice, it could suffice as a simple meal for two.

Some cooks might add sliced bamboo shoot; in Yangzhou I had a version that included both sliced carrot and bamboo shoot, along with fresh green soybeans and wood-ear mushrooms. All of which is to say, go ahead and vary the recipe according to what you have in your fridge or larder.

6 oz (175g) fresh tofu sheets
3 oz (75g) unsmoked bacon, very thickly cut if possible
5 oz (150g) green bok choy
2 cups (450ml) rich chicken or fine banquet stock (see page 318)
1 tbsp lard (optional)
Salt and ground white pepper

Roll up the tofu sheets and cut them into ½–¾ in (12–15mm) ribbons. Cut the bacon across the grain into ½ in (1cm) strips, keeping skin on if you wish. Cut the bok choy into large bite-sized pieces (if you are using baby bok choy, simply halve it lengthways).

Bring a pan of water to the boil, add the tofu and blanch to refresh and reheat. Remove it from the pan with a slotted spoon and drain on paper towels. Tip the bacon into the boiling water and blanch until just cooked. Remove with a slotted spoon. Blanch the bok choy very briefly, just to wilt the leaves. Remove and drain.

Put the stock in a wok or saucepan with the tofu, pork and lard, if using, bring to the boil and boil for about 3 minutes. Season with salt and pepper. Add the blanched greens, heat through and turn everything into a deep serving dish to serve.

Spicy stir-fried tofu with pickles

jia chang xiao chao huang 家常小炒皇

This recipe is based on an unexpectedly delicious dish I tasted once at the restaurant of the Liuying Hotel in Hangzhou. It was made with king oyster mushrooms and a particular pickled mustard from nearby Ningbo. The chef, Niu Youqiang, kindly explained the method to me and this is my attempt to re-create it, but using the more easily available snow vegetable in place of the Ningbo preserve.

King oyster mushrooms (known in Chinese as apricot abalone mushrooms, *xing bao gu*), are sold in many Chinese supermarkets. If you can't find them, use button and/or oyster mushrooms instead. Served with rice, this quick stir-fry makes a simple supper in itself, and it's completely vegetarian if you use vegetarian stock.

4 oz (100g) spiced firm tofu (2 cakes)
6 oz (175g) king oyster mushrooms, or a mixture of button and oyster mushrooms
3 medium-hot dried chillies, or to taste
2 tbsp cooking oil
3½ oz (90g) snow vegetable
1 tsp sesame oil

For the sauce:
¼ tsp dark soy sauce
1 tsp light soy sauce
½ tsp superfine sugar
½ tbsp Shaoxing wine
2 tbsp stock

Holding your knife at an angle, cut the tofu into slices about ⅙ in (5mm) thick. Cut the mushrooms into ⅛ in (3–4mm) slices. Snip the chillies in half with a pair of scissors and shake out the seeds as much as you can. Combine the sauce ingredients in a small bowl.

Heat the cooking oil in a seasoned wok over a high flame. Add the chillies and stir-fry for a few seconds until you can smell them, then add the snow vegetable and continue to stir-fry until it too smells delicious. Tip in the mushrooms and continue to stir-fry. When the mushrooms are tender, add the tofu and heat through. When all is piping hot, give the sauce a stir and pour it in, stirring as the liquid reduces. Turn off the heat, stir in the sesame oil and serve.

Hangzhou breakfast tofu

hang zhou dou hua 杭州豆花

In this delightful recipe, warm silken tofu is seasoned with savory condiments and topped with fresh and crunchy garnishes. It's based on the breakfast tofu I enjoyed near the West Lake in Hangzhou.

Hangzhou breakfast tofu; Suzhou breakfast tofu

10 oz (300g) silken tofu
¼ tsp superfine sugar
2 tsp light soy sauce
1 tsp sesame oil
Chilli oil, to taste
2 tbsp finely chopped Sichuan preserved vegetable

2 tbsp thinly sliced spring onions, green parts only
1 tbsp chopped cilantro
2 tbsp fried peanuts
Salt

Bring enough water to cover the tofu to the boil in a saucepan and salt it lightly. Use a spoon to scoop up large pieces of the tofu and transfer them to the water. Simmer very gently for about 5 minutes to heat it through.

When the tofu is ready, use a slotted spoon to transfer it to a serving bowl and break up the chunks into smaller pieces. Scatter the rest of the ingredients over it and serve. This dish is best eaten with a spoon.

Suzhou breakfast tofu

Instead of the garnishes in the main recipe, put 2 tsp papery dried shrimp and 1 tbsp dried laver seaweed, torn into tiny pieces, in the serving bowl. Add the warm tofu and scatter with 1 tbsp finely chopped Sichuan preserved vegetable, 1½ tbsp thinly sliced spring onion greens, 2 tsp light soy sauce and 1 tsp sesame oil. Mix well before eating. This version is served as part of the lavish breakfast buffet at the Wumen Renjia restaurant in Suzhou.

Buddhist vegetarian tofu rolls

san si juan 三丝卷

On one of my first visits to the Dragon Well Manor restaurant in Hangzhou the chefs prepared a Buddhist vegetarian banquet that took my breath away. Among many delightful dishes, they produced crisp tofu rolls stuffed with shiitake mushrooms, dried bamboo shoot, spiced tofu and fresh cilantro. The rolls were sliced and arranged like the grains on an ear of wheat. I don't expect you to go to such lengths at home, so I've simplified the form, wrapping the stuffing into individual rolls and dipping them in a batter I learned from one of the most wonderful home cooks I know, He Yuxiu. These little packages should delight not only vegetarians, but also your omnivorous friends.

Another similar local delicacy is "jingle bells," made from sheets of tofu skin rolled around a scanty stuffing of minced pork, then cut into bite-sized pieces and deep-fried until crisp and "golden as a cicada's wing." Ethereally light, they collapse like whispers in the mouth. The dish is said to have been named in honor of a man who, upon discovering that the Hangzhou restaurant where he was dining had run out of deep-fried tofu skins, leaped onto his horse and rode off to fetch some. The chef, moved by his determination to eat the tofu, rolled it into the shape of horse's bells—and so the dish entered the classic Hangzhou repertoire.

In the unlikely event that you have any rolls left over, cut them up and add them to a stir-fry of green bok choy. The fried tofu will become soft and juicy, with a fragrant chewiness that sets off the greens.

2–3 sheets dried tofu skin
1 tbsp potato starch mixed with 1 tbsp cold water
Cooking oil, for deep-frying
Chinkiang vinegar, to dip

For the stuffing:
5 dried shiitake mushrooms
3 oz (75g) bamboo shoot
3 oz (75g) spiced or smoked firm tofu
1 spring onion, white part only
A small handful of cilantro leaves
2 slices peeled fresh ginger
½ tbsp Shaoxing wine
2½ tsp light soy sauce
½ tsp dark soy sauce
1 tsp superfine sugar
1 tsp sesame oil
Salt

For the batter:
3 tbsp all-purpose flour
¼ tsp bicarbonate of soda

Put the shiitake mushrooms in a bowl and soak for at least half an hour in boiling water. Cut the bamboo shoot into thin slivers and blanch for 1 minute in boiling water, then drain well. Cut the tofu into thin slivers. When the mushrooms have softened, squeeze them dry, reserving the soaking water, remove the stalks, then thinly slice the caps. Smack the spring onion lightly with the flat side of a Chinese cleaver or a rolling pin to loosen its fibers. Coarsely chop the cilantro. Put the flour and bicarbonate of soda in a large bowl and gradually stir in 4 tablespoons cold water to make a thin batter.

Make the stuffing: heat 1 tablespoon oil in a seasoned wok over a high flame. Add the ginger and spring onion and stir-fry until fragrant, then discard. Add the shiitake to the oil and stir-fry until you can smell them. Stir in the Shaoxing wine. Add the bamboo shoot, stir-fry until piping hot, then add the tofu and 2 tablespoons of the mushroom-soaking water, both soy sauces and the sugar and salt to taste. When the liquid has been absorbed, turn off the heat and stir in the cilantro and sesame oil. Leave to cool.

Cut the tofu skins into 4 x 8 in (10 x 20cm) rectangles. Put one on your board and place about 2 tablespoons of the stuffing along one end. Roll it up, tucking in the ends, and brush the end with the potato starch mixture to seal it. Heat the oil for deep-frying to 350°F (180°C). Use chopsticks to dip the rolls into the batter, then into the hot oil. Fry until golden and puffy, then remove and drain on paper towels. Serve hot with Chinkiang vinegar to dip.

VEGETABLES

On a shining autumn day, chef Zhu Yinfeng took me out into the fields to pick vegetables. There were just a few puffs of floating cloud in the azure sky, a breeze blew gently and birds were singing against a background hum of insects. We walked between rows of green bok choy, slender spring onions and spinach, white butterflies playing among the leaves. Zhu pulled up some heads of bok choy and snipped off bunches of spinach with a pair of scissors, laying them in his basket. He pointed out the alfalfa plants peeping up around the edges of fields of rice stubble, tiny shoots of cilantro and the broad, ragged leaves of potherb mustard. By the time we'd finished, his basket was full and the evening's menu was decided.

The rich landscape of the Lower Yangtze region brings forth an astonishing range of vegetables all year round. Local people take great delight in eating the finest produce of the season: new bamboo shoots, alfalfa sprouts or juicy cattails in the spring; fresh lotus seeds and crisp young chestnuts as autumn draws in; the sweetest spinach after a winter frost. No Jiangnan meal is complete without vegetables, which are usually as delicious as they are healthy and refreshing. Leafy greens are often stir-fried with minimal seasoning or served in soups; the tiny, tender bok choy leaves known as "chicken feather greens" (*ji mao cai*) are particularly sought after. Peas and beans might be paired with pickles or Jinhua ham for umami richness. Root vegetables such as corn-on-the-cob, sweet potatoes and horned water caltrops may be steamed in their husks and skins. Some vegetables, such as pumpkin and sweet potato, are used in both sweet and savory dishes.

Vegetables may be cooked from fresh or after processing. Both soybeans and mungbeans are sprouted, and the Shanghainese adore fava beans that have been soaked until their little shoots poke out. Some vegetables, such as potherb mustard, are almost always pickled before they are eaten. Bamboo shoots, though at their most exquisite when freshly dug out of the earth, may be pickled or dried; the salted, semi-dried shoots known as *bian jian*, greenish and supple, are delicious in soups and stews. In the Yellow Mountain area of Anhui you can buy many kinds of dried bamboo shoot, including what is known as its "clothing": the thin, tender inner layers of bamboo shoot husks. Dried vegetables are prized for their interesting tastes and textures. In Ningbo, one gorgeous speciality is "green for 10,000 years" (*wan nian qing*): dried, deep-green tips of rape or bok choy, which, after a quick soaking, can be used in soups and salads.

The Chinese view strict vegetarianism differently from people in the West. In China, the practice is found mainly in Buddhist monasteries; even lay Buddhists tend to eat meat at home, avoiding it only on religious feast days or when they make offerings at a local temple. Most people see total, ideological "vegetarianism" (*su shi zhu yi*) as a Western phenomenon, while "vegetarian eating" (*su shi*), the habit of eating vegetarian food from time to time but not exclusively, has long been part of Chinese culture. The traditional everyday Chinese diet is led by grain foods and vegetables, with meat, fish or poultry eaten in small quantities for nourishment and savor. Many Jiangnan

vegetable dishes are enhanced by hidden meat in the form or lard or stock. These days, Chinese people who are trying to eat less meat often delight in such dishes, which offer some of the richness of meat but are lighter, healthier and more economical.

Many of the vegetables eaten in Jiangnan are familiar in the Chinatowns of the West, and increasingly in mainstream supermarkets, such as green bok choy, bunched spinach, Chinese leaf cabbage, Chinese chives and taro. Others can be more elusive and may only be available in certain seasons, like yellow hothouse chives and wild rice stem. Still others are local specialities rarely sold outside the region itself, even within China. Here, I've included recipes for many easily available vegetables, as well as a few that are harder to find, but worth seeking out. I've also adapted some local recipes to use easier-to-find vegetables such as kale and chayote, and included one of my favorite Buddhist imitation meat dishes, a stir-fried "crabmeat" made from potato and carrot.

Stir-fried peas with ham

huo tui xiao wan dou 火腿小豌豆

In a tree-lined street in Shanghai's former International Settlement, there's a 1920s Spanish-style mansion that houses one of the best restaurants in the city, Fu 1088. Arrive at the unassuming entrance, and you'll be led through wood-paneled halls and old tiled corridors to a private room decked out in early twentieth-century style. You might end up in a grand dining room with antique clocks on the mantelpiece, or a bedroom under the eaves. At certain hours, your arrival may be accompanied by music drifting up from the grand piano downstairs. Fu 1088 specializes in food from Shanghai and the Jiangnan region, and its executive chef Tony Lu conjures up some of the finest renditions of traditional dishes that you'll find in the city. This is my attempt to re-create one of them, a simple yet delicious stir-fry made with tiny Yunnan peas.

The dark pink of the ham sets off perfectly the emerald green of the peas and gives them an irresistible umami lift. The ivory bamboo shoot adds texture, flavor and color, but the dish will work well without it. If you're using frozen peas, there's no need to defrost them before cooking. Vegetarians may omit the ham, and used diced smoked or spiced tofu, or shiitake mushrooms instead.

½ oz (20g) thickly sliced Spanish or Chinese cured ham, steamed briefly
¾ oz (25g) bamboo shoot
1 tbsp cooking oil
7 oz (200g) small green peas, fresh or frozen
2 tbsp stock or water
½ tsp potato starch mixed with 1 tbsp cold water
½ tsp sesame oil
Salt

Cut the ham into ⅛ in (3–4mm) cubes. Bring a pan of water to the boil. Cut the bamboo shoot into ⅙ in (4–5mm) cubes and blanch them in boiling water; refresh under the cold tap, then drain well.

Heat the cooking oil in a seasoned wok over a high flame. Add the ham, bamboo shoot and peas and stir-fry until the ham smells delicious and the peas are piping hot. Add the stock or water, bring to the boil and season with salt. Give the starch mixture a stir, pour into the center of the wok and mix well. Off the heat, stir in the sesame oil. Serve.

Green soybeans with snow vegetable

xue cai mao dou 雪菜毛豆

This simple, gorgeous recipe is typical of Shanghainese home cooking. Bright green soybeans are tossed in a wok with pickled snow vegetable and slivers of pork and bamboo shoot. It's the kind of dish that, served with plain rice, can be a meal on its own. Shanghainese cooks tend to add a little bamboo shoot for crunch and extra umami, but it can seem like a waste to break open a package of brined bamboo for such a small amount, so feel free to omit this if you wish.

There are other variations on the theme of this dish; some people prefer not to add ginger and garlic, while others might pep it up with a little dried chilli and Sichuan pepper, added to the wok with the garlic and ginger. Vegetarians may simply omit the pork. The same method works well with peas and fava beans.

3 oz (75g) lean pork
1½ oz (40g) bamboo shoot, fresh or brined (optional)
9 oz (250g) shelled green soybeans, fresh or frozen
3 tbsp cooking oil
1 tsp Shaoxing wine
2 tsp finely chopped fresh ginger
1 tsp finely chopped garlic
7 oz (200g) snow vegetable
1 tsp superfine sugar
1 tsp sesame oil
Salt and ground white pepper

Cut the pork into thin slices, then into slivers. Do the same with the bamboo shoot, if using. Bring a pan of water to the boil, blanch the bamboo shoot and rinse it in cold water, then drain. Boil the soybeans for 2 minutes until hot and tender.

Heat 1 tablespoon oil in a seasoned wok over a high flame, add the soybeans and stir-fry over a medium flame until piping hot. Remove from the wok and set aside. Return the wok to a high flame with 1 tablespoon oil, add the pork and stir-fry until the strips have turned pale. Add the Shaoxing wine and allow it to evaporate. Add the ginger and garlic and stir-fry for a few seconds until you can smell them. Tip in the snow vegetable and bamboo shoot and stir-fry until hot and fragrant. Stir in the beans and season with the sugar, a good pinch of pepper and salt if you need it; the salty pickled vegetable may mean you don't. When everything is piping hot and smells wonderful, remove from the heat and stir in the sesame oil. Serve.

Hangzhou green soybeans, pork and pickle

This is a typical Hangzhou supper dish. Cut 100g lean pork into 1cm cubes, add 1 tsp Shaoxing wine and ⅛ tsp salt and mix well. Cut 40g Sichuan preserved vegetable and 40g bamboo shoot into smaller cubes. Boil 250g frozen green soybeans until hot and tender. Heat 1 tbsp cooking oil in a seasoned wok over a high flame. Add the pork, stir-fry until cooked through, then remove and set aside. Stir-fry the preserved vegetable and bamboo shoot until they smell delicious. Add the beans. When everything is piping hot, add the pork and season with salt. Off the heat, stir in 1 tsp sesame oil and serve. Frozen peas can be used instead of soybeans, and can be added directly to the wok.

Steamed green soybeans with ham

huo tui zheng qing dou 火腿蒸青豆

This simple, healthy dish is exquisitely delicious, and looks beautiful too. The recipe comes from the Dragon Well Manor restaurant in Hangzhou, but the basic method is typical of traditional cooking across the region. In the past, farmers would often economize on fuel by cooking a whole meal over a single fire in the wood-burning range. In the bottom of the wok, set into the top of the range, rice would boil and then steam; above it, sitting on a bamboo frame, a few bowls containing other ingredients would also steam in the heat, under a tall wooden lid; everything would be ready to eat at the same moment, with a few homemade pickles from an earthware jar. In Shaoxing they have a specific dialect word (pronounced *hing*) for this way of steaming dishes over the rice.

In characteristic Jiangnan style, the flavor of the fresh vegetable is enhanced by the strong umami taste of a preserve, in this case ham, and some meaty savoriness in the form of stock and lard. The same pattern can be seen in countless dishes: steamed bamboo shoots or sliced taro with ham, Chinese cabbage with salt pork, Asian radish with salted fish, plain silken tofu with fermented amaranth stalks, to name but a few. You might like to try the following recipe with peas, or fava beans. Bacon or sliced Chinese wind-dried sausage may be substituted for the ham. In China they steam the ham before slicing it; this fixes its shape, which makes for neater cutting and a more professional appearance.

Steamed green soybeans with ham; Steamed taro with Chinese wind-dried sausage (page 183)

9 oz (250g) fresh or frozen green soybeans
5 tbsp stock
½ tbsp Shaoxing wine
1 tbsp lard, chicken oil or vegetable oil

1 oz (30g) Spanish or Chinese cured ham, preferably with a little fat, steamed briefly
Salt

Put the beans in a heatproof bowl. Add the stock, wine, lard or oil, season with salt and mix together well. Slice the ham and arrange it on top of the beans.

Put the bowl, uncovered, in a steamer basket and steam over a high flame for 15 minutes (add an extra 5 minutes if cooking the soybeans from frozen). Serve.

Steamed taro with Chinese wind-dried sausage

xiang chang zheng yu tou 香肠蒸芋头

The driver hooted and swerved as he rattled along the country roads at a terrifying pace, but the scenery became pretty and hilly as we neared the Yellow Mountain, and there were glimpses of old Anhui houses through the trees. At the bus station a street vendor was selling wild kiwi fruits, walnuts and dried bamboo shoots, and outside a restaurant yards of homemade sausages were hanging out to dry in the sun.

Wind-dried sausages, made from chunkily cut, salted and spiced fatty pork, are found across southern China. Traditionally, they are made in the last month of the lunar year. They can be simply sliced, steamed and eaten as an appetizer, but they are also used in cooking, as in this recipe, which I learned from chef Chen Xiaoming in Hangzhou. You can make it with any kind of Chinese wind-dried sausage, from the *lap cheong* sold in Chinese supermarkets in the West to the spicy wind-dried sausages of Sichuan.

Think of this recipe as a very simple template for cooking fresh vegetables with salt-cured meat or fish, and vary the ingredients as you please. Taro, incidentally, is an underrated vegetable in the West, but has a lovely silky tenderness to its texture. The people of Jiangnan adore it, and use it in dishes both sweet and savory.

See photograph on page 183

10 oz (300g) taros	5 tbsp stock or water
1–2 Chinese wind-dried sausages	1 tbsp thinly sliced spring onions, green parts only (optional)
1 tbsp light soy sauce	Salt
½ tbsp Shaoxing wine	

Wear rubber gloves to peel the taros (their skin contains an irritant that can cause itching). Slice off any discolored patches, then cut them into ⅛ in (4mm) slices. Cut the sausages at an angle into oval slices about ⅛ in (4mm) thick.

Put the sliced taro in a heatproof bowl that will fit in your steamer and arrange the sausage slices on top. Add the soy sauce, wine and stock or water and season with salt. Put the bowl in a steamer and steam over a high flame for 30 minutes, until very tender. Garnish with spring onions, if desired.

Steamed taro with salted fish

Instead of the wind-dried sausage, use 1 oz (30g) salted mackerel, cut into small pieces. Omit the soy sauce and salt and add 1 tbsp cooking oil or lard to the bowl. The strong, seductive aroma of the salted fish will infuse the taro and the cooking juices. This is based on a dish I enjoyed at the Xianheng Tavern in Shaoxing, thanks to chef Mao Tianyao.

Magical radishes

shen xian cai 神仙菜

The white Asian radish is a favorite Chinese vegetable. It can be fashioned into bright, crisp appetizers, snappy pickles and soothing soups, and it's particularly nutritious. When harvested after a frost, it has a delightful sweetness. Like a number of vegetables, including bamboo shoots and Chinese cabbage, it has a way of absorbing and refining the flavors of any meaty ingredients with which it is cooked. In this recipe, a little fat pork is used to imbue the radish with its luxurious taste and texture and is then removed from the final dish, so the humble radish, enriched with the invisible flavors of the meat, becomes a sumptuous dish fit for immortals, or so its literal Chinese name ("immortal" radish) suggests.

It may sound like an extravagance to make the actual meat vanish from the final dish, but in practice nothing is wasted: at restaurateur Dai Jianjun's Agricultural Academy in Zhejiang, where chef Zhu Yinfeng taught me the recipe, the cooked pork is used for staff meals while the radishes are served to honored guests. This recipe is good for using up raggedy pieces of pork left after making more elegant meat dishes. It's a prime example of *su cai hun zuo,* which loosely translates as "cooking vegetables with a little meatiness for flavor." It also shows you how some of the simplest-seeming Jiangnan dishes are more refined and artful than may at first appear.

1 large white Asian radish (about 1¾ lb/750g)
7 oz (200g) pork belly, skin on
¾ oz (20g) fresh ginger, skin on
2 spring onions, white parts only
1 tbsp cooking oil
1½ tbsp Shaoxing wine
3¼ cups (800ml) stock or water
1 tbsp dark soy sauce
1 tbsp light soy sauce
1 tbsp superfine sugar
1 tbsp thinly sliced spring onions, green parts only
Salt

Peel the radish and then, starting at the pointy end, roll-cut it into 1½ in (3cm) chunks: holding your knife at an angle, cut off a 1½ in (3cm) chunk, then rotate the radish a half-turn toward you and, holding your knife at the same angle, cut off another chunk. Repeat the turning and cutting for the rest of the radish. Cut the pork into 1 in (2cm) chunks. Smack the ginger and spring onion whites with the flat side of a Chinese cleaver or a rolling pin to loosen their fibers.

Bring a pan of water to the boil. Add the radish and blanch for 2 minutes; remove it from the water with a slotted spoon and set aside. Blanch the pork briefly in the boiling water for a minute or two, then drain it well.

Heat the oil in a seasoned wok over a high flame. Add the pork and stir-fry until pale and just tinged with gold. Add the ginger and spring onions and stir-fry until they smell wonderful. Pour in the Shaoxing wine and let it sizzle, then add the stock and bring to the boil. Skim the liquid, then add the radish and all the other ingredients except the spring onion greens, and return to the boil. Cover the wok, turn down the heat and simmer gently for 40 minutes, stirring occasionally.

To serve, remove the pork from the pot (eat it at another meal, perhaps as a topping for a bowlful of soupy noodles). Turn the heat up high to reduce the sauce. Season with a little salt if necessary. Serve with a scattering of spring onion greens.

Sliced chayote with ham and fava beans

can dou fo shou gua 蚕豆佛手瓜

This recipe is based on a seasonal springtime dish served at Old Jesse, one of my favorite Shanghai restaurants. It's a delightful mix of fine, slightly crisp gourd and tender fava beans in a sauce enlivened by ham, spring onion and ginger. At Old Jesse, they make it with the long, shiny, light green variety of calabash gourd known as "blossom-by-night." I haven't been able to find this particular gourd in the US but the chayote, also known as chow chow, makes a magnificent substitute. This vegetable (or, strictly speaking, fruit) is native to the Americas but has been grown since the early twentieth century in southern China, where they call it the "Buddha's hand gourd" because of its row of ridged "knuckles." Chayotes (mostly grown in Costa Rica) are easy to find in Asian and African food shops and are often used by Chinese chefs abroad. The peeled, cored, raw gourd strongly resembles an unripe pear.

In the original recipe the fava beans are cooked only briefly and hold their shape. At home, I like to cook them a little longer because the disintegrating beans add a delicious richness to the sauce. If you'd like the beans to remain whole, stir-fry them briefly before you begin, remove them from the wok and return them when the gourd is just tender, then heat them through and thicken the sauce if desired.

1 chayote (about 10 oz/325g), or a similar amount of long green gourd
8 oz (225g) shelled fava beans (about 1–1⅓ lb/500–600g in their pods)
½ oz (15g) fresh ginger, peeled
2 spring onions, white parts only
1½ oz (40g) thickly sliced lean Spanish or Chinese cured ham, steamed briefly
1½ tbsp cooking oil
1 cup (200ml) hot stock or water
1 tsp potato starch mixed with 1 tbsp cold water (optional)
Salt

Peel the chayote and slice it in half. Cut out and discard the softer core, then cut it into ⅛ in (4mm) slices. If you are using green gourd, simply peel and slice it. Bring a pan of water to the boil, add the shelled fava beans and blanch for 1 minute or so, then drain, refresh in cold water and pop off their skins. Slice the ginger. Cut the spring onion whites, at an angle, into slices. Cut the ham into rectangular slices.

Heat the oil in a seasoned wok over a high flame. Add the ginger and spring onions and stir-fry briefly until they smell wonderful. Add the ham, stir a couple of times, then tip in the fava beans and sliced chayote or gourd. Stir-fry until piping hot, then add the stock or water, bring to the boil and season with salt. Cover and simmer for 3–5 minutes until the gourd is tender, stirring from time to time.

If using the starch mixture to thicken the sauce, mix it well, pour it into the wok and stir briefly over a high flame until the sauce clings to the vegetables. Serve.

Stir-fried fava beans with spring onion

cong hua can dou 葱花蚕豆

On my first visit to Shanghai in the 1990s, Qiu Shuzhen, the sister of one of my cooking teachers in Chengdu, invited me for dinner at her home in one of the old Shanghai lanes, and this was one of the dishes she made: a bright little stir-fry of fava beans and spring onion. It is typical of home cooking in the city, where people adore fava beans, either fresh or dried (after soaking for three days until they sprout, the latter are delicious stir-fried with snow vegetable and then stewed with a little water).

Mrs. Qiu served the beans alongside vegetarian "roast duck," stir-fried river shrimp in their shells, wild rice stem with soy sauce, stewed eel and a potful of dark, caramelized red-braised pork. Do make sure you use young and tender fava beans, which won't require skinning once you've plucked them out of their pods.

2 lb (1kg) young, tender fava beans (about ¾ lb/350g shelled)
1 tbsp cooking oil
2 tbsp thinly sliced spring onions, white parts only
¾ tsp superfine sugar
4 tbsp thinly sliced spring onions, green parts only
Salt

Shell the beans. Heat the oil in a seasoned wok over a high flame. Add the spring onion whites and stir-fry briefly until they are fragrant. Add the beans and toss them in the fragrant oil. Add ¾ cup (150ml) water, sugar and season with salt, and bring to the boil. Cover and simmer over a medium flame for a few minutes, until tender—keep an eye on them to make sure they don't boil dry.

Remove the lid and increase the heat to high to reduce the liquid. When only a couple of tablespoons of liquid remains, add the spring onion greens and stir until they smell wonderful. Serve.

Stir-fried choy sum with wheat gluten

mian jin cai xin 面筋菜心

The rising popularity of gluten-free eating in recent years has given gluten itself a reputation as something aggressive and indigestible. Yet this vital part of our daily bread, the springy, elastic element that the Chinese call the "muscle" of the flour, is rich in protein and valued in China as a nutritious vegetarian ingredient. It often features in Buddhist vegetarian cooking, where its pleasing chewiness gives an almost meaty mouthfeel. This recipe is for a typical Shanghainese supper dish. The deep-fried gluten puffs, cooked in a sauce with juicy greens, are dreamily soft and pillowy, with just a hint of tautness in the bite. Served with rice, the dish can be a simple supper in itself.

Fried gluten puffs can be found in Chinese supermarkets, but they are especially delicious if you make them yourself (see page 324). The same method can be used for other greens, including green bok choy and Chinese cabbage.

5 dried shiitake mushrooms	A few slices of peeled
8 fried gluten puffs	fresh ginger
A few slices of bamboo shoot	1 tsp light soy sauce
(optional)	1 tsp sugar
10 oz (300g) choy sum	1 tsp potato flour mixed with
1 spring onion, white part	2 tsp cold water
only	½ tsp sesame oil
2 tbsp cooking oil	Salt

Cover the dried mushrooms in boiling water and leave to soak for at least half an hour. Remove the stalks and halve the caps. Drain and squeeze, retaining ½ cup (100ml) of the soaking water to use as stock.

Put the gluten puffs in a deep bowl, cover with boiling water and add a small plate with something heavy on top to keep them immersed. Leave for a few minutes to soften. Bring a pan of water to the boil and blanch the bamboo shoot slices, if using.

Cut the choy sum into bite-sized lengths. Smack the spring onion gently with the flat side of a Chinese cleaver or a rolling pin to loosen its fibers.

Bring 1 quart (1 liter) water to the boil and add 1 teaspoon salt and 1 tablespoon of the cooking oil. Add the choy sum and blanch briefly to wilt the leaves. Remove with a slotted spoon and drain well. Add the gluten puffs to the boiling water, return to the boil, then remove, drain and press out as much water as possible.

Heat the remaining oil in a seasoned wok over a high flame. Add the ginger and spring onion and stir-fry briefly until you can smell them. Add the mushrooms and bamboo shoot, if using, and stir-fry for 30 seconds or so.

Add the gluten puffs, ½ cup (100ml) mushroom-soaking water, soy sauce, sugar and ¼ teaspoon salt and mix well. Simmer for about 1 minute, then add the choy sum to the wok. When everything is piping hot, give the potato starch mixture a stir and add just enough to thicken the remaining liquid to a lazy gravy. Remove from the heat, stir in the sesame oil and serve.

Stir-fried celtuce

qing chao wo sun 清炒萵笋

This recipe, along with the celtuce salad in the Appetizers chapter, appears here because of my fervent hope that this exquisite vegetable, a kind of lettuce with thick, truncheon-like stems, will become more widely available outside China (it can currently be found from time to time in Chinese supermarkets and farmers' markets). Simply stir-fried like this in vegetable oil with a little salt, it's fantastically delicious. You may also stir-fry it with other ingredients, or perhaps just a few slices of red bell pepper for color.

2 celtuce stems (about 1½ lbs/700g)
2 tbsp cooking oil
1 tsp sesame oil
Salt

Peel the celtuce stems and discard any fibrous part at their bases. Holding your knife at an angle to each stem, cut it into oval slices 2–3mm thick.

Heat the cooking oil in a seasoned wok over a high flame. Add the celtuce and stir-fry for 1–2 minutes until piping hot. Season with salt. Remove from the heat, stir in the sesame oil and serve.

Green bok choy with dried shrimp

kai yang chao cai 开洋炒菜

This wonderful, quick stir-fry was taught to me by master chef Hu Zhongying in the kitchens of the Hangzhou Restaurant. A handful of dried shrimp lends an umami richness to the juicy greens; a little stock will further enhance their flavor, but you can use water if you don't have any to hand. The recipe may sound similar to the stir-fried cabbage with dried shrimp on page 194, but it has a totally different flavor and mouthfeel.

In Chinese markets, especially in places near the coast such as Ningbo and Zhoushan, you will find great tubs of dried shrimp of different colors and sizes, from the moon-white papery variety to orange-pink creatures as large as the fresh saltwater shrimp that are eaten as a main ingredient. In this dish I use the smallish pink ones that are known as "open ocean," "sea rice" and "rice shrimp" in different dialects. They are sold in most Chinese food shops and keep well in the fridge or freezer. If you wish, you can thicken the cooking juices with potato starch to give it a glossy, professional finish.

The same method can be used for other vegetables, such as choy sum and spinach. If you have the very thick, stalky kind of choy sum, chop it into chopstickable pieces before cooking.

2 tbsp dried shrimp (about ⅓ oz/10g)
1 tbsp Shaoxing wine
10 oz (300g) green bok choy
2 tbsp cooking oil
3 tbsp stock or water
¼ tsp potato starch mixed with 1 tsp cold water (optional)
Salt

Put the shrimp and Shaoxing wine in a bowl and cover with hot water; soak for at least half an hour. Quarter the bok choy lengthways, then cut it into chopstickable lengths.

Heat the oil in a seasoned wok over a high flame. Add the shrimp and stir-fry until they smell delicious, then add the bok choy and stir until the leaves have wilted. Pour the stock or water around the sides of the wok. Bring to the boil, cover and cook for a minute or so to heat through. Remove the lid, season with salt and stir briefly to allow the liquid to reduce. Give the potato starch mixture a stir and mix into the wok, if using. Serve.

Stir-fried round zucchini with dried shrimp

Soak the shrimp as in the main recipe. Cut the zucchini into fairly thin slices. Stir-fry the shrimp in oil until fragrant, add the zucchini and stir-fry until piping hot. Add a little stock and season with salt; cover the wok and cook for a short while until tender. Lift the lid to reduce the liquid, then serve.

Stir-fried green bok choy with wood-ear mushrooms

Soak the mushrooms in boiling water for half an hour to reconstitute, then trim off any knotty bits. Stir-fry with green bok choy. The slippery-crisp mushrooms are a nice contrast to the juicy vegetables.

Stir-fried cabbage with dried shrimp

bao xin cai chao xia pi 包心菜炒虾皮

On my first visit to Ningbo I tasted many marvelous dishes at Cui Guangming's Starfish Harbor Restaurant: raw salted crab; white river shrimp with crisp *tai cai* seaweed; the infamous "stinky trio" (fermented tofu, winter melon and amaranth stalks); tenderly cooked slivers of paddy eel with yellow chives and fava beans; yellow croaker soup; and small octopuses braised in soy sauce. Most of these dishes would be hard to experience outside the region, but there is one I did bring back with me and have been making regularly ever since. It's a stir-fry of cabbage and paper-thin dried shrimp that is unexpectedly intense and delicious.

At the Starfish Harbor restaurant they make it with round white cabbage, but I use the same method at home with thinly sliced spring greens, Savoy cabbage, choy sum, bok choy, sliced Brussels sprouts or Chinese cabbage. This recipe also appears in *Every Grain of Rice*; I've included it here because it's one of my favorites.

A 14 oz (400g) head spring greens, or 14 oz (400g) cabbage of your choice	4 tbsp cooking oil or lard
	6 tbsp papery dried shrimp
	2 tbsp light soy sauce
4 spring onions, green parts only	Salt

Discard any fibrous outer leaves and cut out and discard the thick stem of the spring greens. Cut the rest of the greens or cabbage into very thin slices; cut the spring onion greens into thin slices.

Add 3 tablespoons oil or lard to a seasoned wok over a high flame and swirl it around. Add the shrimp and stir-fry until crisp and fragrant. Remove the shrimp and set aside.

Return the wok to the stove with the remainder of the oil or lard, add the sliced greens or cabbage and stir-fry over a high flame until the cabbage is hot, barely cooked and still a little crisp. Add the shrimp and soy sauce and season with salt if necessary (you may not need any because of the saltiness of the shrimp and soy). Finally, add the spring onion greens, stir them a couple of times, then turn onto a dish and serve.

Stir-fried tatsoi with winter bamboo shoot

ta ke cai chao dong sun 塌棵菜炒冬笋

This beautiful variety of cabbage, its spoon-shaped leaves arrayed in flower-like formation, is a favorite cold-weather crop in the southern Yangtze region. In Chinese it has various names, which mostly allude to its dark green color or the way it grows low and close to the earth; in English you may find it called tatsoi, Chinese flat cabbage, pagoda greens or rosette bok choy (its scholarly name is *Brassica rapa* var. *rosularis*). The Song dynasty poet Fan Chengda, who was born in Suzhou, wrote that tatsoi plucked out of the snow had a flavor as rich and intense as honeyed lotus.

In Shanghai, tatsoi is often paired with another favorite winter vegetable, bamboo shoot, but it can also be stir-fried on its own if you don't have bamboo shoot to hand. Keep an eye out for the vegetable, in season, in farmers' markets and Chinese supermarkets.

5 oz (150g) peeled bamboo shoot (optional)	⅓ oz (10g) fresh ginger, peeled and sliced
10 oz (300g) tatsoi	5 tbsp stock
3½ tbsp cooking oil	½ tsp superfine sugar
	Salt

If using fresh bamboo shoot, slice it in half lengthways, then cut it widthways into 2 in (5cm) sections. Finally, slice it lengthways into 2mm rectangular slices. Bring a pan of water to the boil and cook the shoot for 2 minutes; drain and refresh under the cold tap. (If using packaged bamboo shoot, blanch it in boiling water for a minute or so to refresh.)

Separate the tatsoi leaves and wash them thoroughly. If they are longer than about 4 in (10cm), cut them in half. Bring a pan of water to the boil, add ½ teaspoon salt and ½ tablespoon cooking oil, then blanch the tatsoi briefly—just enough to wilt the leaves. Drain and shake dry.

Heat the remaining oil in a seasoned wok over a high flame. Add the ginger and stir briefly until you can smell its fragrance. Add the blanched tatsoi and bamboo shoot, if using, and stir-fry. When the tatsoi is piping hot, add the stock and sugar and season with salt. Mix well and serve.

Soupy Chinese cabbage with salt pork

bai cai hui xian rou 白菜烩咸肉

There was snow on the ground when I visited the organic farm at Mugongshan in the Zhejiang hills. In a shed, seventeen eager, frenetic piglets that had been born the night before flowed over one another like quicksilver, squealing and squirming, bursting with irrepressible vitality. Outside, the walls were hung with dried chillies and corn cobs from last year's harvest. In another shed dangled a forest of salted hams; enormous clay vats of pickling vegetables sat here and there.

On the land, the terraced fields fell away below us, tiny green shoots peeking up through a frosting of white; bamboo-clad slopes rose all around. There were few vegetables to pick in this season, but the hardy Chinese cabbages stood amid the snow. They looked somewhat ridiculous: huge protuberances of tatty brown leaves tufted with snow, but when farmer Xu Hualong peeled away the rotted leaves, the cabbages inside were tight, crisp and luminous, hidden miracles. He picked one for our lunch.

This is one of the dishes Mr. Xu's wife cooked that day in her farmhouse kitchen, with their own home-salted pork. Chinese cabbage can seem like a watery, rather insipid vegetable, but it becomes dreamily soft and silky when cooked thoroughly in soups and stewed dishes like this one. The cabbage is simply boiled in a good stock with a little salt pork; a smidgeon of lard is a wonderful addition because it emulsifies in the stock and gives it a creamy richness.

14 oz (400g) Chinese leaf cabbage	1 tbsp lard or cooking oil
2 spring onions, white parts only	A few slices of peeled fresh ginger
2½ oz (60g) fat salt pork, pancetta or unsmoked bacon	2½ cups (600ml) stock
	Salt and ground white pepper

Cut the Chinese cabbage widthways into 1 in (2cm) slices. Smack the spring onion whites gently with the flat side of a Chinese cleaver or a rolling pin to loosen their fibers. Remove the rind from the salt pork and cut it into bite-sized slices.

Heat the lard or oil in a seasoned wok over a high flame. Add the spring onions and ginger and stir-fry briefly until they smell wonderful. Add the salt pork and fry briefly until it has become pale. Add the cabbage and stock and bring to the boil. Cover the wok and boil for 8–10 minutes, until the cabbage is silkily tender. After a few minutes, taste the broth and add a little salt if you need to (the salt pork will already have given it some saltiness). Finally, season with a little pepper and serve.

Steamed Chinese cabbage with salt pork

This is a dish from Zhu Yinfeng in southern Zhejiang. Cut the stalky white parts of a Chinese cabbage into evenly sized slices. Blanch, drain and sprinkle them with a little salt. Scrunch the salt into the cabbage with your fingers. Arrange the cabbage in a dish with thin slices of blanched salt pork on top. Add a few tablespoons of stock and a tablespoon or so of lard and season with salt. Steam over a high flame until the cabbage is beautifully tender but not falling apart. Serve.

Stir-fried spinach with sorghum liquor

jiu xiang bo cai 酒香菠菜

This recipe is based on a Shanghai classic: stir-fried alfalfa sprouts with sorghum liquor. Given the difficulty of finding alfalfa, I've followed the example of the Din Tai Fung restaurant in Shanghai by cooking spinach leaves in the same way. The shot of liquor gives the spinach a sharp, edgy aroma that is most delicious.

According to legend, alfalfa was one of the crops introduced to China by the Han-dynasty envoy Zhang Qian after his adventures in Central Asia some 2,000 years ago; it has been cultivated in the Jiangnan region since the fifteenth century. The plant is used mainly to feed animals and as a fertilizer, but its tender spring leaves are enjoyed as a seasonal delicacy in some places, particularly Shanghai, where they are traditionally eaten around Qingming, the Festival of Pure Brightness. If you live in Shanghai or grow your own alfalfa, try using the tender spring leaves instead of spinach.

When making this at home I use a widely available sorghum liquor called *er guo tou*, which can be found in good Chinese supermarkets. Make sure you heat the liquor enough to evaporate the alcohol, leaving only its fragrance behind.

14 oz (400g) bunched spinach
4 tbsp cooking oil
2 tbsp strong sorghum liquor, around 50 proof
1 tbsp light soy sauce
Salt

Thoroughly wash and trim the spinach. If the leaves are large, you may wish to cut them in half lengthways. Dry the spinach as far as possible in a salad spinner or by spreading it out on a clean tea towel.

Heat the oil in a seasoned wok over a high flame until very hot. Add the spinach and stir-fry vigorously until wilted and greatly reduced in volume. Pour the liquor around the edges of the wok so it sizzles, then stir it into the spinach. When everything is hot and fragrant, season with the soy sauce and with salt, if necessary. Serve.

Plain stir-fried greens

qing chao qing cai 清炒青菜

Few recipes are easier than this one, yet it's so delicious. I've included it simply to highlight the use of stir-frying to swiftly cook one of the archetypal Chinese vegetables, one of the great family of brassicas, and to transform it into something not only palatable, but fragrant, juicy and extremely nutritious. You don't need garlic, or ginger, or anything—just try it. Salt is always added at the end of this kind of dish: if you add it too early, it will draw water out of the leaves and result in a watery dish with stringy vegetables.

2–3 heads green bok choy	Salt
2 tbsp cooking oil	

Trim the bok choy and chop it across the line of the leaves into chopstickable lengths.

Heat the oil in a seasoned wok until beginning to smoke. Add the greens and stir-fry over a high flame until hot and wilted. Season with salt and serve.

Stir-fried pea shoots

Sometimes known as "dragons' whiskers" because of their curly fronds, pea shoots are traditionally regarded as a luxurious vegetable in China. In the past they were a banquet delicacy, only available in season and used in soups and stir-fries. They are at their peak in early spring, like tea leaves. They have a beautiful *qing xiang wei* (bright, clear fragrance and flavor) when simply stir-fried with oil and salt, and are also delicious with a smattering of garlic. If you have peas growing in your garden, pluck only the tenderest new leaves for cooking.

Stir-fried lettuce

Crisp lettuces such as romaine are wonderful stir-fried like this.

Stir-fried purple amaranth with garlic

With its deep green, purple-hearted leaves, this vegetable is unmistakable, and can often be found in Chinese food shops. Blanch the leaves in boiling water with a little oil, then stir-fry with finely chopped garlic and salt. The purple of the leaves will give the cooking juices a magnificent magenta color. The vegetable is traditionally eaten around the Dragon Boat Festival in late spring. A handful of fava beans, skinned and then boiled until tender, makes a delightful addition to the dish.

Stir-fried potato slivers with spring onion

cong you tu dou si 葱油土豆丝

A Shaoxing rickshaw driver once told me he had subsisted mainly on potatoes during his rural childhood because his family was so extremely poor. "*Tian a!* (Heavens!)," he said when I told him that many of my own compatriots actually regarded them as a delicious treat and even a staple food.

Although the Chinese don't hold potatoes in the same esteem as my own countrymen, they do have several fine ways of cooking them. This recipe, in which potatoes are simply stir-fried with spring onions and salt, is unexpectedly tasty, and makes a fine accompaniment to rice with another dish or two. I've included it in this collection partly in homage to Mao Cailan, a villager in Zhejiang province who cooked it as part of a radiantly beautiful farmhouse lunch I enjoyed several years ago.

14 oz (400g) waxy potatoes
2 tbsp cooking oil

4 tbsp thinly sliced spring onions, green parts only
Salt

Peel the potatoes. Cut them into ⅛ in (3–4mm) slices, then into ⅛ in (3–4mm) slivers. If not cooking immediately, cover them in lightly salted cold water until needed.

Heat the oil in a seasoned wok over a high flame. Add the potatoes and stir-fry for a few minutes until just cooked but still a little crisp. Season with salt. Add the spring onions and stir to give them a lick of heat, then serve.

Shaoxing potatoes with dried fermented greens

mei gan cai shao tu dou 霉干菜烧土豆

The culinary uses of Shaoxing's most famous preserve, the dried fermented vegetable known as *mei gan cai*, are many and varied, but this dish is one of the most common, and expresses the famous thriftiness of Shaoxing cooking in its use of a cheap pickle to lend rich and satisfying umami flavors to humble vegetables. The *mei gan cai* gives the potatoes an alluring, almost mushroomy flavor, and it's particularly good when reheated the next day, giving the flavors time to deepen. You can buy it in Chinese supermarkets or make your own (see page 332).

The same method can be used to cook green gourds of various kinds, bamboo shoots, fried tofu and French beans. I've made similar dishes with the *mui choy* preserved mustard used in Hakka dishes; the flavor is sweeter than the Shaoxing version, but it's also rather nice.

¾ oz (20g) Shaoxing dried
fermented greens
1 lb (450g) small, tasty new
potatoes, peeled or
unpeeled
2 tbsp cooking oil
2 tbsp thinly sliced spring
onions, green parts only
Salt

Put the fermented greens in a bowl and cover with boiling water; leave for 5 minutes or so to soften, then strain off and reserve the soaking water. Meanwhile, cut the potatoes into thick slices.

Heat the oil in a seasoned wok over a high flame. Add the potatoes and stir-fry for about 1 minute. Add 1⅓ cups (300ml) of the soaking water, topped up with hot water from the kettle if you don't have enough. Bring to the boil, season with salt and cover and simmer until the potatoes are just cooked.

Add the soaked greens and heat for another 30 seconds or so. Adjust the seasoning if necessary, then serve with a sprinkling of spring onion greens.

Hangzhou eggplant with minced pork

rou mo qie zi 肉末茄子

The eggplant may not be a native Chinese plant, but one of the earliest written references to it can be found in the sixth-century Chinese agricultural treatise *Qimin Yaoshu* ("Essential skills for the life of the common people"). Its use in Chinese cookery dates back more than 1,000 years earlier than the tomato, a New World import that is still known in many Chinese dialects as a "barbarian eggplant."

This dish comes from the Hangzhou home-cooking tradition, and was taught to me by chef Hu Zhongying of the Hangzhou Restaurant. It is usually made with long, slender, purple Chinese eggplant, but also works splendidly with the Mediterranean version, which tends to be more widely available outside China. I always salt Mediterranean eggplant before frying, to draw out some of their moisture and limit the amount of oil they absorb, but this is not normally done with Chinese eggplant. If you are cooking for vegetarians, simply omit the pork; the dish will still be delicious.

14 oz (400g) eggplant
About 1½ cups (350ml) cooking oil
2–3 oz (50–75g) minced pork, ideally with a little fat
2 tsp finely chopped fresh ginger
1 tbsp sweet fermented sauce (see page 337)
2 tbsp stock
1 tbsp Shaoxing wine
1 tsp light soy sauce
½ tsp dark soy sauce
½ tsp sugar
¼ tsp potato starch mixed with 1 tbsp cold water
2 tbsp finely chopped spring onions, green parts only
Salt

Cut the eggplant lengthways into 1 in (2cm) thick slices, then cut the slices into long strips. Cut these into 2–2½ in (5–6cm) batons. Sprinkle with a little salt, mix well and leave to drain in a colander for half an hour or so.

Heat the oil to 400°F (200°C). Pat the eggplant dry and deep-fry in a couple of batches until slightly golden. Remove with a slotted spoon and drain on paper towels.

Add 1–2 tablespoons oil to a seasoned wok over a high flame, swirl it around, then add the pork and stir-fry until the meat has lost its pinkness and any liquid that has emerged has evaporated. Add the ginger and stir a few times to release its fragrance. Add the sweet fermented sauce and stir a few times until it smells delicious too. Add the stock, Shaoxing wine, soy sauces and sugar along with the eggplant and mix well. Toss the eggplant in the sauce, then give the potato starch mixture a stir and pour it into the center of the wok, moving briskly to stir it in. Add the spring onion greens, stir a few times and serve.

Lotus pond stir-fry

he tang xiao chao 荷塘小炒

Ponds are an important part of the traditional system of farming in the Jiangnan region. They are used to grow vegetables including lotus, water chestnuts, water caltrops, foxnuts and water shield, and to rear fish and eels, which live on the snails and insects the water also supports. My friend and teacher, chef Zhu Yinfeng, says that when he was a child, the people in his village would catch all the fish in their collective ponds after the rice harvest each year and divide them up according to the number of mouths in the family. They would then drain the ponds and spread the mulch at the bottom on the fields as fertilizer.

This stir-fry, made with two pond-grown vegetables, will perk you up with its surprising and delightful variations on the theme of crispness: the short, sweet, snappy crispness of water chestnuts, the slightly stickier crispness of lotus root, the very delicate crispness of lily bulb, and the tauter, greener crispness of celery.

1 section lotus root (about 7 oz/200g)
1 day lily bulb (about 4 oz/100g)
8 oz (225g) fresh, unpeeled water chestnuts, or 4½ oz (125g) canned
3 celery sticks (about 5 oz/150g)
1 spring onion, white part only
3 tbsp cooking oil
A few slices of peeled fresh ginger
A few slices of carrot or red bell pepper (for color; optional)
Salt

For the sauce:
½ tsp potato starch
½ tsp superfine sugar
3 tbsp stock or water

Peel and trim the lotus root. Halve it lengthways, then cut it into ⅙ in (5mm) slices. Set it aside in lightly salted cold water. Trim the lily bulb and pull apart the petal-like lobes. Wash it thoroughly and trim off any discolored bits. Peel the water chestnuts and cut them into thick slices. Trim and destring the celery; cut it diagonally into lozenge-shaped pieces. Smack the spring onion white lightly with the flat side of a Chinese cleaver or a rolling pin to loosen its fibers. Combine the sauce ingredients in a small bowl.

Bring a pan of water to the boil and add ½ tablespoon cooking oil and ½ tablespoon salt. Tip in the lotus root, celery and carrot or red bell pepper, if using, and blanch for 1–2 minutes, just to "break their rawness." Add the water chestnuts and lily bulb and return to the boil. Tip everything into a colander and drain.

Heat the remaining cooking oil in a seasoned wok over a high flame. Add the ginger and spring onion and stir-fry briefly until you can smell them. Add all the blanched vegetables and stir-fry until piping hot. Season with salt, give the sauce a stir and serve.

Wild rice stem with soy sauce

you men jiao bai 油焖茭白

Bare-legged, chef Zhu Yinfeng stepped into the pond and pulled up what looked like bullrushes. He brought them to show me, their tall, spear-like leaves and swollen stems encased in husks, like bamboo shoots or sweetcorn. He stripped off the leaves and then, more gently, the papery greenness of the husk, to reveal a shiny ivory ziggurat of flesh. Wild rice stem, or water bamboo, (*Zizania caduciflora*) is an extraordinary vegetable, created by the invasion of wild grass stems by a kind of smut fungus (*Ustilago esculenta*) that causes them to swell into crisp white shoots that have the fresh delicacy of bamboo shoots but a softer texture. The plant has been eaten in China since ancient times; its seeds were once considered a cereal crop, but these days only the stems are generally consumed. Along with Chinese perch and water shield, it was known some fifteen centuries ago as one of the three famous foods of the Jiangnan region.

The stems are widely cultivated in Jiangnan today and can also be found in the fresh produce sections of good Chinese supermarkets in the West, where they may be partially peeled; look out for packages of ivory-white shoots with bright green husks, 6–8 in (15–20cm) long. The shoots are normally blanched before cooking.

Wild rice stem is particularly delicious cooked in this Shanghainese way, with rich soy sauce and a hint of sugar sweetness. The same method is often used to cook spring bamboo shoots; if you can buy these fresh, use them as an alternative here.

15 oz (425g) fresh wild rice stem	2 tsp light soy sauce
2 tbsp cooking oil	¾ tsp dark soy sauce
1 tbsp Shaoxing wine	4 tsp superfine sugar
⅓ cup (75ml) stock or water	½ tsp sesame oil
	Salt

Strip off any remaining layers of husk from the wild rice stem, so that you are left with the crisp, pale, ivory-colored stems (the peeled weight will be about ¾ lb/350g). Trim a thin slice off the cut end of each stem, along with any discolored parts. Starting from the tips, roll-cut them evenly into bite-sized pieces: holding your knife at an angle, cut off a chunk, then rotate the stem a half-turn towards you and, holding your knife at the same angle, cut off another chunk. Repeat the turning and cutting for the rest of the stem. Blanch for 1 minute or so in boiling water, then drain well.

Heat the oil in a seasoned wok over a high flame. Add the chopped stems and stir-fry for 1–2 minutes until tinged with gold. Add the Shaoxing wine, stock, soy sauces and sugar, season with a little salt and mix well. Bring to the boil, then cover and simmer over a gentle flame for 3–4 minutes to allow the vegetable to absorb the flavors of the sauce. Remove the lid, turn up the heat and reduce the sauce until syrupy, stirring constantly. Turn off the heat, stir in the sesame oil and serve.

Vegetarian "crabmeat"

qing chao su xie fen 清炒素蟹粉

On the first day of each lunar month people throng the Jade Buddha Temple in Shanghai, lighting incense sticks and kowtowing as they make their ritual offerings. In one of the shrine rooms Buddhist monks chant for the departed soul of an elderly man. His photograph stands on an altar, and his family have laid out dishes of vegetables and tofu, a bowl of rice, a pair of chopsticks and a glass of green tea as sustenance for his afterlife. At lunchtime, visitors pile into the snack restaurant at the back of the temple for a quick bowl of mushroom noodles in stock. A few venture upstairs for a more elaborate set menu of Buddhist vegetarian food: a selection of appetizers that include "roast duck" and "ham" made from tofu and main dishes such as vegetarian "pork chops" and "stir-fried crabmeat." The crabmeat, in particular, is a wonder of culinary artifice: a rich tumble of potato, carrot and egg white infused with the scents of ginger and vinegar, vividly evoking that legendary autumn delicacy, the stir-fried meat of the hairy crab.

For me, this classic dish is an expression of the exquisite creativity of Chinese cooking. A *trompe l'oeil* of color, fragrance, flavor and texture, it mimics the sensation of eating real hairy crab meat in so many details: the pale crab flesh mixed with bright orange coral, the gleaming oil, the white wisps of membrane, the strandy darkness on the outside of the leg meat, the slight sweetness, the aromas of ginger and vinegar. This is my attempt to re-create the particularly amazing version at the Gongdelin vegetarian restaurant in Shanghai.

1 dried shiitake mushroom	4 tbsp cooking oil, plus a little extra
7 oz (200g) carrots	2 tbsp finely chopped fresh ginger
14 oz (400g) potatoes	2 generous pinches of ground white pepper
1 tsp salt	1 tbsp Chinkiang vinegar
1 tbsp superfine sugar	A sprig of cilantro, to garnish (optional)
2 tsp potato starch mixed with 2 tbsp cold water	
2 large egg whites	

Cover the shiitake mushroom in boiling water and leave to soak for at least half an hour. Peel the carrots, but leave the potatoes in their skins. Boil or steam both vegetables until just tender. When cool enough to handle, peel the potatoes and finely chop both them and the carrots. Allow them to cool. Remove the shiitake stalk and slice the cap very finely.

Mix the potatoes and carrots together. Add the salt, sugar and potato starch mixture and mix well. Add the egg whites and stir once or twice with a fork to make a couple of ribbons through the mash—do not mix in thoroughly.

Pour the oil into a seasoned wok over a high flame. Add the ginger and shiitake and stir-fry briefly until the ginger smells wonderful. Add the potato and carrot mixture and stir rapidly, scraping the wok to prevent sticking, until piping hot (make sure it is heated through to cook the egg white and starch mixture). If the mash sticks to the sides of the wok, drip a little extra oil around the edges. Finally, add the pepper and vinegar and stir until thoroughly mixed. Garnish with cilantro, if using, and serve.

Vegetarian "eels" in a sweet-and-sour sauce

xiang you shan si 香油鳝丝

If you visit any fresh-food market in Jiangnan, you will probably see tubs filled with the fluid, yellow-brown snakiness of live paddy eels. Filleted, these savory creatures are the subject of many notable Jiangnan dishes. In Suzhou, people like to make "hissing-oil eels" (*xiang you shan si*) in which the eel fillets, swiftly cooked with soy sauce and sugar, are finished with a great pile of garlic and a libation of fiercely hot oil that produces a puff of steam and the hissing sound of the name. In Ningbo, the eels are cooked most tenderly with yellow chives and peeled fava beans, while in Wuxi they like to deep-fry them crisp and then clothe them in a glossy sweet-sour sauce.

Paddy eels are hard to find outside China, but Buddhist vegetarian restaurants in the region often serve imitation eel dishes like this one, made with strips of dried shiitake mushroom. The following recipe is based on a dish I've eaten at the Gongdelin restaurant in Shanghai.

9 dried shiitake mushrooms
A strip of green bell pepper
A strip of red bell pepper
3 oz (75g) potato starch
Cooking oil, for deep-frying
½ oz (15g) fresh ginger, peeled and cut into slivers
1 tsp sesame oil

For the sauce:
1 tbsp Shaoxing wine
3 tbsp superfine sugar
2 tbsp Chinkiang vinegar
¼ tsp dark soy sauce
2 tsp light soy sauce

Soak the shiitake mushrooms in boiling water for at least half an hour to soften them. Cut the peppers into thin strips. Combine the sauce ingredients in a small bowl.

Remove the mushrooms from their soaking water and squeeze out as much liquid as you possibly can. Remove and discard the stalks and cut the caps into ½ in (1cm) strips. Just before frying them, add the potato starch and toss so that the strips are evenly coated.

Heat the oil for deep-frying to 350–400°F (180–200°C). Scatter the starched mushroom strips into the hot oil and deep-fry briefly until they are no longer floppy. Remove from the oil with a slotted spoon and set aside. Let the oil return to its original temperature, then add the "eels" and fry until golden and crisp. Remove from the oil and set aside.

Return the wok to a high flame with 1 tablespoon of the deep-frying oil. Add the ginger and stir-fry briefly until fragrant. Add the sauce and stir to dissolve the sugar as it boils. Tip the "eels" into the sauce and stir rapidly to clothe them evenly. Add the pepper strips and quickly mix them in. Off the heat, stir in the sesame oil and serve.

Wheat gluten with mixed vegetables

mian jin chao su 面筋炒素

This colorful stir-fry is based on one I learned from my friends Jason Li and He Yuxiu. You can vary the vegetables as you please; add a few slices of waxy potato, Chinese yam or shiitake mushroom, a handful of peas or green soybeans, or some leafy greens.

8–10 fried gluten puffs (see page 324)
A small handful of dried wood-ear mushrooms
A few slices of peeled carrot
¼ red bell pepper
¼ green bell pepper
1 spring onion, white part only
2 tbsp cooking oil
3 slices peeled fresh ginger

8–10 boiled gluten puffs or 3 oz (80g) vegetarian "intestines" (see page 324)
½ cup (100ml) stock or water
1 tsp light soy sauce
1 tsp superfine sugar
1 tsp potato starch mixed with 1 tsp cold water (optional)
½ tsp sesame oil
Salt

In separate bowls, pour boiling water over the fried gluten puffs and the wood-ear mushrooms. When the puffs have softened, rinse them in cool water and squeeze gently to extract most of the water. When the wood-ears have swelled and softened, cut or tear them into bite-sized pieces, discarding any knotty bits. Cut the carrot, on the diagonal, into ⅛ in (3mm) slices. Trim the peppers and cut them into bite-sized squares. Cut the spring onion white at an angle into slices.

Heat the cooking oil in a seasoned wok over a high flame. Add the ginger and spring onion and stir-fry briefly until you can smell them. Add the carrot and stir a few times. Tip in both types of gluten puff and the wood-ears and stir-fry until piping hot. Add the stock or water, soy sauce and sugar and season with salt. Cover and cook over a medium flame for 1–2 minutes.

Stir in the red and green pepper. Remove the lid and turn the heat up high to reduce the liquid; alternatively, if using, give the starch mixture a stir and mix in just enough to thicken it to a sauce that clings to the vegetables. Off the heat, stir in the sesame oil and serve.

SOUPS

Soup is part of the comfort of a Chinese meal. A light broth can refresh the palate, soothe the throat and settle the spirits, which is why food is seldom served without it. At its simplest, such a soup may be no more than a bowlful of stock with a few spring onion greens or strands of seaweed. For greater nourishment and pleasure, rich yet delicate broths are made by simmering whole ducks or chickens for hours to extract their essences, often with tonic herbs. Snack restaurants almost always serve fried noodles, rice or dumplings with a bowlful of broth to cleanse the palate and balance the fragrant oiliness of the food. In Jiangnan, soups are typically served at the end of a meal, in line with the pronouncements of the eighteenth-century gourmet Yuan Mei, who wrote of the proper sequence of dishes:

Salty dishes should come first, bland ones afterwards,
Strong flavors should precede the weak ones,
Dry dishes should come before those that are soupy.

This is part of the typical intention of a Jiangnan meal: to leave those who eat it in a state of wellbeing. While a feast in Europe may conclude with cheeses and rich desserts that induce a state of comatose contentment, the equivalent in Jiangnan is likely to wind down gently with delicate soups, fresh fruit and tea, all of which help to create a feeling of more harmonious satiety that bodes well for a good night's sleep and a refreshing start to the following day.

There are two words for soup in Chinese: light, unthickened broths are known as *tang*, while a *geng* is a soup dense with finely cut ingredients and thickened with starch to give a smooth, satiny liquid. The *geng* stew-soup has a particular resonance in Chinese culture; in ancient times it was not only one of the mainstays of everyday diets, but was also among the most important of the edible sacrifices through which people communicated with their gods and ancestors. The typically crowded assortment of ingredients floating in a *geng* may explain why popular discontent was sometimes described as being "like the bubbling of a *geng* in the pot" (*ru fei ru geng*). In the distant past, such soups were thickened with rice crumbs and mucilaginous vegetables; these days, cooks use powdered starches made from potato and other vegetables.

The Jiangnan region is renowned for its delectable soups. Some defy any attempt at re-creation abroad because of the local particularity of their ingredients, like the famous water shield soup of Hangzhou (*xi hu chun cai tang*). Water shield is a weed that grows in a few Jiangnan lakes, and has oval leaves and buds coated in a layer of transparent mucilage; the tender young leaves, curled up, resemble little gray-green scrolls. The vegetable has little flavor but a delightfully slippery mouthfeel, and looks discreetly elegant in a clear broth, with a sprinkling of finely slivered ham and chicken. For millennia, it has been a prized delicacy, sent in tribute to Chinese emperors and mentioned in poems and letters through the ages; it is one of the foods that inspired the Western Jin dynasty official Zhang Han to abandon his post in northern China and embark on the long journey home to Jiangnan.

Another speciality of Hangzhou is "Immortal duck with Jinhua ham" (*huo zhong shen xian ya*), a sumptuous clay-pot soup made by simmering a whole duck with the lower section of a Jinhua ham. Traditionally, it is said to be ready when three incense sticks have burned away—an old-fashioned method of time-keeping. Suzhou is known for a delicate soup made with the "three whites" from the Tai Lake (whitefish, white shrimp and silvery fish), while Ningbo is the place to try many delicate *tang* broths afloat with local bamboo shoot and vegetables, or grander banquet *geng* soups made with yellow croaker, sea cucumber and other delicacies. The people of Shaoxing, in keeping with their frugal reputation, often make everyday broths by boiling up their beloved dried fermented greens with shrimp or vegetables.

This chapter includes some of the classic soups of the region, such as Mrs. Song's fish soup, as well as some simpler broths for the everyday supper table.

Bok choy broth with pickle

zha cai qing cai tang 榨菜青菜汤

This is a soup I fell in love with during a staff supper at the Dragon Well Manor restaurant in Hangzhou. It is one of those genius Chinese dishes in which humble ingredients yield delightful and sophisticated flavors. In essence, it's a cabbage-and-cabbage soup, but it matches leaf cabbage with stem cabbage, fresh with fermented, so the refreshing juiciness of the green leaves is lit up by the salty-umami undertones of the pickle. Do try it.

2½ oz (60g) Sichuan preserved vegetable
¾ lb (350g) green bok choy
1 tbsp cooking oil
1½ quarts (1.5 liters) stock
Salt and ground white pepper

Rinse the preserved vegetable well to remove any chilli. Cut it into 2–3mm slices, then 2–3mm slivers. Trim the bok choy. If the heads are large, cut them widthways into ½–1 in (1–2cm) ribbons. If they are very small, simply halve or quarter them lengthways.

Heat the oil in a seasoned wok over a high flame. Add the preserved vegetable and stir-fry briefly until it smells wonderful. Add the stock, bring to the boil and boil for a minute or so to allow the pickle to flavor the broth. Add the bok choy and boil until tender. Season with salt and pepper—you probably won't need much salt because the pickle is salty. Serve.

Preserved vegetable soup with slivered pork

Cut some lean pork into slivers add it to the broth with the preserved vegetable; omit the greens.

Simple egg-flower soup

hu lu gua dan hua tang 葫芦瓜蛋花汤

Many traditional Chinese meals include a refreshing soup like this one: a simple broth made with stock, an everyday vegetable and an egg or two. I've written the recipe to use the long, shiny green gourd that's often known by its Indian name, *dudhi*, but silk gourd, chayote or winter melon will give a similar effect. You could also use sliced tomatoes, leafy greens or another vegetable of your choice.

The cooking method allows the beaten egg to set into "flowers"— delicate, frondy blooms that drift among the jade-green slices of vegetable. You can use any kind of stock for this kind of soup. Recently, I used a stock made from the leftovers of a roast duck, which was marvelous. Chinese cooks often add a little lard at the end of cooking to enrich the broth.

1 dudhi or Chinese shiny green gourd (about 1 lb/475g)
2 eggs

1½ quarts (1.5 liters) stock
1 tbsp lard (optional)
Salt and ground white pepper

Peel and trim the dudhi and slice it in half lengthways, then slice it into semicircles about ⅛ in (4mm) thick. Beat the eggs in a bowl.

Bring the stock to the boil. Add the sliced dudhi and boil for about 10 minutes, until tender. Season with salt and pepper and stir in the lard, if using. Turn the heat down low, then drizzle the egg all over the surface of the soup. When the egg has set into "flowers," turn off the heat, stir gently and serve.

Sliced gourd and fava bean soup

chang gua dou ban geng 长瓜豆瓣羹

This is a delightful, easy soup. The original recipe, from a Ningbo cookery book, calls for the local long, shiny green gourd, but I've made it with sliced chayote. The sliced ham gives an umami lift to the soup and sets off its green colors prettily. For best results, steam the ham first.

5 oz (150g) Chinese long green gourd or chayote
1 oz (30g) thickly sliced Spanish or Chinese cured ham, steamed briefly
1¼ quarts (1.2 liters) chicken stock
1 tbsp cooking oil
5 oz (150g) shelled, peeled fava beans (¾–1 lb/350–400g in their pods)
1 tbsp potato starch mixed with 2 tbsp cold water
Salt

Peel the chayote or gourd and cut it neatly into ⅛ in (3mm) slices. Trim off any fat from the ham and cut it into neat little slices. Bring the stock to the boil in a large pan, then keep it warm.

Heat the oil in a seasoned wok over a high flame. Add the fava beans and sliced gourd and stir-fry for about a minute. Add the stock and ham, bring to the boil and simmer gently for 2 minutes until the vegetables are tender. Season with salt. Give the potato starch mixture a stir and add it to the soup in 2 or 3 stages, stirring as the liquid thickens. Add just enough to give the soup a lazy, gravy-like consistency. Serve.

Clear-simmered silkie chicken soup

qing dun wu ji 清炖乌鸡

When it comes to cooking a really good chicken, less is often more. Typically, the most flavorful birds—mature, free-range hens—are "clear-simmered," which is to say stewed gently in water, on their own, for two hours or more, until the flesh falls from the wings and the broth is replete with their delicious essences. Often, a little ginger and spring onion is tucked in to the pot to refine the flavor of the bird; medicinal herbs or goji berries may be added to enhance the tonic properties of the soup. This cooking method encourages appreciation of the *ben wei* or "essential taste" of the bird, without any distractions, and is the kind of which eighteenth-century gourmet Yuan Mei enthusiastically approved: "Every ingredient has its own taste," he wrote, "which should not be confused with that of others … These days, one sees chefs who boil up chicken, duck, pork and goose together in a single broth … creating flavors so blurred that one might as well be munching on candlewax. If chickens, ducks, pigs and geese had souls, I fear they would bring lawsuits against such malefactors in the City of the Wronged Dead."

The finest chicken soups I've ever tasted have been made in the Chinese countryside, from two- or even three-year-old farmhouse birds that produce a divine, golden broth. Seek out good free-range birds, or, as in this recipe, the white-feathered, black-skinned silkie chicken that can be found in Chinatowns and, increasingly, mainstream food shops too. In China, soups like this are typically made in a clay pot.

1 silkie chicken (about 1⅓ lbs/600g)
¾ oz (20g) fresh ginger, skin on
2 spring onions, white parts only
A small handful of goji berries (optional)

Bring a large pan of water to the boil. Leave the chicken whole or chop it, on the bone, into bite-sized chunks. Add the chicken to the pan and blanch it for a minute or so. Remove it from the pan and rinse well under the tap. Discard the blanching water and rinse out the pan. Smack the ginger and spring onions lightly with the flat side of a Chinese cleaver or a rolling pin to loosen their fibers.

Put the chicken in a saucepan or clay pot, cover it generously with fresh water and bring to the boil, skimming well. Add the ginger and spring onion, return to the boil and simmer gently for 2–3 hours. Before serving, add the goji berries, if using, and simmer for a few minutes until plump.

Shanghai double-pork soup with bamboo shoot

yan du xian 腌笃鲜

After a long simmering, the salt pork, fresh pork and bamboo shoot in this Shanghainese soup develop a rich, exquisite sweetness that will make you feel at peace with the world. This was originally a dish for early spring, when the first bamboo shoots of the season would thrust their way up out of the earth, and its glorious scent would drift on the air of many old Shanghai neighborhoods. If you can find fresh spring bamboo shoot, please use it. Otherwise, it is magnificent even when made with bamboo shoot preserved in brine. What is critical is to use really excellent pork.

The name of this dish in Chinese has a delightful ring to it because the words for "salted" (*yan*) and "fresh" (*xian*) rhyme with each other. Although the dish is often regarded as typically Shanghainese, Hangzhou master chef Hu Zhongying tells me it originates in Hangzhou. The character *du* in the name is an onomatopoeic dialect word for simmering over a low flame.

If your salt pork is excessively salty, you may wish to soak it overnight in plenty of cold water before cooking. Some cooks add a handful of tofu knots to the broth for added texture. It is traditionally cooked in a Chinese clay pot.

7 oz (200g) boneless pork belly, skin on	2 spring onions, white parts only
7 oz (200g) gammon (salt pork), with a little fat	2 tbsp Shaoxing wine
5 oz (150g) fresh or brined bamboo shoot	A few lengths of spring onion, green parts only, to garnish
¾ oz (25g) fresh ginger, skin on	Salt

Cut the pork belly into 1 in (2cm) cubes and do the same with the gammon. If using fresh bamboo shoot, peel off the husk, slice away and discard the fibrous part near the base, then roll-cut (see page 350) into 1 in (2cm) chunks. Blanch the bamboo shoot, whether fresh or brined, for a minute or so in boiling water. Smack the ginger and spring onion whites with the flat side of a Chinese cleaver or a rolling pin to loosen their fibers.

Put the pork belly in a pan, cover with cold water, bring to the boil and then blanch for 2 minutes. Drain, discarding the water. Put the pork belly in your cooking pot, along with the gammon and bamboo shoot. Cover with 1½ quarts (1.5 liters) cold water and bring to the boil, skimming if necessary. Add the ginger, spring onion and Shaoxing wine. Boil rapidly for 5 minutes, then half-cover, turn the heat down low and simmer very gently for about 3 hours, by which stage wonderful aromas will fill your kitchen and the broth will taste delicious, with a natural sweetness. Before serving, add a little salt if you need it (you probably won't). Scatter with the spring onion greens, then serve.

Winter melon soup with salt pork

Bring a pan of water to the boil. Add some pieces of salt pork, return to the boil and skim. Add thick slices of peeled winter melon with a dash of Shaoxing wine and, if you like, some green soybeans. Return to the boil, simmer until tender and serve with a scattering of sliced spring onion greens.

Crabmeat, tomato and potato soup

xie fen fan qie tu dou nong tang 蟹粉番茄土豆浓汤

The tomato was known as a "barbarian eggplant" (*fan qie*) by the Chinese coastal people who first encountered it after its long voyage from the Americas (in other parts of China, they call it "Western red persimmon," *xi hong shi*). This substantial soup is made with both tomatoes and potatoes, another New World vegetable, along with the white flesh of saltwater crabs, and is a perfect expression of Shanghai's polyglot history and deep "barbarian" influences. It's a gorgeous sunset of a soup, savory with a hint of sweetness, and finished with a sprinkling of "barbarian pepper," as the Chinese call black pepper. Serve it as part of a Chinese meal, as a European-style first course, or as a meal in itself, perhaps with just bread and a salad on the side.

I often order this soup in two of my favorite Shanghai restaurants, Old Jesse and Fu 1088, and I'm grateful to Fu 1088 executive chef Tony Lu for explaining his recipe to me. At home I make it with freshly picked Cornish crabmeat from my local fishmonger. If you are cooking several dishes and want to make life easier, I suggest you make the soup mostly in advance, and just bring it to the boil and add the starch mixture to thicken when you wish to serve it.

1 lb (475g) potatoes
4 ripe tomatoes (about 1 lb/500g)
1½ quarts (1.5 liters) stock
4 tbsp (60g) butter
1 tbsp cooking oil
9 oz (250g) white crabmeat
3 tbsp tomato paste
2½ tbsp superfine sugar
4 tbsp potato starch mixed with 5 tbsp cold water
Salt and freshly ground black pepper

Bring a pan of water to the boil. Peel the potatoes, steam or boil them until tender, then mash them coarsely. Cut a cross through the skin of each tomato and put them all in a bowl. Cover them with boiling water and leave to cool. When cool enough to handle, peel off the skins, then core them, discarding the seeds, and chop the flesh into fine dice. Bring the stock to the boil.

Heat half the butter with ½ teaspoon cooking oil in a seasoned wok or frying pan. Add the crabmeat and fry until hot and fragrant, then remove and set aside. Heat the remaining butter and oil in the same pan. Add the tomatoes and stir-fry over a high flame until fragrant and partially disintegrated. Add the tomato purée and stir-fry until it smells delicious. Add the hot stock and mashed potatoes and bring to the boil, pressing the potatoes so they spread throughout the soup. Season with the sugar and salt. Add the crabmeat and return to the boil, then give the starch mixture a stir and add it a little at a time, mixing well, to thicken the soup. Serve with a generous scattering of black pepper.

Monk Wensi's tofu thread soup

wen si dou fu geng 文思豆腐羹

Perhaps more than any other dish, this ethereal tofu concoction shows off the dazzling knife skills for which Yangzhou chefs are famed. A single block of silken tofu is cut into paper-thin slices, then into hairlike strands, which drift in a gently thickened broth like some extraordinary subterranean flower, their whiteness set off by wisps of rosy ham and dark wood-ear mushroom.

The dish is named after a Buddhist monk of the Tianning Temple in Yangzhou, who was an accomplished vegetarian cook and originally made it with slivers of tofu, lily flower and mushrooms in a vegetarian broth. Monk Wensi's tofu was one of the dishes served at the lavish Man–Han banquet laid on for the Qianlong emperor in Yangzhou in the late eighteenth century; it was later adopted into the repertoire of the palace kitchen. One modern version of Wensi tofu can be found in the restaurants of Beijing celebrity chef Da Dong, who serves the classic white tofu threads in a black soup colored by squid ink: an utterly beautiful dish.

Do not be disappointed if your tofu threads fail to match up to Yangzhou standards; the soup will be a pleasure to eat anyway! It's a symphony of delicate colors and textures that will soothe and refresh your guests.

Monk Wensi's tofu thread soup; Spinach soup with silken tofu and pork (page 228)

3 dried wood-ear mushrooms
10 oz (300g) silken tofu
¾ oz (25g) Spanish or Chinese cured ham, steamed briefly
3 spring onions, green parts only

1 quart (1 liter) clear stock
3 tbsp potato starch mixed with 6 tbsp cold water
Salt and ground white pepper

Cover the wood-ear mushrooms in boiling water and set aside for at least half an hour.

Turn the tofu out onto a chopping board. Hold a Chinese cleaver or broad cutting knife perpendicular to the board and trim off and discard the sloping end of the block, so you have a clean perpendicular edge. Working slowly and steadily with an up-and-down chopping motion, cut the tofu into the thinnest slices you can—ideally about 1mm thick. Keep the tofu block wet by sprinkling it with a little cold water as necessary. When you have sliced about a third of the block, nudge the slices so they fall on their sides in overlapping layers. Cut them into the thinnest possible strips. Use the side of your cleaver or knife to gently scoop up the tofu slivers and place them in a bowl of cold water. Repeat with the rest of the block.

Drain the wood-ears, trim off any knobbly bits and then cut them into the thinnest possible slivers. Cut the ham and spring onion greens as evenly as possible into very thin slivers.

Bring the stock to the boil in a seasoned wok, skimming if necessary. Season with salt and pepper. Drain the tofu strips in a sieve and gently transfer them to the stock. Add the wood-ears. Bring the liquid back to the boil and adjust the seasoning if necessary. Give the starch mixture a good stir and add it in stages to the soup, stirring gently as the liquid thickens: it's best to do this by nudging the soup with the back of a ladle so you don't break up the tofu. When the liquid has a heavy, lazy consistency that holds the tofu threads easily, transfer to a serving bowl. Sprinkle over the strands of ham and spring onion and stir them in gently. Serve.

Spinach soup with silken tofu and pork

bo cai rou si dou fu geng 菠菜肉丝豆腐羹

This is one of a family of Shanghainese soups that are traditionally made with the herby green leaves of shepherd's purse, a distinctive local vegetable that is most tender in the early spring. If you can find it, do use it in this recipe; otherwise, spinach makes a very satisfying substitute.

Sometimes you will find slippery slices of yellow croaker fish and cubes of tofu suspended in the vibrant green broth; sometimes threads of crab and scallop. In the following recipe, I've given another typical combination that makes an easy supper dish at home: tofu and slivered pork. The broth is thickened with starch so that tiny pieces of each ingredient hang it in like a kaleidoscope.

See photograph on page 227

6 oz (175g) trimmed spinach (about 9 oz/250g before trimming)
4 oz (100g) pork tenderloin
10 oz (300g) silken tofu
1 tbsp cooking oil
½ tbsp Shaoxing wine
1 quart (1 liter) stock
4 tbsp potato starch mixed with 6 tbsp cold water
1 tbsp chicken oil or lard (optional)
Salt and ground white pepper

Bring a pan of water to the boil and blanch the spinach leaves briefly to wilt them. Refresh immediately under the cold tap and then squeeze dry. Chop as finely as possible. Cut the pork into very thin slivers. Cut the tofu into ⅙ in (5mm) cubes.

Heat the cooking oil in a seasoned wok over a high flame. Add the pork and stir-fry until just cooked. Splash in the Shaoxing wine, then add the stock and tofu and bring to the boil. Stir in the spinach and return to the boil. Season with salt and white pepper.

Give the starch mixture a stir and add it in stages to the wok, mixing well as you go, adding just enough to give the soup a silky, heavy consistency—this will ensure that the tofu and spinach are suspended evenly in the soup. Stir in the chicken oil or lard, if using, and serve.

Pig's trotter and soybean soup

zhu ti huang dou tang 猪蹄黄豆汤

The Chinese rarely use unprocessed soybeans in their cookery (except for the tender young beans usually known in English by their Japanese name, edamame). Such beans are somewhat indigestible, their rich proteins locked up a form inaccessible to humans, which is why they are almost always fermented, sprouted or transformed into tofu. However, there are exceptions, as with this satisfying Shanghainese soup, in which soaking and a long simmering renders the beans fragrant and nutritious, and the collagen in the trotters melts away to give a most luxurious mouthfeel.

Do make sure you cook the beans until they're as tender as baked beans: this is important, because undercooked soybeans contain harmful compounds. Trotters are especially popular with Chinese women because they are said to enhance the complexion.

4 oz (100g) dried soybeans
2 pig's trotters
½ oz (15g) fresh ginger, skin on
2 spring onions, white parts only
Salt and ground white pepper

Cover the soybeans in plenty of cold water and soak them overnight. Rinse and drain.

Cut the trotters in half lengthways, then chop them into 1½ in (3cm) chunks, discarding the very knobbly foot end. Blanch them in boiling water for 2 minutes, then rinse them in cold water. Use tweezers to pluck out any remaining bristles. Smack the ginger and spring onion whites lightly with the flat side of a Chinese cleaver or a rolling pin to loosen their fibers.

Put the soybeans and trotter pieces in a pan with 2½ quarts (2.5 liters) cold water and bring to the boil. Skim. Add the ginger and spring onions, then cover, reduce the heat and simmer for about 4 hours, until the beans are completely tender. Season with salt and pepper before serving.

Mrs. Song's thick fish soup

song sao yu geng 宋嫂鱼羹

This soup is a gentle miracle: a swirl of tender fish, golden wisps of egg yolk and slivers of bamboo shoot and mushroom, its savory flavors lifted by a final spritz of vinegar. Like many Hangzhou dishes, this one tells a story. It dates back to the time when the Song dynasty had been driven south to Hangzhou by Jurchen invaders. One day, the emperor took to the imperial boat for a leisurely tour of the West Lake. As he made his progress, he ordered his servants to summon the floating traders on the lake and ask for samples of their wares. One of them boldly introduced herself as "fifth sister-in-law Song," and told the emperor she had followed his court south from the old northern capital Kaifeng, and was making her living by selling thick fish soup on the shores of the lake. The emperor tasted her soup and was overcome by nostalgia for his lost northern capital. Moved beyond words, he thanked Mrs. Song with a gift of rolls of silk shot with silver and gold. Afterwards, they say, local people flocked to Mrs. Song's for a bowlful of soup, "half buying a taste of imperial favor, half buying fish."

The recipe is said to have been based on a northern-style sour-and-hot soup made with carp from the Yellow River, but adapted in Hangzhou to use the mandarin fish or Chinese perch. Sea bass also works like a dream. This recipe is adapted from one in *Hangzhou Cuisine*, with thanks also to chef Hu Zhongying of the Hangzhou Restaurant for his suggestions.

3 dried shiitake mushrooms
1 sea bass (about 1 lb/500g) scaled and gutted
¾ oz (25g) fresh ginger, skin on
3 spring onions, white parts only
1½ tbsp Shaoxing wine
⅓ oz (10g) lean Spanish or Chinese cured ham, steamed briefly
1 spring onion, green parts only

2 oz (50g) bamboo shoot
1 tbsp lard or cooking oil
1 liter chicken stock
1½ tbsp light soy sauce
½ tsp dark soy sauce
2½ tbsp potato starch mixed with 6 tbsp cold water
4 egg yolks, mixed together
1 tbsp Chinkiang vinegar, plus extra to serve
Salt and ground white pepper

Soak the shiitake mushrooms in boiling water for at least half an hour, until softened.

Cut off the head and fins of the fish and slice it along the backbone into two halves. Rinse and shake dry. Place the fish, skin-side down, in a bowl that will fit into your steamer basket.

Take ½ oz (15g) ginger and 1 spring onion white and smack them gently with the flat side of a Chinese cleaver or a rolling pin to loosen their fibers. Tuck them into a bowl with the fish and sprinkle over ½ tablespoon Shaoxing wine. Put the fish bowl in the steamer basket and steam over a high flame until just cooked—about 5 minutes.

When the fish is ready, strain off its juices into another bowl. Gently flake the flesh from the fish, discarding skin and bones, and add it to the cooking juices (chopsticks are good for this).

Smack the remaining spring onion whites to loosen their fibers. Peel the remaining ginger and cut it into thin slivers. Cut the ham and the spring onion green into very thin slivers. Drain the shiitake, discard the stalks and cut the caps into thin slivers. Cut the bamboo shoot into slivers of a similar thickness and blanch for 1–2 minutes in boiling water; drain well. ▸

Heat the lard in a seasoned wok over a high flame. Add the spring onion whites and stir-fry until they are tinged with gold and smell delicious. Add the stock and bring to the boil, then fish out and discard the spring onion whites. Add the mushrooms and bamboo shoot to the wok and return to the boil.

Add the soy sauces and the fish with all its juices, and season with salt. Return to the boil, then turn down to a very gentle simmer. Give the starch mixture a stir and pour it into the center of the wok in about 3 stages, stirring well to thicken the soup—add just enough to give it a creamy, lazy consistency.

Add the egg yolks and stir them into the soup; the yolks will set into flowery wisps. Finally, add the vinegar and heat for just a few moments to fuse the flavors of the soup.

Pour the soup into a serving bowl. Sprinkle with a little pepper and garnish with the slivered ham, ginger and spring onion greens. Serve immediately. Invite your guests to add a tiny dash of vinegar at the table, if they wish.

Milky rice-broth soup with radish and dried shrimp

mi tang zhu luo bo 米汤煮萝卜

Chefs Zheng and Ling and I drove out from Tunxi, near the Yellow Mountain, to the Clove Garden, a restaurant owned by some friends of theirs by the edge of a shimmering lake. I was immediately invited into the kitchen for a lesson in the arts of southern Anhui cooking. Some of the dishes I learned to make that day would be hard to reproduce outside the region—in particular the Yellow Mountain "two stone" soup made with locally gathered stone-ear fungus and so-called "stone chicken" (actually a kind of frog)—but this gentle soup is not. It traditionally relies on that old farmhouse staple known as "rice broth," the silky liquid left after parboiling rice before steaming, but which can also be made by cooking a little rice in plenty of water. Here, slices of radish are simmered in the broth until they are slippery-tender and finally garnished with dried shrimp and spring onions. I would like to thank chefs Gao Yongfei and Feng Jianjin at the Clove Garden for explaining the recipe.

It's a simple, rustic soup and a refreshing balance to, for example, a rich red-braised dish. Think of this recipe as a basic template for all kinds of rice-broth soups, made with any vegetables and odds and ends you might have to hand.

One lovely tonic soup I've enjoyed in Zhejiang is rice broth sweetened with honey and enriched with wisps of beaten egg (*mi tang chong ji dan*): just boil the broth, sweeten it to taste, then stir in a beaten egg over a gentle heat.

½ cup (125g) plain white rice
4 tbsp papery dried shrimp
1½ lbs (650g) white Asian radish
2 tbsp lard or cooking oil

2 tbsp thinly sliced spring onions, green parts only
Salt and ground white pepper

Put the rice in a saucepan with 2 quarts (2 liters) cold water. Bring to the boil, skim and give the pan a good stir to stop the rice sticking. Turn the heat down and simmer for 30 minutes, until the liquid is soft and milky. Strain off and retain the liquid—this is your rice broth. Discard the rice, or use it for something else.

Put the shrimp in a small bowl and add just enough cold water to cover; leave for a few minutes to soften. Peel the radish, halve it lengthways, then cut it into semicircular slices about 2mm thick.

Heat the lard or oil in a seasoned wok over a high flame. Add the radish and stir-fry for 1–2 minutes. Add the rice broth, bring to the boil and simmer for 30 minutes, until the radish slices are completely tender. Stir in the dried shrimp and season with salt and pepper. Serve with a scattering of spring onion greens.

RICE

Rice, the staff of life in southern China, has been at the heart of Jiangnan cooking for millennia. The people of the Neolithic Hemudu culture near Ningbo, some 7,000 years ago, were growers and eaters of rice, and among the earliest in the world to domesticate the grain. The Grand Historian of China, Simaqian, writing more than 2,000 years ago, noted that rice was the foundation of the local diet. Today, to eat a meal is to "eat cooked rice" (*chi fan*); other dishes are seen as secondary accompaniments, to "send the rice down" (*xia fan*).

The paddy fields of Jiangnan, shaped by human hands around the flowing architecture of its hills and valleys, are like a mirror of the seasons, changing with the cycle of planting and harvesting. The bare stubble of winter gives way to flooded fields that gleam like silver in the sun, pricked by the intense green of the new rice seedlings. Paddy eels and loaches lurk in the channels, while ducks paddle and float over the liquid landscape. Later, the grass grows lush and green and the grains swell. At harvest time, the golden stalks are scythed and threshed and the new rice is laid out on bamboo mats to dry in the sun. The straw is bound and piled into haystacks; later, it will be used as animal feed and bedding, and afterwards fertilizer.

Traditionally, plain white rice is cooked either by steaming or by the slow absorption of water in a covered pan. Steamed rice is first parboiled and then steamed in a bamboo pot over a wokful of simmering water; the satiny, milky liquid left over from the parboiling, known as "rice soup," can be drunk on its own or used as a base for soups, ensuring that every possible ounce of nutrition is extracted from the grain (see page 233). Rice cooked by the absorption method is known as "pot-sticker rice" because of the toasty, golden layer that forms where the rice meets the metal of the pan. Most people these days—at least in the cities—use an electric rice cooker, while dreaming nostalgically of the flavor of farmhouse rice cooked on a wood-burning stove.

Leftover rice need never be wasted. It may be reheated with stock or water and scraps of food to make "soaked" or soupy rice, or stir-fried with delicious tidbits to make a meal in itself. Even a few spoonfuls of leftover rice may be mixed with beaten eggs and fried up into a delectable omelet (see page 247). In Shanghai, people love to press their leftover rice into a pot, chill it, slice it thickly, then deep-fry it to make *ci fan gao*: crisp, golden slices that may be seasoned with morsels of ham and spring onion, or eaten sweet with a dip of white sugar. Some people even use the liquid left after washing rice, for example to soak dried bamboo shoot before cooking.

Rice is often eaten as congee, especially for breakfast, when it may be accompanied by salty pickles and other relishes. Another Jiangnan speciality is "New Year's cake" (*nian gao*), made by pounding cooked rice to a smooth, springy mass, which is then cooled and sliced before being used in sweet or savory dishes; the most celebrated version is from the old town of Cicheng, near Ningbo. Sliced rice cake is typically stir-fried or eaten in soup. In Suichang in rural Zhejiang, I once tasted a local kind that had been made from rice soaked in lye water made of plant ashes; the rice cake, sliced and stir-fried, had a yellow tint and a curious alkaline taste from the lye. In the past, people sometimes molded their rice cake into the forms of gold and silver ingots, which were stacked high on red lacquered dishes and displayed as part of the New Year's festivities.

The people of Suzhou, famed for their sweet tooth, prefer to eat larger "bricks" of sweet *nian gao* made from glutinous rice, which arc traditionally eaten at New Year to commemorate a great statesman who lived some two-and-a-half millennia ago, Wu Zixu. According to local lore, the townspeople survived starvation during a siege by digging up the stash of glutinous rice bricks that Wu had buried beneath one of the city gates as an insurance policy.

Pearly glutinous rice is also used to make delicious puddings and savory stuffings. One particular speciality, the "black rice" of Suzhou (*wu mi fan*), deserves separate mention. Steaming hot, enriched with lard and sugar, it looks like black glutinous rice, but is actually made by soaking raw white glutinous rice in water mixed with crushed blueberry leaves; a deep purple color develops as it steams.

In Shaoxing, people often lay raw ingredients directly onto their rice as it cooks, a method known locally as *fan wu*. Food cooked this way is simple but unexpectedly lovely, especially when served with a soy sauce dip. Like many Shaoxing food customs, it has its roots in deprivation. According to local legend, there was once a rich man whose family gorged on meat and fish, but who was so mean-spirited that he fed his servants only rice and vegetables. His daughter-in-law came from a poor household and pitied the servants, but she didn't dare challenge him. She secretly tucked pieces of pork into the rice as it cooked, and seasoned it with just a few pinches of salt. Her father-in-law, thinking that she had given the servants nothing more than rice, commended her frugality, while the servants delighted in their unusually nourishing meals.

Rice is normally served towards the end of a meal, especially on more formal occasions. Many Chinese people avoid eating rice or other grain foods while drinking alcohol because the combination is thought to cause an unhealthy fermentation in the stomach. This is why, if you start eating rice at a Chinese meal, your host may assume that you have drunk your fill of wine or spirits.

When cooking with rice, remember that leftovers should be cooled and refrigerated as quickly as possible, and definitely within four hours (rice that is left sitting around in warm temperatures can cause food poisoning). It's best not to keep cooked rice for more than three days.

Plain white rice

bai mi fan 白米饭

Across southern China, people typically eat long-grain white rice, which is non-glutinous but still somewhat sticky, so it forms chopstickable clumps. Chinese rice vendors often sell Thai fragrant rice, among many other varieties, and since it is also easily available outside China I suggest using it here.

I must admit that I normally make rice in an electric rice cooker, because it makes perfect rice every time and frees me to concentrate on other dishes. This, however, is the most common traditional method for making plain white rice. Quantities depend upon appetite: in general, this amount yields enough to feed 4 people with 2–3 small rice bowls each. Any leftovers may be used to make soupy rice or fried rice.

2½ cups (600g) Thai fragrant rice

1 quart (1.1 liters) water

Put the rice in a bowl, cover it with cold water and use your hand to swirl it around. Drain and repeat until the water is clear. Tip into a sieve and leave to drain completely.

Put the rice in a heavy-bottomed pan with the measured water and bring to the boil over a high flame. Stir to dislodge any grains sticking to the bottom, then boil for a few minutes until the surface of the rice is dry and covered in little round breathing holes. Cover the pan tightly, turn the heat down as low as possible and cook for 12–15 minutes, until tender.

(To make traditional steamer rice, bring your rice to the boil in plenty of water, then simmer for 7–8 minutes, until nearly cooked but still a little hard and starchy in the center of the grains. Drain the rice (reserving the water to use as "rice soup" if desired—see page 233), turn it into a steamer basket lined with clean muslin and steam over a high flame for about 10 minutes, until fragrant and fully cooked.)

Plain short-grain white rice

bai mi fan 白米饭

In Jiangnan, and particularly in Shanghai, people like to eat a short-grain white rice similar to Japanese sushi rice, which absorbs less water than long-grain rice. I often serve sushi rice with Jiangnan food. One delicious and simple way of eating this rice, which was regarded as a treat in times when meat was expensive, is to stir a little lard and soy sauce into hot, freshly cooked rice and sprinkle with finely chopped spring onion greens. This recipe serves around 4.

2½ cups (600g) sushi rice

3⅓ cups (800ml) water

Put the rice in a bowl, cover with cold water and use your hand to swirl it around. Drain and repeat until the water is clear. Tip into a sieve and leave to drain completely. Put the rice in a heavy-bottomed pan with the measured water. Bring to the boil over a medium flame, stir, then turn the heat up high. Boil until holes open up in the surface of the rice. Cover, turn the heat down very low and cook for 20 minutes. Turn off the heat and leave the rice, covered and undisturbed, for 20 minutes, then remove the lid and fluff up the rice.

Plain congee
bai zhou 白粥

Congee is the kindest breakfast food: silky and gentle on the stomach, quiet and soothing. In the Jiangnan region, it is usually served unseasoned, accompanied by steamed buns and perky little relishes such as salted duck eggs, pickles and fermented tofu. Fried or poached eggs or other little dishes, perhaps leftovers from last night's dinner, may also be served. Eat the congee with a spoon and use your chopsticks for the relishes, buns and other dishes.

In China, congee is regarded as the ultimate comfort food. The Song dynasty poet Lu You, who lived in Shaoxing, even suggested that eating it could be a way of achieving immortality. Eating congee can also be a subtle moral statement; the Qing dynasty gourmet Yuan Mei wrote an excoriating description of contemporaries who preferred ostentatious delicacies to plain, well-cooked food, and recounted going home after a confusing banquet of 40 dishes and 16 snacks and having to eat congee to appease his hunger.

Serve your congee with a strong, salty relish, such as cubes of fermented tofu, a dish of pickles (homemade or bought in easy sachets in a Chinese shop) or hard-boiled salted duck eggs. If you like, add steamed buns, sweet or savory, reheated leftover dishes or fried peanuts.

See pages 240–41 for a photograph of a typical Zhejiang congee breakfast. This includes:
  Fried peanuts
  Fried eggs with light soy sauce
  Plain congee
  Red bean paste buns (page 285)
  Hard-boiled salted duck eggs
  Red fermented tofu
  Sweet-and-sour pickled ginger (page 330)

¾ cup (150g) Thai fragrant rice or sushi rice
½ tsp salt
2 tsp cooking oil
2½ quarts (2.4 liters) water

Rinse and drain the rice. Mix it with the salt and oil and set aside for half an hour, then rinse and drain again.

Bring the measured water to the boil in a heavy-bottomed pan over a high flame, add the rice, return to the boil, partially cover the pan with a lid and simmer gently for about 1½ hours, stirring the mixture from time to time. After a while the rice grains will burst open; by the end of the cooking they will have melted into the water to form one soft mass. Serve the congee with your choice of accompaniments.

Black glutinous rice congee

Instead of using just one kind of rice, use 2 oz (50g) black glutinous rice, 2 oz (50g) white glutinous rice and 2 oz (50g) Thai fragrant rice. Omit the salt and oil, but otherwise proceed as in the main recipe. The black rice colors the congee a beautiful purple. This variation is served for breakfast at the Yechun Teahouse in Yangzhou.

Chicken congee

ji zhou 鸡粥

This is a sister dish to the white-chopped chicken on page 70—the two are traditionally eaten together, particularly as a late-night snack. The habit is said to have emerged in Shanghai in the 1920s, and by the 1930s chicken congee and white-chopped chicken were one of the city's most famous "small eats." One street vendor, a Shaoxing native called Zhang Runniu, ran a much-loved stall in Shanghai selling cooked chicken, chicken congee and a broth thick with the jellied bloods of both chicken and duck.

An old cookery book in my collection includes a striking photograph of chicken congee with the traditional condiments and little dishes of all the parts of the poached chicken, including not only meat but also wings, feet, gizzards, intestines, liver, heart, unformed eggs and testicles (the latter two from two different birds, one presumes).

¾ cup (150g) sushi rice
2½ quarts (2.5 liters) chicken stock (see page 317)
Salt

To serve:
Good soy sauce
Thinly sliced spring onions, green parts only
Finely chopped fresh ginger
Sesame oil

Rinse and drain the rice. Put it in a pot with the chicken stock and bring to the boil. Give the rice a good stir, scraping the bottom of the pan to prevent sticking, then half-cover the pan and simmer gently for 1½ hours, stirring from time to time, until the rice grains have burst open and you have a thick congee. Do keep an eye on the pot to make sure the rice doesn't catch on the bottom. Towards the end of the cooking, season lightly with salt.

Serve the congee with a sprinkling of soy sauce, spring onion and ginger and a few drips of sesame oil. If you want to be really Shanghainese, eat it with a dish of white-chopped chicken and soy sauce for dipping (see page 70).

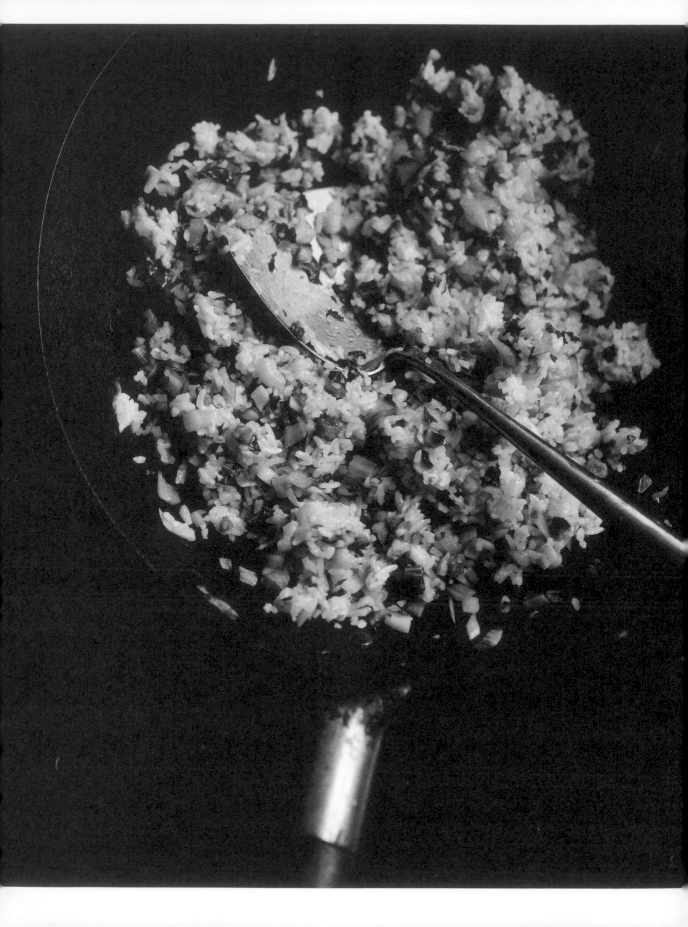

Shanghai fried rice with salt pork and green bok choy

xian rou cai fan 咸肉菜饭

In a backstreet not far from Nanjing Road in the heart of Shanghai, there's a small diner that serves one of the most delicious versions of this classic local rice dish I've tasted. The plump, glossy rice, studded with salt pork, threaded with the bright green of bok choy, is irresistible. Everyone eats it, in the Chinese manner, with a bowl of broth to refresh the palate (a simple stock with sliced spring onion greens will do). This is my version of their recipe, which includes red onion and shiitake mushrooms. This dish is usually made with short-grain white rice—Japanese sushi rice is what I use at home—but it will also taste delicious with long-grain Thai fragrant rice. For the most sizzlingly delicious results, use lard as your cooking oil. Feel free to vary the quantities of pork or vegetables as you please. Spinach may be used as a substitute for the bok choy.

Another traditional way to make this dish is to begin by frying the salt pork and greens, preferably in lard, then add raw washed rice and water. Bring to the boil, then cover and slow cook, as in the recipe for plain white rice.

4 dried shiitake mushrooms
½ small red onion
4 oz (100g) salt pork, pancetta or unsmoked bacon
10 oz (275g) green bok choy (3–4 heads)
3 cups (600g) cooked and cooled sushi rice (1½ cups /300g when uncooked)
2 tbsp cooking oil, preferably lard
1 tbsp finely chopped fresh ginger
1 tsp sesame oil
Salt and ground white pepper

Cover the shiitake mushrooms in boiling water and leave to soak for half an hour. Finely chop the onion. Remove any rind from the pork and chop it into dice. Remove the mushroom stalks and dice the caps. Chop the green bok choy a little more coarsely than the other ingredients. Break the rice up into small clumps to make stir-frying easier.

Heat the cooking oil in a seasoned wok over a medium flame. Add the pork and onion and stir-fry gently until the onion is tender and the pork has released its oil and is fragrant but not browned. Add the mushrooms and ginger, turn up the heat to high and stir-fry briefly until fragrant.

Tip in the rice and stir-fry over a high heat, breaking it up as you go. When the rice is piping hot and smells delicious, season with salt and pepper. (If you are eating the rice as a main meal, it will need to be saltier than if you are eating it with other dishes.) Add the bok choy and continue to stir-fry until the vegetable is piping hot and just cooked. Remove from the heat, stir in the sesame oil and serve.

Vegetarian version

Vegetarians can simply omit the meat in either the main recipe or its variation to make simple *cai fan* ("vegetable rice")—although Chinese cooks would still tend to stir-fry the rice with lard to enhance its fragrance.

Yangzhou fried rice

yang zhou chao fan 扬州炒饭

Late one night, I dropped into my friend Yang Bin's restaurant in the old quarter of Yangzhou for a bowlful of noodles, and happened also to meet his cooking master, Huang Wanqi. Chef Huang started talking about a 2,000-year-old gastronomic text, "The Root of Tastes" (*ben wei pian*), and told me he thought Yangzhou cooking best represented the subtle magic it described. He went on to explain the mysteries of Yangzhou fried rice, the only dish from this ancient gastronomic capital that has so far achieved international fame. He told me how to cook the secondary ingredients in chicken broth, and discussed the different roles that beaten egg could play in the dish. "If you begin by frying the beaten egg, and then add the rice," he said, "you will have 'golden fragments' of egg in the rice (*sui jin fen*). If, instead, you fry the rice and then pour in the egg, the golden liquid coats each grain of rice, so it's like 'silver wrapped in gold' (*jin guo yin*)." Both, he said, were traditional methods.

You don't have to go into such detail to appreciate this dish, one of the finest variations on the fried rice theme. The rice is speckled with little nuggets of delicious ingredients and infused with the umami richness of chicken stock. The following is my version, which omits the hard-to-find luxuries of sea cucumber and freshwater crabmeat, but otherwise follows the traditional method. If you want to make the totally authentic version, add ¾ oz (25g) chopped, soaked dried sea cucumber and ¾ oz (25g) freshwater crabmeat, and substitute tiny freshwater shrimp for the saltwater shrimp.

2 dried shiitake mushrooms
¾ oz (25g) pork tenderloin
¾ oz (25g) small peeled shrimp, fresh or frozen, cooked or uncooked
¾ oz (25g) Spanish or Chinese cured ham, steamed briefly
¾ oz (25g) cooked chicken
¾ oz (25g) bamboo shoot (optional)
3 spring onions, green parts only
1 large egg, plus an egg yolk
2½ cups (600g) cold, cooked Thai fragrant rice (1 cup/250g when uncooked)
5 tbsp cooking oil
¾ oz (25g) fresh or frozen peas or cooked green soybeans
2 tsp Shaoxing wine
1 cup (200ml) chicken stock
Salt and ground white pepper

Cover the shiitake mushrooms in boiling water and leave to soak for half an hour, then remove the stalks. Cut the pork, shrimp, ham, chicken, mushroom caps and bamboo shoot, if using, into small dice. Thinly slice the spring onion greens. Beat the egg and egg yolk with a little salt and pepper. Break the rice up into small clumps to make it easier to fry.

Heat 2 tablespoons of the oil in a seasoned wok over a high flame. Add the pork and shrimp and stir-fry briefly until the pork is pale. Add the ham, chicken, mushrooms, peas or beans and bamboo shoot, if using, and continue to stir-fry for 1–2 minutes, until everything is hot and sizzling. Add the Shaoxing wine, then pour in the stock and bring to the boil. Season with salt, then pour off into a bowl and set aside.

Rinse and dry the wok and return it to the heat with the remaining oil. When the oil is hot, add the beaten egg mixture and swirl it around the base of the wok. When the egg is half-cooked, add all the rice and stir-fry, breaking up any clumps. When the rice is very hot, smells delicious and makes a popping sound around the edges of the wok, add the reserved ingredients in their stock sauce. Mix well and continue to stir-fry for another 30 seconds or so, seasoning with salt or pepper if you wish. Stir in the spring onion greens and serve.

Soy-sauce fried rice

This simple fried rice is popular in Jiangnan; simply stir-fry leftover rice and add soy sauce to taste. A rich, traditional Chinese soy sauce is ideal; otherwise add light soy for salt and flavor, and a little dark soy to provide a deep brown luster.

"Japanese" fava bean rice

yuan guo wo dou fan 原锅倭豆饭

This is my re-creation of a wonderful rice dish served at the Crock-Duck-Dog (*gang ya gou*) restaurant in Ningbo, where they make and serve it in a weighty cast-iron pot. The scent and richness of the salt pork permeate the rice, and the beans make it even more delicious. They are known by an unusual dialect name, *wo dou* or "Japanese" beans, using an archaic and derogatory name for Japan. According to the menu, they acquired this name during the Ming dynasty, when Japanese pirates would harass the people of the Zhoushan archipelago every summer and steal all the fava beans that had just been harvested. Sick of this looting, one year local people poisoned the beans and killed all the pirates, after which they triumphantly renamed the beans.

The dish is traditionally eaten in Ningbo during the Beginning of Summer (*li xia*) solar term of the traditional calendar. It would also work well with peas or green soybeans.

1 cup (250g) sushi or Thai fragrant rice
3 oz (75g) bacon (smoked or unsmoked) or pancetta
1 tbsp lard or cooking oil
5 oz (150g) shelled, skinned fava beans (about ¾ lb/350–400g in their pods)
1 tbsp thinly sliced spring onions, green parts only
Salt

Rinse the rice in several changes of water until the water runs clear. Set aside in a sieve to drain completely. If the bacon has rinds, slice them off and reserve them. Cut the bacon or pancetta into ½ in (1cm) slices or small cubes. Bring a pan of water to the boil, blanch the bacon briefly, then drain it.

Put the lard or cooking oil in a heavy-bottomed pan with a tight-fitting lid and heat over a high flame. Add the meat and rinds, if you have them, and stir-fry until they smell delicious. Remove and discard the rinds, if using. Add the beans and stir them into the fragrant oil. Add the rice and 1⅓ cups (300ml) cold water and season with salt (remember the bacon is already salty). Stir well, scraping the bottom of the pan. Cook over a high flame for a few minutes, without stirring, until small holes appear on the surface. Cover the pan, transfer to a very low flame and cook gently for 20 minutes. Serve with a sprinkling of spring onion greens.

Leftover rice omelet

mi fan ji dan bing 米饭鸡蛋饼

When I was staying on Hangzhou restaurateur Dai Jianjun's organic farm in southern Zhejiang, a young chef made a sweet omelet with leftover rice for breakfast one day. It was unexpectedly delicious—the rice gave the eggs an almost cakey texture—and I've been making versions of it ever since, both sweet, as in the original, and savory. It's a good way of using up irritatingly small amounts of leftover rice. The quantities are not critical, so please use what you have and feel free to improvise. Both versions make a delightful dish for breakfast or a main meal.

On that November morning on the farm, the omelet was just one of a spread of dishes that included congee with black pickled cucumber, slivers of preserved mustard tuber stir-fried with a little pork, fried eggs, sweet potato chips with honey, corn cobs steamed in their husks and little steamed buns.

3 large eggs
½ cup (100g) leftover cooked rice
2 tbsp cooking oil

For the sweet version:
1 tbsp superfine sugar

For the savory version:
A handful of chopped Chinese chives or spring onion greens
Salt

Beat the eggs and stir in the rice, with your choice of sweet or savory additional ingredients.

Heat the oil in a seasoned wok or an omelet pan over a high flame. Pour in the egg mixture and swirl it around the base of the pan. Reduce the heat to medium, cover and fry until the under side is golden. Flip the omelet over.

When the omelet is golden on both sides and just cooked through, remove from the heat. Cut into strips or wedges and and pile them up prettily on a serving plate.

Soupy rice with chopped greens

cai pao fan 菜泡饭

"Soaked" or soupy rice is an excellent way of using up leftovers. All you need to do is reheat yesterday's rice in stock or water with any little tidbits you have hanging around, and perhaps a smidgeon of lard for extra richness. Not surprisingly, there are many variations on this theme. In Zhenjiang I once had a wonderful version made with chopped greens, salt pork and dried shiitake, while a Hangzhou favorite is soupy rice with morsels of intensely flavored soy sauce–cured duck. At home I often make soupy rice with brown rice, which has an even more delightful texture: silky and chewy at the same time. The mouthfeel of soupy rice, with its individual rice grains, is distinct from the mouthfeel of congee, in which rice and liquid fuse into one voluptuous mass.

There's no need to weigh and measure ingredients for this kind of dish: the measurements in the recipe are just a guide. Add enough liquid to generously cover but not overwhelm the rice, which will swell and become juicy in the stock. Season the rice properly if you're planning to make a meal of it; under-season if you'll be eating it with other dishes or just a salty relish—cubes of fermented tofu, perhaps, or a hard-boiled salted duck egg or some pickles.

4 oz (100g) fresh shiitake mushrooms
6 oz (175g) green bok choy
1½ tbsp lard or cooking oil
2½ cups (600ml) stock
1¼ cups (300g) leftover cooked rice (¾ cup/150g when uncooked)
Salt and ground white pepper

Remove the mushroom stalks and thickly slice the caps. Chop the bok choy into bite-sized pieces. Heat the lard or cooking oil in a seasoned wok over a high flame. Add the mushrooms and stir-fry until softened; add the bok choy and continue to stir-fry until just wilted. Set aside.

Bring the stock to the boil in a wok or saucepan. Add the leftover rice, breaking up any clumps, bring to the boil again and cook until just heated through. Stir in the bok choy and mushrooms and season with salt and pepper. Serve.

Stir-fried rice cake with scrambled egg and dried shrimp

qing cai chao nian gao 青菜炒年糕

The Chinese name of New Year's rice cake is *nian gao*, which means "higher every year"—a typically auspicious name for a food traditionally made during the Lunar New Year holiday, but now eaten all year round. It's a squishy, sticky foodstuff made by pounding cooked rice with a wooden cudgel until smooth and elastic, then forming it into cakes that are sliced before cooking, and is a particular speciality of Ningbo and Shanghai. Its culinary applications are many and varied: it can be stir-fried with all kinds of ingredients, simmered in a broth with vegetables, wokked in a brown sugar syrup, or frosted with fine sugar and powdered seaweed. Many Chinese supermarkets sell dried sliced *nian gao*, which must be soaked in cold water to soften it, but I recommend buying fresh or frozen Korean *nian gao*, which is increasingly sold in Chinese supermarkets and can be used directly from the package. It normally comes in the form of oval slices or strips.

This fresh or frozen *nian gao* has become one of my go-to ingredients for fast, delicious, healthy suppers made with whatever odds and ends I have in the fridge. Just keep a pack in the fridge or freezer (unopened, it keeps well in the fridge), and the most fabulous one-dish lunch can be ready in half an hour. At home, I generally stir-fry it with some protein (perhaps an egg, or a little pork or chicken), at least one ingredient for umami flavors (such as dried shrimp or shiitake, or a little bacon) and some fresh leafy greens.

4 dried shiitake mushrooms
7 oz (200g) green bok choy
1 large egg
3 tbsp cooking oil
3 tbsp papery dried shrimp
¾ lb (350g) Korean sliced rice cake
¾ cup (150ml) stock or water
Salt and ground white pepper

Cover the shiitake mushrooms in boiling water and leave to soak for at least half an hour. Drain well, remove the stalks and slice the caps into slivers. Cut the green bok choy across the leaves into ½ in (1cm) ribbons. Beat the egg in a small bowl.

Heat 1 tablespoon of the oil in a seasoned wok over a high flame. Add the egg and stir-fry until barely cooked; remove from the wok and set aside. Return the wok to a high flame with another tablespoon of oil. Add the papery dried shrimp and stir-fry briefly until crisp and fragrant; set aside.

Return the wok to a high flame with the remaining tablespoon of oil. Add the shiitake slivers and stir-fry until fragrant. Add the bok choy and stir-fry until the leaves have wilted. Put the sliced rice cake on top of the greens in the wok, pour the stock or water around the edges and bring to the boil. Cover the wok with a lid, turn the heat down very low and cook gently for 2–3 minutes, until the rice cake has softened and is piping hot. Stir in egg and shrimp and season with salt and pepper. Serve immediately.

"English breakfast" rice cake

This variation is my own invention. Beat an egg and stir-fry until barely cooked; set aside. Stir-fry some chopped bacon until crisp; remove from the wok and set aside. Fry a spring onion white in the bacon-laced oil until fragrant; add soaked and sliced dried shiitake mushrooms and stir until they too smell wonderful. Add chopped choy sum or green bok choy and wilt in the hot oil. Add stock or water and cook gently as in the main recipe. Finally, stir in the egg and bacon with some thinly sliced spring onion greens, and season with salt and pepper.

Stir-fried rice cake with fresh clams

ge li chao nian gao 蛤蜊炒年糕

As you may already have realized, I love cooking with rice cake, which is faintly reminiscent, in its comforting, squishy stickiness, of Italian gnocchi. This is my version of a dish I enjoyed at the Guangming restaurant in Shanghai, where it was made with the strip version of the rice cake. The rice cake breathes in the sea-taste of the cooking liquor, infused with rice wine; the just-cooked clams and bok choy give it a delectable freshness. Think of this, perhaps, as a Shanghainese version of *spaghetti alle vongole*.

In Shanghai they tend to use chopped shepherd's purse, which speckles the entire dish with green, but I've suggested the more easily available green bok choy. (If you can get shepherd's purse, chop it finely and add to the wok just before the clams and liquor; it doesn't need stir-frying first.) You can use more clams if you are feeling extravagant.

6 oz (175g) green bok choy
2 spring onions, white parts only
1⅓ lbs (600g) small clams, in their shells
1½ tbsp Shaoxing wine
¾ lb (350g) Korean rice cake strips
2 tbsp cooking oil
½ oz (15g) fresh ginger, peeled and sliced
Salt and ground white pepper

Slice the bok choy widthways into ½ in (1cm) strips (if you are using small baby bok choy, simply cut them in half lengthways). Smack the spring onion whites with the flat side of a Chinese cleaver or a rolling pin to loosen their fibers.

Wash the clams thoroughly, discarding any that are open. Put them in a saucepan with the Shaoxing wine and 4 tablespoons water, cover with a lid, then steam over a high flame for 2–3 minutes, until the clams have opened. Remove them with a slotted spoon, reserving the cooking liquor. Use chopsticks to pick the clams out of the shells, and set them aside. (If you wish, you can keep a few in their shells.) Bring a pan of water to the boil. Add the rice cake strips and steep over a gentle flame for a minute or so to warm through. Drain.

Heat the oil in a seasoned wok over a high flame. Add the ginger and spring onion and stir-fry until they smell wonderful. Add the bok choy, stir once or twice, tip in the drained rice cake slices and stir-fry until the bok choy has wilted. Add the clam meat and cooking liquor, leaving any grit in the saucepan. Stir briefly to incorporate and season with salt and pepper. Serve.

"Toothless" glutinous rice dumplings with pork and leafy greens

qing cai rou si bie zi tuan 青菜肉丝瘪子团

The best-known glutinous rice dumplings are the sweet ones: wobbly spheres stuffed with sweet black sesame paste known as *tang yuan* that are traditionally eaten at the Lantern festival at the end of the Chinese New Year. In Jiangnan, however, they also like to eat them savory, stuffed perhaps with minced pork or some fragrant preserved vegetable or, as in this recipe, unstuffed but served in a savory soup.

These glutinous rice dumplings bear some resemblance to gnocchi, with dimples that are thought to resemble the sunken cheeks of a toothless person—hence the extraordinary name of the dish. They can be eaten sweet or savory, and are a favorite Suzhou dish, particularly for breakfast; you can vary the vegetable ingredients as you please. Chef Jiang Meizhen taught me how to make them in the kitchens of the Wumen Renjia restaurant in Suzhou.

4 oz (100g) pork tenderloin
1 tsp Shaoxing wine
10 oz (275g) green bok choy
1 cup (250g) glutinous rice flour
1 quart (1 liter) chicken stock
2 tbsp cooking oil or lard
A few slices of peeled fresh ginger
Salt and ground white pepper

Cut the pork into slivers and put it in a bowl with ⅛ teaspoon salt and the Shaoxing wine. Mix well. Trim the bok choy and cut it into bite-sized pieces.

Put the glutinous rice flour in a bowl. Add ¾–1 cup (175–200ml) warm water—just enough to make a cohesive but fairly stiff dough. Knead until smooth. Roll the dough into 2 or 3 cylinders around ½ in (3cm) in diamater. Cut or break off 1–1½ in (2–3cm) pieces and roll them into balls. Flatten each ball between the palms of your hands, then press your index finger into the centers to make deep dimples.

Bring a pan of water to the boil. Add the dumplings, stir once to prevent sticking, then boil for about 2 minutes, until they float to the surface. Remove with a slotted spoon, place in a bowl of cold water and set aside.

Bring the stock to the boil and keep warm. Heat 1 tablespoon of the oil in a seasoned wok over a high flame, add the pork and stir-fry until just cooked. Set aside. Heat the remaining oil in the wok, add the ginger and stir-fry until it smells delicious. Add the stock and the bok choy, bring to the boil and season with salt and white pepper (remember that the dumplings are unseasoned, so the soup should be well salted). Add the dumplings and pork strips, boil to heat through, then serve.

NOODLES

In Suzhou, there's an old noodle shop called Zhu Hongxing that was founded in the 1930s and immortalized in the novella *The Gourmet* by local writer Lu Wenfu, whose greedy protagonist wakes every morning looking forward to his breakfast there. Wooden slats pegged to the wall above the counter announce the names of every dish: soup noodles topped with flash-fried eel or a slice of slow-cooked pork, steamed "soup" dumplings, pickles … Whenever I'm in Suzhou I like to breakfast at Zhu Hongxing. I'll order a bowlful of plain "springtime" noodles in broth (see page 260) with a side dish of heavenly slow-cooked pork or slippery shrimp, a smacked cucumber salad and

pickled radish, and perhaps, if I'm really hungry, a little steamerful of juicy buns.

Across the Jiangnan region, where rice is the staple food, noodles are considered to be a "small eat" (*xiao chi*) rather than a proper meal, a snack to be rustled up at home or eaten in casual restaurants. In the countryside, people sometimes make their own noodles, rolling out a firm wheaten dough, folding it into several layers, then slicing it into slender ribbons. In the cities, they are still often freshly made and eaten.

Some well-known local noodle dishes feature ingredients that are hard to find outside the region, like the "shrimp–exploded–eel" noodles of

Hangzhou and the famous crabmeat and yellow croaker noodles served at A Niang's cafe on a tree-lined street in Shanghai's former French Concession. A Niang's opens at eleven every morning, and by five past the hour the place is crammed with jovial, clamorous people waiting expectantly at their tables. The crabmeat noodles, in particular, are divine, flecked with orange crab coral, laced with ginger, vinegar and a hint of sweetness. In Nanjing, people like to breakfast on a bowlful of slippery bean-thread noodles topped with assorted duck offal and fried tofu puffs (*ya xue fen si tang*), the plentiful offal a side effect of the local obsession with saltwater duck.

Happily, some of the region's classic noodle dishes travel well. Shanghai noodles with dried shrimp and spring onion oil (see page 258) is one of the staples of my own kitchen, and Hangzhou "blanched slice" noodles (see page 262) make a satisfying lunch. If you can, buy fresh Chinese wheat noodles, although dried ones will do. Alkaline noodles made with lye water (*jian shui mian*) have a yellowish tint and a delightfully springy texture. This chapter also includes a couple of recipes for hand-made pastas of different shapes—the "cat's ears" are great fun to make and utterly delicious.

Shanghai stir-fried chunky noodles

shang hai cu chao mian 上海粗炒面

This Shanghainese dish is made with thick, bouncy noodles like fresh Japanese udon, which are given a dark caramel tint by soy sauce and freshened up with barely cooked greens. Pork slivers make a delicious addition, but vegetarians may omit them and still enjoy the dish. In Shanghai, the greens will be the tenderest little sprouts of green bok choy, known as "chicken feather greens"; at home I often use baby spinach because the leaves need to be tender enough to wilt quickly in the heat of the wok. According to some accounts, the recipe was developed by Shanghainese immigrants in Hong Kong.

This is a meal in one dish and makes a quick, satisfying lunch. It serves 2 as a meal, 4 or more if served with other Chinese dishes.

4 oz (100g) lean pork
15 oz (425g) fresh Shanghai noodles or Japanese udon
2½ tbsp cooking oil
9 oz (200g) baby green bok choy or 2 large handfuls of baby spinach
1½ tsp dark soy sauce
1 tbsp light soy sauce

Salt and ground white pepper

For the marinade:
½ tsp light soy sauce
½ tbsp Shaoxing wine
2 tsp potato starch
1 tbsp beaten egg or 1 tbsp cold water

Cut the pork evenly into thin slices, then into slivers. Add the marinade ingredients and mix well.

Bring a pan of water to the boil. Add the noodles and cook for 2 minutes (fresh Shanghai and udon noodles are already half-cooked when you buy them, which is why this doesn't take long). Turn the cooked noodles into a colander and cool under the cold tap. Shake them dry. Drip over ½ tablespoon oil and stir in thoroughly to prevent sticking.

Heat 1 tablespoon of the oil in a seasoned wok over a high flame. Add the pork strips and stir-fry swiftly to separate them. When they are just cooked, remove from the wok and set aside. Clean and re-season the wok if necessary, then return it to a high flame with the remaining oil. Add the noodles and stir-fry until piping hot, adding both soy sauces and seasoning with salt and pepper. Add the bok choy or spinach and continue to stir-fry briefly until wilted. Finally, stir in the pork. Serve.

Shanghai noodles with dried shrimp and spring onion oil

kai yang cong you mian 开洋葱油面

This Shanghainese recipe also appears in *Every Grain of Rice*, but I had to include it here because I find it one of the most indispensable Jiangnan recipes. The combination of oil infused with the fragrance of spring onion and dried shrimp and the umami savoriness of soy sauce is irresistible, however simple it sounds.

I eat this dish so often that I have taken to making the flavored oil in large quantities and keeping it in the fridge—although I'm not even sure it requires refrigeration. I keep fresh Chinese noodles in my freezer too, which means that I can have a bowlful of this gorgeous snack a mere 10 minutes after thinking of it: all that's required is to boil some water, cook the noodles from frozen and dress them in the fragrant oil and light soy sauce. I eat them for breakfast, lunch and midnight feasts, sometimes with a salad on the side. The recipe is said to have been invented by a street vendor near the City God Temple in Shanghai. Serves 2.

2 tbsp dried shrimp
2 tsp Shaoxing wine
4 spring onions
4–5 tsp light or tamari soy
   sauce, to taste
6 tbsp cooking oil
7 oz (200g) dried noodles of
   your choice or 10 oz
   (300g) fresh noodles
Salt

Put the dried shrimp in a small bowl with the Shaoxing wine and just enough hot water to cover them and leave to soak for half an hour. Smack the spring onions slightly with the flat side of a Chinese cleaver or a rolling pin to loosen their fibers, then cut them evenly into 2½–2¾ in (6–7cm) sections. Pour the soy sauce into your serving bowl.

Heat the oil in a seasoned wok over a high flame. Add the spring onions and stir-fry until they are turning a little golden. Drain the shrimp, add them to the wok and continue to stir-fry until the spring onions are well browned and wonderfully fragrant, but not burned. Then set aside this fragrant oil, along with the spring onions and shrimp.

Bring a large pan of water to the boil and cook the noodles to your liking, then drain them well and put them in the serving bowl. Put the spring onions, shrimp and their fragrant oil on top and serve. Mix everything together very well with a pair of chopsticks before eating.

"Springtime" noodles
yang chun mian 阳春面

This is the simplest form of Jiangnan soup noodle, and is made in homes across the region. It consists solely of plain wheaten noodles served in a bowlful of clear stock seasoned with dark soy sauce and garnished with sesame oil and sliced spring onion greens, without any meat, fish or vegetables. The noodles peep shyly out of their dark, aromatic broth.

The name *yang chun mian* literally means "springtime noodles," although some sources suggest it's rather a reference to "Indian summer" (*xiao yang chun*). Eat these as a snack on their own, or with another dish or two on the side. Serves 2.

1 tsp dark soy sauce
2 tsp light soy sauce
½ tsp sesame oil
2½ cups (600ml) stock

10 oz (300g) fresh Chinese wheat noodles
2 tbsp thinly sliced spring onions, green parts only

Divide the soy sauces and sesame oil between 2 serving bowls. Bring the stock to the boil and keep it warm. Bring a pan of water to the boil. Add the noodles, separate them with chopsticks and boil until cooked to your liking. Drain well.

Pour the hot stock over the seasonings in the bowls. Divide the noodles between the serving bowls and garnish with the spring onions.

Hangzhou late-night noodles

rou si ban chuan mian 肉丝拌川面

It was midnight in a Hangzhou backstreet, and Dai Jianjun had taken me to find a famous peripatetic street stall serving *ban chuan* noodles, a favorite local snack. The cook, wild-haired and sweat-faced, stirred at a relentless, machine-like pace. Into her blackened wok she flung handfuls of shredded pork, tofu, pig's kidney and heart, adding some noodles and seasoning with soy sauce and a bright flash of yellow chives, their pungent aromas singing out into the warm autumn air. Her husband, standing behind her, took orders and money, and around them a gaggle of customers sat in near-darkness at ramshackle tables. I couldn't take my eyes off the woman. Like an Olympian athlete of street food, tough and muscular, on and on she toiled, stirring with a brutal, determined rhythm.

Dai told me that the couple's pledge was to "cook each bowlful of noodles separately" (*yi wan mian yi shao*), which is why they were so delicious. Although the woman's work was hard, they made a fortune, enough to send their child to college. Dai and I sat on rickety stools and slurped the strong, bouncy noodles with their sting of offal and the heady fragrance of chives.

This recipe, my tribute to that Amazonian street vendor, is best made with alkaline noodles, which have a yellowish color, a particular taste and a springy texture. If you can't find them, use fresh wheat noodles, or egg noodles if you prefer. For convenience, I've taken the liberty of cooking enough for two, and added mushrooms and preserved vegetable instead of the offal. Serves 2.

4 oz (100g) lean pork
3 oz (75g) spiced or smoked firm tofu
2½ oz (60g) Sichuan preserved vegetable
2 oz (50g) oyster mushrooms
3 oz (75g) Chinese yellow chives
2 spring onions, green parts only
10 oz (300g) fresh Chinese wheat noodles
2 tbsp cooking oil
1 tbsp light soy sauce
1 tsp sesame oil
Salt

For the marinade:
⅛ tsp salt
½ tsp Shaoxing wine
½ tsp potato starch

Cut the pork into slivers. Add the marinade ingredients with 1 teaspoon cold water and mix well. Cut the tofu, Sichuan preserved vegetable and mushrooms into fine slivers. Cut the chives and spring onions into 3 in (8cm) lengths.

Bring a pan of water to the boil. Add the noodles and cook them to your liking, then rinse them under the cold tap and drain well. Heat 1 tablespoon of the cooking oil in a seasoned wok over a high flame. Add the pork and stir-fry until just cooked, then set aside. Return the wok to the flame with the remaining oil. Add the preserved vegetable and stir-fry briefly until you can smell it. Add the tofu and mushrooms and stir-fry until the mushrooms are just cooked.

Return the pork to the wok, add the noodles and stir-fry vigorously to mix everything together, seasoning with the soy sauce and salt (remember the preserved vegetable is salty). When the noodles are piping hot, add the chives and stir-fry briefly until they smell wonderful. Stir in the spring onion greens and then, off the heat, the sesame oil. Serve.

Hangzhou "blanched slice" noodles

pian'er chuan mian 片儿川面

Nearly 1,000 years ago, the Song dynasty court was chased south to Hangzhou by barbarian invaders, which is held to explain some of the northern influences, not only in the city's cooking, but also in the local dialect. Unusually for the southern Chinese, the people of Hangzhou pepper their speech with the burred 'r's normally associated with northern tongues, as in the name of this typical Hangzhou noodle dish, *pian'er chuan*. It's a simple, satisfying concoction of soupy noodles, pickled greens, pork and bamboo shoot. Originally, it was called "blanched slices" (*pian'er cuan*) because the thinly sliced pork and bamboo shoot were briefly cooked in boiling water; later, the character for "blanch" (*cuan*) was replaced by one with a similar sound (*chuan*).

Legend says this dish was inspired by the Song dynasty poet and onetime governor of Hangzhou, Su Dongpo, who famously loved pork but wrote that he would rather renounce it than live in a home without bamboo, that traditional symbol of moral strength and poetic sensibility: "A man may become thin without pork," he wrote, "But without bamboo, he will become vulgar; and while a thin man may regain his plumpness, there is no cure for the scholar who has lost his refinement." Rest assured that in eating this dish of pork *and* bamboo, you can avoid both emaciation and vulgarity. It's a satisfying, hearty dish, and a meal in itself. Chef Dong Jinmu of the Dragon Well Manor restaurant showed me how to make it. Serves 2.

4 oz (100g) bamboo shoot
4 oz (100g) lean pork
1 tbsp cooking oil or lard
½ tbsp Shaoxing wine
4 oz (100g) snow vegetable
1 tbsp light soy sauce
½ tsp dark soy sauce

10 oz (300g) fresh Chinese wheat noodles
Salt
2 tsp lard (optional)
1 tbsp thinly sliced spring onions

Bring a pan of water to the boil. Cut the bamboo shoot into thin, bite-sized slices and blanch them briefly, then refresh them under cold tap water and drain. Cut the pork into thin slices of a similar size. Boil the kettle.

Heat the cooking oil or lard in a seasoned wok over a high flame. Add the pork and stir-fry to separate the slices, adding the Shaoxing wine as the meat turns pale. Add the bamboo shoot, stir-fry briefly, then tip in the snow vegetable. Stir-fry until it's all hot and fragrant, then add the soy sauces and 1⅓ cups (300ml) hot water. Bring to the boil, then turn the heat down low to keep warm.

Fill another pan with boiling water, add the noodles and stir with chopsticks to separate. When they are just cooked, drain the noodles and rinse briefly under the cold tap. Add them to the broth in the wok, with extra hot water if necessary to nearly cover the noodles. Return to the boil and season with salt, along with the lard for extra richness, if desired. Use tongs or chopsticks to transfer the noodles to serving bowls. Spoon over the soupy liquid and the pile the solid ingredients on top. Serve with a sprinkling of spring onions.

Stir-fried sweet potato noodles

ji xi chao fen si 绩溪炒粉丝

While traveling in southern Anhui province a few years ago, I tasted many marvelous and exotic dishes, yet this simple noodle dish from the town of Jixi made one of the deepest impressions. It's a glassy mound of savory noodles tossed with strips of tofu and pork, and infused with the sweet breath of spices from the tofu. Locals sometimes call it "Huizhou shark's fin" because the transparent, snaky strands of noodle resemble the luxurious dried shark's fin once brought home by rich Huizhou merchants from other parts of China. It's both an everyday dish and an essential fixture on the menus of rural feasts and weddings. According to tradition, the noodles should be served uncut as a symbol of long life and lifelong marriage.

Jixi is the hometown of many notable Chinese personages; it's also known as a hotbed of unexpectedly talented chefs or, as they say, "hidden dragons and crouching tigers" (cang long wo hu). Happily, when I visited Jixi I was able to sit down to lunch with six of these dragons and tigers, two of them brothers from a notable family of chefs. The version of this dish served that day was the best I tasted in Anhui, and I've tried to replicate it here. Any Jixi chef will insist that you cannot make the dish without using the plump, bouncy sweet potato noodles made in Jixi itself, but I can assure you that outsiders will adore this version, made with the sweet potato noodles you can find in any Chinatown. Serves 4–6 with rice and other dishes, as part of a Chinese meal.

4 oz (100g) dried sweet potato noodles
3 oz (75g) skinless pork belly
3 oz (75g) spiced firm tofu
2 garlic cloves
3 spring onions, green parts only
¼ red bell pepper, cored and deseeded
1 tbsp cooking oil
1 tbsp Shaoxing wine
1⅓ cups (300ml) stock
1 tsp dark soy sauce
2 tsp light soy sauce
1 tsp sesame oil
Salt

Cover the noodles with cold water and leave to soak for 2 hours or overnight. Cut the pork and tofu into ⅛ in (3–4mm) strips. Peel and slice the garlic. Cut the spring onion greens into 2 in (5cm) sections. Cut the red bell pepper into slivers. Before you start cooking, drain the noodles in a colander.

Heat the cooking oil in a seasoned wok over a high flame. Add the pork and stir-fry until it has turned pale. Add the garlic and firm tofu and continue to stir-fry for a minute or so, until everything smells delicious. Stir in the Shaoxing wine. Add the stock, noodles and soy sauces, stir well and bring to the boil. Season with salt. Cover the wok and continue to cook for 2 minutes, until the stock has almost all been absorbed by the noodles.

Lift the lid and give the noodles a stir once or twice to make sure they don't stick to the wok. Finally, stir in the spring onion greens and red bell pepper, allowing them to feel a quick lick of heat. Off the heat, stir in the sesame oil, then turn the noodles into a serving dish.

Cat's ears

mao er duo 猫耳朵

The Chinese and Italians love to battle it out over who invented noodles (a few years ago, the Chinese claimed to have clinched the argument by discovering a bowlful of 4000-year-old millet noodles on an archaeological site in northern Qinghai province). Perhaps they should take the dispute further to include the origins of orecchiette, or "little ears." In Xi'an in northwest China, home of the Terracotta Warriors, a food writer once welcomed me into his home for a feast of homemade *ma shi*, which turned out to be tiny orecchiette made with a regular Chinese noodle dough, which was cut into small pieces and then rolled with the thumb to make the characteristic "ear" shapes.

In Hangzhou, a famous local snack is "cat's ears" (*mao er duo*), small orecchiette made by exactly the same method but served in typical Jiangnan style in a rich chicken soup ornamented with green peas and little cubes of dark pink ham, white chicken meat and ivory bamboo shoot. It's a characteristically Hangzhou marriage of northern and southern influences that whispers of the flight south of the Song dynasty court in the twelfth century, and brings a delicate southern sensibility to a northern staple food. I've also encountered these little ears in southern Anhui, where Ling Jianjun, the chef who taught me how to make them, called them "white jade silkworm cocoons" (*bai yu yong*). You'll need a clean comb to make them. Serves 4–6 as part of a Chinese meal.

For the ears:
2 cups (250g) high-gluten flour, plus extra for dusting
½ tsp salt
½ tsp cooking oil

To serve:
2 dried shiitake mushrooms
2 oz (50g) bamboo shoot
3 oz (75g) cooked chicken breast
2 oz (50g) Spanish or Chinese cured ham, steamed briefly
3 oz (75g) frozen peas
1½ quarts (1.5 liters) chicken stock
Salt and ground white pepper

Mix the flour and salt together. Make a well in the center and gradually add enough water to make a dough, drawing the flour in from the edges as you go. Knead the dough until smooth and glossy, then cover with a wet tea towel and rest for 15 minutes.

Cut the dough in half. Put one half on a floured board and roll it out into a sheet about ⅛ in (4mm) thick. With a floured knife, cut it into ½ in (1cm) strips. Cut these strips into ½ in (1cm) squares, dusting with flour so they don't stick together. Put a clean comb on the board and dust it with flour, then put a square of dough on the teeth of the comb. Use your thumb to press the square away from you, across the teeth of the comb, and then to the right, so you roll it off the comb. You should end up with a curved "ear" shape with ridges on the outside. Repeat with the rest of the dough, dusting with flour so that the ears don't stick together.

Bring a big pan of water to the boil, salting it as you would for Italian pasta. Tip in the ears and give them a good stir. Boil for 1–2 minutes until the ears float, then drain in a colander and rinse under the cold tap until completely cold. Drain well, add the cooking oil and mix well to coat the ears and prevent sticking. Set aside in the fridge for 2 hours. Cover the shiitake mushrooms in boiling water and leave them to soften for at least half an hour.

Cut the bamboo shoot into ½ in (1cm) cubes and blanch in boiling water. Refresh under the cold tap and drain. Drain the mushrooms, discard the stalks and cut the caps into smaller cubes. Cut the chicken and ham into ½ in (1cm) cubes. Put the bamboo shoot, mushrooms, chicken, ham and peas in a pan with the chicken stock and bring to the boil. Add the cat's ears to the broth. Return to the boil and boil for 30 seconds to reheat. Season with salt and pepper and serve.

Rustic dough-wriggle soup with pickled greens

jia xiang mian ge da 家乡面疙瘩

This quick-fix noodle soup is a homely snack across the Jiangnan region. The pasta pieces are made by using a spoon or chopstick to scrape small pieces of a loose noodle dough directly into a potful of boiling water. In Chinese, the little rags of cooked dough are known as *ge da*, which translates literally as "swelling or lump"; not so appetizing in English, which is why I have taken the liberty of calling them "dough wriggles" instead. You will find variations on the dough wriggle theme across Jiangnan: near the Yellow Mountain in Anhui I lunched on a bowlful of what they called "flour fish," named for the slippery, fishlike qualities of the cooked dough wriggles, in a clear broth with pork, bamboo shoot and mushrooms; in Shaoxing, their dialect name refers to the chopsticks used to scrape the dough into scraps.

The following recipe was told to me by chef Niu Youqiang at the Liuying Binguan restaurant in Hangzhou. If you happen to have a fish stock to hand, the seasonings will suit it rather beautifully, although I've more often used chicken stock or a mixed Chinese stock for this dish. If you like, add some slivers of lean pork to the wok just before you tip in the snow vegetable and bamboo shoot, for extra flavor (no marinade is necessary for the pork). The recipe gives 4 substantial bowlfuls, but will serve 6 with other dishes as part of a Chinese meal.

1¾ cups (400g) low-gluten Chinese flour
2 spring onions, white parts only
2 oz (50g) bamboo shoot (optional)
2 tbsp cooking oil
⅓ oz (10g) fresh ginger, peeled and sliced
5 oz (150g) snow vegetable, chopped
1½ quarts (1.6 liters) stock
Salt and ground white pepper

Put the flour in a bowl and make a well in the center. Gradually add about 1½ cups (325ml) cold water, drawing in the flour from the edges as you stir with a wooden spoon. You should end up with a very wet dough that won't hold its shape. Set aside for about 10 minutes.

Smack the spring onion whites lightly with the flat side of a Chinese cleaver or a rolling pin to loosen their fibers. Bring a pan of water to the boil. Cut the bamboo shoot, if using, into thin slices and blanch for 1 minute, then drain well.

Heat 1 tablespoon of the oil in a seasoned wok over a high flame. Add the ginger and spring onion and stir-fry briefly until they smell wonderful. Add the snow vegetable and bamboo shoot, if using, and stir-fry a little longer until they too are fragrant. Pour in the stock and bring to the boil. Season with salt and pepper and keep warm.

Fill another large pan with water and bring it to the boil. Drip the remaining oil over your wet slick of dough and smear it over the surface. Smear a little oil over the back and front surfaces of a large metal spoon. Hold the bowl of dough over your pan of boiling water and use the spoon to cut narrow strips from the edges of the dough and drop them into the water. Keep rotating the bowl as you nibble away at the dough. Soon the water will be filled with dough scraps diving wildly around like live eels. Continue until you have used all the dough. When the dough scraps have all floated to the surface, scoop them out with a slotted spoon and drop them into the prepared stock. Bring to the boil, then turn into a soup tureen to serve.

DUMPLINGS
AND SNACKS

The Jiangnan region is home to a dazzling variety of dumplings and snacks, known collectively as *dian xin* (or, in the more familiar Cantonese, *dim sum*). If you wander the backstreets of the old Chinese quarter of Shanghai, you will often see cooks raising the lids of great griddle pans packed with juicy potsticker buns with toasty, golden bottoms. In Yangzhou, the Yechun Teahouse does a roaring breakfast trade in the daintiest and most delicious *baozi* (stuffed buns) I've ever encountered, while the people of Ningbo adore their wobbly glutinous rice balls stuffed with black sesame and scented with osmanthus.

Many snacks are prepared for specific festivals or in certain seasons. There are glutinous rice balls, a symbol of family unity, eaten at the Lantern festival at the end of the Chinese New Year, and squishy "green dumplings" (*qing tuan*) made with glutinous rice flour colored green by wild vegetable juice. Traditionally, these are made for the Qingming or "Clear Brightness" festival at the beginning of spring, when people visit family graves to pay their respects to their ancestors. Later, on the fifth day of the fifth lunar month, steamed parcels of glutinous rice wrapped in long indocalamus leaves are eaten on the Dragon Boat Festival or "Double-Fifth."

For the mid-autumn festival of the eighth lunar month, people traditionally worship the full moon

and eat round moon cakes in its honor. Most moon cakes are stuffed with sweet bean paste or sugared nuts, but in Jiangsu they also make them savory with light, flaky pastry stuffed with minced pork. On the ninth day of the ninth month is the Chongyang festival, which is marked with Chongyang cake, a multicolored layering of steamed glutinous rice and red bean paste that is sometimes decorated with colored flags.

One Hangzhou speciality is dainty "Victory Cakes" made from steamed ricemeal pressed into a patterned mold, which were first made, according to legend, during the Southern Song dynasty for the patriotic hero Yue Fei and his soldiers on their return from battle. Far more complicated to master is the Wu Mountain crisp fried pastry, a fragile cone of layered pastry dusted with powdered sugar—just one of a whole family of flaky pastries made from flour and lard. In Shanghai, people adore crisp "golden crabshells" filled with fat pork and spring onion, as well as the golden pinwheel disc known as a "spring onion oil pastry." The latter is a popular street snack, most famously made these days by a hunchbacked trader called A Da in his workshop in the former French Concession.

Prettiest and most frivolous of all were the old "boat snacks" (*chuan dian*) of Suzhou, which are rarely seen in modern times. In the past, the scenic lakes of Jiangnan were dotted with painted wooden boats that could be hired for an outing, along with singing girls and lavish catering. Among the tidbits that people nibbled on these diversions were steamed rice flour dumplings shaped to resemble fruits, vegetables and all manner of creatures. Sha Peizhi, the food scholar who runs a restaurant attached to the Suzhou Food Museum, once invited me for a tasting of traditional boat snacks, including pink "water caltrops," complete with horns and little green stems, glistening white heads of "garlic" filled with candied kumquat and orange "calabash gourds" made with mashed pumpkin and red bean paste.

Among the multitude of snacks of the Jiangnan region, a few remarkable specialities deserve separate mention. In Ningbo, glistening "lye-balls" (*hui zhi tuan*) are made of a glutinous rice flour dough mixed with a strained solution of rice-straw ash; they have a weird, wobbly texture and a sharp alkaline flavor reminiscent of fireworks. Also from Ningbo are the fairylike "dragon-and-phoenix golden cakes" (*jin tuan*), rounds of steamed rice dough that are rolled in pine pollen and then pressed into wooden molds carved with dragons and phoenixes. Another Ningbo speciality is the fabulous steamed rice flour sponge cake, which has the faintly sour taste of its

natural fermentation; it is often toasted and dusted with powdered sugar and powdered *tai cai* seaweed.

The making of most of these snacks is left to the professionals, and many demand a high level of specialist skill. I've included here a small selection of favorites that can be made at home without too much difficulty. Wrapping a *baozi* steamed bun or dumpling, which involves pinching the edge of a round of dough to enclose a stuffing, is a little tricky at first, but once you have grasped the basic technique, you can make them with all kinds of delicious fillings. Professional pastry chefs in Yangzhou may turn out perfectly elegant buns with more than 30 tiny pleats, but all you really need to be able to do is close them tightly so the filling does not escape. If you are making any type of stuffed bun or dumpling for the first time, start by using a reduced amount of filling, which will make the parcels easier to wrap; increase the amount of filling as you get the hang of the technique.

Shanghai potsticker buns

sheng jian man tou 生煎馒头

In the former French Concession of Shanghai, sunlight filters through the wutong trees that arch overhead, dappling the pavements. It's breakfast time, and already the shops and restaurants of Urumqi Street are bustling. A small, hectic cafe is filled with people slurping hot soymilk and dunking deep-fried *you tiao* dough sticks into their bowls. Outside, a tower of bamboo steamers is filled with glutinous rice dumplings and fluffy buns stuffed with pork and radish, hazy in a cloud of steam. In the entrance to her tobacco shop, a woman is frying up *sheng jian man tou*, one of Shanghai's most famous snacks. These golden-bottomed potsticker buns, often known in Chinese simply as "raw-fried" (*sheng jian*), are the heftier yet equally irresistible big brother of Shanghai's dainty *xiao long bao* dumplings. They are made with a leavened dough enclosing a juicy pork stuffing and made by the "potsticker" (*guo tie*) method, in which the raw buns are part-fried and part-steamed in a covered pan.

You'll need a flat frying pan with a close-fitting lid; a heavy-bottomed cast-iron pan or a non-stick pan is best. Makes about 20 buns.

1 tsp white or black sesame seeds, or a mixture of both
2 cups (250g) Chinese low-gluten flour, plus extra for dusting
2 oz (50g) Chinese high-gluten flour
1 tsp active dry yeast
½ tsp superfine sugar
½ tsp baking powder
½ tsp cooking oil, plus extra for cooking
3–4 tbsp sliced spring onions, green parts only
Chinkiang vinegar, for dipping

For the stuffing:
4 oz (100g) jellied stock (see page 320)
¾ oz (25g) fresh ginger, skin on
1 spring onion, white part only
10 oz (300g) pork mince, preferably belly
1 tbsp Shaoxing wine
1½ tbsp light soy sauce
½ tsp salt
⅛ tsp ground white pepper
2 tsp superfine sugar
½ tsp sesame oil

First, make the stuffing. Run a knife or fork repeatedly through the jellied pork stock to break it into small pieces. Smack the ginger and spring onion with the flat side of a Chinese cleaver or a rolling pin to loosen their fibers, put them in a small bowl and just cover with cold water. Put the pork mince in a bowl. Add the Shaoxing wine, soy sauce, salt, pepper, sugar and sesame oil and mix well, stirring in one direction. Gradually add 3 tablespoons of the ginger and spring onion soaking water, stirring as before. Finally, add the chopped jellied stock and mix thoroughly to incorporate. Chill until needed. Toast the sesame seeds in a dry wok or frying pan over a gentle flame until fragrant, then set aside.

Make the dough. Mix the flours, yeast and sugar together in a large bowl and make a well in the center. Gradually add about ¾ cup (150ml) lukewarm water, drawing in the flour as you go, adding just enough water to make a soft but not sticky dough. When the dough is nearly formed, add the baking powder and cooking oil. Mix thoroughly, then knead on a lightly floured surface for about 15 minutes until the dough is pale and smooth. (Alternatively, make the dough in a food processor and knead for a few minutes with a dough hook to achieve the same result.) Cover with a damp tea towel and leave to rest in a warm place for about 20 minutes. ▸

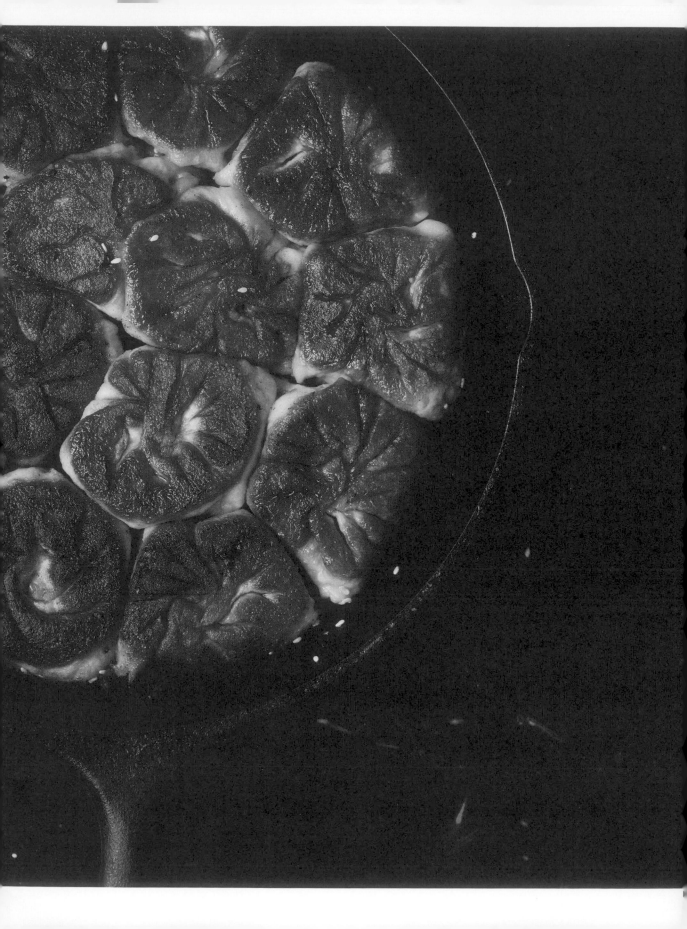

Make the wrappers. Lay out a sheet of parchment paper. Give the rested dough a quick knead, then cut it into two or three strips. Roll each strip into a long cylinder, then cut off pieces of dough the size of walnuts, about 1 oz (30g) each. Dust them lightly with flour. Stand them cut-side up and flatten them into discs with the palm of your hand. Roll the discs into circles about 3 in (9cm) in diameter, dusting with a little flour as required.

Make the buns. Lay a disc of dough in one hand, then use a blunt knife or bamboo spatula to place a heaped tablespoon (¾–1 oz/25–30g) of stuffing in the center. Use your other hand to pinch the edge of the dough to enclose the stuffing (see page 283). Pinch hard to seal the dough, making sure the mouth of the bun is completely closed. Turn the filled bun upside down and place it on the parchment paper. Cover with a damp tea towel and repeat until you have used all the dough. Leave the buns to rise for 20 minutes.

To cook and serve the buns, pour 2 tablespoons cooking oil into a seasoned cast-iron or nonstick frying pan and swirl it around to coat the surface over a high flame. When the oil is hot, take the pan off the heat for a moment while you arrange the upside-down buns in the pan. They should touch each other, so that the surface is covered. Return the pan to the heat and fry for 2–4 minutes until they have toasty, golden bottoms, moving the pan around to ensure even coloring. When they have colored, take the pan off the heat and carefully pour 1¼ cups (250ml) boiling water around the edges of the pan, keeping your face out of the way as this will produce a burst of steam. Cover the pan, return to a high flame and cook for 6 minutes.

Remove the lid to allow any remaining steam to escape, then drizzle another tablespoon of cooking oil around the edges of the pan. Keep cooking the buns until the bottoms have crisped up again—a hearty sizzling sound will be the sign that they are ready. Sprinkle with the spring onion greens and cover the pan for 20 seconds or so. Turn the heat off and sprinkle with the toasted sesame seeds. You can serve them right side up in the pan, as pictured on page 273, or turn them upside-down (pictured opposite) so your guests can admire their golden bottoms. Serve with dishes of Chinkiang vinegar to dip.

Shanghainese steamed "soup" dumplings

xiao long man tou 小笼馒头

At its best, the Shanghainese *xiao long man tou* or "little steamer dumpling," often known outside the region as *xiao long bao* or "soup dumpling," is a work of pastry perfection. You take its twirly neck between your chopsticks and lift it gently from its bamboo steamer, dipping it into vinegar before lowering it into the cradle of your china spoon. You add a few strands of ginger, then you pierce its swollen skirts with a chopstick and out rushes a flush of savory stock.

This snack is a dainty version of the larger stock-filled buns (*tang bao*) found all over the Jiangnan region. A cluster of restaurants around the Guyi Garden in Nanxiang, on the outskirts of Shanghai, claim to be custodians of the original recipe; the women who wrap the dumplings there can each make 400 in an hour. In the autumn hairy crab season, crabmeat is often mixed into the pork stuffing, which gives the dumplings a golden glow. A local Yangzhou speciality is a soup dumpling served in an individual steamer, so generously proportioned that its juices must be sucked out with a straw before it can be lifted.

The key to the juiciness of the dumplings is a jellied stock that melts during the steaming. You can make your own the traditional way from pig's skin or trotters or take a short cut by using gelatine, which is much easier and equally satisfying. Be warned that these are a little fiddly—Chinese people don't normally make *xiao long bao* at home. Makes about 20 dumplings.

1¾ cups (200g) Chinese high-gluten flour, plus extra for dusting
½ tbsp cooking oil, plus extra for the steamer
Chinkiang vinegar, for dipping
1 oz (30g) fresh ginger

For the stuffing:
7 oz (200g) jellied stock (see page 320)

¾ oz (25g) fresh ginger, skin on
1 spring onion, white part only
7 oz (200g) pork mince, preferably belly
1 tbsp Shaoxing wine
1 tbsp light soy sauce
½ tsp salt
⅛ tsp ground white pepper
2 tsp superfine sugar
½ tsp sesame oil

First, make the stuffing. Run a knife or fork repeatedly through the jellied pork stock to break it into small pieces. Smack the ginger and spring onion with the flat side of a Chinese cleaver or a rolling pin to loosen their fibers, put them in a small bowl and just cover with cold water. Put the pork mince in a bowl. Add the Shaoxing wine, soy sauce, salt, pepper, sugar and sesame oil and mix well, stirring in one direction. Gradually add 3 tablespoons of the ginger and spring onion soaking water, stirring as before. Finally, add the chopped jellied stock and mix thoroughly. Chill until needed.

Make the dough. Put 1½ cups (180g) of the flour in a large bowl or a food processor with the cooking oil. Put the remaining ¼ cup (20g) flour in a small bowl. Pour a little boiling water onto the flour in the small bowl, stirring it in as you do so. Add just enough water to transform the flour into a wet, sticky, glistening mass, then scrape this cooked flour into the bowl or food processor with the rest of the flour and the oil. Mix well and gradually add just enough cold water to form a dough that is soft but not sticky. Knead until smooth, shape into a ball, wrap in clingfilm and leave to rest for at least 30 minutes. ▶

Make the wrappers. Cut the dough into strips about 1½ in (3cm) wide, then break off pieces the size of very large cherries, about ½ oz (15g) each. Dust these lightly with flour, stand them cut-side up on a board and flatten them into discs with the palm of your hand. Roll the discs into 4 in (10cm) diameter circles, dusting the board and rolling pin with flour as needed.

Make the dumplings. Brush the base of a bamboo steamer with oil. Holding a circle of dough in one hand, use a blunt knife or bamboo spatula to place about ¾ oz (20g) of stuffing in the center. Use your other hand to pinch the edge of the dough to enclose the stuffing (see page 283). Make sure the mouth of the dumpling is sealed, then pinch it up into a point. Put the finished dumplings in your oiled steamer, leaving gaps of at least 1½ in (3cm) between them.

To cook and serve the dumplings, steam them over a high flame for 8 minutes, either in batches or in stacked layers of the steamer. While they are steaming, peel the ginger and cut it into thin slices, then into fine slivers. Put the vinegar and ginger into dipping dishes. Serve the dumplings in the steamer with the dipping dishes alongside. To eat them, pick one up with chopsticks, dip it in vinegar, then put it in a small bowl or Chinese spoon. Add a few slivers of ginger. Pierce the dumpling with a chopstick and let the stock flow out, then raise the bowl or spoon to your lips and part-bite, part-slurp the dumpling and its juices.

Shanghai pork and vegetable wontons

cai rou da hun dun 菜肉大馄炖

One day my friend Rose took me to visit her aunt in a tiny, higgledy-piggledy cottage on the banks of the Suzhou creek in the Hongkou district of Shanghai. We climbed a narrow wooden staircase to the bright living room, which was filled with Rose's aunts, uncles and cousins. There we drank some cooling chrysanthemum tea while our hostess, Xun Naifen, showed us how to make Shanghainese wontons.

Wontons can be found the length and breadth of China, with different names, forms and fillings—in the Cantonese south they're known as "swallowing clouds" (*yun tun*), in Sichuan as "folded arms" (*chao shou*) and in Shanghai as *hun dun*, a homonym for "primordial chaos." The Shanghainese are known for two kinds of wontons: the "small wontons" made from mere pinches of minced pork loosely gathered into tiny squares of pastry and served in broth; and the "big wontons" of the following recipe, which I've always found more exciting.

Big wontons are typically stuffed with finely chopped shepherd's purse, a wild relative of cabbage. Mrs. Xun had mixed her shepherd's purse with minced pork, uncooked shrimp and a little dried shiitake mushroom to make a delectable stuffing. Shepherd's purse is rarely sold outside Jiangnan, so at home I use blanched kale, the flavor of which recalls the fresh grassiness of shepherd's purse, or bunched spinach, which is also delicious. Large square Shanghai wonton wrappers can be found in many Chinese supermarkets. The same filling can be used to stuff round dumpling wrappers. Makes about 20 wontons.

Two 7 oz (200g) packs square Shanghai dumpling wrappers
A few pinches of dried laver seaweed
1 tsp oil or lard
1 tbsp papery dried shrimp
2 tbsp finely chopped preserved mustard tuber
2 tbsp thinly sliced spring onions
3 cups (750ml) stock (or wonton cooking water)
Salt and ground white pepper

For the filling:
3 dried shiitake mushrooms
9 oz (250g) curly green kale, or 5 oz (150g) bunched spinach or shepherd's purse
¾ oz (20g) fresh ginger, skin on
1 spring onion, white part only
7 oz (200g) minced pork
1½ tsp salt
1½ tsp superfine sugar
½ tbsp Shaoxing wine
1 tsp sesame oil

Cover the shiitake mushrooms with boiling water and leave for at least half an hour to soften. If using kale, remove and discard the thick stalks, so you are left with just leaves. Fill a large bowl with cold water and ice cubes. Bring a pan of water to the boil, add the kale and boil for about 5 minutes, until tender. Drain it well, plunge into the iced water and leave to cool completely. Drain, squeezing out as much water as possible, and finely chop it. (If using spinach or shepherd's purse, prepare them in the same way, just blanch briefly in boiling water.)

Crush the ginger and spring onion with the flat side of a Chinese cleaver or a rolling pin to loosen their fibers and put them in a cup with just enough cold water to cover. Discard the shiitake stalks and finely chop the caps. Put the pork in a bowl and add the shiitake, salt, sugar, Shaoxing wine and sesame oil, along with 4 tablespoons of the water in which you have soaked the ginger and spring onion, which will now have taken on their fragrances. Mix well—it's easiest to do this with one hand. Add the chopped greens and mix well again.

Bring a large pan of water to the boil and fill a small dish with cold water. Place a dumpling wrapper in the palm of your hand and put a generous tablespoon (¾ oz/20–25g) of the pork mixture in the center, pressing it into the wrapper. Dip your finger in the dish of water and run it around the edge ▸

of the wrapper. Wrap the wonton, sealing the edges tightly. Put the finished dumpling on a dry surface. Make the rest of the dumplings.

Tear the laver seaweed into tiny pieces. Put all the serving ingredients except the stock in a deep serving bowl and season with salt and pepper. Bring the stock, if using, to the boil in a separate pan and keep it hot. Drop the dumplings into the boiling water, stirring gently to separate, and cook them for about 5 minutes. Each time the water comes back to a rolling boil, add a small cup of cold water to reduce the temperature, so the dumplings do not jostle too vigorously and fall apart. (You should need to do this a couple of times before the dumplings are cooked.) The dumplings will rise to the surface of the water when they are cooked. Break one open to check that the pork is cooked through if you're uncertain.

When the dumplings are nearly cooked, pour the hot stock into the serving bowl. Remove the cooked dumplings with a slotted spoon and transfer them to the bowl. (Otherwise, simply transfer the wontons and their cooking water to your serving bowl.)

Basic steamed buns

baozi 包子

In the kitchens of the Lu Mansion, once the home of a rich Yangzhou salt merchant and his family, a team of chefs spend their early mornings wrapping *baozi*. Around them sit great basins of different stuffings; a stack of bamboo steamers stands on the end of the table. With a gentle rocking motion, one young chef quickly and effortlessly draws a circle of dough around the stuffing in a series of tiny pleats, finally drawing the dough into a "carp's mouth" and pinching it closed.

Baozi are found all over China but are a staple food in the wheat-eating north, where they tend to be large and substantial. In Yangzhou, pastry chefs make their steamed buns with a dainty southern touch. With a variety of fillings, sweet or savory, they may be eaten as part of a tea breakfast or lunch, the local equivalent of Cantonese *dim sum*. There's a knack to wrapping *baozi*, and it's easier to watch a video or ask someone to show you than to try to learn from the printed page. Once you've grasped the technique, however, they're easy to make and quite addictive.

I usually have some dough or stuffing left over; the remains of vegetarian stuffings can be eaten like salad, while small amounts of meaty stuffings can be stir-fried and served with a bowl of rice or noodles. If it's dough you have left, just make a couple of plain steamed buns. You may like to serve meaty buns with little dishes of Chinkiang vinegar for dipping. I'm very grateful to chef Fu Bing for helping me work out this recipe, which should make 12–14 buns, depending on their size.

For the dough:
2 cups (250g) Chinese low-gluten flour
1 tsp active dry yeast
½ tsp superfine sugar
½ tsp baking powder

1 tsp groundnut oil or melted lard

For the stuffing:
1 quantity stuffing of your choice (see pages 285–88)

Mix the flour, yeast and sugar together in a bowl or on a clean work surface. Make a well in the center and gradually pour in around 150ml lukewarm water (ideally at about 80°F/27°C), drawing the flour in from the sides to make a soft but not sticky dough. When the dough has nearly formed, add the baking powder and oil or lard and mix well. Turn the dough onto a clean work surface and knead briefly until evenly mixed, cover with a damp cloth and set aside in a warm place for 20 minutes. Punch back the dough and knead well until pale and very smooth. Cover with a damp cloth and set aside for another 15 minutes. Brush the layers of a bamboo steamer lightly with oil or lard. Cut out fourteen 2½ in (6cm) squares of parchment paper.

Knead the dough briefly again, then shape it into two sausages with a diameter of 1½ in (4cm). Cut off 1 oz (30g) pieces, stand them on their ends and flatten them with your hand to make fat discs. Roll them into 3½ in (9cm) diameter circles that are thinner around the edges. Take a disc in your left hand (if you are right-handed), place a tablespoon of the stuffing on it and press it down into the center. Use your right hand to draw up and pleat the edges of the circle around the stuffing, turning it in your left hand as you do so. If you're using more than one stuffing, try giving the buns distinguishing features, such as pinching the top into a point or a flat rim of dough, depending on the stuffing.

Seal the buns tightly and put them on the paper squares in the oiled steamer, filling both layers: make sure there is space between them, as they will expand. Cover the steamer and leave in a warm place for 20 minutes to rise. Fill the base with water, bring it to the boil over a high flame and steam, covered, for about 8 minutes, until springy. (The exact cooking time will depend on the size of your buns. You want the stuffing to be heated through and the dough to be cooked but retain a little springiness. If the buns appear flattened and droopy after steaming, they're overcooked.)

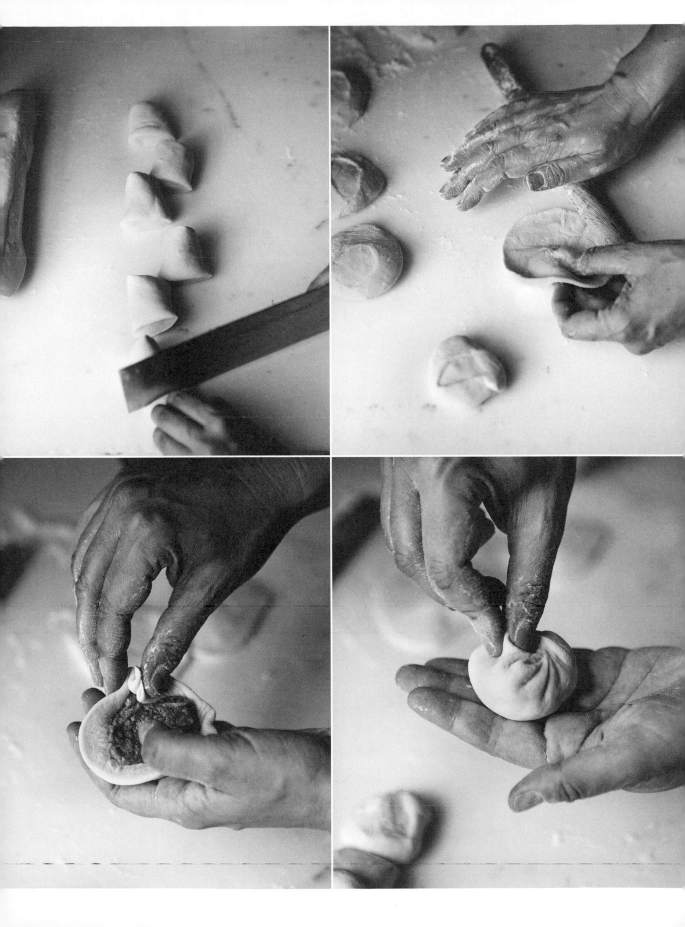

Yangzhou slivered radish buns
luo bo si bao 萝卜丝包

The ritual of early-morning tea and dumplings is not just a Cantonese tradition. Every morning in Yangzhou, people flock to the Yechun Teahouse by the side of the canal for a feast of buns, dumplings and other delectable snacks. Outside, in the yard, retired people listen to performances of local opera, clutching jars of green tea. In the narrow pavilions by the water's edge, the dark wooden tables are covered with bamboo steamers, tea cups and little plates of appetizers, pickles and relishes.

I breakfasted there one morning on little dishes of wild rice stem with shrimp eggs, syrupy jujubes, Zhenjiang pork terrine, juicy shiitake mushrooms with gingko nuts and blanched tofu slivers—and those were just the starters. There were also steamers filled with open-mouthed *shaomai* dumplings, diamond-shaped cakes studded with candied fruits, "soup" dumplings so large their juices had to be sucked out with a straw, and a whole selection of exquisite steamed buns.

This recipe, which makes 12–14 buns, is for one of my favorites, the slivered radish bun, a succulent mix of vegetable and fragrant pork. Yangzhou chef Zhang Hao told me how to make it.

Shanghai vegetarian bun (page 286); Yangzhou "three-cube" buns (page 288); Yangzhou slivered radish buns

1 quantity Basic steamed bun dough (see page 282)	1 tbsp finely chopped fresh ginger
1 white Asian radish, about 2 lbs (900g)	1 tbsp finely chopped spring onion
5 oz (150g) skinless, boneless pork belly	1 tbsp Shaoxing wine
2 tbsp lard or cooking oil	4 tsp light soy sauce
	1 tsp superfine sugar
	Salt

Peel the radish and cut it into 1½ in (3mm) slices, then into slivers. Add 1 tablespoon salt, mix well and set aside for at least half an hour. Cover the pork in cold water, bring to the boil, then simmer gently until cooked through. Remove from the water and leave to cool, then cut it into 2 in (5mm) dice. Drain the radish and squeeze it to get rid of as much water as possible.

Heat the lard or cooking oil in a seasoned wok over a high flame. Add the pork and stir-fry until it smells delicious and is tinged with gold. Add the ginger and spring onion and stir-fry briefly until fragrant. Tip the Shaoxing wine around the edges of the pan and let it sizzle. Remove from the heat, add the radish, light soy sauce and sugar, along with ¼ teaspoon salt, and mix well. Set aside to cool. Use to fill and cook Basic steamed buns (see page 282).

Red bean paste buns

Stuff your buns with red bean paste to make one of the most popular sweet *bao*; buy the paste in a Chinese shop or make your own (see page 327).Stuff and cook as for Basic steamed buns (see page 282).

Everyday pork buns

Make a basic pork stuffing using the ingredients of the Shanghai potsticker bun (see page 272), without the jellied stock. Stuff and cook as for Basic steamed buns (see page 282).

Snow vegetable buns

Stir-fry plenty of snow vegetable with a little finely chopped firm tofu and bamboo shoot, and season to taste with salt and sugar. Stuff and cook as for Basic steamed buns (see page 282).

Shanghai vegetarian buns

xiang gu su cai bao 香菇素菜包

These juicy vegetarian buns are a Shanghainese speciality, served not only in Buddhist vegetarian restaurants but also in mainstream establishments. They make a healthy and delectable breakfast, eaten on their own or with a bowlful of congee. At their simplest, they may be stuffed with just blanched greens and shiitake mushroom, but I like to add a little bamboo shoot or tofu. Some recipes suggest adding small amounts of fried wheat gluten, dried lily flower and wood-ear mushroom. Various kinds of vegetable may be used as the main ingredient, including shepherd's purse and most types of cabbagey greens: I find curly kale works beautifully. Makes 12–14 buns.

See photograph on page 284

1 quantity Basic steamed bun dough (see page 282)
3 dried shiitake mushrooms
1½ oz (500g) curly green kale
1 lb (40g) fresh or brined bamboo shoot
1½ oz (40g) firm tofu (plain, spiced or smoked)
2 tbsp cooking oil
1 tbsp finely chopped fresh ginger
2 tsp plus a pinch of superfine sugar
2 tsp sesame oil
2 tbsp rapeseed or groundnut oil
Salt

Put the shiitake mushrooms in a bowl and soak for at least half an hour in plenty of boiling water. Strip the kale leaves from the stalks, discarding the stalks. Bring a pan of water to the boil, add the kale leaves and boil for about 5 minutes, until tender. Drain and place in iced water until completely cooled, then squeeze out as much water as possible. Chop the kale finely. Bring another pan of water to the boil, add the bamboo shoot and blanch for 1 minute; refresh it under the cold tap, drain well and cut it into tiny cubes. Cut the tofu into tiny cubes too. Drain the mushrooms, retaining their soaking water. Discard the stalks, then cut the caps into tiny cubes.

Heat the cooking oil in a seasoned wok over a high flame. Add the ginger, chopped mushrooms, bamboo shoot and tofu and stir-fry until the ginger and mushrooms smell delicious. Add 2 tablespoons of the mushroom-soaking water along with a pinch of sugar, and season with salt. Stir until the liquid has evaporated, then remove from the heat and add the kale. Add the remaining sugar, sesame oil and rapeseed or groundnut oil and mix thoroughly, seasoning with about 1¼ teaspoons salt; remember that the dough itself is unsalted, so the stuffing should be a bit saltier than if you were eating it alone. Use to fill and cook Basic steamed buns (see page 282).

Yangzhou "three-cube" buns

san ding bao 三丁包

On his tours of the south, the Qianlong emperor was famously unable to resist the lure of Yangzhou, with its lyrical scenery, elegant mansions and—obviously—exquisite food. According to a local tale, the gourmet emperor issued the most exacting demands to the chefs charged with preparing his breakfast. The food should, he ordered, be "nourishing, but not too strengthening; delicious, but not too savory; oil-fragrant, but not in the least greasy; crisp, but not too stiff; and fine and tender while not being too soft." The chefs, so the story goes, were dumbfounded by the complexity of his requirements, until one of them came up with the genius idea of stuffing a steamed bun with small cubes of sea cucumber (nourishing, and not too strong), chicken (delicious, but not in an excessive way), pork (lusciously oily, but not greasy), winter bamboo shoot (crisp, but not stiff) and freshwater shrimp (fine and tender, with a bit of spring to them). The emperor was lavish in his praise of the "five-cube" buns (wu ding bao), and before long they became favorites at the banquets held by the salt merchants and other wealthy denizens of Yangzhou.

Some time later, a dim sum chef at Fuchun Teahouse wanted to give the ordinary people a taste of this imperial delicacy, so he dropped the expensive ingredients—and thus the "three-cube" steamed bun (san ding bao) was born, made just with pork, chicken and bamboo shoot. It is juicy, savory and quite irresistible, like Yangzhou itself. Makes 12–14 buns.

See photograph on page 284

1 quantity Basic steamed bun dough (see page 282)
3 dried shiitake mushrooms
4 oz (100g) chicken breast or thigh meat, with or without skin
6 oz (175g) skinless pork belly
3 oz (75g) fresh or brined bamboo shoot
1 tbsp lard or cooking oil
½ tbsp finely chopped fresh ginger
½ tbsp finely chopped spring onion, white part only
½ tbsp Shaoxing wine
1 cup (225ml) stock
2 tsp light soy sauce
¾ tsp dark soy sauce
1½ tsp superfine sugar
4 tsp potato starch mixed with 3 tbsp cold water
1 tsp sesame oil
Salt

Put the shiitake mushrooms in a bowl and soak for at least half an hour in plenty of boiling water. Bring a pan of water to the boil. Add the chicken and pork, return to the boil, then simmer very gently for about 25 minutes, until just cooked through. Leave to cool. Bring a small pan of water to the boil, add the bamboo shoot and blanch for 1 minute; refresh it under the cold tap and drain well. Cut the chicken into even cubes of about 3 in (8mm), and cut the pork and bamboo shoot into slightly smaller cubes. Discard the shiitake stalks and finely chop the caps.

Heat the lard or cooking oil in a seasoned wok over a high flame with the ginger and spring onion and stir-fry briefly until fragrant. Add the mushroom and bamboo shoot and stir-fry in the fragrant oil, then add the pork and stir-fry until it smells delicious. Add the Shaoxing wine and give everything a stir, then add the chicken, stock, soy sauces, sugar and salt. Bring to the boil. Give the starch mixture a stir and add it in stages, stirring as it thickens the cooking liquid to a gravy. Remove from the heat and stir in the sesame oil. Leave to cool completely; the stuffing will set, which will make it easier to handle. Use it to fill and cook Basic steamed buns (see page 282).

Lotus leaf buns

he ye bing 荷叶饼

Lotus leaf buns, made from a basic steamed bun dough shaped to resemble lotus leaves, are the traditional accompaniment to many rich, meaty dishes, such as Dongpo pork, steamed pork in rice meal and Shaoxing pork with dried fermented greens. They can be made in advance and frozen until you wish to use them. You'll need a clean comb or a serrated knife to decorate them. Makes 15–20 buns.

See photograph on pages 290–91

1 quantity Basic steamed bun   A little cooking oil
    dough (see page 282)

Make the basic steamed bun dough and let it rest. Oil the layers of a steamer. Turn the dough out onto a lightly floured work surface. Knead it briefly, then cut or roll it into a 1½ in (3cm) thick cylinder. Use a knife to cut this into 1¾ in (4cm) sections weighing about ¾ oz (25g) each. Lightly dust your hands with flour, turn each section on its end and flatten it with the palm of your hand, then roll it out into an 3 in (8cm) circle. Repeat with the rest of the dough.

Take a circle of dough and brush the upper side very lightly with oil. Use a chopstick placed across the center to help you fold it in half. Place the folded circle on the work surface and use the teeth of a clean comb or a serrated knife to prick lotus leaf veins into the dough. Use the back of the comb or knife to nudge the rounded edges of the bun in at the end of each "leaf vein." Pinch out the center of the straight edge of the semicircle to make a "stem." Put the buns on the oiled rack of a steamer and leave to rise for 20 minutes.

Steam the buns over a high flame for about 8 minutes, until cooked through. Serve immediately or leave to cool, then refrigerate or freeze. Steam again to heat through before serving.

SWEET DISHES

Although there is no dessert course in a traditional Jiangnan meal, you will find an exquisite multitude of sweet dumplings, pastries and cakes, not to mention sweet soups and potages, across the region. A sweet soup is often served at the end of a banquet, and sweetmeats to symbolize the sweet harmony of married life will always be part of a wedding feast. Otherwise, sweet dishes are mostly eaten as snacks or woven into the broader fabric of a meal. Much of the notorious sweetness of Suzhou and Wuxi cooking is found in what Westerners would consider savory dishes, like sweet-and-sour fish, red-braised pork hock stewed with crystal sugar, and cold shredded ham mixed with toasted pine nuts and crunchy sugar. In Shanghai, a spread of otherwise savory appetizers might include kumquats in syrup or deep-fried peanuts with seaweed and a sprinkling of sugar.

Suzhou is widely known as the headquarters of the Jiangnan sweet tooth. In the heart of the old city, near the Taoist Temple of Mystery, local people queue up at the Caizhizhai sweet shop for multicolored cakes and seasonal treats such as fermented glutinous rice buns stuffed with candied rose petals. The latter are traditionally made for the ancestral sacrifices of early spring and are still only sold in that season. Further south in Jiangsu province, Nanjing is home to some delectable sweetmeats, including lotus root stewed with brown sugar and silky taro bathed in an osmanthus syrup that is glossy and thick with lotus-root starch.

Street vendors and shops selling sweetmeats can be found all over the region. In Shanghai, the food halls and delicatessens around the famous old shopping street, Nanjing Lu, sell not only traditional snacks but also European-influenced cakes and pastries, like sweet biscuits laced with fragrant Ningbo seaweed. Along one of the old canals of Shaoxing, I've seen a man making what must be the progenitors of American fortune cookies by pressing a batter between two round irons and heating them over a fire. The thin egg wafers are wrapped into parcels before they harden; bite into one and you won't find a message, but a glitter of crushed nuts and sugar.

Many traditional Jiangnan sweet dishes lack the cloying sweetness of Western desserts, and have instead just a whisper of sweetness, like the soup of euryale seeds and crisp, gelatinous peach sap that they sometimes serve at the Dragon Well Manor restaurant in Hangzhou. It's a lyrical dish made with mysterious underwater plants, hinting at the silent breathings-out of trees and only faintly sweetened with honey. On the shores of the West Lake, people like to sip a glistening, translucent porridge made from lotus root starch and scattered with sweet osmanthus blooms and slivers of candied fruit (*xi hu ou fen*).

Most Jiangnan sweet dishes are sweetened with cane sugar, which is produced in Zhejiang and Jiangsu, or maltose syrup, the ancient Chinese sweetener often used in nut brittles and snaps. Occasionally, you might be lucky enough to try wild honey like some I tasted once in rural Zhejiang, a dark amber syrup with a staggeringly complex flavor, redolent of old wood, caramel and wildflowers, smoky as an evening by the campfire, peaty as whisky.

This chapter includes a small selection of my personal favorites among the sweet dishes of the region.

Shanghai eight-treasure glutinous rice
ba bao fan 八宝饭

A glistening dome of sweet, sticky rice with a jewel-like pattern of dried fruits and seeds and a dark, secret heart of red bean paste, this gorgeous pudding is a favorite dish in Shanghai and a traditional festive sweetmeat across the region. The "eight treasures" are the fruits, nuts and seeds used to ornament the dish (for savory versions on the "eight treasure" theme, see the relish on page 76 and the stuffed duck on page 116). Traditionally, the pudding is enriched with lard, but I prefer to use coconut oil, which gives it a delicate, enticing aroma and makes it suitable for vegetarians.

Feel free to express your creativity with the decorations. For the photograph, I used five dried jujubes and five dried apricots, a handful of golden raisins, some glacé cherries and a handful of ready-to-use lotus seeds—but do experiment. Many Chinese cooks add pine nuts or strands of multicolored candied fruit; old-fashioned candied angelica would work well. One of my favorite versions of this dish is the one served at the Fu 1088 restaurant in Shanghai, where they use a mixture of black and white glutinous rice and fill the pudding with jujube paste; it is served in tiny individual portions, each with an accompanying cupful of warm walnut cream.

You'll need a steamer, some muslin and a heatproof bowl just large enough to hold the ingredients—around 3 cups (750ml).

1½ cups (250g) Japanese sweet rice
1¼ cups (100g) superfine sugar, plus 3–4 tbsp
1½ oz (40g) lard or coconut oil, or 4 tbsp groundnut oil, plus a little extra

5 oz (150g) red bean paste
An assortment of dried fruits and nuts or seeds for decoration (see headnote)

Rinse the rice in several changes of water until the water runs clear. Cover it in cold water and soak for at least 4 hours or overnight. If you are using very dry dried fruits, cover them in hot water and leave to soften. Cut any large fruits such as jujubes in half and remove the stones.

Line a steamer basket with muslin. Drain the rice and put it in the steamer, spreading it out in an even layer, but without packing it tightly. Steam over a high flame for 20 minutes, until tender. While the rice is still hot, turn it out into a bowl, add 3–4 tablespoons sugar to taste, along with the lard, coconut oil or groundnut oil, and mix thoroughly.

Grease the inside of a heatproof bowl with a little lard, coconut oil or groundnut oil. Arrange the fruits and nuts or seeds in a pretty pattern around the base of the bowl. Carefully place about half the rice in the bowl. Take the red bean paste and pat it with your hands into a circle that will fit onto the layer of rice, with a little space around the edge. Put the bean paste on the rice, then fill the bowl with the rest of the rice and press it down over the bean paste to create a flat surface. Cover the bowl with a small plate and steam over a high flame for 25 minutes.

While the pudding is steaming, melt the remaining 1¼ cups (100g) sugar in ½ cup (100ml) water over a gentle flame, then boil for 1–2 minutes until syrupy. When the rice is ready, remove the plate and replace it with a serving plate. Carefully invert the bowl and turn the pudding out onto the plate. Pour the syrup over it and serve.

Pearly rice balls with sweet glutinous rice wine

jiu niang yuan zi 酒酿圆子

Across the Jiangnan region, people adore this sweet, soothing soup of glutinous rice balls with golden wisps of egg and the delicate aroma of fermented glutinous rice wine, which is especially recommended as a tonic for women after childbirth. In Ningbo, where they call it by a local name (*jiang ban yuan zi*), it's traditionally eaten at the winter solstice, while in Suzhou they add peeled, skinned tangerine segments and eat it on the first day of the lunar new year. Makes enough for about 6 bowls.

1 tbsp goji berries
¾ cup (125g) glutinous rice flour, plus extra for dusting
Around 5 tbsp superfine sugar, to taste
4 tbsp potato starch mixed with 6 tbsp cold water

1 large egg, beaten
½ cup (125ml) fermented glutinous rice wine
1 tbsp candied osmanthus blossoms (optional)

Cover the goji berries with cold water and leave them for half an hour to soften. Put the glutinous rice flour in a bowl and gradually mix in enough tepid water to make a putty-like dough; it should not stick to your fingers. Break off little pieces of dough and roll them into balls the size of shelled hazelnuts. Set aside on a board dusted with a little rice flour.

Bring 1 quart (1 liter) water to the boil. Add the rice balls and simmer until they rise to the surface. Stir in the sugar to taste. Give the potato starch mixture a stir, then gradually add it in stages to the pot, stirring as the liquid thickens—add just enough to give the liquid a slightly heavy, silky consistency. Turn the heat down very low. Drizzle the beaten egg all over the surface of the liquid. Wait for a moment until the egg has set into wisps, then stir in the glutinous rice wine, goji berries and osmanthus blossoms. Serve.

Sweet silver-ear soup with goji berries

yin er geng 银耳羹

Lightly sweetened soups are often eaten as snacks between meals or at the end of a banquet. Some are so exotic that they seem to me like something out of a fairytale. Once, when chef Zhu Yinfeng took me out foraging in southern Zhejiang, we gathered "bamboo bird's nest," a fluffy, sponge-like fungus that grows beneath certain types of bamboo. We washed it and picked it over, then made it into a soup with fresh coconut milk and crystal sugar; its delicate, strandy texture really did evoke the sensation of eating a bird's nest. Other famous Jiangnan sweet soups are made from fresh chestnuts with scented osmanthus blossoms, and euryale seeds with peanuts and jujubes.

It is hard to source some of these ingredients outside China, but this recipe offers the same kind of pleasure with ingredients that can be found in most Chinese food shops. It's a sweet tonic soup dense with soft ripples of silver-ear fungus, scattered with fermented rice grains and scarlet berries, and fragrant with wine. It is magnificently soothing, and said to be beneficial for the lungs. It is sweet but not cloying, and refreshing drunk either hot or cool. Makes enough for about 8 small bowls.

2 whole heads dried silver-ear fungus, about 1½–2 oz (40–50g)
4½–5 oz (125–150g) rock sugar
3 tbsp goji berries

4 tbsp fermented glutinous rice wine
1–1½ tbsp candied osmanthus blossoms (optional)

Cover the silver-ear fungus generously with cold water and leave to soak for an hour or so, until supple. Use a knife or scissors to snip out the tight, hard centers of each head, along with any discolored parts. Use your fingers to break the heads apart into small clumps. Rinse well to remove any grit, then drain.

Put the cleaned silver-ear in a pan, cover with about 2 quarts (2 liters) cold water, bring to the boil and simmer over a very low flame for about 1½ hours, until soft and heavy. Add the rock sugar and stir to dissolve. Simmer for another 30 minutes or so, stirring frequently so the silver-ear doesn't stick to the pan. Set aside, and for best results leave overnight to settle, by which time the silver-ear will be soft and voluptuous, the liquid sleepy and heavy.

An hour or so before you wish to serve the soup, cover the goji berries in cold water and leave them to plump up. To serve, bring the soup just to the boil, stirring constantly. Add a little more hot water if it's too thick. Finally, stir in the goji berries, fermented glutinous rice wine and candied osmanthus, if using, and serve.

Ningbo glutinous rice balls with black sesame stuffing

ning bo tang yuan 宁波汤圆

Large glutinous rice balls stuffed with sweet black sesame paste are known as *tang yuan*. Their origins can be traced back to the Song dynasty, and they are traditionally eaten at the Lantern Festival at the end of the Chinese New Year.

The best *tang yuan* in Jiangnan are said to be made by the Crock-Duck-Dog snack restaurant in Ningbo, where they are the signature dish (the restaurant's curious name puns on the nickname of the man who founded it in 1926). In early spring, *tang yuan* dough may be colored green with Chinese mugwort juice to ward off the ill humors of the season. The rice balls may also have savory stuffings, such as minced pork or shepherd's purse. Makes enough for 6 rice bowls.

2 oz (50g) black sesame seeds
3 tbsp all-purpose flour
2 oz (50g) superfine sugar
3 oz (75g) lard or coconut oil
1½ cups (250g) glutinous rice flour, plus extra for dusting

1 tsp cooking oil
Dried or candied osmanthus blossoms, for sprinkling (optional)

Toast the sesame seeds in a dry frying pan over a low flame until deliciously fragrant, then crush to a coarse powder in a spice grinder, or with a pestle and mortar. Toast the flour in the same way, until it tastes cooked and toasty. Combine the crushed sesame seeds, flour and sugar in a bowl and mix well. Melt the lard or coconut oil over a gentle flame, then stir it into the sesame seed mixture. Leave to cool, then chill in the fridge until set. Roll the set stuffing into balls the size of grapes and dust in glutinous rice flour to prevent sticking. Put in the freezer to harden.

Put the glutinous rice flour in a bowl and gradually mix in the cooking oil and enough tepid water to make a putty-like dough; it should not stick to your fingers. Break the dough into pieces and roll into balls a little larger than the stuffing balls, dusting the work surface with rice flour as necessary. Press your thumb into the center of each ball to make a cup. Press a frozen stuffing ball into each cup and draw up the dough around it to enclose it completely.

Bring a pan of water to the boil, add the rice balls and simmer until they float. Serve about 4 balls per person in a bowl of the hot cooking water. Sprinkle over a few osmanthus blossoms, if you have them.

Pumpkin cakes

nan gua bing 南瓜饼

In the kitchen of Wang's mansion in the old city of Yangzhou is an enormous, old-fashioned cooking range. Built from bricks and whitewashed clay, it rises imposingly at one end of the room. There are five wok stations with fire-beds beneath and cubbyholes behind, for storing seasonings; above, two great chimneys rise to the raftered roof. Perched on top of the range, with a good view of the room, is the Kitchen God's shrine. The Kitchen God (*zao jun*) is the watchman of the Chinese family. Once a year, he reports on their behavior to the Jade Emperor in Heaven, who then decides whether they deserve reward or punishment. To bribe him, family members traditionally make offerings on the twenty-third of the last lunar month of the year, the day of his departure. They light candles and incense before his shrine, burn paper money and, most importantly, give him sweet and sticky things to eat, to seal his lips or, failing that, to sweeten his words.

These gorgeous little pumpkin cakes would do the job perfectly. They are crunchy and golden on the outside, soft and sticky within, with a rich, sweet stuffing. Fill them with red bean paste as in the main recipe, or the jujube paste on page 327.

5 oz (150g) red bean paste
1¾ cups (275g) glutinous rice flour, plus extra for dusting
1 lb (500g) slice of pumpkin
About 1 tbsp superfine sugar, to taste
Cooking oil for deep-frying, plus 2 tsp

Scoop up ⅓ oz (10g) pieces of red bean paste and roll them into balls, dusting them with glutinous rice flour to prevent sticking. Set them aside. Peel the pumpkin and scrape out the seeds. Cut it into thick slices, put them in a dish in the steamer basket and steam until completely tender. Set aside to cool.

Mash the pumpkin to a paste or blitz it in a food processor. Season with sugar to taste—pumpkins vary in their sweetness. When the pumpkin has cooled enough to handle, add 2 teaspoons cooking oil, then the glutinous rice flour in stages, mixing throughly to make a fairly stiff, putty-like dough that does not stick to your hands. You won't need to add water because the pumpkin itself is so juicy. Leave it to rest for 10 minutes.

Break off an apricot-sized lump of dough, about 1 oz (35g). Roll it into a ball, then gently flatten it between your palms. Make an indentation in the center and press in a ball of red bean paste stuffing. Draw up the sides of the dough to enclose the stuffing completely. Roll it into a ball again, then flatten it into a disc about ½ in (1.5 cm) thick. Repeat with the remaining dough and stuffing.

Heat the oil for deep-frying to 300°F (150°C). Fry the pumpkin cakes in batches over a medium flame for about 8 minutes, until golden. The oil should fizz around the cakes, but not too aggressively—you want them to cook slowly enough to melt the lard in the stuffing, and to avoid bursting them open. Serve hot.

Sweet Ningbo rice cake with seaweed

tai cai gui hua nian gao 苔菜桂花年糕

This surprising and delightful sweet dish is a speciality of Ningbo. Sizzly strips of New Year's rice cake are frosted in powdered sugar and seaweed flakes, with a fragrant hint of osmanthus blossom. This combination of umami savoriness and sweetness is one that often occurs in the region's cooking, from the sweet biscuits laced with seaweed on sale in the delicatessens of Shanghai, to another Ningbo speciality: naturally fermented rice flour buns steamed and toasted with powdered sugar and seaweed. I first tasted this delicacy at the Zhuangyuanlou restaurant in Ningbo, where executive chef Chen Xiaoliang was kind enough to let me learn how to make it in the kitchen. Serve it at the end of a Chinese meal, or alongside savory dishes.

1¾ cups (400ml) cooking oil
10 oz (300g) New Year's rice cake, in strips or round slices
3 tbsp powdered sugar

1½ tbsp osmanthus blossom jam or 1 tbsp dried osmanthus blossoms
1½ tbsp aonori-ko seaweed flakes

Heat the oil in a seasoned wok over a high flame to 300°F (150°C). Carefully slide the pieces of rice cake into the oil and deep-fry for 2–3 minutes, until they are slightly puffy. While they fry, use a wok scoop to separate them. Remove the rice cake pieces from the oil with a slotted spoon and set aside. Carefully pour off the oil into a heatproof container.

Return the wok to a high flame with the powdered sugar and osmanthus jam or blossoms. Immediately add the rice cake pieces and toss them in the sugar for 10–20 seconds, by which time the sugar will have melted and coated the slices. Sprinkle the seaweed all over the rice cake pieces and stir rapidly for another 10–20 seconds, until they are evenly coated and smell delicious. Serve immediately.

DRINKS

Dragon Well (*long jing*) green tea and Shaoxing wine are the best-known Jiangnan drinks, but the region is home to many other delicious and unusual beverages. Dragon Well tea is traditionally made from tea leaves gathered around Longjing village on the outskirts of Hangzhou. Infused in hot but not boiling water, it's an exquisite refreshment, simultaneously stimulating and calming. The most sought-after tea is made from the tender young leaves harvested just before the Clear Brightness festival in early spring and, according to aficionados, is brewed with water from the nearby Running Tiger spring.

Although the finest green teas are wildly expensive, everyday tea is part of the social fabric of the region. It's the first refreshment offered when you enter a home or restaurant; lorry drivers and cashiers keep jars of tea at their sides, refilling them at intervals throughout the day. In general, tea is drunk between, before and after meals, although it may sometimes be an accompaniment to them, particularly in the case of the lavish Yangzhou tea breakfast, the Jiangsu equivalent of the Cantonese *yum cha*. Sometimes tea is served with dried fruits, nuts and other "tea snacks" (*cha dian*).

Archaic ways of drinking tea persist in the Jiangnan countryside. In rural Zhejiang, once, after a morning spent catching eels, I was invited back to a farmhouse and greeted as an honored guest with a bowl of green tea that was thick with roasted green soybeans, morsels of dried carrot and salty, toasted sesame seeds. The drink was something between a soup and a cup of tea, crunchy and chewy and refreshing. Aside from real tea, the people of Hangzhou love drinking a tisane made from tiny dried chrysanthemum buds, which are known as "embryonic chrysanthemum" or "chrysanthemum grains." Because of its cooling qualities, this infusion is mainly drunk during the summer months.

Rice wines have been produced in Shaoxing for more than two millennia. They have long been part of the fabric of traditional Shaoxing life; more than eight centuries ago, during the Southern Song dynasty, the poet Lu You wrote of the ubiquity of wine shops in the city. In the old-fashioned taverns of Shaoxing, people took their wine with snacks that might include fava beans flavored with star anise, spiced sparrows' legs, drunken dried fish and deep-fried stinking tofu. You can still catch a flavor of such taverns by visiting the old part of the Xianheng restaurant, which serves Shaoxing wines with typical local snacks and dishes.

The classic Shaoxing wines are "yellow wines" (*huang jiu*), undistilled, amber-colored brews with an alcohol content similar to sherry. They vary in their sweetness; medium sweet and medium dry wines are regarded as the most palatable for drinking. In northern China, people sometimes warm Shaoxing wine with dried plums and ginger; in Shaoxing they drink it neat, either at room temperature or slightly warmed. Traditionally, it is served in pewter ewers. Medium-dry wines, particularly *hua diao*, are used for dishes like drunken chicken and the lavish banquet delicacy Buddha Jumps Over the Wall, both of which are traditionally served in clay wine jars. Cheaper, more basic Shaoxing wines are used in cooking. According to local lore, when drunk in moderation, Shaoxing wine is a medicinal tonic that preserves health and enlivens the blood.

Shaoxing wine production begins in the tenth lunar month with sacrifices to the God of Wine. Glutinous rice is soaked, steamed, then fermented with rich lake water. The resultant mash is pressed to extract the clear wine, which is heat-sterilized and then sealed into jars to mature. The wines are stored and aged in squat clay jars with narrow mouths that are sealed with lotus leaves, bamboo husks and mud mixed with the boozy residue of the wine-making. There are several different types of Shaoxing wine, including "primary red" (*yuan hong jiu*), "added rice" (*jia fan jiu*) and "carved pattern" (*hua diao*). The latter is named because it is stored in jars decorated with elaborate, colorful and auspicious designs.

Many varieties of distilled spirits are also produced in Jiangnan. One particular favorite of mine is Chinese bayberry wine (*yang mei jiu*), made by steeping the raspberry-pink fruits in a strong clear liquor until the wine is heavy and garnet-red. Locally produced drinks aside, beer is a fine accompaniment to Chinese food in general, including that of Jiangnan. If you'd like to drink grape wine, white wines are generally preferable and champagne can be excellent, but oaky chardonnays are best avoided. If you prefer red wine, choose light, fruity wines without much tannin.

Dragon Well tea
long jing cha 龙井茶

The sky shone brightly and the water glittered as I wandered down to the West Lake in Hangzhou one sunny morning. Peach trees and weeping willows lined the shores; cicadas sung amid the branches. Small, canopied wooden boats crossed the surface of the lake, the boatmen pushing through the water with their single oars. On the northern bank, two ladies were singing traditional Yue opera in a wooden gazebo, accompanied by a group of amateur musicians playing the Chinese lute and two-stringed violin. Elderly people sat around them, holding jars of tea and laughing at the witty repartee. I made my way to a teahouse in the garden of an old mansion and took a seat there, gazing out over a meadow of tilting lotus leaves towards the little bridges of the causeway. Around me, noisy pensioners sipped green tea and cracked sunflower seeds between their teeth.

Dragon Well (or *long jing*) tea is the classic Hangzhou drink, and there's no better place to enjoy it than by the side of the West Lake or on a wooden boat that rocks gently on the water. The tea is made only from the tenderest leaves plucked by hand from the tea bushes that run over the Longjing hills. Steeped in hot water, the spear-shaped leaves have a nutty aroma and a delicate, clean taste.

Put 1 tablespoon Dragon Well tea leaves in a mug or tea bowl. Cover with 1–1½ in (2–3cm) water just below boiling point, at 185–195°F (85–90°C) (if you don't have a thermometer, pour boiling water into a cold, empty mug, leave for 30 seconds or so, then pour it onto your tea leaves). Leave to steep until the liquid has been colored by the leaves, then fill the mug or bowl with water at the same temperature.

The leaves will mostly settle at the base of the mug or bowl, so you can sip the clear liquid above them. Keep topping up with fresh hot water for as long as you like; the leaves can be infused several times before their flavor is exhausted.

Jujube and ginger tea

hong zao cha 红枣茶

One of my favorite foot massage emporiums in Shanghai serves this hot fruit infusion, which is delightfully warming on a cold winter's day. You can sweeten it with sugar or honey, but I prefer it unsweetened. It's gorgeous served either hot or cold.

Red jujubes (*hong zao*), also known as Chinese dates, are delectable when eaten fresh in their autumn season, like little apples; dried, the wrinkled, deep-red fruits are used all year round in sweets and tonic dishes. They have been appreciated in the Jiangnan region since Neolithic times—archaeologists found their remains, along with those of rice, water caltrop and calabash gourds, at the Stone Age remains of Hemudu near today's Ningbo. Makes about 1 quart (1 liter).

See page 310 for a photograph that includes soaking jujubes, rock sugar and fresh ginger; the brewed drink is pictured at the bottom of page 311.

4 oz (100g) dried red jujubes	Honey or rock sugar,
¾ oz (20g) fresh ginger	to sweeten (optional)

Break open the jujubes and discard their stones. Put them in a pan with 1½ quarts (1.5 liters) water. Bring to the boil, then cover the pan and leave to steep for a few hours or overnight.

Peel and slice the ginger and add it to the jujubes. Bring everything to the boil and simmer for 45 minutes. Season to taste with honey or rock sugar, if desired. Strain before drinking hot or cold.

Ginger tea with brown sugar

Simmer generous amounts of peeled, sliced fresh ginger in water for at least 10 minutes until you have a peppery infusion. Season to taste with brown sugar. This is a wonderfully warming winter drink, and is particularly advised as a tonic for women during menstruation. Make it as gingery as you like.

Dried Chinese plum and hawthorn infusion

suan mei tang 酸梅汤

In China, many tempting drinks are made from dried fruits. At the Wumen Renjia restaurant in Suzhou they serve a warm, dark, sour-sweet smoothie made from dried apricots and jujubes that have been steamed, blended and diluted with water.

Another gorgeous and refreshing drink is the Hangzhou favorite, cool "sour plum soup." This fruity infusion, sweetened with rock sugar, is made with dried black Chinese plums (*wu mei*), Chinese hawthorn fruit and dried licorice root, all of which can be found in Chinese supermarkets. The wrinkled plums are normally sold whole, while the hawthorn fruit, as small as cherries, tend to be sliced before drying. The infusion is served chilled and would be also be delicious on ice and in cocktails. It keeps in the fridge for a few days. The recipe comes from Hangzhou chef Chen Xiaoming. Makes about 1 quart (1 liter).

1 oz (30g) Chinese dried black plums (10–15 fruits)
1 oz (30g) sliced dried Chinese hawthorn fruit
5 slices dried licorice root
Rock sugar, to taste

Cover the plums, hawthorn fruit and licorice root with cold water and soak for 4 hours or overnight. After soaking, rinse the ingredients, then put them in a pan with 1½ quarts (1.5 liters) water, bring to the boil and simmer for 30 minutes. Sweeten with rock sugar to taste. Strain and chill before drinking.

Warm pumpkin juice with honey

nan gua zhi 南瓜汁

In Hangzhou, the Dragon Well Manor restaurant often serves juices made with the fresh fruits of the season. Perhaps there will be the pale minty-green juice of wild kiwi fruits, the pale gold of loquats, the cool bronze of sugar cane or the milky purity of water chestnuts. Since the Chinese tend to be unencumbered by arbitrary distinctions between fruits and vegetables, they might also offer the warm juices of sweetcorn, pea shoots or pumpkin, lightly sweetened with honey. Drunk before or during a meal, these juices smooth the throat and soothe the spirits.

Pumpkins, which are usually known as "southern squashes" (*nan gua*), are widely grown in China, where they have many culinary uses. In rural areas, people stir-fry the tender leaves of the plant as a vegetable and, in hard times, add their flesh to the rice-pot to make the rice go further. Pumpkin meat may be stir-fried, steamed or made into sweet dumplings. It can also be used to make this golden, satiny drink, which will slip dreamily down your throat. Serves 4.

See page 310 for a photograph that includes a Crown Prince pumpkin; the juice is pictured at the top of page 311.

1¼ lbs (550g) pumpkin, peeled and deseeded	About 4 tbsp honey, or to taste

Put the pumpkin in the basket of a stainless steel steamer and steam over a high flame until completely tender. When the pumpkin is cooked, remove it from the steamer. Put the honey in a small pan with an equal quantity of water from the steamer and stir as you heat it gently to dissolve.

While the pumpkin is still warm, put it in a blender with some of the water from the base of the steamer and blitz until you have a smooth liquid with the consistency of double cream. Season to taste with the dissolved honey. Serve.

Sweetcorn juice

Boil or steam sweetcorn cobs, then cut off the kernels and blend to a smooth, creamy juice. Sweeten with diluted honey, if desired.

Carrot juice

Make it in the same way as the pumpkin juice, with just a hint of added sweetness from diluted honey.

Fresh savory soymilk

dou jiang 豆奖

In the West, people often think of soymilk only as a substitute for cows' milk for vegans and those who are lactose intolerant. In China, it is a common breakfast beverage, often drunk with deep-fried dough sticks (*you tiao*) for dunking. Freshly made, it's a beautiful drink. The best I've ever had is the stone-ground soymilk served at the start of banquets at the Dragon Well Manor restaurant in Hangzhou. Guests there are encouraged first to taste the unseasoned milk to appreciate its intrinsic flavor (*yuan wei*), then to drink it with flavorings of their choice. Some people like it sweetened with sugar, but for me the only choice is to season it with savory condiments: soy sauce, dried shrimp, spring onion greens, pickled mustard and fragments of deep-fried dough stick. This way it's like a soup, and fantastically satisfying.

If you're not drinking the soymilk immediately, you'll notice that a skin will form on the surface as it cools; whip this off with a chopstick and hang it up to dry and you'll have tofu skin, which can be added to a soup or stir-fried vegetables.

You'll need a piece of clean muslin. If you don't have a Chinese dough stick to hand (I usually don't), just omit it. Makes about 1 quart (800ml), or 4 small bowlfuls.

6 oz (200g) dried yellow soybeans
2 drops vegetable oil, plus extra for greasing

To serve (optional):
Superfine sugar, to taste
or
Light soy sauce

Papery dried shrimp
Thinly sliced spring onions, green parts only
Finely chopped Sichuan preserved vegetable
Finely chopped Chinese dough stick

Cover the soybeans with plenty of cold water and soak overnight in a cool place. Discard the soaking water and rinse the beans well.

Bring 1 quart (1 liter) water to the boil and add the vegetable oil (this will help to subdue the foaminess of the soymilk). Put the beans in a blender with about 2 cups (500ml) of the hot water and blitz until smooth.

Lightly grease the inside of a pan with vegetable oil. Line a sieve with muslin and strain the soymilk through it into the pan. Draw the edges of the muslin together and squeeze to extract as much liquid as possible. Use some of the remaining hot water to rinse the residue in the sieve as you go along, and then repeat the squeezing. Add the rest of the hot water to the strained soymilk in the pan and bring it to the boil, stirring to prevent sticking. Simmer for 7–8 minutes. Serve in individual bowls, seasoned with your chosen condiments to taste, and drink it with spoons, like a soup.

If you choose the savory option, for each bowl of soymilk I suggest about 1 teaspoon light soy sauce or organic tamari to taste, and 1 teaspoon each of papery dried shrimp, spring onion greens and Sichuan preserved vegetable (and the dough stick, if using).

BASIC RECIPES

This chapter includes recipes for a few of the most essential stocks, seasonings and pickles of the Jiangnan region. Stock is not only the backbone of many soups, but is also used to enrich and flavor all kinds of dishes. Pickling was until recently part of the rhythm of daily life in virtually every Chinese household. Most rural people, and the older generation in the cities, still make their own pickles and preserves.

If you visit the old towns of Jiangnan during the winter, you may see walls and washing lines festooned with wind-dried meats, salt pork and salted chickens studded with Sichuan pepper, chunky sausages marbled with pink flesh and ivory fat and, in Hangzhou, the mahogany sheen of soy-sauce duck. In urban homes and country cottages, rows of pickle jars stand with swollen waists and narrow mouths, each sealed by an upturned bowl that rests in a channel of water around the rim.

Inside may lurk pickled mustard greens, radishes immersed in sweetened vinegar, or soy sauce-pickled cucumbers so dark they appear almost black.

There are stories and legends connected with many of the region's preserves. None, perhaps, is more poignant than the tale of Peihong, a kitchen servant in a grand Shaoxing household after whom Peihong vegetable (*pei hong cai*), a popular Shaoxing pickle very like snow vegetable, is named. Peihong and her fellow servants, the tale goes, were ill-treated by their master, and given such revolting, spoiled food to eat that they lost their appetites. Peihong worked out a way of preserving tired, wilted greens, transforming them into a mouth-watering pickle. The servants recovered their spirits and their appetites, but their miserly master was so dismayed by the amount they ate that he beat Peihong to death. Her memory, however, lives on in the name of the preserve.

In Ningbo and the other coastal regions, people like to wind-dry fish and other seafood. Sea eels are split open, salted and wind-dried; just steamed with a dash of rice wine, they make a fabulous appetizer. Yellow croakers and other sea fish are salted and wind-dried to make pungent *xiang*, an ingredient that brings a funky thrill to steamed chopped pork or tender tofu. Ningbo is also famous for its salted crab: raw crab that is steeped for a few days in strong liquor with salt and Sichuan pepper, then eaten raw.

Some of the weirdest and most fascinating preserves come from Shaoxing, which is known for its "stinky and rotten" (*chou mei*) delicacies. One of these is rotted amaranth stalks, made by chopping the thick stalks of overgrown amaranth plants into sections and fermenting them until they have a wildly stinky aroma and have partially disintegrated into a pool of smelly green liquid. At this point, the stalks are retrieved and steamed, usually with pork or tofu. They are certainly an acquired taste, but I find them utterly addictive. The malodorous liquid left after their fermentation is a magic potion that is used to ferment other ingredients such as tofu and squash, generating a whole family of stinky—and delicious—foods.

For everyday eating, Shanghainese pickled radish is one of the easiest and most rewarding preserves to make at home. Keep a jar in the fridge and eat it as an appetizer, side dish or relish with your breakfast congee. And although snow vegetable, used widely in Jiangnan cooking, can be bought ready-made in most Chinese supermarkets, the homemade version is worth producing for its fresh perkiness and lively color.

Stock

Chinese cooks say a chef's stock is like the pitch of an opera singer; it is the means by which he expresses his art. Before cheap, pure monosodium glutamate became available in the twentieth century, stocks were among the most important umami flavorings. They were used as a base for soups and stews and, in smaller quantities, to magnify the savoriness of steamed dishes, sauces and stir-fries. In contemporary China, the finest restaurants still rely on traditionally made stocks rather than the quick fix of MSG.

There are no hard-and-fast rules for making stocks, and a good one can be a personal signature, even a secret formula. In the old days, when master chefs were famous for "holding back a trick or two" (*liu yi shou*), they used to sneak ingredients into their stocks when their apprentices weren't looking. Over the past decade or so, I have discussed stock-making with chefs all over the Jiangnan region and gleaned some useful tips. In particular, master chef Dong Jinmu of the Dragon Well Manor restaurant, formerly of the legendary Hangzhou restaurant Louwailou, has shared several of his recipes with me. It was at the Dragon Well Manor restaurant that my eyes were fully opened to the beauty of stock, through the restaurant's insistence on the finest natural ingredients and the total absence of MSG.

There are two broad categories of stocks: clear stocks (*qing tang*) and rich or milky stocks (*nong tang*). A clear stock is often made from chicken, ideally a mature and flavorful hen, or a mixture of chicken and pork. Most importantly, after a stockpot full of ingredients has been brought to the boil, it is simmered over a very gentle flame for at least two hours and sometimes several more, its surface barely murmuring, so that the liquid remains clear. The most exquisite clear stocks will be totally clean and transparent, without a drop of oil; traditionally, they are clarified by using rafts of puréed meat to collect impurities that rise to the surface. Without going to such extreme lengths, you can make an excellent clear stock at home by simmering it very gently,

straining the broth through a fine-meshed sieve or even muslin, then chilling it overnight so the fat solidifies on the surface and can be neatly removed.

A rich or milky stock (*nong tang* or *nai tang*) is made with ingredients that include collagen-rich foods such as pig's feet and skin or, for a fish stock, fish bones. After a period of gentle simmering, the stock is cooked over a medium flame so the fats emulsify into it, and it becomes slightly opaque and creamy in texture—a good rich stock will feel deliciously sticky on the lips. Rich stocks are mainly used in banquet cookery, and can also be used to bring a sense of luxury to understated ingredients such as Chinese cabbage, tofu and stir-fried greens. At home, you can enrich a basic stock by adding a little lard at the end of cooking and fast-boiling it until the fat emulsifies into the broth.

Chinese cooks like to refine their stock ingredients by dispeling the unsavory aspects of their natural tastes, which are known variously as "fishy tastes" (*xing wei*), "off tastes" (*yi wei*) and, in the case of beef, goat and lamb, "muttony tastes" (*shan wei*). This is why most ingredients are blanched in boiling water, then rinsed before simmering for stock. The other chief strategy for purifying the flavor is to add ginger and spring onion, and sometimes a little Sichuan pepper or other spices.

Fish stocks can be made by frying fish bones in lard with spring onion and ginger, splashing in a bit of Shaoxing wine, adding plenty of boiling water, then covering the pot and boiling for 5–10 minutes until the fats emulsify, to yield a rich, milky liquid. The finest fish stocks in China are made from crucian carp, which, sadly, is hard to find in Europe.

Here I offer recipes for some of the classic types of stock, but feel free to tailor them to your own convenience and desires. If you have a pressure cooker, you can make wonderful stocks very quickly, cooking them for 40 minutes at the lower pressure setting, or 30 minutes at higher pressure.

Everyday stock

xian tang 鲜汤

For everyday cooking I normally make stock from free-range chicken carcasses, with pork ribs and perhaps chicken wings if I want something a little richer.

I either use stock fresh or box it up and freeze it in useful quantities. For recipes such as soups, in which stock is a major ingredient, I'd advise you to do the same, or to buy good stock from a delicatessen or butcher. Where stock is used in smaller amounts as a seasoning, it's easier to get away with using a little stock made from good chicken or vegetarian stock cubes, but if you do this, keep an eye on the quantities of any other salty seasonings.

1 oz (30g) fresh ginger, skin on
2 spring onions, white parts only

3–4 raw chicken carcasses
A smaller amount of pork ribs or other bones (optional)

Smack the ginger and spring onions lightly with the flat side of a Chinese cleaver or a rolling pin to loosen their fibers. Bring a large pan of water to the boil. Add the chicken carcasses and pork ribs or bones, if using, and bring back to the boil for about 1 minute. Drain in a colander in the sink, discarding the water, and rinse well under the tap. Rinse out the pan.

Return the carcasses and ribs to the pan, cover with fresh water and bring to the boil. Skim, then add the ginger and spring onions. Turn down the heat and simmer gently for 2–3 hours, uncovered. Strain and discard the solid ingredients, reserving the stock. Allow to cool completely, then chill or freeze.

Chicken stock and chicken oil

Follow the same method as for everyday stock, but use either just chicken carcasses or a whole boiling or free-range chicken to make the broth. After chilling it, you may remove the fat that has solidified on the surface and use this "chicken oil" (*ji you*) to enhance the flavors of your dishes: add a tablespoon or so to a steamed fish, a soup or some stir-fried vegetables just before serving for extra umami richness. I usually freeze chicken oil in thin layers, so I can break it off in small amounts and add it directly to the wok.

Fine banquet stock

gao tang 高汤

In smart restaurants and for special occasions, cooks will make banquet stock (literally "high stock," *gao tang*, or "superior stock," *shang tang*) from chicken and pork enriched with other ingredients that might include lean ham, dried scallops and sometimes duck or pigeon. Some chefs fry their chickens and pork for extra fragrance before making stock, but in my experience this isn't common.

If you can, use a mature hen to make this stock; and as with any chicken, do choose a good free-range bird. A couple of dried scallops, an expensive luxury ingredient, will add an extra umami kick.

1 free-range chicken
1⅓ lbs (600g) pork ribs
2½ oz (60g) lean Chinese or Spanish cured ham
2 oz (50g) fresh ginger, skin on
2 spring onions, white parts only
2 dried scallops (optional)
2 tbsp Shaoxing wine

Bring a large pan of water to the boil. Add the chicken, ribs and ham and bring back to the boil for 1–2 minutes. Drain in a colander in the sink, discarding the water, and rinse well under the tap. Rinse out the pan.

Return the ingredients to the pan. Cover generously with water and bring to the boil. Smack the ginger and spring onions lightly with the flat side of a Chinese cleaver or a rolling pin to loosen their fibers.

When the stock has come to the boil, skim it well. Add the dried scallops, if using, ginger, spring onions and Shaoxing wine. Return to the boil, then turn down the heat and simmer very gently, uncovered, for at least 3 hours, preferably longer. Strain out the solid ingredients. Strain through muslin if you wish, for an even clearer finish. Allow to cool completely before chilling.

Vegetarian stocks
su xian tang 素鲜汤

In Jiangnan, meaty stocks are used to enrich and flavor many vegetable dishes, but pure vegetarian food is served in the restaurants of Buddhist monasteries. Here are a few suggestions for making vegetarian stocks.

Quick vegetarian stock

This is a recipe from the vegetarian restaurant at the Jade Buddha Temple in Shanghai, where they use it for their noodle and wonton soups. Simply season hot water with light soy sauce and a little sesame oil (for 1 quart/1 liter water, about 2½ tsp light soy sauce and ½ tsp sesame oil will do). Simple, but very savory.

Black bean stock

Bring 1 quart (1 liter) water to the boil with 2 oz (50g) black fermented beans, rinsed and drained, then simmer for about 20 minutes. Strain out and discard the black beans if you wish.

Sprouted soybean stock

Sprouted soybeans are a classic vegetarian soup base. The beansprouts, which are longer and thicker than the more common mung beansprouts, are easily available in China but hard to come by in the West, so you may have to sprout your own. To make a "milky" broth, bring a panful of water to the boil, add plenty of soybean sprouts, cover with a lid and boil for 10–20 minutes, until the liquid is richly savory. To make a clear broth, boil the water, add the sprouts, return to the boil and simmer gently, uncovered, for about 30 minutes. Strain the broth, or add the beansprouts to your soups if you wish. (Dried soybeans can also be used to make stock, but they need extremely lengthy cooking to make them digestible—around 4 hours.)

Pickled vegetable stock

If you boil slivers or slices of preserved mustard tuber in boiling water for a few minutes, they will yield a broth with a delicate salty-sour umami flavor. Use this to make simple, cleansing vegetable soups. See page 216 for an example.

Other variations

Other classic ingredients in vegetarian stocks are fresh bamboo shoot, simmered for a while like the soybean sprouts, and shiitake mushrooms. For a rich vegetarian stock, use a mixture of soybean sprouts, peeled bamboo shoot and reconstituted dried shiitake mushrooms.

Easy jellied stock

pi dong 皮冻

Jellied stock is an essential ingredient in steamed "soup" dumplings (*xiao long bao*) and potsticker buns. It's traditionally made from gelatine-rich pig's skin or trotters, but it's much easier, and just as effective, to make it simply by adding gelatine to a good stock. If you have any jellied stock left after making dumpling stuffings, add it to soups, congees and stir-fries for extra savoriness.

2 cups (500ml) clear Everyday or Chicken stock (see page 317)

4 gelatine leaves
Salt and ground white pepper

Bring the stock to the boil, then set it aside. Season with salt and pepper. When the stock has cooled to tea-drinking temperature, put the gelatine in a bowl of cold water for about 4 minutes, until softened and floppy, then stir it into the warm stock until dissolved. Set aside to cool completely, then chill in the fridge overnight to set.

Traditional jellied stock

pi dong 皮冻

This is a recipe for old-fashioned jellied stock made by extracting the natural gelatine from pig's trotters with a long simmering (its name in Chinese means "skin jelly"). It has a rich and wonderful flavor; make more than you need, freeze the surplus and use it to add richness to soups, stews and other dishes.

2 pig's trotters (about 1¾ lbs/750g)
2 chicken carcasses
1 oz (30g) fresh ginger, skin on

2 spring onions, white parts only
1 tbsp Shaoxing wine
Salt and ground white pepper

Ask your butcher to split the trotters in half lengthways. Give them a good rinse. Put the trotters and chicken carcasses in a large pan, cover with cold water and bring to the boil. Boil for 2 minutes, then drain and rinse well. Rinse out the pan. Smack the ginger and spring onion whites lightly with the flat side of a Chinese cleaver or a rolling pin to loosen their fibers.

Return the trotters and carcasses to the saucepan, cover with 3½ quarts (3.5 liters) water and bring to the boil. Skim, then add the ginger, spring onion and Shaoxing wine. Return to the boil, then turn down the heat and simmer gently for 3 hours.

Strain and discard the trotters and carcasses. Boil to reduce the liquid to about 1 quart (1 liter). Season with salt and pepper. Allow to cool completely, then chill in the fridge overnight, or until set.

Lard

zhu you 猪油

Lard is a magic ingredient in Jiangnan cookery, used to add richness and silkiness to soups, stir-fries and noodle dishes. It's also used widely in sweet dishes, especially for flaky pastries and luxuriant stuffings. You can buy lard in supermarkets but it's easy, if time-consuming, to make your own, and I find the homemade version has a cleaner, more neutral flavor.

The best ingredient for making lard is leaf fat, known as "stiff sheet fat" (*ban you*) in Chinese, which surrounds the viscera of the pig, but back fat or belly fat can also be used. Butchers tend not to put their pork fat on display, but can usually supply it if you place an order in advance. If the lard is clean and meat-free, it will keep excellently in the fridge or freezer. I tend to freeze my lard in thinnish layers so I can break off small quantities for use in stir-fries and soups. To save time, you can ask your butcher to mince the fat.

4 lbs (2kg) leaf lard or pork back or belly fat, minced if possible

Preheat the oven to 250°F (120°C). If the fat is not already minced, cut it into 1 in (2cm) strips, then into 1 in (2cm) chunks. Put them in a wide ovenproof pan and add ¼ cup (50ml) water. Put the pan, uncovered, in the oven and cook slowly for about 4 hours, stirring every 30 minutes or so. At first it will make soft, wet, blubbery sounds; later it will gently fizz and seethe as the fat yields up its pale golden liquor. By the end, the fat will be crisp and honey-colored. (These crisp cracklings can be retained and added to other dishes for crunch and umami richness.)

Strain the molten lard through a sieve lined with clean muslin. Pour into sterilized preserving jars and store in the fridge, or allow to cool, then scoop into freezer bags for freezing.

Wheat gluten

mian jin 面筋

In Chinese, gluten is known as the "muscle" of the flour (*mian jin*), which not only expresses perfectly its strong, stretchy qualities, but also hints at the labor required to make it, because transforming wheat flour into gluten—by hand, at least—demands a lot of muscle. It's worth doing from time to time, however, because the taste and texture of homemade gluten tend to be far superior to those of the store-bought variety. Transforming a ball of dough into gluten, then boiling or frying it, is also great fun and rather amazing.

You'll find a colorful recipe for stir-fried gluten on page 213, but feel free to use it in other dishes. Deep-fried gluten makes a delicious addition to red-braised pork, where it absorbs all the rich, meaty juices, and can also be stir-fried with bok choy and other greens. Make sure you knead the dough until it's as smooth as possible, then extract as much starch as you can; this way, your gluten will be smooth, light and pillowy.

A frugal tip: if you wish, you can keep the thick, milky liquid from the first few rinsings of the dough—perhaps 1¾–2 cups (400–500ml). Leave it to settle, then carefully discard the top layer of clear water, leaving a thick starchy liquid. Add to this an egg and a good handful of finely sliced spring onion greens and season with salt. Make this batter into thin pancakes, fried golden on both sides, and serve them alongside other dishes for breakfast, or at any other meal. (In northern China, they steam the thick starchy liquid in layers, and then cut the resulting sheets into the noodles known as "cold skin," *liang pi*.)

8 cups (1kg) strong white bread flour	2 tsp salt

Sift the flour and salt into a large bowl or onto a clean work surface and make a well in the center. Gradually add enough tepid water to make a fairly stiff dough, drawing the flour in from the sides as you do. Knead the dough until very smooth and shiny (you can do this in a stand mixer with a dough hook if you like). Cover with a damp tea towel and leave to rest for at least 1 hour.

Put the dough in a large mixing bowl. Add about ½ cup (100ml) cold water and knead the dough vigorously by hand with the water. You will notice that the liquid quickly becomes milky: this is the starch leaching out of the dough. When the liquid has become thick and white, like light cream, strain it off and discard. Return the wet dough to the bowl and continue adding water in stages, kneading thoroughly between each addition to extract as much starch as possible, and straining off the milky liquid. Make sure you massage out any hard spots in the dough: this is where the starch is lurking.

Keep kneading and rinsing until the water is running pretty clear and you are left with a soft, squishy mass of ivory-colored gluten. The whole process is likely to take around an hour, and you should be left with 2¼–3 cups (300–350g) gluten.

Vegetarian "intestines"

su chang 素肠

This gorgeous little piece of Buddhist trickery not only fools the eye, but also the palate, because the slices of "intestine" so precisely mimic the springy mouthfeel of the real thing. My friends chef Jason Li and his mother, He Yuxiu, taught me how to make them. Add the sliced "intestines" to vegetarian dishes, as you would with regular boiled gluten. Makes 3 "intestines."

To make simple boiled gluten, break it into cherry-sized pieces, drop them into boiling water and cook for 4 minutes, until they float to the surface of the water. Transfer to a bowl of cold water and store in the fridge.

Pictured at the left of the photograph (freshly made gluten pictured top right)

½ quantity Wheat gluten
   (see page 323)

Bring a pan of water to the boil. Take a ball of gluten about the size of a fist and cut it into 3 pieces. Take a pair of natural, unpainted wooden or bamboo chopsticks and hold them together. Wrap one piece of the gluten around the chopsticks, stretching it as you go. You want to end up with a nice bulgy wrapping that extends along most of the length of the chopsticks, without any gaps between the layers of gluten.

Drop the wrapped chopsticks into the boiling water and cook for 4–5 minutes, then transfer to a bowl of cold water. When cool enough to handle, wiggle the chopsticks out of the gluten "intestine," then slice it into ⅛ in (5mm) rings. Keep it in cold water until required. The "intestines" will keep for a couple of days in the fridge, or longer in the freezer.

Fried gluten puffs

you mian jin 油面筋

There is a kind of magic in deep-frying gluten, because when the little pieces enter the hot oil, they puff up dramatically like zeppelins, until they are five or six times their original size and become light, papery and fragile.

Fried gluten puffs, known in Chinese as "oil gluten" (*you mian jin*) are often stir-fried or chopped and added to vegetarian stuffings for buns and dumplings. Sometimes, the puffs themselves are stuffed with pork. Makes 18–20 puffs.

Pictured at the bottom right of the photograph

½ quantity Wheat gluten   Cooking oil, for deep-frying
   (see page 323)

Break the gluten into pieces the size of large cherries. Heat oil for deep-frying to 350–400°F (180–200°C). Working in batches, drop some pieces of gluten into the hot oil. Don't put them too close together, to prevent sticking. Fry, stirring occasionally for even coloring, for 2–3 minutes, until they are puffy and golden and float on the surface of the oil. Drain and set aside. The puffs can be kept for a week or so in the fridge, and longer in the freezer.

Fermented glutinous rice wine

jiu niang 酒酿

The simplest kind of homemade rice wine, this sweet-sour, boozy concoction is a common flavoring for sweet dishes in the Jiangnan region and elsewhere. Known in Jiangnan as "wine ferment" (*jiu niang*), it is made by mixing steamed glutinous rice with a special blend of molds and yeasts, then leaving them to their own devices in a warm, cozy place. Over a few days, the molds transform the rice starch into sugars, and the yeasts then turn the sugars into alcohol and lactic acids, so you end up with a soupy mix of soft, pulpy rice grains and a marvelously aromatic liquid. Unusually, this wine is not strained, but is used along with the residue of the grains. You can find it in Chinese supermarkets, but the homemade version is more delicious. It keeps for ages in the fridge.

You'll need a clean glass or clay jar with a lid, a steamer and a piece of clean muslin.

1¼ cups (250g) long-grain glutinous rice	1 Chinese wine yeast ball (about ⅓ oz/10g)

Rinse the rice in cold water until the water runs clear, then cover it with fresh water and soak it for 3–4 hours or overnight. Drain the rice and put it in a steamer lined with muslin, spreading it out in an even layer, but not packing it tightly. Steam over a high flame for 20 minutes, until tender. Boil the kettle, then leave it to cool.

Take the rice out of the steamer and spread it out so that it cools quickly. Crush the wine yeast to a powder with a pestle and mortar. When the rice is lukewarm, scatter over the crushed yeast and mix it in. Put the mixture into a glass or earthenware jar. Make a hollow in the center of the rice, all the way to the bottom of the jar, so the juices can gather. Sprinkle over 3–4 tablespoons cooled boiled water, then close the jar with a clean tea towel or a loose-fitting lid and leave in a warm place to ferment. The ideal temperature for this is 85°F (30°C) (A Zhejiang farmer who makes this wine professionally warned me not to let it exceed 95°F/35°C, or the wine will sour.)

The wine will be ready after a few days, depending on the ambient temperature. After a day, you can check it: when it is ready, the rice grains will be soft and pulpy but still keep their shape, and the liquid should be beautifully aromatic, with just a gentle hint of sourness. When you reach this stage, top the jar up with cooled boiled water, close with the lid and store in the fridge until needed.

Red bean paste

dou sha 豆沙

Red bean paste, made from little adzuki beans, lard and sugar, is one of the mainstay sweet stuffings for pastries and dumplings all over China. Homemade red bean paste is a real treat, but rather a palaver to make, so you may prefer to buy the tinned version in a Chinese grocery. If you do make it yourself, it stores well in the fridge or freezer. The paste can also be made with coconut oil, which is not authentic but works excellently. Makes approximately 14 oz (400g) red bean paste.

10 oz (300g) dried adzuki beans	5 oz (150g) lard or coconut oil
	10 oz (300g) superfine sugar

Soak the beans overnight in cold water, then rinse and drain them. Put them in a pan, cover with plenty of cold water, bring to the boil, skim and simmer for 30–45 minutes, until completely soft. Drain the beans, reserving the liquid.

Press the beans through a mouli-legumes to remove the skins, adding a little of the cooking liquid if you need it, to help them through. (You can do this using only a pestle and a sturdy sieve, but it's a tedious job, and the amount of bean paste you end up with will depend on the quality of your sieve and the level of your patience.)

Boil the kettle. Melt the lard or coconut oil in a deep pan. Add the beans, sugar and ⅓ cup (75ml) hot water and heat gently to dissolve the sugar, stirring constantly. Increase the heat and stir constantly until the paste is thick and glossy and the water has mostly evaporated, stirring and scraping the bottom of the pan so it doesn't catch. When the paste is ready, it will start to come away from the base of the pan. Do take care while stirring, as the hot paste will spit as it bubbles. Turn the paste into a container and leave to cool. Store in the fridge.

Jujube paste

This delectable variation is made with dried jujubes (also known as Chinese dates), and can be used instead of red bean paste in, for example, the pumpkin cakes on page 300 and the rice pudding on page 294. To make it, split open 10 oz (300g) dried jujubes. Soak them in water for 1 hour. Drain them, put them in a bowl and steam over a high flame for about 30 minutes, until tender. When cool enough to handle, remove and discard the stones, then pass through a mouli-legumes. Place in a pan with 3 oz (70g) lard or coconut oil, ½ cup (100g) sugar and ⅓ cup (75ml) water. Stir constantly over a medium flame to melt the sugar and evaporate the water, as in the main recipe. Makes about 16 oz (450g) paste.

Shanghai soy-pickled radish

jiang luo bo 酱萝卜

This crisp, juicy pickle is totally addictive, and a wonderful standby to keep in the fridge. In Shanghai, I've often eaten it as an appetizer alongside other dishes; at home, I might have a few slices with breakfast congee or, in a non-Chinese context, with cold meats or cheese. Just a slice or two perks up almost any meal. Do make it with fresh, firm, clean-looking radishes, ideally those picked after a winter frost, when they are sweetest. Don't use radishes with flesh that is holey or cottony in texture. Some people add a dried chilli or two to the pickling brine. In restaurants, they often arrange the curved slices of pickled radish in concentric circles on the serving dish, like the petals of a flower.

Shanghai soy-pickled radish; Shanghai pickled radish skin; Snow vegetable (bottom left); Shaoxing dried fermented greens (bottom right)

1 fresh, clean, firm white
    Asian radish (about 1¾
    lbs/750g)
2 tsp salt
A little sesame oil, to serve

For the pickling liquid:
⅓ cup (90ml) light soy sauce
½ cup (100ml) cooled boiled
    water
4 tbsp superfine sugar
3 tbsp Chinese red or rose
    vinegar

Wash the radish well, but don't peel it. Trim off and discard both ends, along with any whiskers or blemishes. Cut in half lengthways and then, holding the knife diagonally, cut each half into ⅙ in (5mm) slices. Put the slices in a non-reactive container, add the salt and mix well. Cover with a small plate, then weigh this down with a heavy stone or weight. Leave in the fridge or another cold place for 24–48 hours to press out much of the liquid.

Mix the ingredients for the pickling liquid together, stirring to dissolve the sugar. Drain the radishes, squeezing out as much liquid as possible. Immerse the radishes in the pickling liquid in a non-reactive container; use a small plate to keep them covered by the liquid and keep in the fridge for 2 days before eating. The pickle will keep well in the fridge for at least several weeks.

To serve, remove some of the radish from the pickling liquid and dress with a tiny amount of sesame oil.

Shanghai pickled radish skin

Many Jiangnan people adore the pickled skin of the radish, because it has a tighter, more distinctive crispness. Take 3 white radishes and trim, top and tail them as described above. Put each radish on your chopping board and thickly slice off one of its sides, including the skin and about ½ in (1cm) of flesh at the thickest part. Rotate the radish by 90 degrees and do the same again. Repeat twice, so that you end up with one long baton of inner radish that is square in cross-section, and four long, thick strips of skin. Use the inner flesh of the radish for other recipes (it will be delicious in soups and stews, or slivered and made into a salad – see page 41). Put a piece of radish skin on your chopping board and cut it diagonally into ½–1 in (1–2cm) strips. Salt and pickle it in the soy-sauce brine as in the main recipe.

Sweet-and-sour pickled ginger

tang cu pao jiang 糖醋泡姜

This is a perky little relish from the Dragon Well Manor restaurant in Hangzhou: sweet, sour and peppery from the ginger. Chef Yang Aiping taught me how to make it. Serve this pickle with appetizers or breakfast congee, or just have a piece between dishes to refresh your palate, like a sorbet. Many Chinese people would advise that it's best to eat ginger in the summer, according to the adage: "Eat radish in the winter, ginger in the summer" (*dong chi luo bo xia chi jiang*).

7 oz (200g) fresh, plump, tender ginger	8 tbsp red Chinese vinegar
1 tsp salt	6 tbsp superfine sugar

Peel the ginger and cut it lengthways into ⅛ in (5mm) slices, then into ⅛ in (5mm) strips. Add the salt, mix well and set it aside for 1 hour to draw out some of the pepperiness. Bring a little water to the boil, then set it aside to cool.

Drain off any liquid from the ginger, then rinse it in the cooled boiled water. Squeeze out as much liquid as possible from the ginger, then squeeze dry. Put it in a non-reactive pot or jar with the vinegar and sugar. Steep for at least 2 days before using. The pickle will keep in the fridge for a few weeks at least.

Soy-pickled ginger

This is a recipe from my Shanghainese friend and teacher, He Yuxiu, who advises that it should be eaten in the morning rather than the evening. Enjoy it with breakfast congee or steamed buns. Peel 7 oz (200g) fresh, plump ginger and cut lengthways into fairly thin slices. Salt, rinse and squeeze as in the main recipe, then put it into a jam jar. Mix 4 tbsp light soy sauce with 1 tbsp sugar and 2 tbsp cooled boiled water, and pour over the ginger. Steep for at least 2 days before using.

Snow vegetable

xue cai 雪菜

This brisk, salt-sour, mustardy pickle is one of the staples of the Jiangnan kitchen, and is extremely easy to make. In the region, they make it with Chinese potherb mustard (*xue li hong*), but local chefs working abroad achieve similar and very satisfactory results with radish tops and small mustard greens. When freshly made, the pickled greens are emerald-bright; after a week or two they will fade to a darker, dimmer green. The pickle derives its curious name from the fact that potherb mustard flourishes in cold, snowy weather. Local people say the vegetable should be gathered and pickled before Li Chun, the Beginning of Spring, while its leaves are still young and tender.

This is one of the easiest Jiangnan pickles to make and has myriad culinary applications. It has a particular affinity with fish and seafood—just try steaming a fish or some clams with some of the juices from your pickle jar, a dash of Shaoxing wine and a little crushed ginger and spring onion, for a simple and delicious dish.

Once you've seen how easy and rewarding it is to make snow vegetable, you'll probably find yourself keeping a constant supply on hand, as I do. This is a fresh, quick pickle that is ready to eat after a week. I worked out this recipe with the guidance of chefs Hu Zhongying and Zhu Yinfeng.

See photograph on page 329

1¾ lbs (750g) small mustard greens, potherb mustard or radish tops	1 tbsp salt

Wash the greens thoroughly, then thread them onto a coathanger or a length of string and hang them to dry overnight in a cool place. (Many people advise sun-drying the greens for half a day before pickling; if you wish to do this, hang them up or lay them out on bamboo trays in strong sunlight.)

The following day, chop the greens coarsely into ½ in (1cm) pieces and put them in a large basin. Sprinkle with the salt, then scrunch it into the greens, using similar movements to those you would use if kneading bread dough (your eyes may water slightly from the hot, mustardy fumes). Knead until the salt is thoroughly incorporated, and the greens look wet and are already exuding their juices.

Pack the greens into a sterilized glass jar with a tight-fitting lid. Use the end of a wooden rolling pin to press them tightly into the jar, so they are covered with a thin layer of their own liquid. Seal with the lid and leave at room temperature to ferment. Open the jar once a day to allow any gases to escape during the initial fermentation. You want the greens to acquire a delicious sour-savory taste; the exact timing will depend on temperature, but I've found about a week at room temperature is fine, with less time when the weather is hot, and more in a colder place. When the pickle is ready, keep it in the fridge for a month or two, or store it in the freezer.

Shaoxing dried fermented greens

mei gan cai 霉干菜

The dried fermented pickle known as *mei gan cai*, or sometimes *wu gan cai* (black dried vegetable), is the heart and soul of Shaoxing cooking. It has a rich, intense flavor reminiscent of soy sauce, but with a pleasingly tart edge.

According to local chef Mao Tianyao, who loves *mei gan cai* so much he has written two books about it, it's like a Mah Jong wildcard because you can play it any way you like, so plentiful are its culinary applications. Most famously, it is slow-cooked with pork belly (see page 93) but after a quick soaking it can also be used in stir-fries, soups and dumpling stuffings. In the past, *mei gan cai* was a poor man's food, used to lend umami flavors to cheap vegetarian ingredients like potatoes (see page 202) or simply boiled in water to make a flavorful and nourishing broth.

Many vegetables can be used to make *mei gan cai*, including round green cabbage, mustard greens, potherb mustard and green bok choy, each of which gives a pickle with a different shade and aroma. (One Shaoxing market vendor said he knew of forty varieties; the smell of one of his pickles reminded me of oolong tea, another, sleek and dark, of Marmite.) Often, *mei gan cai* is mixed with dried bamboo shoot to make "shoot dried vegetable" (*sun gan cai*).

After their initial pickling, the greens are sun dried, which darkens them and intensifies their flavor until they taste almost mushroomy. They keep indefinitely and their flavor matures over time. The smell given off as they dry is marvelous and bewitching.

See photograph on page 329

2 lbs (1kg) small mustard greens or potherb mustard	4 tsp salt

Wash the greens thoroughly, then thread them onto a coathanger or a length of string and hang them to dry overnight in a cool, shady place.

The following day, cut the greens into 2 in (5cm) lengths. If there are any thick stalks, cut them lengthways into very thin slices. Put all the greens in a large basin. Sprinkle with the salt, then scrunch it into the greens, using similar movements to those you would use if kneading bread dough (your eyes may water slightly from the hot, mustardy fumes). Knead until the salt is thoroughly incorporated, the greens look wet and are already exuding their juices.

Pack the greens very tightly into a sterilized glass jar. Cover them with a plate and a heavy stone or weight to weigh the plate down (I use a large old-fashioned weight). Cover the jar with a clean tea towel and leave in a shady place to ferment for a few days at room temperature, until they have turned a darker green and exude a heady fermented fragrance. Make sure the plate covers them all and weighs them down, or the top layer may go moldy.

On a day with strong sunlight, use chopsticks to remove the greens from the jar and spread them out in a thin layer on broad bamboo trays, or solid trays lined with clean tea towels. Unravel any tight knots of green leaves so that they dry more quickly. Leave them to dry in direct sunlight, turning them from time to time so they dry evenly (if the sun is not strong enough, they may taste moldy). If the weather changes, and in the evening, bring the trays indoors. Repeat the process until the greens are bone dry—this should take a few days, depending on the weather. Bag up the greens and store them until needed.

Sichuan pepper salt

jiao yan 椒盐

This classic dip is made with Sichuan pepper, which is gently roasted with salt until both are marvelously aromatic. The seasoning is particularly good with roasted meats and deep-fried foods, but can also be used in sweet dumplings and pastries, where the combination of sugar with a hint of salt and spice is delightful.

The dip will be most delicious soon after making; you can keep it in a sealed jar, but the pepper flavor dims over time.

1½ tbsp salt	½ tbsp whole Sichuan peppercorns

Put the salt and Sichuan peppercorns in a dry wok and stir gently over a very low flame for a few minutes, until your kitchen has filled with the gorgeous aroma of the toasted pepper and the salt has yellowed slightly. Tip the mixture into a mortar and grind it to a fine powder. Sift the powder through a tea strainer or a small sieve to remove any remaining woody pepper husk. Store in a sealed container.

Sweet fermented sauce dip

tian mian jiang 甜面酱

This sleek, dark sauce is used as a dip for various foods, including fresh cucumber batons, and also as a relish to be served with roast meats. It keeps indefinitely at room temperature.

1 tbsp cooking oil	1 tbsp white sugar, or to taste
5 tbsp sweet fermented sauce (see page 337)	

Boil the kettle. Heat the oil in a seasoned wok over a medium flame. Add the sweet fermented sauce and stir-fry for a minute or so until fragrant. Add ¼ cup (50ml) hot water and bring to the boil. Season with the sugar. Continue to stir until the sauce thickens to the consistency of tomato ketchup, then remove from the wok and set aside.

鼎中之变
精妙微纤
口弗能言
志弗能喻

The transformations that occur in the cooking pot are
so supremely wonderful and delicate that the mouth cannot
express them in words, nor the mind comprehend them.

Legendary chef Yi Yin, quoted in *The Root of Tastes*
by Lu Buwei (third century BC)
吕不韦, 吕氏春秋本味篇

PLANNING A MENU

There are no hard-and-fast rules for planning a Chinese menu; the key is to create a balance of ingredients and cooking methods that will leave your guests feeling happy and satisfied. So a rich dish of red-braised pork is best balanced with some light, refreshing vegetables; a juicy or soupy dish is a delightful counterweight to something deep-fried. Try to avoid repetition of main ingredients, colors and cooking methods.

Jiangnan meals tend to begin with cold dishes, most of which can be prepared in advance. Hot dishes are then served as they emerge from the kitchen, with soup and rice offered towards the end of the meal. In China, a meal normally concludes with fruit rather than sweet dishes; in a Chinese home you may be given whole fruits and a knife to peel them; in restaurants, fruit is usually cut and arranged beautifully on a serving platter. Dessert in the Western sense is not part of a traditional Chinese meal, but you may offer a Chinese sweetmeat in its place if you please. I like to combine traditions by serving seasonal fruit alongside chocolates, baklava or something else that hits the sweet spot. You may also like to greet your guests when they arrive with cups of green tea and "tea snacks" (*cha dian*), which might include dried fruits, nuts and seeds.

From the point of view of the cook, it's always worth including cold dishes that do not demand last-minute attention and at least one slow-cooked soup or stew that can be prepared in advance and reheated at dinner time. (Remember, also, that it's easy to increase quantities of cold dishes and stews, and more difficult to do the same with stir-fried dishes—see the tips on stir-frying on page 351.)

It's also worth keeping in mind that Jiangnan dishes can be deliciously combined on a menu with dishes from other Chinese regions. I often serve a mixture of Jiangnan and Sichuanese dishes at a single meal.

SERVING QUANTITIES

The dishes in this book are mostly intended to be shared with rice as part of a Chinese meal, rather than eaten individually. For this reason, serving quantities are not included. When planning a meal, the most important thing is to make sure that there is enough rice for everyone to eat their fill, while the number and amount of the accompanying dishes are more flexible. In general, try to think in terms of having one dish per person plus one extra, or more if you're feeling generous. The advantage of this method of calculation is that if an extra guest suddenly appears, you can simply add another place setting to the table.

The exceptions to this are noodles, which are typically served as a main meal in individual bowls (I have specified servings for noodle recipes), some sweet dishes, and dumplings and buns, for which I have indicated the approximate number of pieces each recipe makes, since the number eaten is normally a matter of personal appetite.

INGREDIENTS

ESSENTIALS

These few ingredients are the essentials of the Jiangnan kitchen, and are used in many of the recipes in this book. They are easy to find in most Chinese supermarkets. More details about each ingredient are given over the following pages.

Soy sauce, light and dark: A rich tamari soy sauce may be used instead of light soy sauce, especially for dipping.

Chinkiang vinegar: This dark brown rice vinegar can be found in most Chinese supermarkets.

Shaoxing wine: A basic cooking wine will do for most dishes, but where Shaoxing wine is a key flavoring, please use a drinking-quality wine.

Sesame oil: Pure toasted sesame oil can be found in Chinese shops and mainstream supermarkets. It is used in tiny quantities as a seasoning, so a bottle lasts for ages.

Potato starch or cornstarch: Potato starch can be found in most Chinese supermarkets; cornstarch can also be used.

A few spices: Start with cassia bark and star anise.

Dried shiitake mushrooms

Fresh ginger and spring onions

SEASONINGS, SAUCES AND COOKING WINES

食盐
Salt (shi yan)

Fine table salt is most suitable for use in the recipes in this book.

胡椒粉
White pepper, ground (hu jiao fen)

White pepper is favored in Chinese cookery because it is often used in so-called "white-flavored" (bai wei) dishes: pale-colored dishes made without soy sauce, which would be marred by a speckling of black pepper. I follow Chinese practice in my recipes, but if you prefer to use black pepper, do go ahead.

鲜汤
Stock (xian tang)

Stock is a vital ingredient in soups and stews, and is used to amplify umami flavors in other dishes. I make my own stocks from chicken carcasses and/or pork bones and store them in batches in the freezer (see pages 316–21). Canned unsalted chicken stock or bouillon cubes can also be used (when using the latter, which tend to be salty, you may need to reduce the amount of salty seasonings in a recipe). In the recipes here, use stock made from chicken, or chicken and pork, unless otherwise specified. Vegetarians may wish to substitute a vegetarian stock where stock is used in otherwise vegetarian dishes.

酱油
Soy sauce (jiang you)

Soy sauce is made by fermenting cooked soybeans, sometimes with wheat, innoculating them with mold spores and immersing them in brine, a process that breaks down their proteins to create delicious flavors. Traditionally, Jiangnan cooks use a single soy sauce that is both umami-salty and dark, but these days many chefs use Cantonese light and dark soy sauces instead. For the sake of convenience, I've suggested using the easily available light and dark soy sauces in my recipes. (At home, I sometimes use an organic tamari soy sauce, which is similar to traditional Jiangnan soy sauces, wheat-free and particularly delicious when used for dipping. If you wish to use tamari, use the same quantities suggested in the recipes for light soy sauce.) Whichever soy sauces you use, make sure they are naturally fermented.

生抽
Light soy sauce (sheng chou)

Light soy sauce is made from the first liquid run-off from fermented soybeans. It has a thin consistency and is very salty. It is used mainly for its salty-umami flavor, in cooking and as a dip. "Premium" and "deluxe" soy sauces are far superior to the basic versions, and well worth the extra expense.

老抽
Dark soy sauce (lao chou)
Dark soy sauce is made from the heavy liquid that can be drawn from a vat of fermenting soybeans after the light soy sauce has been taken. It has a heavy, syrupy consistency and an extremely dark color; it is also less salty than light soy sauce. It is used mainly where a rich color is required. At home, I use a mushroom-flavored dark soy sauce, which was recommended to me by one of my favorite Shanghai restaurants.

白糖
Superfine sugar (bai tang)
Aside from its use in sweetmeats, sugar often appears as a seasoning in Jiangnan dishes. Even where sweetness is not a dominant note, very small amounts of sugar may be used to round out or harmonize flavors (he wei). In my recipes, sugar always means white superfine sugar unless otherwise specified. Until very recently, Chinese chefs used burned sugar (tang se) to color their stews and sauces, but this has fallen out of favor because of concerns over the potentially carcinogenic effects of burned foods; nowadays dark soy sauce is used instead.

冰糖
Rock sugar (bing tang)
Rock sugar (its Chinese name translates as "ice sugar") has a mellow caramel flavor and is often used in slow-cooked or tonic dishes. Sometimes the crystals are very large and need crushing before use with a pestle and mortar.

镇江醋, 陈醋
Chinkiang vinegar or brown rice vinegar (zhen jiang cu, chen cu)
The city of Zhenjiang in Jiangsu province (also known as Chinkiang) produces one of China's most famous vinegars, a heady brew of glutinous rice colored dark brown by charred rice, with a rich, mellow flavor. It is somewhat reminiscent of lighter Italian balsamic vinegars, which can be used as a substitute.

大红浙醋, 玫瑰醋
Red or rose rice vinegar (da hong zhe cu, mei gui cu)
Paler in hue than Chinkiang vinegar, this variety is known in Chinese as "rose vinegar" (mei gui cu) because of its pinkish tint, or Zhejiang vinegar (zhe cu) because it's a speciality of Zhejiang province. It is used both in cooking and as a table condiment.

甜面酱
Sweet fermented sauce (tian mian jiang)
This thick, dark paste is made from fermented wheat and salt, sometimes with added soy, and has a rich, earthy taste with a hint of sweetness. It is used in cooking and to make a dipping sauce. Confusingly, it is often sold with the English names "sweet bean sauce" and "hoisin" sauce, so look out for the Chinese characters to make sure you're buying the right thing. Jiangnan cooks also use a similar paste made from soybeans (dou ban jiang); for the sake of simplicity, I've used only sweet fermented sauce in this book.

蒜茸辣酱酱
Chilli and garlic sauce (suan rong la jiao jiang)
In general, Jiangnan food is not spicy-hot but the Shanghainese, in particular, do like to add a hint of chilli heat to some dishes. Chilli and garlic sauce works well; you could also use sambal oelek or another pickled chilli paste.

绍兴酒, 黄酒, 料酒
Shaoxing wine (shao xing jiu, huang jiu, liao jiu)
Glutinous rice wine with a distinctive amber color, known as "yellow wine" in Chinese, is the most famous product of Shaoxing, which has been renowned for its brews for more than 2,000 years. Basic Shaoxing cooking wines can be found in virtually any Chinese supermarket, and are perfectly adequate for use in small quantities (medium-dry sherry can be used as a subsitute). However, for dishes where wine is a key flavoring, such as Dongpo pork and drunken chicken, do use wine of drinking quality, such as Huadiao wine.

花雕酒
Huadiao wine (hua diao jiu)
The finest medium-dry Shaoxing wines are sometimes stored in carved and painted clay jars, hence the name "carved-decoration" (hua diao) wine. You should be able to find Huadiao wine in better Chinese supermarkets, along with the "added rice" (jia fan 加饭) and "red daughter" (nu'er hong 女儿红) varieties, the latter named because of the custom of laying down a jar of wine upon the

birth of a daughter, and bringing it out for her red-bedecked wedding. Any of these may be used in dishes such as Dongpo pork and drunken chicken.

高粱酒, 白酒
Sorghum liquor
(gao liang jiu, bai jiu)

Fierce, burning liquors made from sorghum and other grains are typically drunk in toasts at formal dinners, and used only occasionally in cooking. In Jiangnan, small amounts of such liquors may be used to add fragrance to "drunken" foods, and also to refine the flavors of vegetable dishes. At home I use Red Star *er guo tou* sorghum liquor, which is 55 proof.

酒酿, 甜酒, 醪糟
Fermented glutinous rice wine
(jiu niang, tian jiu, lao zao)

This gentle, sweet-sour, aromatic liquor is made by fermenting cooked glutinous rice with a special wine yeast that is sold in balls in good Chinese supermarkets (see below). The wine is easily recognizable because it still contains the softened, denatured rice grains that remain after fermentation. Known by various names in China, and in Jiangnan as *jiu niang*, it can easily be made at home (see page 326). It is mainly used in sweet dishes.

酒曲
Wine yeast *(jiu qu)*

This is the essential ingredient for transforming cooked glutinous rice into fermented glutinous rice wine (see above). It is sold in pale lightweight balls or tablets, and should be crushed with a pestle and mortar.

SPICES

八角, 大茴香
Star anise *(ba jiao, da hui xiang)*

Star anise, often paired with cassia bark, is one of the key spices in Jiangnan cooking. It has a powerful flavor and should be used sparingly.

桂皮
Cassia bark *(gui pi)*

Often used with star anise, these strips of bark from the Chinese cassia tree have a cinnamon-like flavor. Cassia bark is easily found in Chinese supermarkets; cinnamon sticks can be used instead.

香叶
Bay leaves *(xiang ye)*

Known simply as "fragrant leaves" in Chinese, bay leaves are often used alongside other spices, particularly in five-spiced dishes.

草果
Tsao-kuo or black cardamom *(cao guo)*

These dark ridged seed pods, nutmeg-sized, have a cool, cardamom-like flavor and are often used in Chinese spice mixes. Although sometimes known in English as false or black cardamom, they are usually sold as *tsao-kuo* or *amomum tsao-kuo*. Before use, crack them partly open by smacking gently with the flat side of a Chinese cleaver or a rolling pin.

五香粉
Five-spice powder *(wu xiang fen)*

This seasoning, made from an assortment of spices (not necessarily five), often includes Sichuan pepper, cassia bark, star anise and fennel seeds.

山奈, 沙姜
Sand ginger *(shan nai, sha jiang)*

This spice looks like dried ginger, but is actually made from the sliced, dried rhizome of another plant in the same family, a kind of galangal known in Chinese as sand ginger or *shan nai* (*Kaempferia galanga*). It has a peppery aroma and is used in spice mixtures and some dishes, including beggar's chicken.

甘草
Dried licorice root *(gan cao)*

Dried sliced licorice, known as "sweet grass" in Chinese, can be found in most Chinese supermarkets.

花椒
Sichuan pepper *(hua jiao)*

Jiangnan cooks use Sichuan pepper in salt cures and to make salt-and-pepper dip (see page 333).

干辣椒
Dried chillies *(gan la jiao)*

Dried chillies are occasionally used in Jiangnan cookery, especially in Shanghai and in rural, mountainous areas. Avoid using fiery Thai and Indian chillies in Jiangnan dishes; choose instead milder, more fragrant Sichuanese varieties.

PICKLED AND CURED VEGETABLES

雪菜
Snow vegetable *(xue cai)*

Pickled potherb mustard, or "snow vegetable," is used in many Jiangnan dishes for its refreshingly sour, delicately pungent flavor. It is made with a raggedy-leafed variety of mustard (*Brassica juncea* var. *crispifolia*) that is normally pickled before eating. The vegetable, harvested in the middle of winter, is known in Chinese as *xue li hong*, which translates as "red-in-snow" or "luxuriant-in-snow," depending on the characters used. Chinese supermarkets in the West sell snow vegetable that has been chopped before packaging. At home I make my own snow vegetable, with the small mustard greens (*xiao jie cai* 小芥菜) that I can buy in Chinatown instead of potherb mustard (see page 331). Chinese chefs abroad sometimes use radish tops. In the recipes, I assume that snow vegetable is already chopped.

霉干菜
Shaoxing dried fermented greens (mei gan cai)

This dark dried pickle is made by salt-pickling various types of mustard green, then sun-drying them until they look like large, unruly tea leaves. The leaves are soaked briefly in water before use. Often, they are boiled up with sliced bamboo shoot and then sun-dried again to make "bamboo shoot dried vegetable" (*sun gan cai*), which has an extra dimension of deliciousness. This preserve keeps indefinitely. You may find it in Chinese supermarkets, but don't confuse it with the sweeter, moister *mei cai* or *mui choy* used by Hakka and Cantonese people. If you can't find it, you can make your own (see page 332).

榨菜
Sichuan preserved vegetable (zha cai)

Sichuan is the best-known producer of this crisp, salty-sour pickle, made from a variety of stem mustard, but it's also found in the Jiangnan region. It is used in garnishes, stir-fries and soups. Its Chinese name means "pressed vegetable" because the salted stems are squeezed to remove excess water before they are seasoned and packed into jars to ferment. This pickle is usually sold in Chinese supermarkets in tins or plastic pouches as "Sichuan preserved vegetable." It should be rinsed well before use and keeps well in the fridge.

CURED MEAT, FISH AND EGGS

火腿
Ham (huo tui)

Dark cured ham is used widely in Jiangnan cookery for its umami flavor and pretty pink color. The finest hams, made in Jinhua, Zhejiang province, are not available in the West, but Spanish serrano ham makes an excellent substitute. In the United States, locally made Chinese ham can be found in Chinese supermarkets. Chinese cooks normally steam their ham to cook it through before they chop it—otherwise, slices or strips of raw ham curl up during cooking and look less elegant in the final dish. At home I buy a thick slice of Spanish ham, steam it, cut it into pieces and store it in the fridge or freezer until needed.

咸肉
Salt pork (xian rou)

Salt pork, like ham, is often used to add umami flavors to vegetable dishes, but it's less expensive, which is why it's used more widely in home cooking. It has a lighter cure, paler color and softer texture than ham, and is still sometimes made at home. In China, salt pork often requires soaking overnight in cold water to reduce the saltiness. At home I use gammon, unsmoked ham or pancetta in Chinese salt-pork dishes, none of which require pre-soaking.

虾米, 海米, 开洋, 虾皮
Dried shrimp
(xia mi, hai mi, kai yang, xia pi)

Dried shrimp have an intense, salt-savory flavor. They come in many different sizes but can be divided into two broad types. The first are the tiny, pale, paper-thin shrimp known in Chinese as "shrimp skin" (*xia pi*), and referred to as "papery dried shrimp" in this book. They can be added directly to dishes, but are more delicious after a brief stir-frying to bring out their fragrance. The second are the pinker, more substantial dried shrimp (*kai yang, xia mi, hai mi*), which should be soaked in hot water before cooking, ideally with a dash of Shaoxing wine. Dried shrimp keep for ages in the fridge or freezer.

鲞
Salted fish (xiang)

Salted, sun-dried yellow croaker has a strong, funky taste that is adored in Zhejiang province and is a great foil to fresh ingredients. Bone-dry yellow croakers can be found in Chinese supermarkets and are best soaked for a few hours or overnight in cold water to soften before use. At home, I've taken to using frozen Vietnamese salted mackerel, which has a similar flavor and softer texture, so it doesn't require soaking. Be warned that these fish have a pungent aroma!

干贝, 瑶柱
Dried scallops *gan bei, yao zhu*
Dried scallops are used for their umami deliciousness. An expensive luxury, they are often known in Chinese as "jade pillars" (*yao zhu*).

咸鸭蛋, 腌蛋
Salted duck eggs
(*xian ya dan, yan dan*)
Curing duck eggs in a strong brine or paste made from ash or mud mixed with salt intensifies their flavors and enables longer storing. Hard boiled, they may be cut in half on the shell and eaten as an appetizer or a relish with congee. Salted duck eggs can be found in most Chinese supermarkets. Gaoyou in Jiangsu province is known for its double-yolked salted eggs.

DRIED, BRINED, CANNED

香菇, 花菇
Shiitake mushrooms
(*xiang gu, hua gu*)
Dried shiitake mushrooms have a profound flavor and are one of the staple umami seasonings in Chinese cookery, particularly in vegetarian dishes. Soak them in hot water for at least half an hour before use: strained, the soaking water can also be used to add flavor to dishes. The stalks are

normally sliced off and discarded, but can be used in vegetarian stocks. Some dried shiitake have crisscross fissures on their caps: these are known as "flower mushrooms" (*hua gu*).

木耳
Wood-ear or Chinese black fungus (*mu'er*)
These slippery black mushrooms grow like ears on old, damp wood, hence the name. Flavorless, they are used for their color and crisp, slippery texture. Soak in hot water to reconstitute, then trim off any knots and knobbles. A tiny amount of these dried mushrooms will expand extravagantly after soaking.

银耳
Silver-ear fungus (*yin'er*)
This gorgeous mushroom, a traditional tonic food, looks papery and yellowish when dry, but after a good soaking subsides into slippery, transparent waves. It is used mostly in sweet dishes.

竹笋
Bamboo shoot (*zhu sun*)
Fresh bamboo shoot of various types is one of the most exquisite pleasures of Chinese cuisine and widely used in Jiangnan cooking, but sadly rarely available in the West. Dried bamboo shoot of various kinds is also used in Jiangnan dishes, and equally hard to find abroad. Those available in the West are mostly brined and sold in tins or plastic pouches, and bear little comparison to the fresh shoot. For this reason, I've only included recipes in which bamboo shoot is a minor ingredient, used for crunch and color. The best type I've found

outside China is individually packaged winter bamboo shoot sold in Japanese groceries. Both packaged and fresh bamboo shoot should be blanched in boiling water before use. Once opened, brined bamboo shoot can be kept for a few days in lightly salted water in the fridge.

黄花菜
Day lily flowers (*huang hua cai*)
These long, golden dried flowers, the blooms of the day lily plant, are typically used in Buddhist vegetarian and tonic dishes. Look out for supple, pale golden flowers; they darken and harden with age. They should be soaked in cold water for at least half an hour before use. In season, the fresh flowers can sometimes be found in China; they can be stir-fried after a quick blanching, perhaps with slivers of pork and bamboo shoot.

荷叶
Lotus leaves (*he ye*)
In the Jiangnan region, fresh lotus leaves are used to wrap meat, fish and poultry, usually before steaming; they have a bewitching fragrance that infuses the food as it cooks. Enormous dried lotus leaves can be found in good Chinese supermarkets and can be used after a quick dunking in boiling water. After cooking, the leaves, which are not eaten, can be added to congee to lend it a most delicious flavor and a pale green tint.

莲子
Lotus seeds (*lian zi*)
In season, lotus seeds are sold in their pods and can be peeled and nibbled like nuts. Outside China, the ivory-colored seeds are

conveniently sold peeled in vacuum packs, or dried. Dried lotus seeds should be soaked overnight in cold water before use; vacuum-packed seeds can be used directly. Lotus seeds are a traditional fertility symbol because their name sounds the same as "successive sons."

枸杞子
Goji berries (gou qi zi)

These tiny bright-red berries, also known as wolfberries, are the fruit of two species of boxthorn, *Lycium barbarum* and *Lycium chinense*, and are cultivated mainly in northern China. Recently marketed as a "superfood" in the West, they have long been considered a tonic food in China. One of their dialect names in China, *gou nai zi*, sounds similar to their standard name but means "dog nipples"—remarkably apt, when you look at them.

红枣
Jujubes (hong zao)

These crinkled, dark-red dried fruits (*Zizyphus jujuba*), also known as Chinese dates, are often used in sweet and tonic dishes. When fresh, in their autumn season, they are pale green and brindled with brown, their flesh bright and crunchy like a sweeter, softer kind of apple. The dried fruits are sold in most Chinese food shops. Each fruit has a single stone, like an olive.

乌梅
Chinese dried black plums (wu mei)

These aromatic dried fruits can be found in Chinese supermarkets. They can be eaten as a snack or made into a refreshing drink.

山楂干
Dried hawthorn fruits (shan zha gan)

Hawthorn fruits can be made into fruit leather, wafer-like snacks or a thick jam reminiscent of Spanish *membrillo*; they are also used to make fruit infusions. Sliced dried hawthorn fruits can be found in larger Chinese supermarkets.

红豆
Adzuki beans (hong dou)

Adzuki or azuki beans are simply known as "red beans" in Chinese. They are often used in sweet dishes, especially in the form of red bean paste (see below). They should be soaked overnight in cold water before cooking.

豆沙
Red bean paste (dou sha)

Red bean paste, known in Chinese as "bean sand," is one of the most popular sweet stuffings for dumplings and other snacks. It is made from mashed cooked adzuki beans, lard and sugar. Tinned red bean paste can be found in East Asian food shops, or you can make your own (see page 327).

糖桂花
Osmanthus blossom jam (tang gui hua)

Tiny scented yellow osmanthus blossoms are one of the most important flavorings in Chinese sweet dishes, and are particularly beloved in the Lower Yangtze region. They are normally sold in the form of a runny jam, speckled with the tiny flowers.

龙井茶
Dragon Well tea (long jing cha)

Dragon Well tea, a Hangzhou speciality, is not only a beautiful drink, but is also used in some dishes, such as the stir-fried shrimp on page 160. Other loose-leaf green teas can be substituted.

SEAWEEDS

紫菜
Laver seaweed (zi cai)

Dried laver seaweed is sold in dark, crinkly circles; break off a tiny bit and add it to broths, where it will expand greatly. It has a delicate umami flavor and a pleasantly slippery texture; it also adds a dark color note that can complement pale ingredients.

苔菜, 苔条, 浒苔
Branched string lettuce (tai cai, tai tiao, hu tai)

This umami-delicious and wonderfully fragrant variety of grass kelp or gutweed (*Ulva prolifera*) is a particular speciality of Ningbo. Sometimes known in English as "sea moss," it grows in grassy fronds in the shallows of coastal areas, and is dried before it goes to market. I've never found *tai cai* for sale outside China, but Japanese *aonori-ko* flakes contain grass kelp, have a similar flavor and make an excellent substitute for the seaweed in flaked form. In other dishes where the seaweed is not flaked, this won't work, so I suggest you either omit it or do as countless Chinese restaurants in the UK do, and transform cabbage leaves into "crispy seaweed"! This sounds like an unlikely solution, but works surprisingly well (see page 36).

RICE AND FLOUR

粳米
White rice (*jing mi*)

Plain white, non-glutinous rice is at the heart of most meals in Jiangnan and across southern China. The Chinese favor slightly sticky varieties such as long-grain Thai fragrant or jasmine rice, which are easily picked up with chopsticks. In Jiangnan, people prefer a sushi-type rice with rounder, plumper grains. I often serve sushi rice with Jiangnan dishes.

糯米
Glutinous rice (*nuo mi*)

Raw glutinous rice looks chalkier and more opaque than non-glutinous rice, and has a stickier texture when cooked. In China it is often used in sweet dishes, and is always soaked before steaming. The glutinous rice sold in Chinese supermarkets tends to be long-grain, but short-grain Japanese "sweet rice" is closer to the type used in Jiangnan. You can use either here, though sweet Japanese rice gives a more authentic appearance and mouthfeel.

糯米粉
Glutinous rice flour (*nuo mi fen*)

This starchy white flour is mixed with water to make a putty-like dough used in many sweet dishes.

高筋面粉, 底筋面粉
Chinese high-gluten and low-gluten flours (*gao jin mian fen, di jin mian fen*)

Chinese supermarkets sell flours with different gluten contents for different purposes. High-gluten flour is best for some dumplings, while low-gluten flours are best for steamed buns. Some recipes use a mixture of the two. You can use ordinary strong white bread flour and all-purpose flour, respectively, as substitutes, but the Chinese flours tend to be finer and paler and give more elegant results, which is why I recommend them.

红曲粉
Red yeasted rice (*hong qu mi*)

The Chinese have been innoculating rice grains with the yeast *Monascus purpureus* for more than a thousand years. The yeasted rice is a deep purple, and can be used as a natural food coloring for a dramatic pink color. To use the rice in cooking, grind it to a powder, or soak it in hot water for a few minutes, then strain off the bright pink juices.

米粉, 蒸肉粉
Rice meal (*mi fen, zheng rou fen*)

This is rice that has been dry-roasted with spices and ground to the consistency of fine couscous. It is mostly used to coat ingredients for steaming. Make your own (see page 96) or buy it in Chinese supermarkets, where it is often sold as "steam powder."

年糕
New Year's rice cake (*nian gao*)

There are different versions of New Year's rice cake (*nian gao*) in different parts of China. In Shanghai and Ningbo, it is typically made with non-glutinous rice that is steamed and then pounded to form a smooth, elastic dough. This is made into flattened sausage shapes and often imprinted with auspicious designs. Happily, this kind of rice cake can now be found in good Chinese supermarkets in the West. At home, the best I can find is Korean, sold frozen or chilled, cut into slices or strips and ready to use. If you can only find dried rice cake, soak it in cold water overnight before cooking.

生粉
Potato starch (*sheng fen*)

The flavorless white powdered starches known collectively as *sheng fen* are the key to thickening Chinese sauces, and are also used in coatings for fried foods. Various types can be used, including cornstarch, pea starch and potato starch. I use potato starch, which you can find in any Chinese supermarket; if you wish to use cornstarch, which has slightly different properties, increase my quantities by half.

NOODLES AND DUMPLING SKINS

面条
Wheat noodles, fresh or dried (*mian tiao*)

Typically, noodles in the Jiangnan region are made from a wheat flour dough that is cut or extruded into fairly thin strands. Alkaline lye water (sodium hydroxide) may be added to the dough, giving the noodles a distinctive fragrance, a yellowish tint and a bouncy texture. In my recipes, you may use fresh or dried Chinese wheaten noodles, plain or alkaline, as you please. I tend to use noodles without egg, but egg noodles should work fine too.

上海面

Shanghai noodles

(shang hai mian)

One Shanghainese speciality, rarely seen elsewhere in Jiangnan, is thick, bouncy noodles that resemble Japanese udon. They can be found in the refrigerator section of some Chinese supermarkets. Japanese udon noodles may be used as a substitute.

粉条

Sweet potato noodles *(fen tiao)*

These brownish translucent noodles are made by forcing a hot paste made from sweet potato starch through a holey vessel into boiling water. They are flavorless but have a delightfully slippery, springy mouthfeel. They are sold in dried form and should be soaked in cold water for several hours or overnight before use.

馄炖皮

Wonton wrappers *(hun dun pi)*

Regular wonton wrappers can be found in the refrigerator section of good Chinese supermarkets. Shanghainese wonton skins, which are normally labeled as such, are larger and thicker (4 in/10cm square); if you can't find these, use regular wonton skins instead.

OILS AND FATS

Cooking oil

For stir-frying, and Chinese cooking in general, you need a neutrally flavored cooking oil with a high smoke point. At home I use a clean-tasting organic rapeseed oil, and occasionally groundnut oil, both of which I recommend. (In Jiangnan, one old-fashioned cooking oil is camellia oil, also known as tea oil or tea seed oil, which is made from the oil-rich seeds of the *Camellia oleifera* tree. These days it is hard to find and relatively expensive, so it is used mainly as a speciality oil for its gorgeous nutty flavor and nutritional richness. It's sometimes referred to as the "oriental olive oil.")

猪油

Lard *(zhu you)*

A small amount of lard can add a dash of luxury and umami deliciousness to vegetable dishes. Many Jiangnan cooks use it as a stir-frying oil—either on its own or mixed with vegetable oil—or to enrich steamed dishes and soupy noodles. You can also add lard to a soup, boiling it briefly to emulsify the fat and make the liquid almost creamy. Lard is also used as a fat in pastries and sweetmeats. It's easy to make your own (see page 322).

香油, 麻油

Sesame oil *(xiang you, ma you)*

Toasted sesame seed oil, which has a dark caramel color, is used in tiny quantities as a flavoring, and not as a cooking oil. It is added to hot dishes right at the end of cooking because high heat destroys its fragrance, and is also used in dressings for cold dishes. Always buy pure rather than blended sesame oil. Good toasted sesame oil can be found in mainstream supermarkets as well as Chinese shops.

鸡油

Chicken oil *(ji you)*

Chicken oil is the golden oil made from rendered chicken fat, which has a gorgeous umami flavor. Make it by gently heating the yellow fat from a free-range chicken carcass until the oil has run out and the solids are crisp and brown, then strain off the oil. Alternatively, keep the solid layer of fat that collects on a chilled chicken stock. I freeze my chicken oil in thin layers, then break off small, tablespoon-sized pieces, which I add directly to soups, stir-fries and steamed fish just before serving.

椰子油

Coconut oil *(ye zi you)*

Coconut oil is not a traditional cooking oil in the Jiangnan region, but it's particularly wonderful in sweet dishes, where it makes a fine vegetarian substitute for the traditional lard.

TOFU

Tofu, otherwise known as beancurd, is an important part of the Jiangnan diet and one of the essentials of Buddhist vegetarian cookery. At its simplest, it's made by soaking dried yellow soybeans, grinding them with water, straining the resulting liquid to make soymilk, then heating and curdling the milk with a coagulant of gypsum or mineral salts (known in Japanese as *ngari*). The soft fresh curds may be eaten just as they are or pressed into a more solid form, which may then be deep-fried, smoked, spiced or fermented. Tofu stalls in China sell many different varieties; the following are those used in this book.

豆腐

Plain white tofu (dou fu)

Plain white tofu is made from curds that have been pressed so that they hold their shape and can be cut into thick slices or cubes with a knife, but remain tender. It can be found in most Chinese shops, usually packaged in water. Before cooking this kind of tofu, steep it in very hot, lightly salted water for 5–10 minutes to warm it through and refresh its flavor. After opening a package, keep any leftover tofu immersed in fresh water and use within a day or so.

豆花

Silken tofu (dou hua)

Silken tofu is made from unpressed curds and has a delicate, custardy consistency. It is commonly known in Chinese as "bean flower" (dou hua) and can be eaten with sweet or savory seasonings. It is sold in Chinese and Japanese food shops.

豆腐干

Firm tofu (dou fu gan)

Known in Chinese as "dry tofu," this is made by pressing the soymilk curds to extract as much water as possible, giving it a firm, almost cheese-like texture. Firm tofu can be sliced or slivered and holds its shape well enough to be stir-fried.

烟熏豆腐干

Smoked tofu (yan xun dou fu gan)

Wood-smoking gives firm tofu a marvelous flavor. Cut into slices or slivers, it can be stir-fried with many different vegetables and is particularly excellent with celery or Chinese chives. It can also be used in salads.

香干

Spiced tofu (xiang gan)

Firm tofu is often steeped in a spiced broth that may be colored with dark soy sauce or caramelized sugar. Like tofu, spiced tofu can be sliced or slivered and used in stir-fries, or eaten on its own.

百叶, 千张

Tofu sheets (bai ye, qian zhang)

Known as "hundred leaves" or "thousand sheets" in Chinese, these ivory-colored sheets of tofu are made by pressing fresh soymilk curds in thin layers between sheets of muslin (you'll notice they bear the imprint of the cloth). They can be used to wrap chopped foods into parcels or tubes, or cut into ribbons and used in salads and cooked dishes.

豆腐皮

Dried tofu skin (dou fu pi)

These thin, translucent golden sheets are made by drying out the protein-rich skin that gathers on the surface of soymilk; the Japanese call them yuba. They are widely used in Jiangnan cookery, most notably in making vegetarian "duck" and "goose" but also as wrappers for various deep-fried tidbits. Store them in the fridge or freezer. Always make sure you have more than you need for a recipe, since some sheets may be broken. Scraps can be soaked briefly in hot water, then added to soups, stews and stir-fried dishes for a bit of extra protein. If the sheets are too stiff to be pliable, lay a clean, damp tea towel over them, or steam them for a minute or so.

豆腐乳, 南乳, 红腐乳

Fermented tofu and red fermented tofu

(dou fu ru, nan ru, hong fu ru)

This almost cheese-like relish is made by allowing cubes of firm tofu to grow moldy, then sealing them into jars with salt, wine and spices to ferment. The tofu is often eaten straight as a condiment with congee or soupy rice, but can also be used in cooking. There are various types; the most distinctive of Jiangnan is known in Chinese as "southern" or "red" fermented tofu (nan ru or hong fu ru), and comes in a brine colored a deep pink by red yeasted rice. It's referred to in these recipes as red fermented tofu.

GLUTEN

Wheat gluten is extracted from a wheat flour dough by kneading it in water to wash away all the starch, leaving behind pure protein. The yellowish gluten may be boiled or deep-fried, or leavened and steamed before use. It has a pleasingly soft, springy texture, absorbs flavors well and is often used in Buddhist vegetarian dishes. To make your own, see page 323.

水面筋, 油面筋

Boiled or fried gluten

(shui mian jin, you mian jin)

When fresh gluten is boiled as a prelude to cooking, it is known as "water" gluten (shui mian jin); when deep-fried, it is known as "oil" gluten (you mian jin). Deep-fried gluten puffs can be found in Chinese supermarkets, and should be soaked briefly in boiling water to soften before cooking. You may also find gluten in Japanese shops, where it is called *seitan*.

烤麸
Leavened wheat gluten *(kao fu)*
Kao fu, a particular speciality of Shanghai, is made by leavening wheat gluten, then steaming it in great blocks that look a bit like sponge cake. It has a pleasingly bready texture and soaks up flavors beautifully. The fresh version is hard to find outside Shanghainese communities; the dried version, which should be soaked before use, is more readily available.

GREENS

青菜, 上海青菜, 小棠菜
Green bok choy *(qing cai, shang hai qing, xiao tang cai)*
Sometimes known as Shanghai bok choy, this cabbage variety (*Brassica campestris* ssp *chinensis*) is one of the most ubiquitous vegetables of the Jiangnan region and, happily, is also widely available outside China. In Shanghai, the tender young sprouts of this and other leafy vegetables are known as "chicken feather greens" (*ji mao cai*). Green bok choy is paler in color than the other common variety of bok choy, which has fleshy white leaf stems surrounded by dark green leaves.

大白菜, 黄芽菜
Chinese leaf cabbage
(da bai cai, huang ya cai)
Chinese cabbage (*Brassica campestris* ssp *pekinensis*) is one of the most important winter vegetables and can be eaten fresh or pickled, raw or cooked.

塌菜
Tatsoi or Chinese flat cabbage
(ta cai)
This loose, dark-leafed, flower-like cabbage (*Brassica rapa* var. *rosularis* or *Brassica narinosa*), which is popular in Shanghai, is increasingly available in Chinese supermarkets and farmers' markets in the West.

蒿菜, 茼蒿
Garland chrysanthemum leaves
(hao cai, tong hao)
These edible leaves of a variety of chrysanthemum known as crown daisy have a refreshing herby flavor and are used in salads, soups and stir-fries. There are two varieties with differently shaped leaves, which can be used interchangeably. They are increasingly sold in Chinese supermarkets outside China.

芥菜
Mustard greens *(jie cai)*
Mustard greens (*Brassica juncea*) are often sold by their Cantonese name, *gai choy*. They have large, broad green leaves and a slightly mustardy flavor and are usually pickled before eating. When fully grown, the clusters of leaves often appear twisted. Small mustard greens (*xiao jie cai*, 小芥菜) make a fine substitute for potherb mustard in pickled snow vegetable (see page 331).

莴笋, 青笋
Celtuce/stem lettuce/asparagus lettuce *(wo sun, qing sun)*
This variety of lettuce, which has scanty leaves and a truncheon-like stem, is widely eaten in the Jiangnan region. The leaves are delicious stir-fried but the real attraction is the stem, with its

delectable crispness, beautiful jade-like color and exquisite flavor. The stem should be peeled before use in salads, soups, stir-fries and stews.

豆苗
Pea shoots *(dou miao)*
Once regarded as a seasonal luxury, these delicate, whiskered little shoots are now widely available, and they are delicious stir-fried or added to soups.

苋菜, 米苋
Amaranth leaves
(xian cai, mi xian)
Amaranth leaves, which come in both green and purple varieties, are popular across southern China. The type with purple leaves edged in green is most often sold in Chinese shops in the West; when stir-fried it produces the most beautiful pink juices. The Shanghainese love to stir-fry young green amaranth leaves, which they call *mi xian*, or 'rice amaranth'. Woody, overgrown amaranth stalks are fermented to make an extraordinary pickle in Shaoxing (see page 315).

ROOTS AND SQUASHES

萝卜
White Asian radish *(luo bo)*
Often sold as daikon or mooli, the long white Asian radish is an important Chinese vegetable and delicious in pickles, salads, soups and stews. Choose plump, stiff, smooth-skinned radishes.

佛手瓜
Chayote *(fo shou gua)*
This green fruit, a type of squash, is native to the Americas but appreciated by Chinese chefs

for its delicate, crisp flesh, which is similar to that of the shiny green gourd (*hu zi* 瓠子, *ye kai hua* 夜开花), a favorite Chinese vegetable that can be hard to find abroad. Peeled and deseeded, it is wonderful in salads, stir-fries and soups. It can be found in East Asian, African and Caribbean food shops, where it is sometimes sold as "chow chow."

冬瓜
Winter melon (*dong gua*)
These huge melons have dark green skin with a thin, frost-like coating and delicate pale flesh. They are typically used in soups and braised dishes. Most shops sell them ready-cut into slices of a reasonable size.

丝瓜
Silk gourd (*si gua*)
Silk or loofah gourds come in two varieties: smooth-skinned and angular. After peeling and cooking the flesh becomes soft and spongey, which is why it is often used in soups and soupy dishes.

芋艿, 芋头
Taro (*yu nai, yu tou*)
Taro is an underrated vegetable in the West, but much loved in southern China. After peeling and boiling or steaming, the bristly brown corms have a delightful texture, like a whiter, more slippery version of potatoes. Choose smaller corms where possible and wear rubber gloves when peeling them, because the raw skin contains a mild toxin that can cause itching. Taro can be found in Chinese, Caribbean and African food shops.

WATER VEGETABLES

藕
Lotus root (*ou*)
Lotus "root," actually the underwater stem or rhizome of the lotus plant, has a crisp texture and can be cut into pretty, holey slices. It is used in stir-fries, soups and salads, or chopped up to give a bit of crunch to meatballs. In Zhejiang, it is also made into a white starch that can be eaten as a kind of porridge.

荸荠, 马蹄
Water chestnuts (*bi qi, ma ti*)
Water chestnuts have a bright, crisp texture and a very delicate sweetness when fresh. Peeled, they can be eaten as a fruit and are also used to add crunch to cooked dishes. Do use fresh water chestnuts if you can: canned ones are pleasantly crisp but lack flavor.

茭白
Wild rice stem (*jiao bai*)
The swollen stem of a type of water grass, which has a crisp texture and delicate flavor, is widely used in Jiangnan cooking, both as a vegetable in its own right and to add crunch and color contrast to all kinds of stir-fries. It can sometimes be found in Western Chinese supermarkets. An alternative name for it is "water bamboo."

FRESH AROMATICS

韭菜
Chinese chives (*jiu cai*)
Also known as garlic chives, these long, flat, spear-like leaves have a bright, pungent taste and are delicious in stir-fries and dumpling stuffings. They can be found in most Chinese food shops.

韭黄
Yellow chives (*jiu huang*)
Like chicory or rhubarb, when Chinese chives are deprived of sunlight they grow pale, delicate and yellow and acquire a beautiful pungency of flavor. They are wonderful when stir-fried with meat, poultry, scrambled eggs or firm tofu. They tend to be less easy to find outside China than green Chinese chives.

韭菜花
Flowering chives (*jiu cai hua*)
The slender flowering stems of Chinese chives are sold separately from the leafy chives themselves, in bunches. They are generally stir-fried with meat, eggs or firm tofu.

葱
Spring onions (*cong*)
Long green onions with straight white bases rather than swollen bulbs are one of the most essential seasonings of the Jiangnan kitchen. In China, you can buy large spring onions (*da cong*), which are used in marinades and cooking, and small spring onions (*xiao cong*), which are used as a garnish. In general, if you are using regular spring onions, the tender green part is best used as a garnish, and the more robust white part in cooking.

姜, 生姜
Fresh ginger (*jiang, sheng jiang*)
Often used with spring onion, fresh ginger is one of the essential aromatics in Jiangnan cookery. Try to buy plump, smooth-skinned, fresh-looking ginger.

大蒜
Garlic *(da suan)*

Garlic plays a relatively minor role in Jiangnan cooking, especially when compared with Sichuan and the north, but is used in some dishes, particularly in Shanghai.

香菜
Cilantro *(xiang cai)*

Fresh cilantro is used as a garnish in Jiangnan cooking, and in some salady dishes.

OTHER VEGETABLES

百合
Fresh lily bulb *(bai he)*

This gorgeous vegetable, which somewhat resembles heads of garlic, may be sold in vacuum packs in the refrigerated section of Chinese supermarkets, and keeps for weeks in the fridge. It has a marvelously delicate, crisp texture. To use, peel the bulbs into individual lobes and rinse well, discarding any discolored parts. Cover with cold salted water if not using immediately.

青豆
Fresh green soybeans *(qing dou)*

Fresh young soybeans have a particularly delicious flavor and a vibrant green color. They are widely available frozen, either in their pods or podded. In their furry pods, they are known in Chinese as 'hairy beans' (*mao dou*), and in English by their Japanese name, edamame.

蚕豆
Fava beans *(can dou)*

The people of Jiangnan have a particular love of fresh fava beans, which are used in many appetizers, soups and stir-fries. In most dishes, they are shelled and then peeled before cooking. To peel shelled fava beans, blanch them for a minute or so in boiling water, refresh them in cold water, then pop them out of their skins. Happily, some Chinese supermarkets sell ready-skinned fava beans in their freezer sections.

For photographs of many of these ingredients, please visit fuchsiadunlop.com

EQUIPMENT

COOKING VESSELS

Wok and lid

A wok is ideal for stir-frying because its narrow base and high sides make it easy to turn pieces of food over a high flame. Traditional Chinese woks have rounded bases, and can only be used on gas stoves and specialist induction cookers. If you don't have a gas stove, use a wok with a flat base. Some modern woks have non-stick surfaces; I prefer the traditional version, made from uncoated carbon steel or cast iron. For home use I recommend a wok 12–14 in (30–35 cm) in diameter. Woks may have two "ear" handles on either side, one long handle or a combination. Long-handled woks are easier to move around, while woks with two "ears" are more stable. Woks can be used not only for stir-frying, but also for boiling, steaming, dry-roasting and deep-frying. If you are filling a wok with hot water or oil, do make sure it is stable. You can use a wok stand (see below). If you don't have a wok, use a frying pan with high sides for stir-frying. You'll need a wok lid if you want to use your wok as a steamer. A wok lid is also useful for slow cooking and fast boiling, for example when emulsifying a stock.

Preparing a new wok

If you buy a traditional carbon steel wok in a Chinese supermarket, begin by scrubbing the interior with steel wool, then wash thoroughly with soapy water. Rinse, wipe dry, then heat over a high flame. When the metal is really hot, switch off the heat, pour in a little cooking oil and use a thick wad of paper towels to carefully smear it all over the surface. Let it cool slightly, then repeat this seasoning process twice with fresh paper and oil. Your wok is now ready for cooking. With use, the color of a wok will gradually darken, and the surface will develop a patina that makes food less likely to stick.

Maintaining your wok

After use, a quick scrub under the tap is normally sufficient to clean a wok. When cleaning a hot wok, use a brush with natural-fiber bristles; if you are using a plastic brush, cool the surface slightly with cold water before scrubbing. If you do have to scrub a traditional wok more aggressively to remove food that has stuck, you may strip off its protective patina, in which case re-season the surface before storing it (see above). The surface should also be reseasoned after you have used a wok for boiling or steaming. If you don't keep the surface seasoned and your wok becomes rusty, simply scrub off the rust with steel wool, rinse well and re-season with oil.

Bamboo or metal steamer with lid

Layered bamboo steamers and lids can be bought cheaply in Chinese supermarkets. Stand them above boiling water in a stable wok and use them for steaming buns, dumplings and all kinds of dishes. If you're steaming food in a dish, make sure there is enough room around it for steam to circulate. Metal steamers may also be used, but condensation tends to gather on the underside of their lids and drip onto any uncovered food.

Clay pot

In China, clay pots (*sha guo*) are often used for slow-cooked soups and stews. Most traditional clay pots have glazed interiors but are otherwise unglazed, and therefore fragile. They retain heat well but cannot tolerate sudden changes of temperature, so should be warmed up gently. Before using a traditional clay pot for the first time, immerse both pot and lid in cold water and soak overnight. Modern fully glazed pots, which are less fragile, can also be found in Chinese supermarkets and are equally good for soups and stews. Dishes made in clay pots are usually served in them too—use a heatproof mat to protect your table.

Electric rice cooker

An electric rice cooker is a good investment because it cooks rice perfectly every time, allowing you to concentrate on the rest of the dishes. More sophisticated rice cookers can make congee, sticky rice and brown rice as well as plain white rice.

UTENSILS

Chinese cleaver

You can use any sharp knife for cutting, but a cleaver is ideal. The Chinese cutting cleaver, which is known as a "vegetable knife" (*cai dao*), is thinner and lighter than the kind of chopper used in butchery. It may appear intimidating at first, but it's an addictively wonderful tool. Aside from cutting, you can use the flat of the blade to smack ingredients like fresh root ginger to loosen its fibers and to scoop up pieces of food and move them around. If you wish to chop through bones, you'll need a heavier chopping cleaver (*kan dao*) too.

Wok scoop

A wok scoop is ideal for stir-frying because it enables you to scoop up and turn ingredients. This is the implement most Chinese people use for stir-frying at home.

Chinese ladle

Chinese professional chefs tend to use a ladle rather than a wok scoop because of its versatility: a ladle can be used not only to move food around the wok, but also as a bowl for mixing seasonings into a sauce, and to scoop up water or oil.

Strainer

Metal strainers, also known as spiders or skimmers, are useful for scooping pieces of food out of hot water or oil.

Plate tongs

These metal tongs are incredibly useful for transferring a hot dishful of food from a steamer basket to the table for serving. They can be found in good Chinese supermarkets.

Rolling pin

Chinese rolling pins are small and light and usually have tapered ends. They are the best tool for rolling out the wrappers of dumplings and buns.

Bamboo or wooden chopsticks

Chopsticks are useful for separating pieces of food in deep-frying oil, as well as for tasting. Long-handled cooking chopsticks can be found in Chinese supermarkets.

OTHER EQUIPMENT

Wok rack

These little trivets will transform your wok into a steamer – simply rest one in the base of the wok, pour in water up to the top of the trivet and bring to the boil. Place a dish of food, uncovered or covered with a plate or aluminum foil, on the trivet, cover the wok with a lid and steam.

Wok stand

If you have a round-bottomed wok, a wok stand will keep it stable, either on the stovetop or the work surface.

Wok brush

A wok brush made from strips of bamboo is good for brushing out a hot wok (plastic brushes may melt if the metal is still very hot).

Whetstone

Rectangular whetstones are usually sold alongside cleavers in Chinese supermarkets. They have a fine-grained and a coarser side. To use a whetstone, wet it and rub it with a drop of dish detergent. Place it on a wet cloth at right angles to the edge of a work surface. You will notice that the blade of your cleaver is flat on one side and angled on the other. Lay the flat side almost flat across your whetstone and push it backwards and forwards on the stone, moving the knife from side to side as you do this for even sharpening. Turn the blade over and hold it at a very narrow angle to the stone. Push backwards and forwards over the stone as before, until the blade is sharp. If your knife is fairly blunt to begin with, start by using the coarser side of the whetstone, then sharpen it up on the finer side.

Bamboo mat

Bamboo mats, which can be bought in many Chinese supermarkets, are used when slow-cooking to prevent ingredients from sticking to the base of a clay pot or saucepan. Simply cut them to size and place them in the base of your pan before adding the ingredients. They can be washed and reused, although they don't usually last long.

Oil or sugar thermometer

A thermometer is invaluable for judging when deep-frying oil has reached the right temperature (although with experience you may be able to judge this without it).

TECHNIQUES

CUTTING

The art of cutting is fundamental to Chinese cooking. Most ingredients are cut into small, chopstickable pieces, and when stir-frying, even cutting helps ensure that every piece of food will be cooked to perfection at exactly the same moment. Precise cutting also enhances the visual and tactile beauty of a dish. Accomplished Chinese chefs cut their ingredients into pieces of startling uniformity. Although such delicate precision is unusual in domestic cookery, it's worth trying to cut your food as evenly as possible. Quite apart from the culinary benefits of well-cut food, quiet, methodical cutting can be one of the many pleasures of Chinese cooking. If you are cutting meat, especially fatty meat, you will find it much easier if you freeze it for an hour or two beforehand to firm it up. There is a whole vocabulary to describe the shapes into which food may be cut; these are a few of the most essential.

Slices

There are many kinds of slice, including the small "thumbnail slice" of garlic or ginger, the larger "domino slice" and the wide, very thin "ox-tongue" slice.

Slivers

Chop spring onions into sections, then cut them lengthways into very thin slivers or "silken threads." For other ingredients, cut them into slices, overlap the slices on a board, then cut into slivers.

Spring onion "flowers"

Cut the green part of spring onions widthways into thin slices or "flowers" to make a bright, refreshing garnish.

Fine chopping

Garlic and ginger are often finely chopped into tiny "rice grains," while ham can be reduced to "fine choppings" for a garnish.

Roll-cut chunks

A shape for carrots, taro, bamboo shoot and other vegetables that increases the surface area of the pieces. Place your vegetable on a chopping board. Hold your knife at an angle and cut a thick chunk. Roll the vegetable a quarter turn towards you and repeat. The motion is like sharpening a thick pencil.

Strips

Cut ingredients into fairly thick slices, then into strips.

Smacking vegetables

Use the flat side of a Chinese cleaver or a rolling pin to smack vegetables to loosen their fibers so that they release their flavors or absorb a sauce.

Small cubes

Cut ingredients into thickish slices, then into strips, then into small cubes.

SALTING

Vegetables that contain a lot of water, such as radishes, may be cut into pieces, mixed with salt and set aside for half an hour or so, then squeezed to extract water. Salting gives vegetables a pleasing texture somewhere between suppleness and crunch.

BLANCHING

Cut vegetables are often boiled briefly before cooking, either to "break their rawness" so they may be swiftly stir-fried, or to dispel bitter or peppery flavors, for example in the case of radish. Blanching leafy greens reduces their volume, which can make stir-frying easier in a modestly sized domestic wok. Some vegetables, such as bamboo shoot, may be blanched to remove natural toxins. Blanching is also used to refresh the flavors of canned or packaged ingredients, such as bamboo shoot and tofu. When blanching, take care not to boil your vegetables for too long, so that they retain a bit of crunch. When vegetables are not being cooked immediately after blanching, they are usually flushed in cold water to arrest the cooking process, then drained and set aside.

MARINATING

Chinese cooks marinate ingredients both to refine their flavors and dispel "fishiness," and to give them a base flavor or color. Seasonings such as salt, Shaoxing wine, ginger and spring onion are used for the first purpose, soy sauce commonly for the latter. When food is cut into small pieces for stir-frying, a lengthy marinade is not required: simply slice your main ingredient, add the marinade seasonings and set aside for the time it takes to prepare everything else.

COATING IN STARCH

Before cooking, pieces of meat, fish, seafood or poultry are often clothed in a batter made from starch mixed with water or egg. Sometimes, ingredients are coated in a light batter and then pre-cooked in oil at a low or moderate temperature, or—less commonly—in simmering water, before a final stir-frying. This technique is often known as "velveting" because it gives the food a soft, slippery texture. A thicker batter may be applied as a prelude to deep-frying, to preserve the succulence of the food in the hot oil. Dry starch may also be used to coat food before deep-frying.

STIR-FRYING

Stir-frying is one of the most essential Chinese cooking methods, both in restaurants and domestic kitchens. It's fast, economical, and superb for preserving the bright crispness of vegetables and the succulence of meat and poultry. Stir-frying is also the perfect cooking method if you wish to serve several dishes from a single pan, because a succession of simple dishes can be rustled up with only a quick rinse of the wok between them.

The most common general term for stir-frying is *chao*; specific terms include *hua chao*, "slippery stir-frying," in which pieces of food are clothed in starch and fried at a low or moderate temperature ("velveted") before fast stir-frying, to preserve their tenderness; and *sheng chao*, "raw stir-frying," in which the main ingredient is not coated in starch. *Bian* is another word for stir-frying, often used for fragrant, dry dishes with no sauce. While it's impossible to achieve the fiery heat of a Chinese restaurant wok in a normal home kitchen, there are a few ways to make the most of stir-frying on any stovetop.

Be prepared. Make sure you have all your ingredients and seasonings cut evenly into small pieces, marinated and close at hand before you begin. Blanch vegetables that take a little longer to cook, such as carrot and celery, before you stir-fry them.

Have a serving dish at the ready.

Do not overload the wok with ingredients. If you try to cook too much at once the heat will be insufficient and you may end up steaming the food in its juices rather than stir-frying. If you want to double quantities of a stir-fried dish, it's usually faster and more effective to make the same dish twice than to cook everything at once.

Season your wok carefully (see page 348) and make sure it's smoking hot before you add your cooking oil and start to stir-fry.

"Fry-fragrant" your aromatics. After seasoning the wok, add the cooking oil, swirl it around and immediately add any aromatics such as garlic, ginger or chilli. If you allow the oil to overheat before adding them, they will color and burn almost immediately. Stir-fry very briefly until fragrant, then add the other ingredients.

Use enough cooking oil. The hot oil helps to cook the food, and remember that if you follow Chinese custom and use chopsticks to help yourself from a serving plate, most of the oil will remain on the plate.

STEAMING

Steaming is one of the most typical Chinese cooking methods, and a mainstay of Jiangnan rural kitchens. At its most basic, it's one of the simplest and most economical ways of cooking; all you have to do is place ingredients in a bowl with a few seasonings, put them in a steamer and steam. In farmhouse kitchens, people often place a bamboo rack over their steaming rice, then set a few dishes on it so that rice and dishes steam together. Steaming preserves the innate taste and nutritional richness of ingredients, without the transformations of searing, browning or tossing at high temperatures in a wok. In Jiangnan, people often steam fresh vegetable ingredients, such as soybeans, bamboo shoot or taro with a little of something cured and strongly flavored, such as ham or dried fish; the essences of the ingredients mingle in the steam to delicious effect. There's something very gentle and nourishing about steamed food. I find a supper of steamed soybeans with ham (see page 182) and steamed rice to be the perfect antidote to a stressful day or an excessive meal.

With a bamboo steamer

Use a steamer with a lid that will fit into your wok. Select a bowl or a dish that will sit in the steamer basket with enough room around it for steam to circulate. The dish should be deep enough to hold any juices that emerge during cooking. Buns and dumplings can be laid directly onto the oiled slats of the steamer, or placed on pieces of blanched cabbage leaf or parchment paper. Place the wok on the stove and make sure it's stable. Fill it with enough water to reach the bottom edge of the steamer basket, but not the slats on which your dish will rest. Bring the water to the boil, then place your dish of food in the steamer, cover with the lid and steam. Keep an eye on it and top up with boiling water if necessary. After steaming, you'll need to re-season the surface of your wok to prevent it from rusting.

Without a bamboo steamer

Place a metal trivet in the base of a wok or a broad saucepan (if you don't have a trivet you can improvise by using a small tuna can with both ends removed). Pour in enough water to reach the top of the trivet and bring it to the boil. Place your dish on the trivet, cover the wok or pan with a lid and steam. If you use a metal lid to cover your steamer, condensation can gather on its underside and drip onto the food. To prevent this, you can cover the dish with its own lid, an upturned plate or aluminum foil. You can also use a metal saucepan with a steamer insert.

DEEP-FRYING

Deep-frying, with its extravagant use of oil, is used more in restaurants than in domestic cookery; most home cooks only deep-fry when they are entertaining guests. Nonetheless, as everyone knows, it's a fabulous method for bringing out the fragrance of food and for creating crisp, crunchy textures. You need far less oil to deep-fry in a wok than in a saucepan because of its narrow base: if you cook your food in small batches, you can often get away with as little as 1¾ cups (400ml oil). Ingredients are often deep-fried twice, once to "fix their shape" (*ding xing*) and cook them through, and a second time to give them a crisp, golden finish. If you are deep-frying in a wok, do make sure that it's absolutely stable—a wok ring is essential if you use a round-bottomed wok on a stove without a wok cradle, and a wok with two short handles is more stable than one with a single long handle. An oil or sugar thermometer is extremely useful for judging the temperature of deep-frying oil (if you don't have one, it's useful to know that a stale cube of bread browns in about 60 seconds at 350°F/180°C, the temperature required for many dishes.) When deep-frying, remember that you can re-use the same oil to season your wok for any stir-fried dishes.

PRESSURE COOKING

Pressure cooking is a brilliant way of making stocks and stews more quickly. It can dramatically reduce the time it takes to make steamed, boiled and braised dishes, while reducing the effort because you don't have to worry about the pan boiling dry.

RED-BRAISING

Red-braising is one of the most characteristic Jiangnan cooking methods, although it's not exclusive to the region. "Red" refers to the deep color that soy sauce lends to a dish. Typically, the ingredients are cooked with dark soy sauce, Shaoxing wine and sugar, with a little ginger and spring onion. Towards the end of cooking, the liquid is reduced over a high flame until dark and syrupy. The juices of red-braised dishes are utterly delicious when trickled over plain white rice. Any leftover sauce can be saved and reheated with some tofu (deep-fried or plain) or a vegetable of your choice. Virtually any ingredient can be red-braised, but the method is most closely associated with pork and fish. Because of the final reduction of the cooking liquid with red-braised dishes, you should avoid adding too much soy sauce or salt at the start: you can always add more to taste at the end, as you reduce the sauce. In Jiangnan, cooks often use traditional soy sauces that are both dark in color and salty; at home I use a mixture of dark and light soy sauces to achieve a similar effect. I also follow the example of one of my favorite Shanghai restaurants and use a mushroom-flavored dark soy sauce in red-braised dishes.

"SMOTHERING"

The term *men* is used to describe cooking in a closed pot for a "smothering" effect, allowing the food to absorb the flavors of a sauce as it cooks. Sometimes ingredients are stir-fried as a prelude to smothering in a covered wok; Chinese chefs often talk about letting food in a wok "smother a little" as an intermediate stage of cooking.

STEEPING

Steeping (*jin*) is one of the most ancient Chinese cooking methods and is typical of the Jiangnan region, where it often takes the form of immersing raw or cooked ingredients in a brine made from Shaoxing wine or the mulch left over from its fermentation. A fermented sauce made from shrimp (*xia you*) may also be used. In the past, steeping was used as a way of preserving fresh ingredients, but for a shorter time than actual pickling.

THICKENING SAUCES AND SOUPS

Chinese cooks usually thicken sauces and soups right at the end of cooking by stirring in a mixture of starch and cold water. With stir-fried dishes, this thickening makes the sauce cling glossily to the ingredients rather than pool on the serving dish. Always give your starch mixture a stir before adding it to a hot liquid to ensure that the starch is evenly distributed in the water. The starch mixture should feel thin and milky—if it's too thick and you add it suddenly to the wok, it can set into sticky clumps. For the same reason, pour the starch mixture into the center of the wok, because it will set into clumps if you pour it directly on to the hot metal around the edges. Add the starch mixture gradually, in stages. Always err on the side of caution when thickening sauces and soups—too much starch can make them gloopy. You can always add a little more, but you can't take it away. Home cooks may not bother with thickening the scant juices of stir-fried vegetables, but it gives a professional finish, which is why it's a common practice in restaurant kitchens.

"GLEAMING OIL"

In Jiangnan restaurants, chefs often finish a wok-cooked dish by stirring in a little oil to enhance its luster; this practice is known as "gleaming oil" (*ming you*). Sometimes they use ordinary cooking oil, sometimes an oil infused with spring onion, crushed ginger and spices. The practice is rare in domestic cooking and I don't generally do it at home, but I've made an exception for the splendid "squirrel fish" on page 143 so you can see how it works.

VINEGAR AS A TABLE CONDIMENT

Vinegar is often the only condiment on a Jiangnan dinner table. It may be used as a dip for deep-fried foods, to which it brings a spritz of acidity and brightness. It is also used to "dispel fishiness," particularly though not exclusively in fish and seafood (this is why vinegar is an essential condiment for crab and shrimp). The application of vinegar to Jiangnan food, particularly deep-fried delicacies and seafood, is somewhat reminiscent of the use of lemon juice in Mediterranean cookery.

OTHER COOKING METHODS

There are many other cooking methods in Jiangnan cuisine, some of which are quite specific. *Dun* refers to the long simmering of ingredients to make a soup; *hui* to boiled dishes in which all the ingredients are finely slivered; *kao* to roasting, like the famous Beggar's chicken; and *cha shao* to impaling an ingredient, typically a huge slab of pork belly, on a roasting fork and roasting it slowly over a pile of embers.

INDEX

FURTHER READING

The vast majority of the books I have consulted in the course of writing this book are in Chinese and largely unavailable outside China. For this reason, a full bibliography would be of little use to most readers, and would have stolen space away from the recipes, so you will find one on my website, fuchsiadunlop.com, rather than in this book.

Here follows a select bibliography of suggestions for English-language reading that I found particularly useful in understanding the culture and cuisine of the Jiangnan region.

Cao Xueqin, *The Story of the Stone* (also known as *The Dream of the Red Chamber*), Vols 1–5, translated by David Hawkes (Vols 1–3) and John Minford (Vols 4–5) (Penguin Books, London). This classic Chinese novel is ostensibly set in northern China, but describes the leisured upper-class life of Jiangnan, where Cao Xueqin spent his early life.

Chang, K. C., *Food in Chinese Culture: Anthropological and Historical Perspectives* (Yale University Press, 1977). Especially the chapter by Michael Freeman on Song dynasty food, which is largely devoted to the gastronomic life of old Hangzhou.

Gernet, Jacques, *Daily Life in China on the Eve of the Mongol Invasion, 1250–1276*, (George Allen and Unwin, London, 1962). Gives a vivid picture of life in thirteenth-century Hangzhou.

Huang, H. T., *Science and Civilisation in China. Volume 6: Biology and Biological Technology. Part V: Fermentations and Food Science* (Cambridge University Press, Cambridge, 2000). A remarkable, scholarly work filled with fascinating information about Chinese food in general, with much that is relevant to Jiangnan.

Jullien, François, *In Praise of Blandness: Proceeding from Chinese Thought and Aesthetics*, tr. Paula M. Varsano (Zone Books, New York, 2008). A concise philosophical work that brilliantly explains the Chinese love of subtlety and understatement.

Polo, Marco, *The Travels*, tr. Ronald Latham (Penguin Books, London, 1958). Including his accounts of thirteenth-century Jiangnan.

Shen Fu, *Six Records of a Floating Life*, tr. Leonard Pratt and Chiang Su-hui (Penguin Books, London, 1983). An exquisite, though unfinished, work by a member of the Jiangnan literati.

So, Yan-kit, *Classic Food of China* (Macmillan, London, 1992). A well-researched collection of classic Chinese recipes with a particularly useful introduction.

Waley-Cohen, Joanna, "The quest for perfect balance" in Freedman, Paul (ed.), *Food: The History of Taste* (Thames & Hudson, London, 2007).

You may also like to read some of my other writings on Jiangnan food culture:

"A Dream of Red Mansions" in *Shark's Fin and Sichuan Pepper: A Sweet-Sour Memoir of Eating in China* (Ebury Press, London, 2008), about Yangzhou and its food.

"Garden of Contentment" in *The New Yorker* (November 24, 2008, issue), about Dai Jianjun and the Dragon Well Manor restaurant.

"The Seduction of Stink" in *Saveur* (issue 177, October 2015), about the stinking foods of Shaoxing.

"Kicking Up a Stink" in *Financial Times Weekend* (May 20, 2011), about a tasting of smelly cheeses in Shaoxing.

"The Delicate Flavours of Suzhou Cuisine" in *The Financial Times Weekend* (September 11, 2010).

ACKNOWLEDGMENTS

This book has been fed and nourished by the amazing generosity of my friends in China. First and foremost, I would like to thank Dai Jianjun of the Dragon Well Manor in Hangzhou, who has encouraged me since the beginning, allowing me into his kitchens, introducing me to countless classic dishes, and opening my eyes to the wonders of Jiangnan cooking. It is to him that this book is dedicated.

The staff of the Dragon Well Manor and Dai's organic farm in southern Zhejiang have been like a second family to me. I have been honoured to learn from veteran chefs Dong Jinmu, Guo Ma and Yang Aiping in the Manor's kitchens, as well as the current head chef, Chen Xiaoming, who has been tireless in answering my questions. Down on the farm, Chef Zhu Yinfeng has taken me foraging and harvesting, fed me unforgettable delicacies and shared with me his deep knowledge and contagious enthusiasm for the art of cooking. Uncle Zhou, Master He, Master Hong and "Summer" have let me tag along on their visits to farmers and fisherman all over the region, while Jiang Li, Xue Yan, Yang Waining and Qian Lu have been unstinting in their kindness.

Also in Hangzhou, veteran master chef Hu Zhongying has welcomed me into his kitchens and greatly enriched my knowledge of Zhejiang cuisine. I will always be grateful to chef Fu Yueliang for sending me to the Dragon Well Manor for lunch more than eight years ago. Chefs Niu Youqiang and Liu Guoming also helped me on my way.

In Shaoxing, Mao Tianyao has been an inspirational teacher. Also in Shaoxing, I would like to thank Hu Feixia, Xianheng chefs Sun Guoliang, Zhou Guoxiong and Wu Jianmiao, and local winemaker Han Jianrong.

In Suzhou, Sha Peizhi and her colleagues Jiang Yuanxiang, Jiang Meizhen and Zhang Shuchao have all taught me more than I can express; I would also like to thank Zhu Anling, veteran chefs Su Fugen and Lu Qiancai, noodle chef Qu Guiming and the head chef of the Deyuelou.

In Yangzhou, I was privileged to be taken under the wing of local food expert Xia Yongguo, who fed and entertained me and tutored me in the history and culinary culture of that historic city. Chefs Zhang Hao and Ge Hualin and their colleagues Shen Wei and Yang Zhaohui let me study in their kitchens, where I learned, among other things, how to bone and stuff a duck and how to make lion's head meatballs. Chef Yang Bin gave me a guided tour of a local market. I would also like to thank Liu Guangshun for an incredible dinner of Yangzhou snacks.

Jason Li, a gifted chef who runs a Shanghainese supper club in London, has been boundlessly generous with his culinary knowledge. He and his mother He Yuxiu, who lives in Shanghai, have been an inspiration to me and have taught me much of what I know of Shanghainese home cooking. My friend Rose Leng has been another guiding light in my work on Jiangnan food: she gave me my first taste of the region at the Ningbo Residents' Association restaurant in Hong Kong more than fifteen years ago, and has introduced me to many fabulous restaurants and enticing delicacies in Shanghai. I have also been lucky to be helped by Rose's extended family, particularly her aunt Xun Naifeng and cousin Liang Liang, who took much trouble to arrange for me to visit a tofu factory. Chef Tony Lu of Fu 1088 introduced me to many local delicacies.

In Ningbo, master chef Chen Xiaoliang let me into his kitchens, while one of his staff, chef Bao Haimin, gave me a tour of the local food scene. Also in Ningbo, I would like to thank restaurateur Cui Guangming and chef Liu Hongyuan, as well as the manager and staff of the Crock-Duck-Dog snack shop. In Zhoushan, Rose Leng's cousin Lin Wei introduced me to the delights of the local seafood, both in restaurants and in his own kitchen, while his friend Chen Xinfang drove us around.

In Nanjing, I am much obliged to Peng Dongsheng, Fan Meng and Lingling.

In Anhui, chef Zheng Chengjiang was an assiduous host and Ling Jianjun was a brilliant explainer of Huizhou food culture and culinary techniques. Thank you also to chefs Feng Jianjun and Gao Yangfei; chefs Zhou Xiaozhong, Wang Zhiguo, Zhou Yongzhong and Tang Niandong in Jixi; chef Sun Wenping and manager Hu Guangsheng in Xidi; and chef Zhang Wanghe near Hongcun.

In Chengdu, I would like to thank my old friends Wang Xudong and Liu Yaochun for their help. I would also like to thank Liu Guangwei and Simon Liu of East Eat magazine, and Liu Wei and Sansan from Changsha. In Shanghai, Francesca Tarocco and Nunzia Carbone have put me up (and put up with me!) on numerous occasions, while Gwen Chesnais and Davide Quadrio have shared with me many Jiangnan adventures. Thanks also to Susan Jung and Nigel Kat in Hong Kong for their hospitality.

I would not have been able to complete this book without the support of Lucy Walker and Nikki Johnson at the BBC. My friends and colleagues of the Barshu Group have helped me with so many things: a huge thank you to Shao Wei and Juanzi, Sherrie Looi and Anne Yim. Barshu chefs Zhang Huabing, Zheng Qingguo and Fu Bing were kind enough to assist me with the photo shoots,

and Fu Bing helped me to develop my bun-making skills. I would like to thank my principal guinea pigs, Cathy Roberts, Sam Chatterton Dickson, Adam Lieber, Jimmy Livingstone, Sophie Munro, Kai Wang and Simon Robey for tasting dishes and giving me their opinions. Paul Michael, Mara Baughman, Vicky Franks and Augustyna Hawro have all helped to keep the show on the road. Anissa Helou has been a fantastic comrade in food and work. My mother, Carolyn Dunlop, was kind enough to help me with recipe testing. Thanks also to Rebecca Kesby, Penny Bell, Xiaoming Wu and Seema Merchant for being such great friends. A particular thank you to Lambros Kilaniotis for his love and support, and for believing in me and this book on the many occasions when I didn't.

I've been extremely lucky to work with Bloomsbury Publishing, and the brilliant editors Natalie Bellos, Alison Cowan and Richard Atkinson, as well as Xa Shaw Stewart, Alison Glossop and Marina Asenjo. Thanks also to Laura Gladwin for her meticulous editing—and patience. It was a joy working with Yuki Sugiura and Cynthia Inions on the photo shoots. In the United States, it's been a privilege to be published by Maria Guarnaschelli at W. W. Norton, and I'm also very grateful to Erin Sinesky Lovett. And thanks, as always, to my wonderful agent, Zoë Waldie.

Finally, I know that my friends and teachers in China have been waiting patiently for this book for

a very long time. Thank you all for trusting me with your recipes and stories. I have done my best to translate into words and recipes a little of your extraordinary culinary tradition, although I knew I would never do it justice. I hope you will forgive my mistakes and omissions, and that the book will bring back some happy memories of the times we have spent together in beautiful Jiangnan.

ABOUT THE AUTHOR

Fuchsia Dunlop trained as a chef in China in the mid-1990s and has been cooking, researching and writing about Chinese food ever since. Her work has appeared in numerous publications, including the *Financial Times*, *Observer Food Monthly*, *The New Yorker* and *Saveur*, and she has received awards from the Guild of Food Writers, the James Beard Foundation and the International Association of Culinary Professionals. Fuchsia's previous books include *Every Grain of Rice*, *Sichuan Cookery* and *Shark's Fin and Sichuan Pepper*.

For information about permission to reproduce selections from this book, write to Permissions, W. W. Norton & Company, Inc., 500 Fifth Avenue, New York, NY 10110

For information about special discounts for bulk purchases, please contact W. W. Norton Special Sales at specialsales@wwnorton.com or 800-233-4830

Manufacturing by RR Donnelley Asia Printing Solutions Limited
Book design by carolineclark.co.uk

ISBN 978-0-393-25438-9

W. W. Norton & Company, Inc.
500 Fifth Avenue, New York, N.Y. 10110
www.wwnorton.com

W. W. Norton & Company Ltd.
Castle House, 75/76 Wells Street, London W1T 3QT

1 2 3 4 5 6 7 8 9 0